Inscribing the Hundred Years' War
in French and English Cultures

SUNY series in

Medieval Studies

———————

Paul E. Szarmach, editor

INSCRIBING THE

HUNDRED YEARS' WAR

IN FRENCH AND ENGLISH CULTURES

Edited by

DENISE N. BAKER

STATE UNIVERSITY OF NEW YORK PRESS

Published by
STATE UNIVERSITY OF NEW YORK PRESS
ALBANY

© 2000 State University of New York

All rights reserved

Printed in the United States of America

No part of this book may be used or reproduced in any manner whatsoever without written permission. No part of this book may be stored in a retrieval system or transmitted in any form or by any means including electronic, electrostatic, magnetic tape, mechanical, photocopying, recording, or otherwise without the prior permission in writing of the publisher.

For information, address
State University of New York Press,
90 State Street, Suite 700, Albany, NY 12207

Production, Laurie Searl
Marketing, Patrick Durocher

Library of Congress Cataloging-in-Publication Data

Inscribing the Hundred Years' War in French and English cultures / edited by Denise N. Baker.
    p. cm. — (SUNY seres in medieval studies)
"International Congress on Medieval Studies at Kalamazoo, Michigan on May 8, 1994"—P.
Includes bibliographical references and index.
ISBN 0-7914-4701-4 (acid free : alk. paper) — ISBN 0-7914-4702 (pbk.-acid free : alk. paper)
    1. French literature—To 1500—History and criticism—Congresses. 2. English literature—Middle English, 1100–1500—History and criticism—Congresses. 3. Hundred Years' War, 1339–1453—Literature and the war—Congresses. 4. France—Relations—England—Congresses. 5. England—Relations—France—Congresses. I. Baker, Denise Nowakowski, 1946– II. International Congress on Medieval Studies (29th : 1994 : Kalamazoo, Mich.) III. Series.

PQ188 .I57 2000
820.9′001—dc21

00-021409

10 9 8 7 6 5 4 3 2 1

Contents

Acknowledgments		ix
Introduction		1
	Denise N. Baker	
1	Warmongering in Verse: *Les Voeux du heron*	17
	Norris J. Lacy	
2	Inscribing the Body with Meaning: Chivalric Culture and the Norms of Violence in *The Vows of the Heron*	27
	Patricia DeMarco	
3	Meed and the Economics of Chivalry in *Piers Plowman*	55
	Denise N. Baker	
4	Chaucer's Tale of Melibee: Contradictions and Context	73
	Judith Ferster	
5	Chaucer after Retters: The Wartime Origins of English Literature	91
	John M. Bowers	
6	Politics and the French Language in England during the Hundred Years' War: The Case of John Gower	127
	R. F. Yeager	

7	THE UNCERTAINTY IN DEFINING FRANCE AS A NATION IN THE WORKS OF EUSTACHE DESCHAMPS *Earl Jeffrey Richards*	159
8	THE POLITICAL POETICS OF THE *DITIÉ DE JEHANNE D'ARC* *Anne D. Lutkus and Julia M. Walker*	177
9	CLOTHING AND GENDER DEFINITION: JOAN OF ARC *Susan Crane*	195
10	A PACIFIST UTOPIA: *CLERIADUS ET MELIADICE* *Michelle Szkilnik*	221
11	THE HUNDRED YEARS' WAR AND NATIONAL IDENTITY *Ellen C. Caldwell*	237
	LIST OF CONTRIBUTORS	267
	INDEX	269

To Lee and Andi

ACKNOWLEDGMENTS

This collection of essays had its inception in a session on the Hundred Years' War and the literatures of France and England presented at the International Congress on Medieval Studies at Kalamazoo, Michigan, on May 8, 1994, the day, coincidentally, that the Chunnel between London and Paris opened. The enthusiastic response of the audience to this topic encouraged me to undertake this project. I wish to thank two of the original panelists, John M. Bowers and Ellen C. Caldwell, as well as the other contributors whose essays are included in this anthology.

I am also grateful to Paul Szarmach, Director of the Medieval Institute at Western Michigan University and editor of this SUNY series in Medieval Studies, for the support and advice he graciously gave me as this manuscript was submitted for review. James Peltz, editor of SUNY Press, his assistant Katy Leonard, and production editor Laurie Searl were always prompt and thoughtful in their dealings with me.

My colleagues Mary Ellis Gibson, Robert Kelly, and Russ McDonald, as well as Patricia DeMarco and the two readers for SUNY Press, offered valuable suggestions for revising my introduction and the essays in this anthology.

Gregory Tredore, my research assistant, exercised great patience in helping me prepare this manuscript for publication. I very much appreciated his good humor and careful attention to detail.

I am grateful to three presses for allowing me to reprint the following essays or revisions of them.

Susan Crane, "Clothing and Gender Definition: Joan of Arc," *Journal of Medieval and Early Modern Studies*, 26:2 (Spring 1996): 297–320. Copyright 1996 Duke University Press. All rights reserved. Reprinted with permission.

Judith Ferster, "Chaucer's *Tale of Melibee*: Advice to the King and Advice to the King's Advisors," from *Fictions of Advice: The Literature and Politics of Counsel in Late Medieval England*, by Judith Ferster. Copyright 1996 University of Pennsylvania Press. Reprinted by permission of the publisher.

Norris J. Lacy, Introduction to *The Vows of the Heron*, ed. John L. Grigsby and Norris J. Lacy, Garland Library of Medieval Literature 86, series A. Copyright 1992 Garland Publishing. Reprinted by permission of the publisher.

Anne Lutkus and Julia Walker, "PR pas PC: Christine de Pizan's Pro-Joan Propaganda," in *Fresh Verdicts on Joan of Arc*, ed. Bonnie Wheeler and Charles Wood, The New Middle Ages 2. Copyright 1996 Garland Publishing. Reprinted by permission of the publisher.

INTRODUCTION

From 1337, when Philip VI confiscated Aquitaine from Edward III, until 1453, when the English lost the duchy for good, France and England engaged in the intermittent military conflict that historians have named, somewhat inaccurately, the Hundred Years' War. This period of hostilities coincided with a remarkable efflorescence of vernacular literature in both countries. French literature, which had come to dominate the secular culture of Christendom in the twelfth century, continued to flourish in texts by authors such as Machaut, Deschamps, and Christine de Pizan, the first woman known to earn her living as a writer. In England, over which France had exercised cultural hegemony since the Norman Conquest, a renaissance of literature in the native language occurred during the second half of the fourteenth century with texts by such authors as the anonymous *Gawain* poet, Langland, Gower, and Chaucer, the father of English literature. The intersection between these two contemporaneous phenomena, the sociopolitical circumstances of the Hundred Years' War and the production of vernacular literature in France and England, is the subject of this collection of essays.

These essays participate in the "turn toward history" that has marked literary studies during the last decade.[1] As will be apparent, their analyses have been enabled and invigorated by the recent conversation about historical criticism. Like the old historicism, these essays assume that a text speaks of the period during which it was composed, but they also insist that it speaks to its time, questioning as well as articulating its culture. Like Marxist and cultural-materialist criticism, these essays explore the nexus between literature and sociopolitical conditions, but without subscribing to a particular model of the historical process. And like the New Historicism and cultural poetics, these essays acknowledge the textuality of history. They agree with Paul de Man that "the bases for historical knowledge are not empirical facts but written texts," but they reject the dismissal of the material reality of the past implicit in the concluding clause of his sentence: "even if these texts masquerade in the guise of wars or revolutions."[2]

Despite their debt to these diverse methodologies, the essays in this collection heed Lee Patterson's warning that "historical criticism must abandon the hope of any theoretical foundation and come to rest instead upon its own historically contingent moment and upon convictions that find their final support within experience."[3] After analyzing the limitations of both Marxist and New Historicist practices, Patterson concludes by identifying the dilemma for historical critics: "the question was—and remains—whether cultural analysis is possible without an explicit commitment to a specific philosophy of history, a specific definition of the real. Can history be written without causality? And if not, is causal explanation possible without a foundational commitment to some narrative of historical action, be it the fulfillment of the Spirit, the rise of a heroic bourgeoisie, or the class struggle entailed by social inequality?"[4] In response to this dilemma, Patterson proposes a critical historicism, informed by the investigator's self-reflection about his or her own historicity and validated by its political rather than its theoretical efficacy.[5] Such a critical historicism assumes that literary and critical texts can interrogate as well as bespeak their cultures and that they can perform local and small-scale interventions to challenge the dominant social and political formations of their own historical moment.

Although she does not use the term *critical historicism*, Gabrielle Spiegel formulates a methodology for textual analysis that incorporates many of the premises which Patterson articulates. She enjoins historical critics to concentrate upon what she terms the social logic of texts as "situated uses of language."[6] Instead of assuming the dominance of either history or literature, she explores the reciprocity of context and text as mutually constitutive. "All texts occupy determinate social spaces," Spiegel explains, "both as products of the social world of authors and as textual agents at work in that world, with which they entertain often complex and contestatory relations. In that sense, texts both mirror and generate social realities, are constituted by *and* constitute the social and discursive formations which they may sustain, resist, contest, or seek to transform depending on the case at hand."[7] By recognizing the complex interdependence of text and context and the possibility that the text might oppose as well as acquiesce to dominant ideologies, Spiegel implicitly acknowledges the agency of authorship without claiming that the author can act entirely independent of cultural constraints. As Patterson argues, critical historicism must recognize that this antinomy between the individual and the totality can never be resolved, for, as he succinctly puts it, "the self may be made, but it is also self-made."[8]

Concurring with Patterson, Spiegel insists that historical critics should focus on the local and contingent rather than the global; they must forgo both master narratives of history and preconceptions about the text's relationship to its culture. "There is no way to determine a priori the social function of a text or its locus with respect to its cultural ambience. Only a minute examination of the form and content of a given work can determine its situation with respect to broader patterns of culture at any given time."[9] Spiegel thus balances the claims of history and literature by calling for a criticism that respects the specific and unique details of both the context and the text. "What this means," she explains, "is that a genuine literary history must always to some extent be both social and formalist in its concerns, must pay attention to a text's 'social logic' in the dual sense of its site of articulation and its discursive character as articulated *logos*."[10] By combining historicist and formalist analysis, Spiegel recognizes the aesthetic dimension of literary texts without implying that it allows access to a transcendental truth.

In fact, Spiegel insists on the historicity of literature by contending that this dual perspective on the text's social logic can best be achieved by concentrating on the moment of its inscription, "that is, on the ways in which the historical world is internalized in the text and its meaning fixed."[11] She distinguishes inscribing from recording by emphasizing the mediation of the author. In contrast to recording, inscribing "represents the moment of choice, decision, and action that creates the social reality of the text, a reality existing both 'inside' and 'outside' the particular performance incorporated in the work, through the latter's inclusions, exclusions, distortions, and stresses."[12] Spiegel thus contends that the text constructs its context as much as the context constructs the text.

It is precisely this reciprocity between literature and history that the following essays explore. Concentrating on the moment of inscription, they investigate the social logic of texts that speak of and speak to the Hundred Years' War. Examining the ways in which these texts manifest the sociopolitical conditions under which they were produced and analyzing the work they perform in their cultural economy, these essays demonstrate how history influences literature and how literature intervenes in history.

Any effort to scrutinize the reciprocity between history and literature must begin by situating the texts under consideration in the chronology of the Hundred Years' War. Historians usually divide these 116 years into four periods: 1337–1360, 1360–1396, 1396–1422, and 1422–1453.[13] Important treaties or truces in 1360, 1396, and 1420 were soon breached and hostilities were renewed. English dominance in the first and third periods alternated with increased French resistance in the second and fourth.

Although historians debate the fundamental causes of the Hundred Years' War, the immediate catalyst was the feudal and dynastic disputes between Edward III and the French monarchy. As duke of Aquitaine, Edward, like his predecessors back to Henry III, owed liege homage to the French king. In 1328, a year after Edward assumed the throne, the French monarch died without a direct heir. As nephew of the deceased Charles IV, Edward asserted a right to the French crown. Although the French nobility chose Philip of Valois as king, Edward's royal lineage through his mother conflicted with his feudal position. According to Prestwich, "The claim to the French throne transformed the whole basis of disputes between the rival sovereigns. No longer would Edward III appear as a rebellious vassal, disregarding the terms of his homage; rather, as a claimant to the throne he was the equal of Philip VI."[14] With Edward's renewal of his homage to the new French king in 1329 and 1331, though, the dispute seemed settled. Fundamental differences, however, remained unresolved.

According to contemporaries, the event which ignited the hostilities was the vowing game dramatized in the anonymous French poem of the 1340s, *Les Voeux du heron* (*The Vows of the Heron*).[15] This poem purports to record the incident that provoked Edward III to wage war on France: an imputation of his cowardice by Robert d'Artois. Although no other evidence confirms that the poem's vowing session actually occurred, both contemporary chroniclers and recent historians acknowledge Robert d'Artois's role as an actual or an ostensible cause of the hostilities between England and France. Banished by Philip VI, he received asylum from Edward III in 1336. According to Froissart, Robert d'Artois incited the English king to assert his claim to the French throne; in the final revision of the *Chroniques* extant in the Rome manuscript, Froissart even alleges that Robert dictated the declaration of Edward's hereditary right read before the Parliament in March of 1337.[16] Indeed, Philip VI cited Edward's refusal to extradite Robert d'Artois as the evidence of a breach of fealty that justified the French confiscation of Aquitaine in May of 1337. Recent historians, however, regard Robert d'Artois as the excuse for, rather than the instigator of, the hostilities, even though they disagree about whether it was the English or the French king who used the banished aristocrat to rationalize his own conduct.[17]

Although it was composed in the first decade of the Hundred Years' War, *The Vows of the Heron*, as the essays by Norris Lacy and Patricia DeMarco demonstrate, foreshadowed the ruthlessness of the English troops and the suffering of French civilians in the century to come. Until Henry V changed the strategy in the second decade of the fifteenth century, the English army's primary tactic of *chevauchée*, or prolonged raid, not only undermined the authority of the French king but also wreaked devastation, or *damnun*, on the populace of the invaded country. It was also during this period that the English won most of their great military victories: Sluys in 1340; Crécy in 1346; the successful siege of Calais in the subsequent year; and Poitiers in 1356, when King John II was captured by the Black Prince. Through these spectacular victories, Edward III and his son gained their renown as military leaders. For the French, though, as Ellen Caldwell shows, these defeats came to represent, at least from the nineteenth century on, their courage and endurance in such powerful works of art as Delacroix's painting, *La Bataille de Poitiers* (1829–30), and Rodin's sculpture, *Les Bourgeois de Calais* (1884–86).

Encouraged by the domestic havoc in France and the failure of the peace negotiations, Edward III returned to Calais in 1359 and set out for Rheims, where he must have planned to be crowned king. After almost two months of extreme privation during the dead of winter, Edward abandoned the seige of Rheims and turned his troops toward Burgundy. In the meantime, however, a young *valettus*, or yeoman, named Geoffrey Chaucer, serving under Prince Lionel, was captured outside Retters (Réthel). As John Bowers argues, this wartime experience may well have changed the course of English poetry by inciting Chaucer's reaction against the French literature that had exercised cultural hegemony in his homeland since the Conquest. After a terrible storm in April of 1359 while the English army was encamped near Chartres, Edward agreed to relinquish his claim to the French throne in return for full sovereignty in Aquitaine and neighboring territory and a ransom of three million *écus* (£500,000) for King John. Signed in 1360, this Treaty of Brétigny (or Calais) brought to a close the first period of the Hundred Years' War.

In England, though, the Treaty of Brétigny proved controversial. Those who had benefitted financially from the war objected to Edward's relinquishment of his claim to the French crown. Composing the A-text of *Piers Plowman* between 1368 and 1374, Langland, one of the earliest opponents of the Hundred Years' War, criticized these militarists, I argue, in the debate between Meed and Conscience in Passus III. The Treaty of Brétigny held for less than a decade. In 1369 Edward responded to Charles V's intervention in a dispute between the Black Prince and some of the nobility of Aquitaine by resuming the title of king of France, and Charles retaliated by confiscating the duchy. The second period of the Hundred Years' War had begun.

In the 1370s the English did not attain the military success of the preceding period. Rather Charles V and his constable, Bertrand du Guesclin, gradually reoccupied the land ceded by the Treaty of Brétigny, and the French navy began to raid the southeast coast of England. "For the first time," Desmond Seward writes, "the Plantagenets faced an enemy who was their superior."[18] In 1376 the Black Prince died, and the following year, Edward III died. Richard II assumed the English throne in 1377 at the age of ten. Three years later du Guesclin and Charles V both passed away, but they had managed to win back most of the territory conquered by Edward III.

During this decade and the following one, French and English public opinion turned against the war because of the high taxes required to sustain it and the wastefulness of the nobility. Domestic problems as well as personal inclination led both Richard II and Charles VI, who succeeded his father in 1380, to favor peace. As Allmand observes, though, "both kings came to be surrounded by uncles who sought to further war for their own ends. Each, in his own way, reacted against avuncular pressure."[19] In England, Richard II's disinterest in the war together with his favoritism toward his friends angered one of his uncles and his allies. After successfully pressing charges of treason against five of Richard's advisers and friends in the Merciless Parliament, these Appellant lords gained control of the council in 1388 and tried, unsuccessfully, to reignite the war. Their efforts, as Judith Ferster contends, explain the veiled allusions that Chaucer makes in his enigmatic Tale of Melibee. By the 1390s, though, both Richard and Charles were seeking ways to end the hostilities. Their efforts culminated in 1396 in a twenty-eight year truce and the marriage of Charles's daughter Isabella to Richard II. The second period of the Hundred Years' War thus drew to a close.

The truce negotiated between Richard II and Charles VI, however, was broken by the end of the century as both kings lost control of their governments. The recurring bouts of mental illness that Charles VI suffered since 1393 weakened his rule, and in 1399 Richard was deposed by his cousin, Henry. The instability of the last decade of the fourteenth century and the first decade of the fifteenth is reflected is the canons of Eustache Deschamps and John Gower. Charles VI's madness and the competition for power between his uncle, the duke of Burgundy, and his brother, the duke of Orléans, divided the French into two factions and would ultimately culminate in thirty years of civil war. France's identity as a nation-state had not yet been formed, as Earl Jeffrey Richards's analysis of Deschamps's poetry demonstrates. Likewise, in England in the late 1390s John Gower reverted to French in his last works despite the rapid ascendancy of English as a literary language and his own use of the vernacular for his *Confessio Amantis* at the beginning of the decade. His choice, Robert Yeager argues, was governed by political motives: the increasingly autocratic behavior of Richard II and Gower's knowledge of the preferences of Henry IV.

Domestic problems in both France and England limited full-scale warfare until Henry V ascended to the throne in 1413 and reinstated the English claim to the French crown the following year. By 1419 Henry had captured all the important towns of Normandy in four years of siege warfare. His defeat of the French forces at Agincourt in 1415 has been regarded since the time of Shakespeare, as Ellen Caldwell demonstrates, as the epitome of English heroism. Henry V's spectacular success in the Hundred Years' War culminated in the Treaty of Troyes of 1420. According to its terms, Henry became heir to the crown of France and was to assume the throne at the death of Charles VI. In the meantime, Henry would marry Catherine, Charles's daughter, and act as regent. This "Final Peace," as the English termed it, failed, however, when Henry V died in August of 1422, two months before Charles VI. His heir, Henry VI, was less than a year old.

The fourth period of the Hundred Years' War stretches from the death of Henry V to the expulsion of the English from Normandy and Aquitaine in the middle of the fifteenth century. Under the remarkable leadership of a peasant girl, Joan of Arc, the French broke the English seige of Orléans, and the dauphin was able to journey to Rheims to be crowned Charles VII in July of 1429. The English claim on the French throne, ratified in the Treaty of Troyes, had been refuted. Despite his debt to "la Pucelle," Charles betrayed her hopes for France, a fact that was not lost on Christine de Pizan, the first French woman to support herself through her writing, who ended her career with a poem in praise of Joan. In the *Ditié de Jehanne d'Arc* (*The Tale of Joan of Arc*) Christine, as Anne Lutkus and Julia Walker carefully explain, endorses the Maid's strategy rather than the monarch's. Within two years of her success at Orléans, though, Joan was captured by the Burgundians and their English allies and brought to trial for heresy. One of her characteristics that intrigued the interrogators, as Susan Crane reveals, was Joan's insistence on wearing men's clothes, a fact that raises questions about conceptions of gender in the late medieval period. Burned at the stake in the

English-held city of Rouen, Joan's death led to a period of stalemate as both diplomatic and military efforts to settle the war fell short during the 1430s and 1440s.

Cleriadus et Meliadice, the anonymous French romance whose hero becomes king of England through marriage, expresses, as Michelle Szkilnik explains, the longing for peace throughout this period. Prospects for a settlement seemed to increase with the Truce of Tours in 1444, by the terms of which Henry VI married Margaret of Anjou, a niece of the French monarch. "Once again," Allmand remarks, "it was hoped to postpone a settlement and place faith upon a personal union between the royal families of the two countries to resolve the outcome of the old dispute between them."[20] Once again, however, these hopes were disappointed. Within five years the war resumed, and the English soon lost Normandy and then Aquitaine to the French. Though most contemporaries at the time may not have realized it, the Hundred Years' War was over when Bordeaux finally fell in July 1453, and the English were expelled from France.

As this overview of the Hundred Years' War reveals, this was a momentous century marked by controversy and turmoil. Inscribed during these tumultuous times, the texts under consideration here engage, either overtly or covertly, in the debates about war policy, military practices, and national identity that raged throughout the period. Investigating this imbrication of literature and history, the essays in this collection demonstrate, as Spiegel puts it, how "texts both mirror and generate social realities, are constituted by *and* constitute the social and discursive formations which they many sustain, resist, contest, or seek to transform depending on the case at hand."[21] The relationship of a specific text to the particular case at hand is precisely what each of the following essays attempts to elucidate.

The first pair of essays investigates the intersection of the literary and the historical in *Les Voeux du heron* (*The Vows of the Heron*). With its fictive account of the events that precipitated the Hundred Years' War, this poem exemplifies the overt political uses to which literary texts could be put in the Middle Ages. As Norris Lacy and Patricia DeMarco show, though, these uses are often problematic for readers unfamiliar with the contemporary scene upon which the poem comments. Their complementary essays enact a critical conversation that situates *The Vows of the Heron* in its historical and cultural context.

In "Warmongering in Verse: *Les Voeux du heron*," Norris Lacy, the poem's most recent editor, provides the historical context needed to appreciate the complexity of the political agenda informing *The Vows of the*

Heron. Although this poem was probably composed during or after 1346, the vowing game it dramatizes is set in September of 1338. Its participants are clearly identified as historical personages associated with the inception of English hostilities against France. Lacy demonstrates that the temporal displacement of this fictive banquet to the decade before the early battles of the Hundred Years' War enables the poet to develop numerous discrepancies between the oaths made by the poem's speakers and their actual subsequent exploits. This gap between fiction and fact, story and history constitutes the poem's irony and, coupled with the escalating violence promised by the later vows, leads Lacy to conclude his essay with speculation about the *Vows*' critique of militaristic posturing.

In the second essay of this collection, "Inscribing the Body with Meaning: Chivalric Culture and the Norms of Violence in *The Vows of the Heron*," Patricia DeMarco confirms Lacy's speculation by exploring several different perspectives for establishing the critical purpose of the poem's irony. Acknowledging that the graphic representation of violence in a chivalric text does not per se indicate the author's censure, she provides the grounds for evaluating the *Vows*' many depictions of the war's devastation of noncombatants, particularly women. Examining the poem's violation of the function of the wounded body in chivalric literature, its questioning of English motivation according to the principles of just war theory, and the defamiliarization of war's horrors achieved by the pregnant queen's final vow, DeMarco concludes that the *Vows of the Heron* critically reflects on chivalric violence even though the poet can offer no alternate ethos to counteract it.

The second pair of essays shows that the militarism of the nobility was also criticized by two of the most popular Middle English authors, William Langland and Geoffrey Chaucer. Unlike the French author of *Les Voeux du heron*, though, these London writers are more oblique in their criticism in order to avoid the reprisals of the powerful English magnates who favored war. In our respective essays, Judith Ferster and I analyze Chaucer's and Langland's covert endorsements of efforts to make peace with France in the 1360s and 1380s.

In "Meed and the Economics of Chivalry in *Piers Plowman*," I contend that Langland discloses the material incentives for war occluded by chivalric ideology during the debate between Conscience and Meed in the first dream vision of the A-text of *Piers Plowman* (circa 1368–1374). I demonstrate that Langland ascribes to his character Meed the same arguments against the Treaty of Brétigny (1360), according to which Edward III was to relinquish his claim to the French throne, that are expressed in contemporary discourses opposing the king's withdrawal from the war. Comparing Meed's defense of the profits that accrue to military leaders with the economic practices of Edward III and the nobility during the first phase of the hostilities from 1337 to 1360, I establish that Langland uses Meed's objections to this treaty to question the motives of the king and his magnates for waging war on France.

Judith Ferster's essay, "Chaucer's Tale of Melibee: Contradictions and Context," resolves the debate between formalist and historicist critics about Chaucer's purpose in assigning to his own persona in *The Canterbury Tales* his translation of Albertano of Brescia's *Liber consolationis et consilii*. She reconciles the paradoxes and contradictions that seem to deconstruct this treatise with the apparent topicality of its message by situating the Melibee in the controversy provoked by the Appellant lords from 1386 to 1389 over advising the king. Displeased by Richard II's overtures of peace with France, these powerful magnates insisted that they serve as the king's councillors and that he pursue the war. In this context, Ferster concludes, the Tale of Melibee's deconstruction of the Appellants's ideology of advice signals Chaucer's cautious allegiance to the king and to peace.

The next three essays examine the formative influence of the Hundred Years' War on nationalism in England and France. This period of military hostility coincided with the first phase in the emergence of the nation-state and impelled the development of distinctive nationalist ideologies in both countries.[22] Although the process was only initiated during the Hundred Years' War, both the English and the French begin to identify themselves against the other, their opponent in the intermittent conflict that lasted for over a century.

In the case of England, the differentiation from France occasioned a reaction against the ascendancy of the enemy's literature and language and incited the development of a native, vernacular culture. As Turville-Petre observes: "The emergence of the fully-fledged nation involves a process by which a unifying culture is widely disseminated throughout the population.... The use of English was a precondition of the process of deepening and consolidating the sense of national identity by harnessing the emotive energy of the association between language and nationalism."[23] John Bowers and Robert Yeager analyze how this nascent ideology of Englishness affected the canons of the period's preeminent poets, Geoffrey Chaucer and John Gower. Acquaintances living and writing in or near London during the last quarter of the fourteenth century, both were associated in some capacity with the royal court and informed about the various debates regarding English war policy. While Chaucer's entire *oeuvre* is in Middle English, Gower remained a trilingual poet, composing in French even at the end of the fourteenth century.

Using postcolonial theory in "Chaucer after Retters: The Wartime Origins of English Literature," John Bowers analyzes Chaucer's literary productions through *The Legend of Good Women* as reactions against French artistic hegemony. Despite the prestige of the opponent's culture among the aristocrats of Edward III's court, Bowers speculates that the young Chaucer's humiliating captivity near Rheims for several weeks, if not months, in 1360 spurred him to dissociate his poetry from the dominance of his French contemporaries. Bowers correlates Chaucer's canon prior to *The Canterbury Tales* with the events of the Hundred Years' War and demonstrates that his relationship to the French tradition has political as well as artistic dimensions.

In "Politics and the French Language in England during the Hundred Years' War: The Case of John Gower," Robert Yeager addresses an anomaly in this trilingual poet's career: his abandonment of English in the texts he composed after the *Confessio Amantis*. Unlike Chaucer's canon, Gower's manifests no clear evolution toward Englishness, despite the increasing popularity of the native language and the growing antagonism toward France. Yeager resolves this apparent discrepancy by carefully establishing the probable chronology of Gower's works and their extant manuscript copies. Dividing the poet's career into three periods, he demonstrates the correspondence between Gower's choice of language and the immediate political circumstances, especially changes in the reigning king's policy toward France.

Because its language and literature had enjoyed preeminence throughout Europe since the twelfth century, the process of establishing French national identity was not primarily linguistic. Rather, during the fifteenth century the conflict between France and England was increasingly conflated with salvation history as the French came to regard themselves as God's chosen people. Earl Jeffrey Richards examines the differences between the traditional conception of a 'nation' and this nascent nationalism in his essay, "The Uncertainty in Defining France as a Nation in the Works of Eustache Deschamps." He demonstrates that Deschamps is a transitional figure, foreshadowing the emerging concept of national identity, but nonetheless emphasizing conventional Christian universalism and estatist hierarchy. Although he denounces France's enemy using the traditional rhetorical epithets of Englishmen with tails and perfidious Albion, Deschamps ultimately attributes the Hundred Years' War to sin on both sides. His cosmopolitanism is manifest, Richards concludes, in his praise of his English contemporary, Geoffrey Chaucer.

The next pair of essays focuses on the role of two extraordinary French women, Christine de Pizan and Joan of Arc. Despite their differences of age, class, and experience, both Christine de Pizan and Joan of Arc excelled in professions that were regarded as the exclusive domain of men in the late Middle Ages. Their paths crossed in 1429 when, at the end of her long and distinguished career, Christine wrote her final poem, *Le Ditié de Jehanne d'Arc* (*The Tale of Joan of Arc*), in honor of the extraordinary peasant girl who had just led the military victory over the English that made possible the dauphin's coronation at Rheims.

In contrast to the guarded references to the Hundred Years' War made by Langland and Chaucer, Christine de Pizan earned her living and her fame writing texts that engaged in political polemic. During the first quarter of the fifteenth century, she distinguished herself both as an opponent of misogyny and a proponent of the monarchy. In "The Political Poetics of the *Ditié de Jehanne d'Arc*," however, Anne Lutkus and Julia Walker contend that in her final text Christine de Pizan, disregarding possible reprisals, voices her opposition to a monarch she had formerly supported, Charles VII. They demonstrate that Christine intervenes during late August or early September of 1429 in support of Joan of Arc in her debate with the newly crowned king about whether to take Paris. Arguing that the usual date of "the last day of July" for the poem's completion ignores the chronology of the events it refers to, Lutkus and Walker show that in the *Ditié de Jehanne d'Arc* Christine engages in her last act of political propaganda on behalf of Joan and France, not Charles VII and the monarchy.

In "Clothing and Gender Definition: Joan of Arc," Susan Crane interrogates the textual traces of "la Pucelle" in the transcripts of her trial to investigate the significance of cross dressing to her self-conception. After evaluating the reliability of the various transcripts of Joan's own, admittedly coerced, responses, Crane examines the meaning assigned to her transvestism both by her inquisitors and by the accused herself. Transgressing the gendered oppositions within the semiotics of clothing, Joan's cross dressing, Crane concludes, troubles her sexuality. Like the other essays in this collection, Crane's demonstrates the imbrication of history and literature, but from a different angle: she shows that historical documents, rather than offering unmediated access to the past, are as ambiguous as literary texts; nonetheless, if they are interrogated critically, they can afford us at least a partial glimpse, if not an extended gaze, of the past.

Michelle Szkilnik, like Crane, also investigates the impetus that the Hundred Years' War afforded for imagining a radical revision of social formations. In "A Pacifist Utopia: *Cleriadus et Meliadice*," she reads this French romance of the 1440s as a counterpoint to Froissart's *Chroniques*; through its contrasting fiction of France and England at peace, it complements the chronicle's commemoration of chivalry on the battlefield. A realistic romance, *Cleriadus et Meliadice* invokes familiar names of places and personages to create the same texture of historicity that Froissart does. As Szkilnik establishes, however, the violence that erupts in the *Chroniques'* narrative of the Hundred Years' War is, in the romance, either directed toward the heathen other or contained by the chivalric exploits of its exemplary hero, Cleriadus. Through her exploration of its attempt to recuperate the chivalric idealism discredited by the grim realities of a century of warfare (as shown in the preceding essays on *Les Voeux du heron* and *Piers Plowman*), Szkilnik accounts for the remarkable popularity of this late-medieval romance, which is extant in nine manuscripts and five editions printed between 1495 and 1529.

The final essay of this collection, Ellen Caldwell's "The Hundred Years' War and National Identity," traces the long shadow that this conflict has cast on constructions of nationalism in England and France. Examining both visual and verbal representations of the war, ranging from the *Apocalypse* tapestries commissioned by the duke of Anjou in 1373, to Shakespeare's *Henry V* and *Henry VI, Part 2* as well as Olivier's and Branagh's films of the former, to Delacroix's painting and Rodin's sculpture depicting French defeats, Caldwell demonstrates how the Hundred Years' War has been used to write "analogue history." Later events, such as the two world wars in this century, have been inscribed in terms of the national paradigms established by the Hundred Years' War: France's victimization and endurance in contrast to England's glorious conquests. However, as Caldwell shows through her analysis of Shakespeare's *Henry VI, Part 2* in the second half of her essay, representations of the Hundred Years' War have also critiqued nationalism and the sacrifices that subjects have been required to make on behalf of the state.

Clearly these essays are connected not only by their common focus on texts that respond to the Hundred Years' War, but also by certain recurrent themes that these texts share: a critique of the aggressive violence and excessive greed of men-at-arms, the need to express such criticism of powerful military and political figures covertly, and the role that war plays in imagining social change and constructing national identity. Most surprising, though, may be the antiwar sentiments that several essays expose in texts like *Les Voeux du heron*, Langland's *Piers Plowman*, Chaucer's Tale of Melibee, and *Cleriadus et Meliadice*. Perhaps the opposition of French writers to the Hundred Years' War is to be expected, given the great suffering imposed on the populace by the English *chevauchées*. However, it may seem anachronistic to attribute pacifist attitudes to fourteenth-century English authors like Langland and Chaucer; one might well suspect that the critic, an American academic in the post-Vietnam era, is imposing his or her own values on these Middle English texts.

Although political historians have recognized that popular opposition to the Hundred Years' War in both England and France was primarily a protest against increased taxation, few have discussed other motives for objecting to the military conflict. Recently, however, social historians have found new evidence of antiwar sentiments in the sermons, religious treatises, and literature of the century. John Barnie argues that at least by the 1380s "peace became a matter of overriding concern to men of conscience."[24] Ben Lowe takes this claim even further: "Without too much exaggeration it can be said that a true movement, albeit an uncoordinated one, swept across England in the later Middle Ages, determined to end the war with France and tending toward a reevaluation of the whole practice of war itself."[25] Indeed, both Lowe and Barnie identify Gower, Langland, and Chaucer as among the major proponents of this new "intellectual environment wherein we find the first sustained discourse of peace."[26] Thus, while the Hundred Years' War has long been regarded as the beginning of the traditional enmity between the English and the French, it also provided, as these essays demonstrate, the impetus for a new conception of the possibility of peace.

NOTES

1. For J. Hillis Miller's use of this phrase in his survey of the critical terrain in his 1986 Presidential Address to the Modern Language Association, see "The Triumph of Theory, the Resistance to Reading, and the Question of the Material Base," *PMLA* 102 (1987): 283.

2. Paul de Man, *Writing and Difference*, trans. Alan Bass (Chicago: University of Chicago Press, 1978), 298.

3. Lee Patterson, *Negotiating the Past: The Historical Understanding of Medieval Literature* (Madison, Wisconsin: University of Wisconsin Press, 1987), 48.

4. Patterson, *Negotiating the Past*, 68.

5. Patterson introduces this term in "Critical Historicism and Medieval Studies," in *Literary Practice and Social Change in Britain, 1308–1530*, ed. Lee Patterson, The New Historicism: Studies in Cultural Poetics 8 (Berkeley: University of California Press, 1990). Although he chooses to leave the term open-ended, so that "*critical historicism* is able to refer to a wide range of historicist initiatives while still asserting the crucial fact of initiation itself, of work that conceives of itself as something other than business as usual" (2), Patterson distinguishes his own practice from New Historicism and Marxist criticism.

6. Gabrielle M. Spiegel, "History, Historicism, and the Social Logic of the Text in the Middle Ages," *Speculum* 65 (1990): 77.

7. Spiegel, "The Social Logic of the Text," 77.

8. Patterson, *Negotiating the Past*, 74.

9. Spiegel, "The Social Logic of the Text," 77.

10. Spiegel, "The Social Logic of the Text," 77–78.

11. Spiegel, "The Social Logic of the Text," 84.

12. Spiegel, "The Social Logic of the Text," 84.

13. This summary of the major events of the Hundred Years' War draws upon Christopher Allmand, *The Hundred Years War: England and France at War c. 1300–c. 1450*, Cambridge Medieval Textbooks (Cambridge: Cambridge University Press, 1988), 6–36; May McKisack, *The Fourteenth Century, 1307–1399*, Oxford History of England 5 (Oxford: Clarendon Press, 1959), 105–49; Michael Prestwich, *The Three Edwards: War and State in England, 1272–1377* (London: George Weidenfeld & Nicolson, 1980; London: Routledge, 1990), 165–87; Nigel Saul, *Richard II* (New Haven: Yale University Press, 1997); and Desmond Seward, *The Hundred Years War: The English in France 1337–1453* (New York: Atheneum, 1978).

14. Prestwich, *The Three Edwards*, 170.

15. John L. Grigsby and Norris J. Lacy, eds., *The Vows of the Heron (Les Voeux du heron): A Middle French Vowing Poem*, Garland Library of Medieval Literature 86, series A (New York: Garland Publishing, 1992), 7.

16. Jean Froissart, *Chroniques de J. Froissart*, ed. Siméon Luce et al. (Paris: Société de l'histoire de France, 1869–1975), I:118–19, 359–60.

17. For the differences of opinion about Robert d'Artois's role, see McKisack, *The Fourteenth Century*, 115, 120, 124, 126; Prestwich, *The Three Edwards*, 168–69; W. M. Ormrod, *The Reign of Edward III* (New Haven: Yale University Press, 1990), 9–10; and Jonathan Sumption, *The Hundred Years War: Trial by Battle* (London: Faber and Faber, 1990; Philadelphia: University of Pennsylvania Press, 1991), 170–73, 184, 274–75, 293.

18. Seward, *The Hundred Years War*, 103.

19. Allmand, *The Hundred Years War*, 24.

20. Allmand, *The Hundred Years War*, 35.

21. Spiegel, "The Social Logic of the Text," 77.

22. See Colette Beaune, *The Birth of an Ideology: Myths and Symbols of Nation in Late-Medieval France*, trans. Susan Ross Huston, ed. Fredric L. Cheyette (Berkeley: University of California Press, 1991), for a discussion of the myths and symbols of nationhood developing in France during this period; Thorlac Turville-Petre, *England the Nation: Language, Literature, and National Identity, 1290–1340* (Oxford: Clarendon Press, 1996), examines the beginnings of English nationalism in the half-century prior to the Hundred Years' War. Both authors discuss competing conceptions of nationalism in their introductions.

23. Turville-Petre, *England the Nation*, 10.

24. John Barnie, *War in Medieval English Society: Social Values in the Hundred Years War 1337–99* (Ithaca, N.Y.: Cornell University Press, 1974), 129.

25. Ben Lowe, *Imagining Peace: A History of Early English Pacifist Ideas, 1340–1560* (University Park, Pa.: Pennsylvania State University Press, 1997), 146; for a discussion of the continental peace discourse, see 72–79.

26. Lowe, *Imagining Peace*, 71; for discussions of Gower, Langland, and Chaucer, see 82–102; Barnie, *War in Medieval English Society*, 122–31; and Robert F. Yeager, "*Pax Poetica*: On the Pacifism of Chaucer and Gower," *Studies in the Age of Chaucer* 9 (1987): 97–121.

CHAPTER 1

WARMONGERING IN VERSE

LES *VOEUX DU HERON*

NORRIS J. LACY

Les Voeux du heron (*The Vows of the Heron*), a French vowing poem from the 1340s, narrates in its 422 alexandrines an event that ostensibly occurred in September of 1338 and precipitated the Hundred Years' War.[1] The anonymous poet tells us that Robert d'Artois, banished from France by Philippe de Valois, publicly labels Edward of England a coward for failing to maintain control over France. Robert then instigates a vowing session (over a cooked heron, a bird that is a traditional symbol of cowardice) during which the English king is incited to invade France, burn the countryside, and defeat his enemy Philippe de Valois. A number of others at the court then pronounce vows that affirm their support, with varying degrees of enthusiasm, for the cause Robert is promoting.[2]

Les Voeux du heron has been largely neglected by scholars, having generally been accorded the status of a footnote, at most, in literary history. Until it was recently re-edited, the newest edition dated from 1921, and although it is occasionally mentioned as part (generally a minor part) of the tradition of vowing poems, serious assessments of its literary value are virtually lacking.[3]

This poem surely does not merit such neglect. Historians will understandably continue to know it, if at all, as little more than a mere curiosity, for it is not history and only ironically purports to be that. Literary scholars, however, should find it more than deserving of their attention. First, it offers a fascinating example of the metamorphosis of history into fiction, and in the process it dramatizes an amusing burlesque of the historical personages,[4] reflecting in each case, and often inverting or exaggerating, a biographical detail presumably known to its audience. Second, it is of interest for the ingenuity of the protagonist, Robert, who uses his considerable skill and, where necessary, his subtlety to transform a jovial social occasion into a provocation to war and carnage. The resulting poem will not, in fact, teach us much; rather, it is our knowledge of the war that will assist us in a proper, literary appreciation of *Les Voeux du heron*.

That prerequisite knowledge is primarily an acquaintance with the *dramatis personae* of the historical event. All the characters named in the text actually existed, and most are known to have performed actions related, though far from identical, to those they vow to undertake; those actions occurred just before or during the early years of the Hundred Years' War.[5]

The cast of characters, with their historical counterparts, is as follows:

- The king known in the poem as Edward Louis is Edward III, who invaded France in 1339. Although the text tells us that the events took place in September of 1338, Edward was on the continent at that time.

- Robert d'Artois had been exiled from France and hospitably received by Edward. It is clear that Robert made efforts to incite Edward against Philippe de Valois, the French king (who also happened to be Edward's cousin), but there is no indication that the poem is an accurate reflection of his methods. Robert took part in Edward's military campaigns in France and was at the head of an English army in July of 1340. He was wounded in battle in 1342 and died late in that year.

- William of Montacute had recently (in March of 1337) received the title of Earl of Salisbury; he is called Salebrin in the poem. About him we know, among other facts, that he had lost an eye in battle four years earlier.

- In the poem Salisbury is with a young woman, the daughter of the Earl of Derby (Derbi). The latter, who received his earldom at the same time as Salisbury, in fact had two daughters, although Whiting thinks it unlikely that either had a liaison with Salisbury.[6] In 1337 Derby had participated in an attack against Louis of Flanders on the island of Cadsant.

- Walter of Manny (or Mauny) was a native of Hainaut who enjoyed an excellent reputation as a military man.

- Suffort in the poem was the Earl of Suffolk (Robert Ufford), who was captured by the French at Lille in 1340, along with the Earl of Salisbury; according to some writers of the period, they were released only after the king of Bohemia intervened on their behalf.

- John of Hainault (or of Beaumont, as in the poem) was associated with the king of Bohemia, first as his ally, later as his enemy; moreover, in July of 1346, Beaumont officially shifted his allegiance from Edward to Philip.

- Jean de Fauquemont (or Faukemont), also known as John of Valkenberg, took part in the 1339 invasion of the Cambrésis; he and John of Hainault (our Beaumont) achieved notoriety for the atrocities they committed in war.

- Edward's queen, Philippa, gave birth to her fifth child, christened Lionel of Antwerp, on November 29, 1338.

The points of most interest in the present context are, as noted, the skill and subtlety employed by the central figure, Robert, to incite the other characters to war, and the progressive intensification of those characters' sentiments as jests turn into bloodthirsty boasts. A systematic review of the poem's events and progression will demonstrate the process by which an adroit protagonist shows himself able to manipulate sentiments and people with comparative ease.

Seasonal introductions to poems most often concern spring, when the trees put on new leaves, the birds start singing, and the flowers bloom. Here, it is instead autumn, and the inversion of the traditional motif extends to the poet's noting that the birds have ceased to sing and that the trees have lost their leaves; the meadows are now bare of flowers (1–4). The action of the poem takes place in September, and the autumnal setting foreshadows the ominous turn that events will take.

Following the introduction, the poem records vows pronounced by ten people.[7] Its structure is circular, as the king begins the sequence, or opens the circle, that will be closed by the queen's vow. Robert d'Artois himself offers the second vow, and the following sections include (in order) vows spoken by the Earl of Salisbury, then by the woman he loves (the daughter of the Earl of Derby), followed by Walter of Manny, the Earl of Derby himself, the Earl of Suffolk, John of Valkenberg, John of Beaumont, and finally the queen.

The essential question to be asked in an evaluation of the poem concerns its author's apparent intent. There are two keys that will yield the answer to that question. First, there are the strained relationships and the complicated alliances that become increasingly evident on a court occasion that, replete with feasting, drinking, and boasting, ought in theory to foster and reinforce camaraderie among the participants. The fact that such camaraderie is initially strained and eventually almost absent has an unsettling effect and implies that something is seriously amiss here.

The second key is the discrepancy we can observe between what we now know about the characters and what they say and do in the poem. Indeed, we can identify such a discrepancy in most *laisses* of the poem, but its extent and effect vary widely and illustrate both the increasing tension and violence of the events and, especially, the literary uses of history and historical biography.

First, Robert accuses the king of cowardice and thus evokes the latter's vow. The narrator tells us that Edward reacts to the accusation with anger and resentment (87), but in fact outrage is not easy to find in his vow. He announces that he will invade France, where, curiously, he will wait for a month to learn whether the French will attack him (103–4). His words appear even more seriously understated when he threatens to impose a tax or tribute such as was never instituted by a *damoiseau* or a marquis, though the threat by a king to outdo a young man and a midlevel noble in demanding tribute sounds either hollow or humorous. The king, in other words, reacts angrily and then makes a vow that is either ironic or, at very least, half-hearted.

That vow, however, apparently suffices to convince Robert that his plan will work, and he vows that he himself will someday return to France. His only threat of specific action is offered in a single line (142): he will do battle. Robert may be confident of success, but it will not come immediately: the following sections do little to advance his cause.

The next vow is peculiar indeed: the Earl of Salisbury swears not only that he will fight and set fires, but that he will keep his eye closed during the entire war, and the narrator assures us that he succeeded (191–94, 206). The nature of his vow indicates that the author must have known of Salisbury's earlier loss of an eye, and it consequently suggests that, with cruel humor, he is amusing himself and his reader at the expense of the Earl of Salisbury. We cannot know whether the vow actually equates the closed eye with the blind one—he will necessarily keep the eye closed, because it has already been lost—or whether it is a reference to his one good eye, a prospect that evokes the spectacle of poor Salisbury fumbling around in France with one eye gone and the other closed. It does not matter greatly which of these the narrator intended, though, because once we know the historical reality, we can draw confident conclusions about the tone of the passage and about the reaction it was expected to elicit from readers: laughter at the expense of the half-blind Salisbury.

The fourth vow is made by the woman with Salisbury; she is the daughter of the Earl of Derby. Hers is a mild oath indeed: she will wait for Salisbury to accomplish his vow, and if he returns safely, she will then belong to him (217–18). The only evident purpose of her vow is to ensure that the man with her will complete what he has sworn to do. Her function therefore parallels the queen's, even though, as we shall see, the latter's vow is far stronger, indeed violent.

Walter of Manny pronounces the fifth vow, taking us to the midpoint of the session. It is at this moment that a different tone chillingly intrudes into the text. Walter announces his intention to destroy a city and "kill the people and leave them with gaping mouths" (244). The violence of the image is new to the poem. Yet, like many of the other vows, it is not exactly what it appears to be. Froissart noted that Walter of Manny, a renowned military figure, had in fact sworn to be the first to invade France, but when he did so, the actual result of his raid was "abortive and more than a little ridiculous."[8] The *Heron*'s image is thus cuttingly ironic.

Next, the Earl of Derby vows to challenge Louis of Flanders to a joust (271–72). Whiting informs us that when the historical Derby attacked Louis (as his poetic counterpart has here sworn to do), "the earl, with more bravery than caution, dashed ahead, slipped, and fell prostrate."[9] Burdened down by heavy armor, he had to be rescued from this dangerous, not to mention embarrassing, situation.

The poem had begun in unsurprising fashion, with the king's vow followed by Robert's (spoken *sotto voce*) and in rapid order by four others, which are ironic, amorous, and largely inconsequential. In a single case (Derby), the tone is threatening, but it is a threat that dissolves in irony if we know what actually happened to him. To this point we also have a perfectly conventional structure: a group of knights and nobles in obviously jovial spirits, making the kind of boasts we might expect to accompany drinking (see 361) and merrymaking.

But complications quickly multiply. The Earl of Suffolk's vow, the seventh in the series, provokes an immediate response from Jean de Beaumont.[10] Suffolk has vowed to do battle with the son of the king of Bohemia (293–99), who happens to be a friend of Beaumont, and the latter vows to take the side of his friend against Suffolk (305–14). As would prove to be the case in the war itself, relationships and alliances are confused, and this passage illustrates the ease with which the vowing session, whether intended as a drinking game or serious affirmation of political and military support, can get out of hand and lead to unanticipated conflicts. Suffolk responds in conciliatory fashion to Beaumont, pointing out that they have after all a common purpose, which is to challenge the king of France; nonetheless, the exchange between the two suggests that matters are taking an unsettling turn, though clearly a turn devoutly wished and cleverly plotted by Robert.

Indeed, the next vow, made by John of Valkenberg (Fauquemont), is noticeably more violent and bloodthirsty than those that preceded it. Other characters had vowed at most to set a fire or engage someone in battle; Salisbury will do both (and with one eye—or is it two?—closed all the while), and the woman he loves simply agrees to accept him if he accomplishes his vow. The most shocking of the vows before *laisse* IX was that of Walter of Manny, who expressed his determination to burn a city and kill its inhabitants. That violence is now reflected, but greatly magnified, in Valkenberg's oath that he will burn churches and kill pregnant women and even his own friends (337–45).

Significantly, scholars have, to my knowledge, discovered nothing about the historical Valkenberg that would let us read this passage as ironic. All indications are that Valkenberg "carried out the spirit as well as the letter of his vow."[11] Oddly, though, Whiting is intent on interpreting the entire poem as humorous to a degree, and while admitting the correspondence of literary detail and historical reality in this sequence, he insists on seeing "savage humor" in the contrast of this passage with its less serious environment. I suggest instead that we are now confronted by pure savagery, bereft of humor.

In fact, if we seek consistency throughout the poem, we inevitably miss the central point of the composition. Robert could not have realized his project had the text remained static and humorous from beginning to end. He begins by presenting the symbol of cowardice or passivity (the heron) when the king and his subjects are in the properly pliant mood: conviviality reinforced, if not provoked, by drink. The king's vow is hardly ominous, and the next several are lighthearted and amusing. Clearly (for Robert), this situation must change, and as the participants get into the spirit of the vowing session and try to outdo one another, the vows also become more serious and more ominous. With Valkenberg, matters are reaching fever pitch, and Robert is close to achieving his objective of inciting his companions to immediate bellicose action.

At the same time, matters become more complicated in another way as well. We have already seen that indiscriminate boasting by Suffolk had brought him into conflict with Beaumont, troubling the conviviality of the occasion and casting doubt on the clarity of allegiances. Now Beaumont proves himself the voice of reason (or, from Robert's viewpoint, of dangerous skepticism). He belittles boasting that is provoked by strong wine and attractive women, noting that the courage displayed under those twin influences is sure to wither when one is confronted by the cold of weather and the heat of battle; then, he says, the braggart will wish for the safety of a dark cellar somewhere (see 358–75). Beaumont's caution may in fact be the most accurate prediction of all: much will go wrong; beginnings are easy, but completing what one undertakes and returning safely are no easy matters.

His reservations notwithstanding, Beaumont, too, agrees to offer a vow, but it is a conditional one, reflecting again the complexities of alliances and loyalties at the time: he will serve as the marshal of the king's army, unless he is recalled from exile by the king of France. In fact, history tells us that, shortly before the Battle of Crécy, he realigned his allegiances and agreed to serve the French king.

And finally, there is the queen's chilling vow (416–27). Nothing in the preceding scenes, and particularly in the comparatively reasonable attitude of Beaumont, could prepare us for her words. They not only close the circle of vows begun by the king, but they punctuate the series by threatening violence, as no other vow had done, against the speaker herself. In fact, her vow proves to be the catalyst needed to transform the occasion definitively from an idle boasting contest into military action. Specifically, in order to persuade her husband the king to take her along as he goes off to accomplish his vow, she announces that she is pregnant and swears that if she is not on the continent when the infant is about to be born, she will kill both herself and her child with a long steel knife.

Here it should be noted that two of the ten participants are women; one makes her vow near the beginning; the other is last. The contrast between them is striking. The first supports the man with her, vowing only to wait for him and, if he executes his vow, to give him her love. The queen, by contrast, takes matters into her own hands, offering a vow that is rendered particularly chilling by its specificity and by the objects of the threatened violence. In part, the queen's vow is a closural device—it causes Edward to bring the vowing session to an abrupt halt—but the increasing violence of the words both underlines the psychological preparation for war and, at the same time, illustrates the danger of vows that get out of hand. The contrast is dramatic between a man who vows not to open his eye and a woman willing to kill herself and her unborn child.

As soon as the session ends, part of the heron is consumed (as was customary in poems belonging to the vowing cycle), and then the king makes the necessary preparations and leads his knights and his queen to the continent. At Antwerp her child is born and is named Lionel of Antwerp. She has accomplished her vow, but the poet warns that before the others are accomplished, much blood will be shed. Robert, on the other hand, has achieved his goal: "Adont parti li cours des Englés par dela" (442) [Thus the English court set out across the sea].

Authorial technique depends largely, as noted, on the knowledge we bring to our reading; without such knowledge of the historical characters and events, the poem means little. Particularly in the early sections of the text, the narrator sets up apparently heroic situations and then undoes them, with us as privileged observers. As the poem progresses, that irony assumes a sharper, even brutal edge, conveying the fundamental absurdity of the war and the tragic ease with which it can be provoked. It may be going too far to call the work an antiwar poem, but as Beaumont's condemnation of idle boasting in *laisse* X indicates, it is surely a text whose cutting irony undermines the validity of militaristic posturing.

Any contention that *Les Voeux du heron* is a neglected masterpiece would be extravagant. Yet, it is by no means without merit. The poet, whoever he was, was a writer of far more than passable skill who responded admirably to the demands his subject made on him. The result is a text that is far more complex than a casual reading would suggest, a text that effectively dramatizes the sinister process by which political manipulation, cynically but expertly conducted by the protagonist, transforms a jovial court gathering into the prelude to a calamitous war.

NOTES

1. Vowing poems were popular in late-medieval France, and we have a series of them in which vows are pronounced over a bird. The best known and most important of these compositions is *Les Voeux du paon* (*The Vows of the Peacock*), composed by Jacques de Longuyon sometime before 1313; see *Les Voeux du Paon*, ed. Graeme R. L. Ritchie, in *The Buik of Alexander by John Barbour*, vol. 1 (Edinburgh: Scottish Text Society, 1925). For a brief discussion of the cycle within which it stands, see Renate Blumenfeld-Kosinski, "The Poetics of Continuation in the Old French *Paon* Cycle," *Romance Philology* 39 (1986): 437–47. The other vowing poems, including, *Les Voeux du heron*, were doubtless written in imitation of Jacques's poem. This essay is based on a section of the introduction to John L. Grigsby and Norris J. Lacy, eds., and Norris J. Lacy, trans., *The Vows of the Heron*,

Garland Library of Medieval Literature 86, series A (New York: Garland Publishing, 1992), 8–18. All line references, given parenthetically, are to this edition. Permission of the publisher is gratefully acknowledged.

2. The same events are recounted in a later Latin text, the *Chronographia Regum Francorum*, ed. H[enri] Moranvillé, 3 vols. (Paris: Sociètè de l'histoire de France, 1891–97), which probably drew on the *Vows of the Heron*. The Latin text (which incidentally gives the date as 1337 rather than 1338) is printed as Appendix II in Grigsby and Lacy, *The Vows of the Heron*, 98–100.

3. The text has been transmitted in five fourteenth-century manuscripts (in addition to two nineteenth-century transcriptions). The manuscripts are S (Bern, Burgerbibliothek, 323, the base manuscript for the 1992 Grigsby-Lacy edition); R (Brussels, Bibliothèque Royale, 10433); U (Brussels, Bibliothèque Royale, 11138); X (Brussels, Bibliothèque Royale, IV, 601); P (Paris, Bibliothèque Nationale, fonds français 9222). Although published over a half-century ago, B. J. Whiting, "The Vows of the Heron," *Speculum* 20 (1945): 261–78, remains one of the more useful studies available. Measuring textual developments against historical fact, Whiting concludes that the *Heron* is a "grimly satirical document" in which the characters are generally associated with "unsuccessful, mean or revolting acts" (278). (Oddly, as I note below, he also sees humor in the text from beginning to end.) I suggest instead that the text is "grim" only toward the end and that its effect is more striking and dramatic precisely because it has begun as a lighter, almost jesting (if somewhat cynical) poem that then takes a dark turn and ultimately leads to calamity.

4. Except one, Fauquemont/Valkenberg (concerning whom see below).

5. Some writers of the time recounted incidents that correspond roughly to those that the *Voeux du heron* protagonists vow to undertake. Jean Froissart, for example, by commenting that Sir Walter Manny had vowed in England that he would be the first to enter France, implied (but of course did not establish) that something like the poem's vowing session may really have taken place; see Jean Froissart, *Chroniques de J. Froissart*, vol. 1, *1307–1340 (Depuis l'avènement d'Edouard II jusq'au siège de Tournay)*, ed. Simèon Luce, Sociètè de l'histoire de France (Paris: J. Renouard, 1869).

6. Whiting, "The Vows of the Heron," 270.

7. The poem is in *laisse* structure, composed of stanzas of unequal length; the longest is 118 lines, the shortest only fourteen.

8. Whiting, "The Vows of the Heron," 271.

9. Whiting, "The Vows of the Heron," 271.

10. Since Robert d'Artois did not invite Beaumont to make a vow at this time (but will do so later), and since Beaumont's speech does not include the customary formulaic elements (e.g., "I vow and promise"), it appears to fall outside the primary vow structure of the poem and thus was not included in my enumeration of ten vows.

11. Whiting, "Vows of the Heron," 273.

CHAPTER 2

INSCRIBING THE BODY WITH MEANING

CHIVALRIC CULTURE AND THE NORMS OF VIOLENCE IN *THE VOWS OF THE HERON*

PATRICIA DeMARCO

The Vows of the Heron (*Les Voeux du heron*), a mid-fourteenth-century poem, has often been cited as one of the medieval period's few direct critiques of chivalric violence. And in the history of the *Vows*' reception, one moment in the poem has consistently captured the attention of editors and critics. In the final *laisse*, the pregnant Queen Philippa offers a vow to rip open her womb should the fetus within attempt to be born before her husband, King Edward III, has an opportunity to engage militarily with the French:

"Je sai bien que piecha
Que sui grosse d'enfant, que mon corps sentu l'a.
Encore n'a il gaires qu'en men corps se tourna.
Et je veue et promech a Dieu qui me crea,
Qui nasqui de la Virge que ses corps n'enpira,
Et qui morut en crois, on le crucefia,
Que ja li fruis de moy de mon corps n'istera
...
Et s'il en voelt isir quant besoins n'en sera,
D'un grant coutel d'achier li miens corps s'ochira:
S'ara m'ame perdue et li fruis perira."[1]

> [I have known for some time / That I am pregnant; my body has felt it. / It moved in my body only a short while ago. / And I vow and promise to God, who created me, / Who was born of the Virgin (whose body remained whole), / And who died on the cross, crucified, / That my fruit will never leave my body. . . . And if it should desire to be born before that time, / With a great steel knife my body will slay itself. / Thus will my soul be lost and the fruit will perish.]

Beginning with the earliest nineteenth-century editors, this remarkable scene has been taken as a rare example of the critical perspective so hard to locate within the chivalric tradition.[2] In this essay, my object will be to specify the kinds of critical energies which are being released here and to ask further what role gender plays in both the scene itself and in the history of critical assessments of the poem. None of the vows which precede that of the queen have ever engendered the outrage and confident condemnation that her vow has provoked; in essence, her vow has been taken to be the very negation of chivalry, an ideology usually able to accommodate all possible negations. Why has this vow been so troubling?

To address these critical issues, the first section of this essay begins by sketching out the normative parameters within which chivalric literature conceived of the violence of warfare. Using the theoretical work of Elaine Scarry, I will suggest how casualties in war may or may not be invested with meaning and hence legitimacy in chivalric descriptions, and I will argue that, assessed against these parameters, the representation of violence in the *Vows of the Heron* stages a rejection of the usual methods through which chivalry inscribed the wounded body with meaning. The second section of this essay will turn to a contemporary philosophical background for these texts, the extensive theological writings concerning just war theory, and consider how the poet's familiarity with the concepts of intent and agency in this body of writing opens up an avenue through which to critique aristocratic violence. I will also suggest here that the poet confers a "positive," alternative meaning to chivalric violence, one built upon an emergent category of civilian immunities.[3] In the third and final section, I will return to the queen's vow in order to unpack the unspoken assumptions that inform the poet's representation of the pregnant woman as an agent and as an object of war's violence.

THE NORMS OF VIOLENCE

The Vows of the Heron was written either during or after the year 1346, well after the Hundred Years' War had begun. The events narrated by the poem itself, however, are set explicitly in September of 1338. On this, the eve of the Hundred Years' War, the poem tells the story of a dinner at which an exiled French nobleman, Robert of Artois, shames the English king Edward III into declaring war against France.[4] Eager to set the war in motion, Robert instigates a courtly vowing game in which each member of Edward's court offers a vow "in the name of a heron" to perform great deeds of arms against the French. From its opening lines, the violence of the early campaigns of the Hundred Years' War is vividly rendered.

> Ensi en avint il en che propre termin
> Par un gentil vassal qui estoit de grand lin.
> Robers d'Artois ot non, ce dïent palasin.
> Chiex commencha la guerre et l'orible hustin
> Dont maint boin chevalier fu jeté mort souvin,
> Mainte dame en fu vesve et maint povre orfelin,
> Et maint boin maronnier a courchiét son termin,
> Et mainte preudefeme mise a divers destin,
> Et tante bele eglise fu arse et mise a fin
> Et encore sera, se Jhesu n'i met fin (17–26).

[Thus it occurred at that time, / Because of a noble vassal who was of high lineage: / His name, according to the courtiers, was Robert of Artois. / He began the war and the terrible strife, / In which many fine knights were struck down dead, / Many ladies were made widows, and there were many orphans, / And many fine seamen had their lives shortened, / And many good women were forcibly corrupted; / And a great many churches were burned and destroyed—/ And many more will be, unless Jesus bring this to an end.]

The poem's direct and nonidealized representation of the destruction occasioned by the Hundred Years' War might seem to offer compelling evidence of a critical dimension in this poem. But, as many have observed of similar passages in chivalric biographies and chronicles, such descriptions must be handled with care.[5] In chivalric narrative, dramatic and graphic depictions of war's casualties are regularly rendered without the slightest indication of a critical tone, and laments over the horror of war often coexist comfortably with strident defenses of the necessity and righteousness of war.[6]

This is not to say that chivalric narratives were not circumscribed by an implicit but powerful sense of what might be thought of as normative and what improper violence. The dividing line between these categories is very difficult to demonstrate, however, largely because it is never so simple a question as the nature or quantity of violence which is at issue. The propriety of any violent act—the sense of normative parameters—is determined, rather, by the way in which a given action may or may not derive its meaning from larger systems of honor, regardless of the action. To understand the flexibility of this system, it may be useful to refer to Elaine Scarry's work on the semiotic functions of the wounded body. In *The Body in Pain*, Scarry suggests that the wounded body plays an important role in deciding and verifying contested issues such as disputes about the possession of territory. She maintains that the wounded body's primary function, one which is exercised outside of the immediate environment or moment of conflict, is "to substantiate whatever outcome was produced" as a result of a given conflict.[7] In a given territorial dispute, for instance, the populace's investments are given concrete form as they are inscribed with extreme literalness on the body. Attached to the "disembodied" ideas of warfare, the wounded body functions to verify and to memorialize aspects of national consciousness, political belief, and self-definition.[8] In her analysis, this process is made possible by the profound referential instability of the body itself. Since the body is incontestably real but also lacking any intrinsic meaning, the wounded body easily becomes "an attribute of an issue that at that moment has no independent reality of its own."[9]

Scarry's powerful account of the signifying potentiality of the body can help us to examine the function of the wounded body in chivalric texts which idealize warfare as the privileged arena for the performance of chivalric identity.[10] Following Scarry's suggestion that the material effects of war (i.e., the wounded body) are central to the processes of perception through which war comes to have meaning, we can observe how the injured body becomes a central component in chivalric literature's project of inculcating chivalric values and securing the identity of the chivalric man-at-arms. Let me consider briefly here two characteristic texts in order to establish the normative parameters through which chivalric writers understood the meaning of violent practices.

The Chandos Herald's chivalric biography of the Black Prince will provide our first case in point. Composed in the 1380s by an English writer with firsthand knowledge of the battlefield and considerable sympathy for the combatants on both sides of the Hundred Years' War, *The Life of the Black Prince* details the brutal tactics of war used by the English against the French.[11] Even the sympathetic voice of the Chandos Herald, however, comments with admiration on the manner in which the English "overrode and wholly burnt and laid waste" the French countryside.[12] Describing such acts explicitly as deeds of "prowess, valor, and hardihood," the Chandos biographer seems untroubled by the fact that these tactics were frequently directed against noncombatants, as when the English, while enroute to Paris, "to disport themselves, put everything to fire and flame. There they made many a widowed lady and many a poor child orphan."[13]

Despite the measure of sympathy expressed here, the legitimacy of an attack on civilians passes by unquestioned, suggesting that such tactics were considered a normative practice of the Hundred Years' War.[14] There is little, moreover, in the Chandos biographer's account to suggest that such practices were thought to be incompatible with proper chivalric behavior. Indeed the Chandos biographer expresses admiration for the single-minded brutality of his enemy: "Whoso saw coming the puissance and power of the King of France, great marvel would he have to relate! Inflamed with ill-will and anger they set forth to encounter together, bearing themselves in such true knightly fashion that never since Christ's coming did one behold fiercer battle."[15] Such passages remind us that within the chivalric community, violent self-assertion might draw admiration regardless of national or state boundaries. As the Chandos poet's lists of the wounded and the dead further witness, the chivalric ethos was capable of sustaining an acknowledgment of war's brutal realities without any sense of incompatibility with chivalry's highly idealized vision of its own practices.

Our second case will be that of the *Chronicles* of Jean Froissart. Here I would like to consider two passages, both of which describe knightly interventions on the behalf of civilians. The first comes from the account of an Anglo-French battle in 1346 in which Froissart describes the slaughter of the citizens of Caen by English forces.[16] In the midst of the slaughter, the English knight Sir Thomas Holland arrives. Froissart says that he "rode into the streets, and saved many lives of ladies, demoiselles, and cloisterers from defiling, for the soldiers were without mercy."[17] A similar moment of chivalric intervention is highlighted in Froissart's discussion of the vow made by Edward III to wreak vengeance on the inhabitants of Caen for the death of his beloved knights. Froissart says there that Sir Godfrey of Harcourt convinced the king to put aside his right to vengeance and further implies that chivalric virtue had won the day as Godfrey proceeded through Caen, commanding in the king's name that "none to be so hardy to put fire in any house, to slay any person, nor to violate any woman."[18]

We might make several observations here. The first involves an apparent inconsistency between Froissart's account and that of the Chandos Herald. At first glance Froissart's censorious account of the ransacking of Caen and his admiring recollection of the merciful deeds of the English might seem to provide a stark contrast to the Chandos Herald's admiration for the brutal tactics of the Black Prince. Although one might account for this difference by simply invoking the possibility for very different ethical codes within examples of a single type of historical work, I would argue here that these apparently very different accounts actually evaluate military actions according to the same set of chivalric principles and are both indebted to a common understanding of the meaning of the death and destruction occasioned by war. To put the case simply, in both accounts any given action (i.e., attacking civilian populations) may be judged noble when it is recognized as instantiating the chivalric virtue of the knight (i.e., his prowess, his assertiveness) and ignoble when the act is held to demonstrate the lack of such virtues (i.e., his lack of mercy or generosity). As Scarry's meditations on the body remind us, deeds of arms lack any intrinsic ethical coding. Within the tautologies of chivalric culture, acts of violence are dependent, at least in part, upon a deed's place in realizing chivalric identity. They are condoned to the degree that an act of injury is suffused with the meaning of honor, reprehensible without the citation of the chivalric ethos.

As Scarry observes, the wounded body's meaning, though fundamentally arbitrary, is neither disposable nor predetermined. Indeed the referential instability that is the hallmark of the body, the fact that the body's hurt requires a "separate specification" to endow it with meaning (e.g., honor), always allows the body to be "translated into another language," to be "relocated elsewhere."[19] This is just the possibility which is realized in the opening *laisse* of the *Vows of the Heron*, as the poem depicts the dead bodies of sailors and soldiers, the raped bodies of good women, and the widows and orphans who are the living witnesses to war's injuring practices. But what seems significant in the *laisse* is not the mere presence of the lifeless body (or of the ransacked church, for that matter) but rather the absence of a chivalric discourse which would give these bodies meaning within the chivalric ethos of honor (whether understood individually, as the knight's honor, or collectively, as the honor of England). In other words, whereas warfare in the chivalric biography provides an occasion for the knight to perform his chivalric identity, and whereas the bodies of the dead and wounded function to materialize that identity, giving it the meaning of honor and prowess, in the opening *laisse* of the *Vows of the Heron* the poet has severed the body from the chivalric ethos which would give it meaning. With this displacement, he has also suppressed the power of the chivalric vow to effect a meaningful reality.

AGENCY, INTENTIONALITY, AND
MEDIEVAL THEORIES OF THE JUST WAR

This separation between the body and its meaning cannot be sustained, however, once the poet turns to the knights' vows. To understand this, I would like to consider briefly the very peculiar nature of the chivalric vow. The vow is a classic example of what J. L. Austin defined as a performative utterance, a speech act in which saying something is doing it: "Let there be light," "I thee wed," "I declare war."[20] From Austin's classic formulation to the discussions of Jacques Derrida and Judith Butler, one important feature of the performative has been stressed: its presupposition of a fully endowed agent.[21] As Judith Butler has argued, the founding fiction of the performative utterance is that its power to instantiate reality originates with the speaking subject. More than other sorts of discourse, the performative implies an immediate and transparent agent who is fully capable of effecting reality with mere words. Thus, as performative utterances, vows must accomplish two things successfully: first, they must secure the fiction of the self-endowed agent; and second, they must substantiate the meaning of the vow—in this case, as an instantiation of honor—through a verifying material reality. In the *Vows of the Heron*, however, the agency of each avower is variously troubled. In order to explain these troubles, let me offer a brief explanation of some late medieval ideas about intentionality as they are outlined in the theory of the just war.

Discussing the tendency of critics to read the alliterative *Morte Arthure*'s realistic and graphically violent rendition of King Arthur's military campaigns as evidence of the poet's critical attitude toward warfare, Juliet Vale has commented that "according to the laws of war, injury to the non-combatant, or the havoc caused by an army on *chevauchée* is not in itself good or bad: condoned in support of a just cause; unpardonable without such justification."[22] According to the tenets of just war theory, there were two primary ways in which the destruction of war could be justified, both of which had been established by Augustine and carried into the fourteenth century through the writings of Gratian, Aquinas, and the school of legists associated with the Post-glossators.[23] In Augustine's treatment of the just war, the suffering experienced by noncombatants had to be understood within the larger purposes of divine providence.[24] Whether a given war was divinely authorized or undertaken without the sanction of divine will, it functioned in either case to execute divine justice. For Augustine, the death and destruction inflicted in warfare, although it might appear to be arbitrary from the limited viewpoint of humans, was in truth a local instance of the higher workings of divine providence.[25] Consequently, the suffering of both civilian and combatant in the just war had a higher purpose. The destruction inflicted upon an enemy, for instance, could function to deliver retribution for sinful behavior while the suffering of the just could work to test the patience of the faithful.[26]

At the level of individual ethics, the just war was distinguished from simple violence through an examination of intent. We have already touched upon the way in which Augustine had made central to his account the claim that warfare functioned to institute justice. For Augustine warfare was only just when it was conducted with a motive and a disposition consistent with this higher purpose.[27] Consequently, Augustine denied the right of private persons to exercise violence (in war or in self-defense) on their own authority and accorded the status of justness only to those wars initiated and conducted by the sovereign who, Augustine argued, was most capable of undertaking violent action with a just and charitable disposition.[28] Thus the theology of the just war gave birth to a potent and extremely influential conceptual division between the just, public warfare of the ruler and the unjust, private violence of the individual.

Whereas Augustine, writing for a Christian populace under the secular jurisdiction of the Roman Empire, was troubled by the capacity of kings to act tyrannically and to use warfare to advance illicitly their own material interests or to feed their sinful lusts for territory, the fourteenth-century legists who inherited Augustinian and Thomistic theories of the just war wrote as the civil servants of Christian states seeking to expand the monopoly powers of the sovereign state over the exercise of violence.[29] Their formulations of the just war consequently stressed the destructive character of violence exercised by the individual acting outside of sovereign authority. Augustine's foundational distinction between the public war of the sovereign state and private acts of war was thus developed to produce elaborate conceptual schema by which the private violence exercised by aristocrats (in the pursuit of vengeance, as an extralegal defense of land claims, etc.) and by mercenaries and disbanded groups of soldiers (who enroute to war pillaged and looted their way through towns and villages) could be condemned.[30] Moreover, in their concern to justify the containment, and in some formulations the criminalization, of private violence late medieval just war theorists extended Augustine's understanding of the defining power of intentions, stressing the problem of the unjustly motivated combatant acting within the sphere of the just war.

Using intentionality as a criterion to distinguish acts of licit and illicit violence, fourteenth-century legists such as John of Legnano and Honoré

Bonet struck at the heart of chivalric identity, threatening to render illicit much of what a late medieval reader of chivalric literature would have understood as proper knightly activity. In the sphere of the public war, for example, Legnano defined military service motivated by "the intention of plundering" as both unjust and "dishonorable."[31] In the sphere of private warfare, Legnano and Bonet challenged the knight's right to assert his interests and his honor with recourse to direct, independent and passionate violent action.[32] Seeking to limit the nobleman's right to exercise private violence, both Legnano and Bonet condemned acts of violence motivated by either the angry drive for vengeance or the chivalric desire for repute.[33] The criterion of intentionality could be used to assess the conduct of the knight in both public and private warfare, thus providing a potent weapon with which to critique the destruction occasioned by noble violence.

This theoretically useful technique was given concrete form by Honoré Bonet in an attempt to provide a foundation for the immunity of civilians from warfare. Bonet's *L'Arbre des Batailles* provides an illuminating point of comparison with *The Vows of the Heron*, especially in the symptomatic rhetoric which Bonet uses to represent death and destruction. Having defended the doctrine of civilian immunities in a lengthy section, Bonet concludes his argument with an important caveat: "if sometimes the humble and innocent suffer harm and lose their goods, it cannot be otherwise, for as I have said above, all the weeds cannot be uprooted from among the good plants without some of the latter coming to harm, because they are too close and neighboring one to another."[34] The difference here between Bonet's figuration of the body of the civilian and that which we have observed in our previous examples is striking. Where the Chandos biographer unabashedly portrays the destruction wreaked on civilians, acknowledging that the main purpose of war is to injure and to destroy, Bonet vacillates in *L'Arbre* between condemning violence against civilians and masking the centrality of such practices to even the just war. In the passage just cited, the metaphorical representation of the death of civilians occludes the material fact of war's destruction. As the extended conceit of weeds and uprooting displaces what would be the disturbing presence of the massacred civilians, Bonet's treatise asserts that the death of civilians is an unfortunately frequent but essentially unintended aspect of war.[35] With the emphasis on just intentions, the theologian's and the legist's justification of warfare becomes insufficient to the task of legitimating the death of civilians, making it increasingly difficult to acknowledge explicitly that the central purpose of warfare is to injure and to kill.

Such a displacement is effectively refused by the *Vows* poet who, as we have seen in examining *laisse* one, makes it possible to see the bodies of civilians as war's victims. In returning to the *Vows*, we will now explore how the poem reveals the civilian as war's *intended* victim, enabling a critique of the chivalric man-at-arm's violent practice of arms within the context of the just war.

On its surface, *The Vows of the Heron* presents the Hundred Years' War as a *bellum hostile*, a war justified by its initiation by a sovereign prince and by that prince's genealogical claim to the French throne.[36] The poet establishes this history in two separate passages in the text: in the first, Robert of Artois suggests that Edward has just cause for initiating war against France (82–85), and in the second, Edward himself considers and repudiates challenges leveled by many contemporary writers against his claim to possess just cause in his war against France (108–17).[37]

But although the *Vows of the Heron* presents Edward III's own claim for the Hundred Years' War's status as a just war, the poem suggests that lurking below the public rhetoric of the just war lay the unjust motivations and impulses of private vengeance. Indeed it is the desire for private vengeance that sets the plot of the poem into motion and leads the French noble, Robert of Artois, to bring a heron before the courtly Edward III, accusing the English king and his court of cowardice. As the narrator notes in introducing Robert's inciting speech, Robert of Artois had been banished from his home in France by the French King Philip (34–36). Robert admits that he will find his revenge only when he has successfully prodded Edward into declaring war against Philip. Laughing, Robert says to himself:

> ... "Or ai je men avis,
> Quant par ichel hairon que au jour d'ewy ay prins
> Commenchera grant guerre, selonc le mien avis.
> Je doi bien avoir joie par Dieu de paradis,
> Car a tort du boin roy fuy sevrés et partis;
> Et banis fui de Franche, le nobile païs,
> Et desevrés a doel de tous mes boins amis.
> ...
> Je m'en iray en Franche, n'en suy mie esbahis,
> Et si me conbaterai ains que soie partis" (119–26; 141–42).
>
> [Now I have my wish, / Since on this heron that I caught today, / A great war will begin, according to my desire. / I should be happy, by God in heaven, / For I was wrongly separated and divided from the good

king. / And I was banished from the noble land of France / And grievously separated from all my good friends / ... I will go to France—I am not frightened— / And I will do battle before I leave there.]

Far from having any interest in Edward III's claim to the throne or in the common good of England, Robert is motivated by the passion for vengeance, a passion which leads him to manipulate and transform Edward's concern for public honor and for the claims of genealogy into a war which serves his own interests.

The drive for vengeance highlighted in this opening scene is also invoked twice later when Robert prods the nobles at Edward's court to partake in the courtly vowing game and join Edward in the war against France. These two remarks occur at significant moments in the narrative: first, following Walter of Manny's promise to destroy a French city and kill its inhabitants (225–28), and second, after the Earl of Derby's vow to joust with Louis of Flanders (279–83). Robert's declaration of his interest in vengeance in both of these vowing scenes works to associate the chivalric passion for deeds of arms with the motive force of vengeance. And through this association the poet casts a shadow on Edward's claim for a just *causa belli* in the Hundred Years' War.

Another challenge to the status of Edward's war is delivered in the narration of the vows made by the nobles at his court. Three of these vows show a particular emphasis on the conception of warfare as an occasion for the performance of chivalric deeds: Walter of Manny's vow to set fire to the inhabitants of a fortified city "long held" by Godemars du Fay (238–40); the Earl of Derby's vow to "joust" against "a powerful and much feared count," Louis of Flanders (273); and the vow of the Earl of Suffolk who, taking up his "heart's desire to do battle," promises to seek the "son of an emperor who has much goodness in him" and make him feel the force of his lance or sword (294–98). In each of these cases, interest in prosecuting the sovereign's war derives from the opportunity war provides for winning repute through personal combat. One could imagine such portraits being given in praise of chivalric heroism were it not for the fact that, as Norris Lacy has convincingly demonstrated, these are portraits deeply marked by irony.[38] As an audience reading this poem in the 1340s would be likely to know, each of the vows met with miserable failure in historical reality.[39] In establishing this ironic perspective, the poet strips the chivalric veneer from the knightly vow. All that remains are a series of bombastic assertions marked by self-interest and the drive for personal reputation.

To further understand the poet's purposes here, we will need to attend to both the language of these knightly vows and the implications of this language in establishing the "justice" of Edward's war. The vows of Manny, Derby, and Suffolk are all marked by the romance idiom, a point further highlighted in the language of Robert's challenge to John of Valkenberg as he summons him to "vow to the heron the right to *adventure*" (my emphasis). For a French audience reading the *Vows* in the 1340s, Valkenberg was an infamous figure. Along with another of the poem's knightly avowers, John of Hainault, he was notorious for having committed wartime atrocities as part of the English invasion of Cambrésis in 1339. Indeed, Valkenberg's vow has him promise to do deeds very much like those of which he was accused in contemporary accounts:[40]

> ". . . se li rois englés passoit dela le mer,
> Et parmi Canbresis voloit en Franche entrer,
> Que g'iroie le fu par devant li bouter,
> Et si n'espargneroie ne moustier ne autel,
> Femme grosse n'enfant que peüsse trouver,
> Ne parent ne ami, tant me peüst amer,
> Pour tant que il vausist roy Edouart grever.
> Pour son acomplir vorray mon cors pener.
> Or aviegne qu'aviegne, je voel *aventurer*" (338–46, my emphasis).

> [if the English king crossed the sea / And wanted to enter France through the Cambrésis, / I would go and set the land ablaze before him; / And I would not spare church or altar, / Or any pregnant woman nor child I might find, / Or any relative or friend, however much he loved me, / Should he stand in the way of King Edward. / To accomplish this I am willing to suffer. / Now come what may, I wish to go *adventuring*.]

In Valkenberg's vow, the true motive spurring his participation is shown to be the preeminent right of the romance hero to adventure. And, as the tenor of the courtly vowing game reaches a violent pitch in Valkenberg's vow, the poem demonstrates once again the way in which chivalric adventures bring about the destruction of civilians (pregnant women and children) and of communal bonds (relatives and friends).

As I have already suggested in discussing the views of Honoré Bonet, there is nothing unusual per se about the acknowledgment of the death of civilians in war. There are, however, several features of the *Vows of the Heron*'s portrait which distinguish it from more typical contemporary representations of war and chivalry. In much of the literature of the period, when the death of civilians or the destruction of property is mentioned, responsibility for such acts is placed on the free companies and on nonnoble troops who were frequently portrayed rioting and looting their way to and from war. For example, the previously cited passage from Froissart attributed responsibility for the brutal ransacking of Caen to the "soldiers," clearly distinguishing the brutal acts of the unchivalric nonaristocrat from the merciful deeds of the English knights.[41]

The Vows of the Heron, by contrast, not only blames the nobility for such brutal deeds, it does so in such a way as to stress the clear *intent* behind such destruction. John of Valkenberg *plans* to kill pregnant women and to destroy churches. Thus where a text like Bonet's *L'Arbre des Batailles* conceives of these deaths as unfortunate and unintended, *The Vows of the Heron* insists that they are both the inevitable consequence and the intended action of the chivalric classes at war. Within the defining parameters of just war theory, as we have already noted, these are actions which clearly fail to meet the criterion of just intentions. Moreover, by suggesting that the Hundred Years' War is fueled by the drive for vengeance, the *Vows* poet refuses the conceptual separation of the just war and the war of private vengeance. The complex strategy whereby the poet exposes the blurred boundary between the just public war and the unjust war of private vengeance can be witnessed in the vow of Valkenberg. Valkenberg yokes the "desire to adventure" ("je voel aventurer") to the king's cause ("par son veu acomplir"). This declaration is, of course, a re-enactment of Robert's earlier performance in which he moved Edward to declare war by tying the language of sovereign rights and titles to the chivalric discourse of honor, shame, and vengeance, rendering them indistinguishable.

As we have seen, *The Vows of the Heron* both attests to the private interests which fueled aristocratic support for warfare and also shows a critical awareness of how easily such illicit aristocratic practices and motives could be united to the cause of the king's just war. In both instances, the *Vows* attempts to forge a critical perspective from which a contemporary audience would be brought to reflect critically not only upon the destructive character of war, but also upon the destructive practices of the chivalric man-at-arms. As we shall see, however, *The Vows of the Heron* ultimately fails to resolve the problems it reveals. For although the poem exposes the drive for vengeance as the dark underside of the just war, it also suggests that the alternative to the brutal, vengeance-driven chivalrics of a Robert of Artois or a Valkenberg is itself deeply problematic.

THE COURTLY LOVER, THE LADY,
AND THE LIMITS OF CRITIQUE

As we have already seen, *The Vows of the Heron* brings the drive for private vengeance under intense critical scrutiny, but well before the reader encounters the violent chivalrics of Manny and Valkenberg, she or he is presented with four vows which have been described by Norris Lacy as "ironic, amorous, and largely inconsequential." They are innocuous as well, providing a surprising introduction to the militant chivalrics that we have just surveyed. Noting the peculiarly disproportionate concern of these vows with courtly love, Lacy has suggested that the interest in love in this poem "offer[s] an ironic counterpoint to the primary scenes being played out."[42] We might put this point even more forcefully, observing that *The Vows of the Heron* does much to highlight the incommensurabilities between devotion to love and devotion to warfare.

Indeed, the poem suggests that the amorous devotions of the knight are the root cause of the inconsequential character of his promised deeds. As Robert of Artois first enters Edward's court, he disparages and shames the English by asserting that those "cui amours ont sousprins" [who are ruled by love] and "qui sont soubgis / As dames amoureuses" [who are the subjects / Of fair, amorous ladies] are cowards whose vows to perform deeds should be made on the heron, the most cowardly of birds. Having declared that only "li preu amoureus, qui d'amours sont garnis" [the valiant lovers, who are furnished with love] should vow to the heron (69–73), Robert directs his shaming indictment of the English at Edward III, a king portrayed as being more interested in love and leisure than in war:

> Li roys seoit a table sans penser mal engin,
> En pensees d'amours, tenant le chief enclin.
> Du gentil roy de Franche s'apeloit il cousin
> Et le tint en chierté com son loiel voisin;
> Envers li ne pensoit bataille ne hustin (10–14).
>
> [The king was seated at table, without evil thoughts; / With his head bowed, he was thinking of love. / He was cousin to the good king of France / And held him dear, as his loyal neighbor; / He had no thought of war or strife against him.]

In this opening portrait of the English court, Edward's lack of interest in warfare is presented as an extension of his courtly demeanor. The peaceful character of the one devoted to love contrasts sharply with the militant character of Robert of Artois:

> ... un gentil vassal qui estoit de grand lin.
> ...
> Chiex commencha la guerre et l'orible hustin
> Dont maint boin chevalier fu jeté mort souvin ... (18–21).
>
> [a noble vassal who was of high lineage: / ... he began the war and the terrible strife, / In which many fine knights were struck down dead....]

While Edward prefers to pass his time feasting with his courtiers, his thoughts bent on love and leisure, men like Robert of Artois do the real business of war. Here the poet presents the reader with a contrast made familiar in the courtly romances of Chrétien de Troyes and best known to students of late medieval English literature through the chronicler Walsingham's protest that Richard II favored "the knights of Venus rather than the knights of Bellona," those "more valiant in the bedchamber than on the field, armed with words rather than weapons, prompt in speaking but slow in performing the acts of war."[43]

If it is clear that the opening vows of the poem function satirically to mock the courtly knight and his preoccupation with women and amorous dalliances, it is far more difficult to account for the poet's purposes in setting forth such a series of courtly vows as a prelude to the more violent promises of Manny and Valkenberg. Walsingham's indictment of the courtly knight presumes a standard of normative judgment which argues implicitly for the valorization of the knight of Mars. Preoccupation with women, leisurely lounging, and talk of love are signs of degeneration from a masculinist norm of aggressive action and competitive assertiveness; moreover, the only defense against charges such as Artois's and Walsingham's is one which requires that the knight undertake direct and militant action. This is the logic, of course, behind Robert of Artois's introduction of the vowing game and the purpose animating his shaming remarks. But is this also the poet's logic? The poet's detailed satire of the courtly knight suggests that it is, but, as we have seen, much of the poem is also devoted to exposing the brutal tactics of the militant, vengeance-driven knight. With such incommensurable objects of critique, one might conclude that the poem is marked by a fundamental contradiction.

To unfold this contradiction, we may consider the vow made by the Earl of Salisbury, who is described as a model of the amorous courtier. Seated next to his lady, "ou grant amours apent, / Qui fut gente et courtoise de biau contenement" [the object of great love, / who was appealing and courtly and of fair countenance] (159–60), Salisbury asks her to place her finger over his eye. He then vows to perform valiant deeds—he will burn the French countryside "ou il a boine gent" [where there are good people]—all the while keeping his eye closed. In itself, Salisbury's vow could well seem properly chivalric. The voluntary closing of an eye is meant to suggest that the knight is taking on an extra burden in warfare, making his performance all the more remarkable. In actuality, however, the historical Earl of Salisbury had been blinded, as was well known, years earlier during a military engagement in the Scottish wars.[44] Salisbury's vow thus must have a sharp impact on our sense of knightly agency. As I suggested earlier, the power of the performative vow to instantiate identity requires the avower to be a fully endowed agent. But this is precisely what Salisbury is not. It is not in his power to take on blindness because he has already been blinded. With such an ironic casting of the courtly knight's pretensions to honorable action, the poet undercuts the illusion of agency at the heart of the chivalric vow.

A similar ironic casting animates the poet's depiction of Edward III in the final *laisse* of the poem, the same *laisse* as that in which Queen Philippa will deliver the vow with which we began this essay. Invited by Robert of Artois to make a vow, the queen protests at first that it would be shameful of her to comply ("Et honnis sont li corps que ja i pensera") [And cursed be the person who would even think I would vow] for

> "Dame ne peut vouer puis qu'elle signeur a,
> Car s'elle veue riens, son mari pooir a
> Que bien puet rapeller chou qu'elle vouera" (407–9).
>
> [A lady cannot vow when she has a husband, / For if she vows something, her husband has the power / To revoke the vow she has made.]

As a female, a body [li corps] who lacks the capacity to realize words in deeds, the queen cannot enact a vow, and thus her "mari," Edward, offers to acquit her vow with his own (masculine) body. He replies encouragingly to her, "Voués ... mes cors l'acquitera / Mes que finer en puisse, mes cors s'en penera!" (412–14) [Make your vow, my body will acquit it; / So that it will be accomplished, my body will labor] (my translation). The queen then delivers her vow:

> "Je sai bien que piecha
> Que sui grosse d'enfant, que mon corps sentu l'a.
> Encore n'a il gaires qu'en men corps se tourna.
> Et je veue et promech a Dieu qui me crea,

Qui nasqui de la Virge que ses corps n'enpira,
Et qui morut en crois, on le crucefia,
Que ja li fruis de moy de mon corps n'istera" (416–22).

[I have known for some time / That I am pregnant; my body has felt it. / It moved in my body only a short while ago. / And I vow and promise to God, who created me, / Who was born of the Virgin (whose body remained whole), / And who died on the cross, crucified, / That my fruit will never leave my body.]

The object of the satirical portrait at this moment is to make Edward's adoption of an aggressive, militant stance against France analogous to his claim to uphold his wife's vow, revealing his inadequacies on both counts. Like the courtly Salisbury, Edward is first aligned with the female body which cannot itself accomplish a vow and, then, as he offers to prove her vow with his body, threatened with the very same disability she possesses: her inability to turn words into deeds may become his. As in Salisbury's case, the only remedy to the disabilities incurred by preoccupation with women is direct, aggressive action. Faced with the specter of the queen's female body, bursting with child, the courtly king and husband must quickly declare war against France and turn his own words into deeds before an untimely delivery makes a mockery of his capacity for heroic agency.[45]

Unsurprisingly, at this point Edward puts an abrupt end to the vowing game: "Et quant li rois l'entent moult forment l'en pesa, / Et dist: 'Certainement nulz plus ne vouera'" (428–29). [When the king heard this, he was very distressed, / And he said, "Certainly, there will be no more vows."] In one manuscript version of the text, Edward directly silences the queen, exercising his prerogative as her husband to annul her vow. In such a response the poem registers the psychic consequences of condemning the violent practice and motives of the aristocracy, expressing the fear that to indict violent action is to undermine the very foundations of aristocratic masculine identity, leaving it no foundation upon which to perform either its difference from the feminine body or its privileged relation to power and authority.[46] Viewed in relation to the poem's critical meditation on the way in which violent action founds masculine identity, the poem's abrupt closure signals the limits of its critique.

Despite the possibility of containment here, I would like to suggest that, in one important way, the queen's vow maintains the poet's critical reflection on war's destructiveness. By returning to the final lines of the queen's speech, we can see that the vow also challenges chivalric violence against women and children, thus providing a foundation for an emergent ideal of civilian immunities.

Having sworn to hold her child within her womb until Edward accomplishes his vow in France, the queen offers this final concluding remark,

> "Et s'il en voelt isir quant besoins n'en sera,
> D'un grant coutel d'achier li miens corps s'ochira:
> S'ara m'ame perdue et li fruis perira" (425–27).
>
> [And if it should desire to be born before that time, / With a great steel knife my body will slay itself. / Thus will my soul be lost and the fruit will perish.]

With this conclusion to the queen's vow, the poem highlights two ways in which chivalric culture contributes to war's horrors. In the first instance, the queen's vow emerges as the logical outcome of a chivalric ritual, the vowing game, which demands and inspires ever more brutal acts of violence. Beginning with Salisbury's vow to engulf the good people in flames, reaching a fevered pitch in Valkenberg's promise to destroy churches and to kill pregnant women, and culminating in the queen's vow to do violence to her womb, the poet suggests that the competitive spirit of chivalric culture inspires ever more horrific acts of violence.

Considered as an exemplary instance of the behavior fueled by chivalric culture, the queen's vow also works to suggest how the wounded body is inscribed with meaning within the chivalric ethos. If warfare demands that the knight put his body at risk, and if vows to fight with one eye closed are understood metonymically as an expression of the combatant's willingness to inscribe his body with the meaning of victory (or honor, or any other meaning typically inscribed on the wounded body), then the queen's offer of her own body must also be considered a chivalrous sacrifice of the body to warfare. As such it highlights the sacrificial logic through which the chivalric nobility offered their own bodies to warfare.[47]

Most readers have not, of course, deemed the queen's vow to be a chivalrous one. Critical consensus is all but unanimous on this point.[48] From the poem's earliest editors, Chalon and Delecourt, who condemned the vow in disgust, to Johan Huizinga, who described it as "the extreme of savagery," to the more recent assessment of John Grigsby and Norris Lacy, who suggest that the "shocking vow made by the queen" is designed to "underline and intensify the sinister process" by which an "apparently carefree court gathering" might be transformed into "a calamitous war," critics have concurred that the vow is an aberration from the codes of chivalry.[49] But what distinguishes this vow from those preceding it? One possible distinction is that the queen's vow is made "particularly violent by its specificity and by the objects of the threatened violence."[50] But is this exactly right? As we have seen, Valkenberg's vow is also quite directly rendered, and its object of violence is fundamentally the same as the queen's—a pregnant woman. And so we are left with one final question: why has the poet placed the last vow (or indeed any vow) in the mouth of a woman?

First, we may observe that the queen's gender functions to reinforce the idea that certain classes of persons should be exempt from war's violence. At the beginning of her vow, the queen observes that she has known for some time "Que sui grosse d'enfant, que mon corps sentu l'a. / Encore n'a il gaires qu'en men corps se tourna" (417–18) [That I am pregnant; my body has felt it. / It moved in my body only a short while ago.] This reference to quickening endows the fetus with a measure of personhood that was not accorded to it in Valkenberg's vow.[51] It also helps to articulate an ideal of an innocent, wholly vulnerable victim of war. As we have seen, the idea that civilians should be exempt from war's violence was tenuous at best in this period. In an Augustinian framework, the destruction of an enemy population was justified by a diffuse notion of subjective *culpa* or "war guilt," one that did not distinguish between soldiers and civilians.[52] In the queen's vow, the poet provides a category of civilian that could not easily be said to bear such *culpa*.[53] Furthermore, if, as I have been suggesting, developments in late medieval just war theory made it increasingly difficult to acknowledge explicitly that the central purpose of warfare is to injure and to kill, the queen's vow makes that purpose strikingly apparent and disturbingly intentional.

This poem is a significant attempt to reflect critically upon the violence of war, especially when viewed in relation to a courtly-chivalric tradition known for its idealizing tendencies. And yet the ideal of civilian immunities articulated by the *Vows* has a troubling foundation. It rests on another ideal, an assumption of which the poet is probably not conscious, but which is nevertheless central to the poem's ability to forge its critique of chivalric violence through the queen's vow. This is an assumption about women's agency.

Throughout the Middle Ages, women had a diminished agency before the law. Although in daily practice, individual women found ways to evade the restrictions on their independent legal and economic agency (and indeed while widowed women possessed a far greater range of legal rights as independent persons under the law), the general conception of women as diminished persons has been well established in historical studies. In a group of legal cases cited by Barbara Hanawalt and Paul Strohm, for instance, women who had committed homicide were assumed to have been incapable of contriving such deeds themselves and were regularly reported to work with male accomplices.[54] In such legal proceedings, the agency of women was minimalized and marginalized, rendered dependent upon the agency of those classes of men whose status as persons fully endowed with customary rights was legally assured and culturally acknowledged.

We see the *Vows'* concern with the agency of its female avower in the way it frames the queen's vow. When the queen is asked to offer her vow, she does not do so immediately, but first demurs, remarking, "Dame ne peut vouer puis qu'elle signeur a, / Car s'elle veue riens, son mari pooir a / Que bien puet rappeler chou qu'elle vouera" (407–9). [A lady cannot vow when she has a husband, / For if she vows something, her husband has the power / To revoke the vow she has made.] Despite these momentary hesitations, the queen does, however, offer a vow which she is able to accomplish through her own agency. This, the spectre of a woman disposing of her body as she sees fits, is, I would suggest, precisely what helps to elicit a critical response to her vow: to see it as an aberration, a willful refusal of women's normatively nurturing, maternal agency.[55]

To see her vow in this manner, however, requires a fundamental misrecognition: a substitution of the illicit nature of the performative agency of the pregnant woman for the illicit nature of the act itself. And the implications of this misrecognition are far broader than this local textual moment or the historical era marked by the Hundred Years' War. As Susan Bordo has recently argued, there is a striking disparity in the way in which contemporary legal judgments apply the concept of personhood to men and women, especially in legal cases where rights of bodily integrity are at issue.[56] Citing a growing number of cases before the American courts in which pregnant women have been accused of felonious child abuse for drinking alcohol or for refusing surgical and medical interventions, Bordo documents the ways in which women's legal status as persons are abbreviated, at times wholly evacuated, in order to protect the life of a potential person.[57] In the case of the *Vows*, a similar dynamic is enacted as the social valorization of maternity is invoked to support an ethical ideal of civilian immunities.

I have suggested that an implicit sense of women's proper, maternal agency invites a horrified response to the queen's vow and helps to solidify the poet's condemnation of the chivalric culture that inspires and indeed demands inscriptions of violence on the body of civilians. It is significant that in the portrait of the queen's vow, the poem has not disentangled violence from its constitutive role in founding aristocratic masculinity. By representing the greatest violence in the poem as that promised by a woman, the poem effects a final displacement of the aristocratic male's role in contributing to war's horrors even as the poem has made it possible for its readers to see, to name, and to protest these horrors. Such contradictions, as we have seen in examining the treatise of Honoré Bonet, are a reminder of the limits of critical reflection within late medieval writings on war. The poet of the *Vows of the Heron* will not privilege (perhaps because chivalric culture itself is not yet capable of privileging) the knight of Venus over the knight of Mars. But if, in the end, the *Vows* poet has not fully imagined an alternative to Robert of Artois within chivalric literature and culture, the brutal inscription of chivalric meaning on the bodies of pregnant women remains as a troubling and destabilizing image of the wounded body that is not wholly recuperable within the chivalric ethos.

NOTES

1. *The Vows of the Heron (Les Voeux du heron): A Middle French Vowing Poem*, eds. John L. Grigsby and Norris J. Lacy, trans. Norris J. Lacy, Garland Library of Medieval Literature 86, series A (New York: Garland Publishing, 1992), 416–22, 425–27. All quotations from the poem are cited by line number from this edition, hereafter referred to as *Vows*. For ease of reference, I cite Lacy's English translation, but occasionally offer my own translation in braces for the purpose of emphasis. I wish to thank David Aers, Denise Baker, Lisa Kiser, Ethan Knapp, Lee Patterson and Ann Marie Rasmussen for their insightul comments on various forms of this essay.

2. See, for instance, *Le voeu du héron, poème publié d'après un manuscrit de la Bibliothèque de Bourgogne, avec les variantes d'un autre manuscrit de la même bibliothèque et celles du texte donné par La Curne de Sainte-Palaya*, eds. Renier H. G. Chalon and Charles J. B. Delecourt, Socièté des bibliophiles de Mons (Mons: E. Hoyois, 1839). B. J. Whiting, "The Vows of the Heron," *Speculum* 20 (1945): 261–78, offered the first sustained reading of the poem as an antiwar poem and used the queen's vow to suggest that warfare is a "struggle productive only of destruction, frustration and suffering" (278).

3. By using the word *positive*, I do not mean here to indicate an ethical valuation. Rather I use the term to indicate a statement or representation which goes beyond critique and negation to assert an alternative meaning to those made available within chivalric discourse.

4. See Lacy's discussion in the previous essay in this collection, "Warmongering in Verse," based on his introduction in *Vows*; and Whiting, "The Vows of the Heron."

5. Juliet Vale, "Law and Diplomacy in the Alliterative *Morte Arthure*," *Nottingham Medieval Studies* 23 (1979): 31–46; and Elizabeth Porter, "Chaucer's Knight, the Alliterative *Morte Arthure* and Medieval Laws of War: A Reconsideration," *Nottingham Medieval Studies* 27 (1983): 56–78.

6. For compelling discussions of this problem, see Derek Brewer, "Chaucer's Knight as Hero, and Machaut's 'Prise d'Alexandrie,'" in *Heroes and Heroines in Medieval English Literature*, ed. Leo Carruthers (Cambridge: Boydell and Brewer, 1994), 94–95; Winthrop Wetherbee, "Chivalry under Siege in Ricardian Romance," in *The Medieval City under Siege*, ed. Ivy A. Corfis and Michael Wolfe (Woodbridge, Suffolk: The Boydell Press, 1995), 212; and Lee Patterson, *Chaucer and the Subject of History* (Madison, Wisc.: The University of Wisconsin Press, 1991), 175.

7. Elaine Scarry, *The Body in Pain: The Making and the Unmaking of the World* (New York: Oxford University Press, 1985), 120.

8. Scarry, *Body in Pain*, 125.

9. Scarry, *Body in Pain*, 125.

10. Lisa Kiser has kindly drawn my attention to Donna Crawford's useful account of the representation of injuring in the Breton lay tradition, one which also draws upon the work of Elaine Scarry. See "'Gronyng wyth Grysly Wounde': Injury in Five Middle English Breton Lays," in *Readings in Medieval English Romance*, ed. Carol Meale (Woodbrige, Suffolk: D. S. Brewer, 1994), 35–52.

11. Mildred K. Pope and Eleanor C. Lodge, eds., introduction to *Life of the Black Prince by the Herald of Sir John Chandos* (Oxford: The Clarendon Press, 1910), 1–lx. All subsequent references to the Herald's text are to this dual language edition. Line numbers referring to the French text are followed by page numbers indicating Pope and Lodge's translation of the text cited here.

12. *Life of the Black Prince*, 169–72: 136.

13. *Life of the Black Prince*, 236–39: 137.

14. See Michael Prestwich's most recent discussion of this tactic in *Armies and Warfare in the Middle Ages: The English Experience* (New Haven: Yale University Press, 1996), 198–204. Similar attitudes may be found in contemporary chronicles such as the *Brut*. Enroute to Crécy, for instance, Edward III is said to have "distroyed by the way tounes wiþþe peple duelling þerinne;" *The Brut or the Chronicles of England*, ed. Friedrich W. D. Brie, Early English Text Society, o. s., 136 (London: Oxford University Press, 1960), 2:298. See, too, Jean le Bel's account of how Salisbury, Suffolk, and Hainault converged on Marle, "ardirent les fausbours et la bonne ville de Cressy en Lannoys, et tout le pays d'entour;" *Chronique de Jean le Bel*, ed. Jules Viard and Eugène Déprez, Société de l'histoire de France (Paris: Librairie Renouard, 1905), 1:160–61. *The Chronicle of Jean de Venette*, ed. Richard Newhall, trans. Jean Birdsall (New York: Columbia University Press, 1953) is typically cited as an exceptionally sympathetic record of the destruction inflicted on the French peasant population

during the Hundred Years' War. But note, for instance, Venette's account of the noblemen, footsoldiers and burgesses from Normandy and Flanders who "sacked and burned" Winchelsea and "slew" the civilian inhabitants, an attack represented without any sense of impropriety. He frames the event with a traditional Augustinian gloss, observing that the French invaded England with the hope that they "who had not been able, by reason of God's disfavor or perchance of their own demerits, to defend themselves on their own ground ... might with humility and diligence recover on foreign soil the fame and wealth lost at home and return with honor and renown by God's aid" (97).

15. *Life of the Black Prince*, 310–17:137.

16. Jean Froissart, *The Chronicles of Froissart*, trans. John Bourchier (New York: Macmillan Company, 1904), 97.

17. Froissart, *Chronicles*, 97.

18. Froissart, *Chronicles*, 97.

19. Scarry, *Body in Pain*, 124.

20. For J. L. Austin's formulation, see *How to Do Things with Words* (Cambridge, Mass.: Harvard University Press, 1962), 4–11. Helen Solterer observes that the medieval philosopher, Nicolas Oresme (1320–1382), termed such a category of speech acts *mos actisans* [activating words]; see her discussion in "Flaming Words: Verbal Violence and Gender in Premodern Paris," *Romanic Review* 86 (1995): 357.

21. See Austin, *How to Do Things with Words*, 4–11; Jacques Derrida, "Signature, Event, Context," in *Limited, Inc.* (Evanston, Ill.: Northwestern University Press, 1988), 13–19; and Judith Butler, *Bodies that Matter: On the Discursive Limits of 'Sex'* (New York: Routledge, 1993), 9–13.

22. Vale, "Law and Diplomacy," 38.

23. See Frederick H. Russell, *The Just War in the Middle Ages* (New York: Cambridge University Press, 1975).

24. See Augustine, *Concerning the City of God against the Pagans*, trans. Henry Bettenson (Harmondsworth, England: Penguin Books, 1972), 4:34; and "Reply to Faustus the Manichean," in *The Political Writings of St. Augustine*, ed. and trans. Henry Paolucci (Chicago: Gateway Editions, 1962), 22:75.165 and 170. I offer here an admittedly selective overview of just war theory's development, one which does not touch upon the important transitional role of Bernard of Clairvaux and the impact of Aquinas's concept of culpability. For a fuller account of this development, see Russell, *The Just War*, esp. chapter 3. Robert F. Yeager provides an excellent overview of these developments in relation to John Gower's defense of peace in "*Pax Poetica*: On the Pacificism of Chaucer and Gower," *Studies in the Age of Chaucer* 9 (1987): 97–121.

25. It is worth noting here the similarities between the arbitrary, yet meaning-generating character of the wounded body in Scarry's account and the character of

the death and destruction caused by war in Augustine's theological conception. In both accounts the material object or event is inherently arbitrary; only the context provides a guide to the meaning of the wounded and dead body or the destroyed object. Augustine, however, presumes the possibility of a universal meaning for the death and destruction of warfare, one that does not rely upon the confirming belief of the individual within (or outside of) the Christian community.

26. On warfare as an instrument of punishment for sins, see Augustine, *City of God*, 19:7; and "Reply to Faustus," 22:75.165.

27. On the requirement of just intentions, see Augustine, "Reply to Faustus," 22:74.164 and 22:79.176–77.

28. On the illegitimacy of private acts of violence, see Augustine, "Reply to Faustus," 22:78.176; and on the distinction between war conducted with charity and with hatred, see 22:74.164.

29. On Augustine's concern with the "lust for dominion," see *City of God*, 4:4–5. For an extended discussion of the civil function of fourteenth-century legists such as Honoré Bonet, see N. A. R. Wright, "*The Tree of Battles* of Honoré Bouvet and the Laws of War," in *War, Literature and Politics in the Late Middle Ages*, ed. C. T. Allmand (Liverpool: Liverpool University Press, 1976): 12–31, esp. 19–21 and 25–29. On the reliance of French monarchs on the advice of fourteenth-century Italian jurists, see C. T. Allmand, *The Hundred Years' War: England and France at War, c.1300–1450* (Cambridge: Cambridge University Press, 1988), 112–13.

30. These distinctions are clearly laid out in the chapter organization of Legnano's treatise; see Giovanni da Legnano, *Tractatus de Bello, de Represaliis et de Duello*, ed. Thomas Erskine Holland, trans. James Leslie Brierly (Oxford: Oxford University Press, 1917), 195–205. On the dissemination of Legnano's writings on the just war, see Holland's introduction, x–xxi. For a discussion of the evidence for Legnano's influence in France during the period in which *The Vows* was composed, see G. W. Coopland, introduction to *The Tree of Battles of Honoré Bonet* (Cambridge, Mass.: Harvard University Press, 1949) 25–34.

31. Legnano, *Tractatus de Bello*, 3:1.263–64.

32. Legnano, *Tractatus de Bello*, 5:124.308 and 5:157.326; see also Bonet's remarks in *Tree of Battles*, 4:82.175.

33. See, for instance, Legnano's attempt to delimit the sphere in which duels could be licitly undertaken by nobles in *Tractatus de Bello*, 6:170.332. Bonet, who otherwise follows Legnano's treatise closely, reduces Legnano's extensive treatment of private violence to a few passages and, by denying private violence a central place in his treatise, effects his own far more emphatic denial of its legitimacy. For an exemplary instance of Bonet's attitude toward warfare motivated by anger, see *Tree of Battles*, 4:132:213. Bonet also condemns warfare motivated by a concern for glory (4:32) and profit-seeking (4:34).

34. Bonet, *Tree of Battles*, 4:48.154. A similar metaphor is found in a speech of Henry IV to the prelates in which he describes his violent suppression of traitors, suggesting that he has gathered up the "tares and cast them out and set good plants in my garden;" see *Chronique de la Traison et Mort de Richard Deux Roy Dengleterre*, ed. B. Williams, English Historical Society, (London, 1846;Vaduz: Kraus Reprints, 1964), 93.

35. Compare the passage cited above with Bonet's remarks throughout Book 4 of *Tree of Battles*, chapters 86–102.

36. For a full discussion of the various types of warfare and their defining criteria, see M. H. Keen, *The Laws of War in the Late Middle Ages*, (London: Routledge & Kegan Paul, 1965), especially 69, 81 and 104–10. For a more recent account, one which stresses the increasing importance of distinctions between types of warfare, see Prestwich, *Armies and Warfare*, 238–43.

37. For a discussion of the status of the Hundred Years' War, the standard account is May McKisack, *The Fourteenth Century, 1307–1399*, Oxford History of England 5 (Oxford: Clarendon Press, 1959), 107–26.

38. See Lacy, "Warmongering in Verse," in this collection, or his introduction to *Vows*, 11–13.

39. See Whiting's detailed account in "The Vows of the Heron," 270–72; and Thomas Wright's earlier remarks in his edition of *Political Poems and Songs*, vol. 1 (London: Longman, Green, and Roberts, 1859), xiv–xviii.

40. Two contemporary accounts of the Cambrésis campaign are relevant here: the first, from an account preserved in the municipal library at Cambray, observes how the English "enforchoient femmes gisans d'enfans, femmes mariées et bonnes filles et aux jeunes enfans copoient à l'ung un pied, à l'autre les oreilles et aux aultres le nez et à aulcuns crevoient les yeux et disoient chest pur che qu'il vous souvienne que le roi d'Angleterre et les Anglois ont esté en Cambrésis" (Henry Dubrulle, *Cambrai à la fin du Moyen Age* [Lille: Lefebvre Ducrocq, 1903], 285, n.1); the second, from Gilles le Muiset's chronicle (1272–1352), provides essentially the same details: "et habuerunt Anglici spolia et lucra infinita, et violaverunt mulieres, et infantibus truncabant uni pedem, alteri manum, alteri aurem; et, membratim truncates eos, dicebant: 'Sic apparebit quod rex Anglie fuit in hiis partibus,' alia plura enormia faciendo" (Gilles le Muiset, *Chronicle*, ed. H. Lamaître, Société de l'histoire de France, [Paris: Librairie Renouard, 1906], 118; discussed by Whiting, "The Vows of the Heron," 273). The explicit reference by Muiset to the memorializing function of these violent deeds is remarkable.

41. For another instance of this tendency, see *Chronique de Jean le Bel*, 70:72; see also the series of violent incidents attributed to mercenaries and nonnoble men-at-arms cited by B. J. H. Rowe, "Discipline in the Norman Garrisons under Bedford, 1422–35," *The English Historical Review* 46 (1931): 194–208.

42. Lacy, introduction to *Vows*, 13, 17. In Lacy's reading, in contrast to my own, love and prowess are ultimately understood as compatible dispositions. While there

can be little question that medieval courtly writers often portrayed the two interests as mutually supportive, they also recognized the potential conflicts and frequently thematized the tensions between these two facets of knightly identity.

43. Thomas Walsingham, *Historia Anglicana*, ed. H.T. Riley, Rolls Series, No. 28 (London, 1863–64), 2:156. See also Chrétien de Troyes, "Eric and Enide," in *The Complete Romances of Chrétien de Troyes*, ed. and trans. David Staines (Bloomington: Indiana University Press, 1990; First Midland Book Edition, 1993), 31–33 (lines 2432–78), and "The Knight with the Lion," 286–87 (lines 2486–2540). Line numbers cited here refer to the French edition on which Staines's translation is based, *Les Romans de Chrétien de Troyes*, ed. Mario Roques (Paris: Les Classiques Français du Moyen Age, 1952–75).

44. A point made by Whiting, "The Vows of the Heron," 269–70, and Wright, *Political Poems and Songs*, xiii–xiv. See also Lacy's discussion of Salisbury's vow in "Warmongering in Verse," in this collection, or his introduction to *Vows*, 11–12.

45. Here and at lines 431–36, the poet is again building irony with his reader's knowledge of the historical outcome of each vow. See the contemporary chronicle, *Scalacronica: The Reigns of Edward I, Edward II, and Edward III as Recorded by Sir Thomas Gray*, ed. and trans. Herbert Maxwell (Glasgow: J. Maclehose & Sons, 1907), 105, which reports that in 1338 Edward, after having declared war against France, spent fifteen months on the continent and especially in Antwerp where he lay "without making any war, only jousting and leading a joly life." Gray records the birth of Lionel at this time and discreetly suggests that Edward's leisurely preoccupations were the cause of the English defeat at Presfen and of the naval disasters at Southhampton and Middleborough. Such a record of contemporary opinion may explain the apparent discrepancy which critics have noted between the fact that Edward only invaded France in 1339 and the poem's own dating of its events to 1338 (*Vows*, 5). If we follow the *Scalacronica*'s lead, there is no discrepancy, only yet another suggestion that the *Vows of the Heron* is determined to undermine the illusion of aristocratic self-sufficiency and agency.

46. On the vicissitudes of masculine identity formation in the knightly class, see David Aers, "Masculine Identity in the Courtly Community," *Community, Gender, and Individual Identity: English Writing, 1360–1430* (New York: Routledge, 1988), 117–52.

47. My formulation of this dynamic as a sacrificial one has benefitted from discussion with Alan Frantzen and Daniel Kline and from consideration of their collaborative essay, "The Anti-Sacrifice of Isaac: Violence and Subverting the Law of the Father" (paper presented at the annual conference of the Centre for Medieval Studies, University of Toronto, October 1998).

48. The exception is John Carmi Parsons, "The Pregnant Queen as Counsellor and the Medieval Construction of Motherhood," in *Medieval Mothering*, eds.

John Carmi Parsons and Bonnie Wheeler (New York: Garland Publishing, 1996), 39–61. Parsons reads the queen's vow as a celebratory portrait of a royal wife upholding male honor.

49. Chalon and Delecourt, *Le voeu du héron*, xi–xii; J. Huizinga, *The Waning of the Middle Ages* (New York: Anchor Press Doubleday, 1949), 91; Lacy, introduction to *Vows*, 15, 18. See also Whiting's discussion, "The Vows of the Heron," 277–79.

50. Lacy, "Warmongering in Verse," 23, or introduction to *Vows*, 15.

51. Thanks to Ann Marie Rasmussen for drawing my attention to this detail. For contemporary understandings of the endowment of the fetus with motion and ensoulment, see the late thirteenth- or early fourteenth-century text, *De secretis mulierum*, with two of its sixteenth-century commentaries in *Women's Secrets: A Translation of Pseudo-Albertus Magnus's "De Secretis Mulierum" with Commentaries*, ed. Helen Rodnite LeMay (Albany, N.Y.: State University of New York Press, 1992), 79, 86, 106.

52. Russell, *The Just War*, 19.

53. Compare Chaucer's portrait in The Tale of Melibee in which Melibee is advised by an old wise counselor to choose peace over warfare: "For soothly, whan that werre is ones bigonne, ther is ful many a child unborn of his mooder that shal sterve yong by cause of thilke werre"; *The Riverside Chaucer*, ed. Larry D. Benson, 3rd ed. (Boston: Houghton Mifflin, 1987), 219.

54. See Paul Strohm's chapter, "Treason in the Household," in *Hochon's Arrow: The Social Imagination of Fourteenth-Century Texts* (Princeton, N.J.: Princeton University Press, 1992), 128–34; and Barbara Hanawalt, "The Female Felon in Fourteenth-Century England," *Viator* 5 (1974): 253–68.

55. In the poem, God's redemptive act of creation and Mary's birthing of Jesus are offered as "corrective" ideals of reproductive acts; see *Vows*, 419–20. Parsons presents an alternative reading of the role of inversion in "The Pregnant Queen as Counsellor," 52.

56. See Bordo's chapter, "Are Mothers Persons? Reproductive Rights and the Politics of Subjectivity," in *Unbearable Weight: Feminism, Western Culture and the Body* (Berkeley: University of California Press, 1993), 71–97.

57. Bordo, "Are Mothers Persons?" 81, 85–88.

CHAPTER 3

MEED AND THE ECONOMICS OF CHIVALRY IN *PIERS PLOWMAN*

DENISE N. BAKER

In the first dream vision of the A and B-texts of *Piers Plowman*, Langland has Meed defend herself against Conscience's indictment by accusing him of cowardice in persuading the King to surrender his claim to the French throne.[1] Through this character's topical allusion to the harsh conditions of the Normandy campaign of 1359–1360 and the specific provisions of the ensuing Treaty of Brétigny,[2] Langland engages in the debate about Edward III's war policy that took place in the 1360s and early 1370s. References to the Treaty of Brétigny in several works contemporary with the A-text of *Piers Plowman* indicate the range of such contestation and reveal Langland as one of the earliest opponents of the hostilities with France. Although public opinion turned against the war when the English began to suffer defeats after its resumption in 1369, his position remains distinctive, for, through Meed's objections to the Treaty of Brétigny, Langland interrogates the ideology of chivalry that Edward III so successfully cultivated to gain baronial support for the war.[3]

According to the Treaty of Brétigny (sometimes called the Treaty of Calais), negotiated in 1360, Edward III agreed to relinquish his claim to the French throne in exchange for three million écus (£500,000) in ransom for King John and full sovereignty over an expanded duchy of

Aquitaine, Ponthieu, Guines, Montreuil, and Calais with its environs.[4] Before the treaty was ratified at Calais in October of 1361, however, the clauses requiring each king's concession were removed to a separate letter which stipulated that the renunciations would be made after the territories had been exchanged, but no later than November of 1361. In the meantime, both kings would retain but not exercise their respective rights. For reasons that can only be speculated about, the renunciations were not officially made. The war recommenced in 1369 when Charles V violated Edward's claim to sovereignty by summoning the Black Prince as a vassal to Paris in response to complaints from his subjects in Aquitaine and Edward retaliated by formally resuming the title of king of France.[5]

Since he composed the A-text of *Piers Plowman* sometime between 1368 and 1374,[6] Langland's original allusion to the Hundred Years' War is contemporaneous with the period during which the Treaty of Brétigny failed and the second phase of the war was initiated. He ascribes to Meed the same objections to the treaty that are registered in three texts of the 1360s, the *Prophecy of John of Bridlington*, the *Anonimalle Chronicle*, and the *Scalacronica*. Because Langland has gradually established his critical attitude toward Meed by Passus III, this character's opposition to peace serves to interrogate the values typically espoused by the warrior class and Edward III himself. Contextualization of Meed's objections to the Treaty of Brétigny thus reveals that the first dream vision of *Piers Plowman* is more controversial and daring than might otherwise be appreciated. For despite Conscience's repudiation of "mede mesurles" (III.225), the King's support for Meed in her debate with Conscience (IV.1–3) and his continued insistence, until the Peace episode in Passus IV, that these two personifications should wed indicates Langland's critique of Edward III's complicity with the legal and social corruption depicted in the poem.[7]

Langland represents Meed as an opponent of the Treaty of Brétigny. She criticizes its terms as unfavorable to the King and blames Conscience for persuading him to accept them. "[Cowardly þou consience conceiledest him þennes] / To leuen his lordsshipe for a litel siluer, / þat is þe riccheste reaume þat re[yn] ouer[houip]" (III.193–95). Meed disavows the treaty because, she asserts, the King has renounced the great wealth promised by his claim to the French throne for a paltry sum, probably an allusion to the ransom of three million *écus* to be paid for King John. If she had been in charge of the war effort as marshal,[8] Meed claims, she would have advised the King against such an inequitable exchange.

> "Hadde I be march[al] of his men, be marie of heuene,
> I durste han leid my lif & no lesse wed
> He shulde haue be lord of þat lond in lengþe & in brede,
> And ek king of þat kiþ his kyn for to helpe,
> þe leste brol of his blood a barouns pere" (III.188–92).

By accepting the terms of the Treaty of Brétigny, Meed contends, the King betrayed his own best interests as well as those of his followers.

In ascribing such criticism of this treaty to Meed, Langland not only presents this personification acting in character, but also has her echo a view expressed by a significant proportion of Edward III's subjects in the 1360s. "[T]o those who supported the war," Barnie observes, "the ultimate act of betrayal was the Treaty of Brétigny. England had not suffered a defeat in the field for a decade and a half, and France was thought to have avoided conquest by the use of the deceitful diplomacy for which she was renowned."[9] The earliest documented criticism of the Treaty of Brétigny occurs in the *Prophecy of John of Bridlington*, composed sometime between November 13, 1362, and April 8, 1364, by John Erghome, Austin Friar of York.[10] Although he does not explicitly condemn the recently ratified treaty, Erghome's "chief purpose in writing the prophecy was to incite the king to fresh efforts to win his maternal inheritance."[11] Making a strong case for the legitimacy of the English claim in the first chapter of the first distinction and glorifying the king's past successes in battle with France throughout, Erghome prophecies that a reformation in old age will bring Edward to reassert his right and ends by predicting that the Prince of Wales will be crowned king of France in 1405. A piece of prowar propaganda, the *Prophecy of John of Bridlington* opposes the Treaty of Brétigny in the name of one of the most powerful magnates of the period, Humphrey de Bohun, to whom Erghome dedicated this text. In 1363 this Bohun inherited from his father William, Earl of Northampton and constable of England, a valuable estate that had been considerably enlarged by the profits of war.[12]

Another contemporary but more explicit criticism of the treaty, remarkably similar to Meed's, is expressed in the *Anonimalle Chronicle*. Though its origin is uncertain, the single surviving manuscript of this chronicle belonged to St. Mary's Abbey in York. The entries for 1349–1376 are based on a lost Latin original composed soon after the events occurred. This source, as Gransden notes, gives the *Anonimalle Chronicle* "especial value because no other contemporary chronicle covers the last years of Edward III's campaigns and writers of the next generation were subject to strong biases."[13] After presenting a detailed and often unique account of the campaign of 1359–1360 ending with the terms of the Treaty of Brétigny, the *Anonimalle* chronicler reports with regret Edward III's order, after the signing at Calais, that the English surrender towns and castles they had conquered in France "to the great loss and harm of the king of England and his heirs for ever, for nearly the whole of the community of France was in subjection and ransom to them; and within a brief period the said captains and their men could easily have conquered the kingdom of France to the advantage of the king of England and his heirs, if he had allowed them"[14] [a graunt perde et damage al roy Dengleterre et a ses heirs pur toutz iours, qare bien pres toute la communalte de Frauns fuist en subieccion et raunsoun a eux et si purroient les ditz captayns od lour gentz deinz brieff avoir conquis la roialme de Frauns al oeps le roy Dengleterre et ses heirs sil les voldroit avoir soeffre]. The *Anonimalle* chronicler's confidence that Edward III could have achieved ultimate victory in France resembles Meed's boast that, had she been marshal, "[The King] shulde haue be lord of þat lond in lengþe & in brede, / And ek king of þat kiþ his kyn for to helpe, / þe leste brol of his blood a barouns pere" (III.190–92). By having Meed express the opinion that the King's relinquishment of his claim to France was premature, Langland was obviously giving voice to one side of the contemporary debate about the Treaty of Brétigny.

The *Scalacronica* of Sir Thomas Gray, completed before his death in 1369, expresses even greater dissatisfaction with the terms of the treaty than the *Anonimalle Chronicle*. A chivalrous history of England covering the reigns of the three Edwards from 1274 to 1363, the *Scalacronica* was composed by Sir Thomas Gray of Heton, Northumberland, a soldier who distinguished himself in both the Scottish and French wars. As a participant in Edward III's last campaign, he provides an eyewitness account of the war in France in 1359–1360. In the *Scalacronica*, he opposes the Treaty of Brétigny for reasons similar to Meed's. Because he is criticizing Edward III, however, Gray masks his objection as a general rather than a specific complaint. He begins by admitting that a peace motivated by "virtue and [a desire] to please God, without being inspired, strengthened or constrained by any [other] influence, especially by no wish for ease nor carnal desire, but virtuously and righteously for the common weal, . . . cannot but be profitable and good." Gray condemns, however, a treaty negotiated from less noble motives: "as when one is conscious of his right and yet fails to maintain it through indolence and a desire to avoid discomfort, wishing and hoping to find more pleasure in another direction; or as when one abandons [his right] through want of means, or through the weariness of people's hearts in persevering, or through growing old—this [manner of] putting an end to a war is not often profitable in the outcome."[15] Although his criticism remains general, many of the motives that Gray mentions could be attributed to Edward III. Like Meed, he implies that Edward renounced a legitimate claim to the French throne for an ignoble reason, be it indolence, lack of steadfastness, or simply old age.

Sir Thomas Gray goes on to criticize kings who fail to wage war because of "want of prudence, of hardihood and of [means of] liberality." As he defines these three deficiencies, the resemblance between his position and the one Langland ascribes to Meed becomes even clearer. "Want of prudence—as when one does not inquire whether God will show him grace in advancing his cause and does not press the same in reasonable measure through the willing accord of his people, and with such hardihood as shall not be daunted at a crisis by fear of disaster or of damage to property during war; endurance of which things in a bold way, [brings] honour, profit and cheerfulness, so that the hand shall be liberal in rewarding those who deserve it, for the encouragement of others to do the like—the one thing in the world most helpful in waging war."[16] Although Gray does not explicitly mention the Treaty of Brétigny, his inclusion of this criticism of an ignoble peace near the end of his account of the Normandy campaign of 1359–1360, a campaign in which he participated, implies that he is referring to Edward III's withdrawal from the war and relinquishment of his claim to France.

Sir Thomas Gray's castigation of the king's lack of liberality anticipates Meed's conclusion to her criticism of the Treaty of Brétigny.

> "It becom[iþ] a king þat kepiþ a reaume
> To ȝiuen hise men mede þat mekly hym seruen,
> To alienes, to alle men, to honoure hem with ȝeftis.
> Mede makiþ hym be louid & for a man holde.
> Emperours & Erlis & alle maner lordis
> þoruȝ ȝeftis han ȝonge men to [ȝerne] & to ride" (III.196–201).

In giving such advice to the King in *Piers Plowman*, Meed is simply describing the practice of Edward III, who announced the resumption of the war in the Parliament of 1369 with a promise that those who participate will be rewarded with conquered land "to be held by them and their heirs and successors, from the King and his heirs, Kings of France"[17] [a tenir a eux & lour heirs & successeurs, de Roi & ses heirs Rois de France]. Both Langland and Edward III clearly understood the economic motive undergirding chivalric culture: the opportunity for lucrative financial gain was a perquisite of English military service in the Hundred Years' War.

The first phase of the Hundred Years' War, from 1337 to 1360, had indeed proved profitable to many of the English soldiers, both common and noble. "Almost all the chroniclers who report the campaigns of the 1340s and 1350s," Barnie observes, "comment on the great fortunes to be made from the war, and much of their information must have been gleaned from the impressions of returning soldiers and from the rumours which spread abroad after the completion of a successful campaign."[18] The greatest beneficiaries of the war profits were, of course, the military leaders from among the nobility. Service in France provided several kinds of financial opportunities for this class. As Allmand explains, "In a very real sense war was becoming an important supplementary source of livelihood, for which the nobility increasingly sold their services to the king in return for wages and promises of opportunities of obtaining what were euphemistically known as the 'advantages' of war: the profits of ransoms; booty; and grants of land seized from the conquered."[19] As the following examples demonstrate, during the first phase of the Hundred Years' War from 1337 to 1360, Edward III and his son the Black Prince had indeed followed Meed's advice by providing their military commanders with ample opportunities to acquire such recompense.

Wages were the least reliable and profitable of these remunerations. By the reign of Edward III, military service had changed from a feudal obligation to a voluntary employment as the procedures for recruitment by contract developed.[20] The nobility served as military contractors, mustering fighting men and distributing the wages collected from the Exchequer to them. For the campaign of 1359, for example, the contractors included some of the most prominent members of the higher nobility: four of the king's sons as well as the earls of Lancaster, Northampton, Warwick, Oxford, Suffolk, Salisbury, March, and Stafford.[21] The schedule of wages specified all ranks, from earls to archers. Ranging from "a mark a day for a duke to a shilling a day for a man-at-arms below the estate of knight,"[22] these wages, when paid, were enough to cover the soldier's expenses. Captains of retinues who had opportunities to earn additional bonuses, either legally or illegally, might even turn a profit.[23]

Far greater gains, though, accrued from plunder or ransom, both of which were regarded as legitimate supplements to or substitutes for wages. By specifying the terms for the division of such spoils among the troops and war leaders, contemporary indentures or contracts for military service provide clear evidence, as Allmand observes, "that the profit motive in the conduct of war was accepted by the society of the day."[24] The chronicles which cover the first phase of the war from 1337 to 1360 abound with accounts of the booty taken from France. As McFarlane remarks: "Letters from the captains of Edward III's armies, preserved in Avesbury's chronicle, tell the same exultant story of organized and highly successful pillage. Booty was one of the chief military objectives, and no one, peasant or townsman, clerk or knight, was immune from loss at the hands of enemy raiders; civilians were as fair game as combatants."[25] The English commanders in the field often encouraged such plunder as an integral tactic of the *chevauchée*, the purpose of which was to wreak devastation or *damnum* on the French.[26] For example, in his *Chronicon*, completed shortly before his death in 1358, Geoffrey le Baker paraphrases the Black Prince's exhortation to his troops before the battle of Poitiers to fight for honor and for wealth.[27] "To the victor go the spoils" was a literal statement of the outcome of medieval warfare.

Ransom was even more profitable than plunder. In his *Life of the Black Prince*, the Chandos Herald describes the scramble for prisoners at Poitiers: "You might see many an archer, / many a knight, many an esquire / running in every direction to take prisoners"[28] [Veïssiez courir maint archier, / Maint chevalier, maint escuier, / De toutes parz prisoniers prendre]. Although common soldiers sometimes captured prisoners, the lion's share of ransoms went to the nobility, including the royal family. Lack of documentation makes it difficult to trace the profits of privately negotiated ransoms; however, many captives were sold to the king or the Black Prince for considerable sums.[29] As Hewitt observes, "Ultimately, by one channel or another, nearly all the noble prisoners mentioned in the Treaty of Brétigny as having been taken at the battle of Poitiers, became the king's property. It was under his direction that their ransoms were negotiated."[30] The king, moreover, claimed a right to the most important and lucrative of the prisoners, such as the members of the French royal family or the enemy war leaders. By exerting this claim over King John, who was captured at Poitiers, for example, Edward III was able to negotiate a ransom in the Treaty of Brétigny of 3,000,000 *écus* or £5000,000, "some five or six times what the English crown might receive from its ordinary revenues, including the wool subsidy, together with the lay and clerical subsidies, a staggering sum even when we recognize that, in the end, less than half of it was paid."[31] The opportunity to take prisoners provided a compelling financial incentive for military service, particularly among the nobility, including Edward III himself.

The most lucrative rewards for service in France, however, were appointments, annuities, and grants of land either in conquered territories or in England given by the king. Since conquered castles and towns belonged to him, he could reward his most distinguished followers with their revenues. Henry of Grosmont, Duke of Lancaster, for example, built the Savoy Palace in London with the income granted him by the king from the town and castle of Bergerac which he captured.[32] After the battle of Poitiers, the Prince of Wales lavishly rewarded many of his troops with annuities, some of which were temporary "until the prince shall have provided him with an equivalent of land and rent elsewhere."[33] Even the Cheshire archers received modest gifts like grants of pasture or timber from the prince's forest.[34]

All of these advantages of war—plunder, ransoms, profits from appointments and direct gifts—are in theory awarded by the war leader or king. Even the booty and prisoners captured by individual soldiers, according to the medieval laws of war, are the king's possessions to distribute. Although the captor had a claim to a certain share of the moveable loot he took in pillage, he was first required to turn the goods or money over to the king or his representative, the war leader. In the *Tree of Battles* composed during the last quarter of the fourteenth century, Honoré Bonet explains the principles informing this division of spoils: "what a man gains from his enemies belongs to him, if we bear in mind that previously it belonged to his enemies, who have lost their lordship over it; but it does not belong to the captor to the extent that he is not obliged to hand it over to the duke of the battle; and the duke should share the spoils out among his men, to each according to his valour."[35] As Keen clarifies, this seemingly contradictory law of war was intended to protect both parties, "its object being to adjust rights in spoil to the extent of involvement in the risks of its capture."[36] Because the king took the greatest risk in war, he had the sole right to all captured lands, castles, and towns.[37] The king and the captain could also claim one-third of the moveable loot acquired by their soldiers. Up until the early 1370s, according to Ayton, "when *restauro equorum* [compensation for horses] was offered, as with major expeditions to France, the superior contracting party would receive half of his immediate subordinates' profits."[38] The remainder of the spoils were distributed among the troops according to their rank.[39] Likewise, according to the terms of the indenture or contract, any ransom paid by a prisoner was to be shared in and distributed by the king or war leader.[40] During the Hundred Years' War the loot and ransoms gained in battle were, at least in theory, to be considered meed from the king just as surely as the appointments and gifts he more directly bestowed.

Although the system of rewards for military service endorsed by Meed was the standard practice of Edward III, Langland criticizes both the warriors who receive such meed and the king who grants it. Through Meed's allusion to the Treaty of Brétigny, he not only acknowledges that the king appeals to the greed of his soldiers, he also implies that avarice rather than honor is Edward III's own motive for waging war against France. Langland alludes to the king's share in the profits of war when he has Meed take credit for initiating the expedition of 1359–1360. He levels this charge in a somewhat puzzling passage which switches from the disastrous conclusion of this campaign to its promising inception with a reference to Calais. Meed contrasts Conscience's cowardly pillaging as he retreated from France with her earlier encouragement of the King as he set out on the expedition:

> "Wiþoute pite, pilour, pore men þou robb[ed]est,
> And bar here bras on þi bak to caleis to selle,
> Þere I lefte wiþ my lord his lif for to saue,
> And made hym merþe mournyng to leue,
> And bateride hym on þe bak, boldite his herte,
> Dede hym hoppe for hope to haue me at wille" (III.182–87).

Although lines 184–85 may seem to allude to Edward's departure from Calais after the terms of the Treaty of Brétigny were negotiated, the immediate context indicates that they refer to his setting out from Calais at the beginning of the expedition.[41] Langland subversively suggests that Edward's motives were decidedly mercenary with Meed's boast that she "bateride [the King] on þe bak, boldite his herte, / Dede hym hoppe for hope to haue me at wille" (III.186–87). Through Meed's claim that she encouraged and emboldened the King, Langland calls attention to the great wealth Edward III acquired during the first phase of the war up to 1360. Although the expenses of the war were high, this financial burden was borne by the French and by the English taxpayers. As McFarlane remarks, "The gains of war, and some of the wages, were paid by the enemy. The rest of the wages and the cost of equipping the troops was borne by the English Exchequer. Not, it must be emphasized, by the English king, but by taxation for which the war was the excuse. When Edward III won advantage by his arms, he didn't pay it into the Exchequer; he treated it as he treated John of France's ransom; he put it in his own pocket."[42] By identifying the King's desire for meed as the motive for the hostilities, Langland implicitly contests Edward

III's official declaration that the war was being fought to pursue his legitimate claim to the French throne.

In questioning the king's motives, Langland anticipates the debate among modern historians about Edward's war aims. As McKisack points out, "Those who contend that his real objective was the Crown of France have to meet the awkward facts of his voluntary liege homage to Philip VI in 1331 and of his readiness to relinquish the title, not only at Brétigny and Calais but in the two draft treaties drawn up in London in 1358 and 1359, when most of the cards were in his hands."[43] Langland, like McKisack, recognizes that Edward's willingness to give up the claim to the crown of France in the Treaty of Brétigny contradicts his alleged reason for waging war.

No matter what his aims were, though, Edward took precautions to squelch any skepticism about his motives through a carefully orchestrated propaganda campaign. As McKisack goes on to explain: "There can be no doubt, however, that Edward wished his claim to be taken seriously by his own subjects; for if he were the rightful king of France, then his war could be depicted as essentially defensive; and the success of such propaganda measures may be read in the pages of the chronicles and of the parliament rolls."[44] Implying that the king was motivated by avarice rather than honor, Langland, in contrast to the chroniclers, disputes such propaganda about the legitimacy of the war.

Given the widespread propaganda about the validity of Edward III's claim to the French throne, though, many of Langland's contemporaries were puzzled by his willingness to accept the terms of the Treaty of Brétigny. In having Meed attribute the King's decision to qualms of conscience, Langland may either be reflecting or shaping a debate which continued among the chroniclers through the rest of the fourteenth century. Alluding to the harsh conditions of the 1359–60 campaign, Meed accuses Conscience of cowardice in persuading the King to relinquish his claim to France.

> "In normandie was he nouȝt anoyed for my sake,
> Ac þou þiself, soþly, asshamidest hym ofte;
> Crope into a caban for cold of þi nailes;
> Wendist þat wynter wolde han last euere;
> And dreddist to be ded for a dym cloud,
> And hastide[st]þ þe homward for hunger of þi wombe" (III.176–81).[45]

Meed's reference to the dim cloud which aroused dread among the troops has long been recognized as an allusion to the storm that devastated the English army on April 14, 1360, a week after Easter as they camped outside

Chartres.⁴⁶ Describing the terrible suffering and extensive destruction caused by the torrential rains, hail, and lightning, the *Anonimalle Chronicle* refers to this day as "evil Monday."⁴⁷ Sir Thomas Gray's *Scalacronica* gives much the same account of the horrible devastation of this storm: "On Sunday the 13th of April it became necessary to make a very long march toward Beauce, by reason of want of fodder for the horses. The weather was desperately bad with rain, hail, and snow, and so cold that many weakly men and horses perished in the field. They abandoned many vehicles and much baggage on account of the cold, the wind and the wet, which happened to be worse this season than any old memory could recall."⁴⁸ While the *Anonimalle Chronicle* and the *Scalacronica*, both contemporary with the A-text of *Piers Plowman*, describe the havoc wreaked on the English troops by this storm, neither of them suggests, as Langland's Meed does, that it caused Edward III to have qualms of conscience.

Later chronicles, however, address the king's response to the devastation explicitly, either denying or asserting that the hardships of the campaign, and particularly the storm of Black Monday, persuaded Edward to negotiate with the French. In the English continuation of the *Brut* covering 1333 to 1377, for example, the vivid description of this storm ends with an assertion that it did not frighten the king. As the English soldiers ravaged the countryside on their way toward Orleans, "there fell upon them such a storm and tempest that none of our nation ever heard of or saw anything like it; because of it thousands of our men and their horses on their journey (as it were through vengeance), suddenly were slain and perished, but these very strong tempests did not frighten the King, or many of his people, and they continued in the journey they had begun"⁴⁹ [þere fil oppon hym suche a storme & tempest þat non of our nacioun herd ne sawe neuere non such; thurght þe whiche, þousandeȝ of our men & of hers horses in here iourneying (as it were þorugh vangeaunce), sodenly were slayn & perisshed, þe which tempestes ful mich ȝet ferid not þe Kyng, ne myche of his peple, þat þey ne wenden forth in her viage þat þey had begunne.] Although the *Brut* chronicler acknowledges the speculation that this storm was divine retribution "(as it were þorugh vengeaunce)," his denial that Edward was frightened suggests that the king's interpretation of the event was an issue under contention.⁵⁰

In contrast to the *Brut* chronicler, Froissart, writing in the early 1390s, ascribes Edward's willingness to accept the terms offered by the French, just as Langland's Meed does, to qualms of conscience resulting from the fear incited by the storm. While the English and French ambassadors were negotiating unsuccessfully, there occurred what Froissart describes as a grand miracle which very much humbled and broke [Edward's] courage, for . . . storms, tempests and lightning so great and so horrible descended from the sky on the host of the king of England, that it seemed very properly to all those who accompanied that time was about to be ended, because there fell from the air stones so large that they killed men and horses, and the most hardy of them were terrorstriken. And then the king of England gazed toward the church of Notre Dame of Chartres, and he himself vowed and yielded devoutly to Our Lady, and promised, so as he said and confessed afterwards, that he would be accorded to peace.[51]

[un grant miracle qui moult le humilia et brisa son corage, . . . uns orages, uns tempès et uns effoudres si grans et si horribles descendi dou ciel en l'ost le roy d'Engleterre, que il sambla bien proprement à tous ceulz qui là estoient, que li siècles deuist finer, car il cheoient de l'air pières si grosses que elles tuoient hommes et chevaus, et en furent li plus hardi tout eshidé. Et adonc regarda li rois d'Engleterre devers l'eglise Nostre Dame de Chartres, et se voa et rendi devotement à Nostre Dame, et prommist, si com il dist et confessa depuis, que il s'accorderoit le pais.]

Froissart interprets the storm as a sign of "the grace of the Holy Spirit who worked here also" [le grasce dou Saint Esperit qui y ouvra ossi].[52] Prior to the storm, Edward was not willing to heed Henry of Grosmont's advice that "while you have the power to withdraw in honor, you ought to accept the offers that have been presented to you; for, my lord, we may lose more in one day than we have gained in twenty years"[53] [entrues que vous en poés issirà vostre honneur, vous en issiés et prendés les offres que on vous presente; car, monsigneur, nous poons plus perdre sus un jour que nous n'avons conquis dedens vingt ans.] Such an appeal to the king's greed, it seems, could not work without an accompanying fear instilled by the storm.

As this evidence from the chronicles demonstrates, Edward III's contemporaries debated his reasons for agreeing to relinquish his claim to the French throne in the Treaty of Brétigny. Although it is impossible to ascertain whether Langland was repeating or initiating rumors, he seems to be the first commentator to associate the "dym cloud" of Black Monday with the English king's qualms of conscience. By the end of the century Froissart provides a detailed and dramatic narrative of how this severe storm aroused Edward's scruples.

Whatever its historical accuracy, the purpose of Langland's explanation within the context of Meed's speech is clear. As the spokespersonification for those who benefitted financially from the war, Meed seeks to discredit her critic Conscience both by charging him with cowardice and by alleging his complicity in the atrocities of war. "Wiþoute pite, pilour, pore men þou robb[ed]est, / And bar here bras on þi bak to caleis to selle" (III.182–83). While this *ad hominem* argument certainly points to the fallibility of Conscience as a moral guide, Langland's irony is directed against Meed. Though she mocks Conscience's newfound sympathy for the victims of pillage, Langland uses her speech to expose the economic incentives for war with France occluded by the ideology of chivalry.[54] Such mercenary motives, he implies, corrupted the moral judgment of the warrior class.

At the very time that Edward III was promoting the cult of chivalry at court in order to win baronial support for the war,[55] reports of English *chevauchées* through France were disclosing the brutal reality masked by this idealization of knighthood. As Allmand remarks, "Society was faced with two images of the soldier. On the one hand was the traditional knight of chivalry, the figure of romances, and, more recently of the new chivalric order, one of whose social functions was the defence of those in physical need and danger. . . . On the other hand was the image, conveyed with increasing frequency by the chroniclers, of the common soldier as a symbol of something to be feared, the perpetrator of violence and destruction, whether this took the form of attacks on property (pillage and arson) or on people (murder and rape)."[56] Langland's expression of sympathy for the victims of war and his critique of the economic system that spurred such destruction challenge the policies of Edward III and the tactic of *chevauchée* during the first phase of the Hundred Years' War. By making Meed an opponent of the Treaty of Brétigny, Langland exposes the greed of the warrior class. In creating this character to give voice to the prowar position, he satirizes the most powerful group within late fourteenth-century society, Edward III and his magnates. Meed's self-defense is, in fact, an indictment of the economics of chivalry.

NOTES

1. George Kane, ed., *Piers Plowman: The A Version*, rev. ed. (London: Athlone Press, 1988), III.176–99; and George Kane and E. Talbot Donaldson, eds., *Piers Plowman: The B Version*, rev. ed. (London: Athlone Press, 1988), III.189–212. All subsequent quotations of *Piers Plowman* will be from the A version and will be documented parenthetically in the text. Although Langland also alludes to the war with France in the C-text, the corresponding passage has been extensively revised and

will not be discussed in this essay. For clarity, I capitalize *king* when referring to the character in Langland's poem and use lowercase to identify historical personages such as the English king.

2. Walter W. Skeat identified this allusion to the Treaty of Brétigny in the notes to his parallel text edition, *The Vision of William concerning Piers the Plowman* (Oxford: Oxford University Press, 1886), 2:48–49. Skeat's identification is disputed by Bernard Huppé, "*Piers Plowman* and the Norman Wars," *PMLA* 54 (1939): 37–64; and John Selzer, "Topical Allegory in *Piers Plowman*: Lady Meed's B-Text Debate with Conscience," *Philological Quarterly* 59 (1980): 257–67. Assuming that Meed represents Alice Perrers, Edward III's mistress after the death of Queen Philippa in 1369, Huppé and Selzer argue that this passage refers to a campaign in the 1370s. J. A. W. Bennett, "The Date of the A-Text of *Piers Plowman*," *PMLA* 58 (1943): 566–72, refutes Huppé by showing that the description of winter privations in Normandy at A.III.176–79 fits contemporary accounts of the campaign of 1359–1360; somewhat incongruously, though, Bennett accepts Huppé's identification of Meed with Alice Perrers. Although I do not interpret Meed as the personification of the over-powerful noble or Langland's poem as an endorsement of absolutist monarchy, my essay amplifies Anna Baldwin's discussion of Meed's opposition to the Treaty of Brétigny in *The Theme of Government in Piers Plowman* (Woodbridge, Suffolk: D. S. Brewer, 1981), 37. For the text of the Treaty of Brétigny, see A. R. Myers, ed., *English Historical Documents 1327–1485*, vol. 4 of *English Historical Documents*, ed. David C. Douglas (New York: Oxford University Press, 1969), 103–8.

3. Juliet Vale, *Edward III and Chivalry* (Woodbridge, Suffolk: Boydell Press, 1982); M. H. Keen, *England in the Later Middle Ages* (London: Methuen & Co., 1973), 144–46.

4. John Palmer, "The War Aims of the Protagonists and the Negotiations for Peace," in *The Hundred Years War*, ed. Kenneth Fowler (London: Macmillan, 1971), 59–62; May McKisack, *The Fourteenth Century, 1307–1399*, Oxford History of England 5 (Oxford: Clarendon Press, 1959), 140–42.

5. McKisack, *The Fourteenth Century, 1307–1399*, 140–45; Keen, *England in the Later Middle Ages*, 140–42.

6. George Kane, "The Text," in *A Companion to Piers Plowman*, ed. John Alford (Berkeley: University of California Press, 1988), 184.

7. Richard W. Kaeuper, *War, Justice, and Public Order: England and France in the Later Middle Ages* (Oxford: Clarendon Press, 1988), demonstrates how the war effort diminished the resources available for the domestic administration of justice; his study affirms the historical veracity of the connection that Langland makes in this first dream vision between the corruption of the royal court and the legal system and the king's war policy.

8. For a discussion of the marshal's responsibilities as one of the chief organizers of the war effort, see Michael Prestwich, *Armies and Warfare in the Middle Ages: The English Experience* (New Haven: Yale University Press, 1996), 171–75.

9. John Barnie, *War in Medieval English Society: Social Values in the Hundred Years War, 1377–99* (Ithaca, N.Y.: Cornell University Press, 1974), 13.

10. Sister Helen Margaret Peck, "The Prophecy of John of Bridlington," Ph. D. Dissertation, University of Chicago, 1931, 4–51; "John of Bridlington," in *Political Poems and Songs*, ed. Thomas Wright (London: Longman, Green, and Roberts, 1859), 1:123–215.

11. Peck, "The Prophecy of John of Bridlington," 57–58.

12. G. A. Holmes, *The Estates of the Higher Nobility in Fourteenth-Century England* (Cambridge: Cambridge University Press, 1957), 22–24; Prestwich, *Armies and Warfare*, 171.

13. Antonia Gransden, *Historical Writing in England ii: c. 1307 to the Early Sixteenth Century* (Ithaca, N.Y.: Cornell University Press, 1982), 111.

14. *The Anonimalle Chronicle 1333 to 1381*, ed. V. H. Galbraith (Manchester: Manchester University Press, 1970), 49; translated in Barnie, *War in Medieval English Society*, 13–14.

15. Sir Thomas Gray, *Scalacronica: The Reigns of Edward I, Edward II, and Edward III*, ed. and trans. Herbert Maxwell (Glasgow: J. Maclehose & Sons, 1907), 164–65.

16. Gray, *Scalacronica*, 165.

17. *Rotuli parliamentorum*, vol. 2 (1369) (n.p., n.d.), 301, my translation.

18. Barnie, *War in Medieval English Society*, 33; see also Keen, *England in the Later Middle Ages*, 147.

19. Christopher Allmand, *The Hundred Years War: England and France at War c. 1300–1450* (Cambridge: Cambridge University Press, 1988), 47. The actual profitability of the war for the English nobility has been a subject of debate among historians; see, for example, the opposing arguments offered by K. B. McFarlane, "War, the Economy and Social Change: England and the Hundred Years War," *Past and Present* 22 (1962): 3–13; and M. M. Postan, "The Costs of the Hundred Years' War," *Past and Present* 27 (1964): 34–53. Michael Powicke, "The English Aristocracy and the War," in *The Hundred Years War*, ed. Kenneth Fowler (London: Macmillan, 1971), 130–34, reviews both sides of the debate and concurs with McFarlane's assessment.

20. The most thorough discussion of the changing remunerative practices during the reign of Edward III is provided by Andrew Ayton, *Knights and Warhorses: Military Service and the English Aristocracy under Edward III* (Woodbridge, Suffolk: Boydell Press, 1994), 96–137. Prestwich, *Armies and Warfare*, 83–96, 111–12, argues that wages began being paid for military service during the Norman period, but other historians date the prevalence of this practice to the reign of Edward III; see also Michael Prestwich, *The Three Edwards: War and State in England, 1272–1377* (London: George Weidenfeld & Nicolson, 1980; London: Routledge, 1990), 200–1; H. J. Hewitt, *The Organization of War under Edward III, 1338–62* (Manchester: Manchester University Press, 1966), 33–37; C[hristopher] T. Allmand, "War and Profit in

the Late Middle Ages," *History Today* 15 (November 1965): 762; and K. B. McFarlane, *The Nobility of Later Medieval England: The Ford Lecture for 1953 and Related Studies* (Oxford: Clarendon Press, 1973), 23–27.

21. Hewitt, *The Organization of War under Edward III*, 34 with a reference to the list of six nobles on 32, cites these names from the *Calendar of Patent Rolls*, 1358–61, but Prestwich, *Armies and Warfare*, 93, claims that contracts were not needed for Edward III's own expeditions to France, including the one of 1359.

22. McFarlane, *The Nobility of Later Medieval England*, 23; see also Keen, *England in the Later Middle Ages*, 147–48.

23. McFarlane, *The Nobility of Later Medieval England*, 24–27; and Prestwich, *Armies and Warfare*, 95.

24. Allmand, "War and Profit in the Late Middle Ages," 763; see also Keen, *England in the Later Middle Ages*, 147–48; Prestwich, *The Three Edwards*, 201–3.

25. McFarlane, *The Nobility of Late Medieval England*, 33; see also Keen, *England in the Later Middle Ages*, 146.

26. Hewitt, *Organization of the War under Edward III*, 99–118.

27. *Chronicon Galfridi le Baker de Swyndbroke*, ed. Edward Maunde Thompson (Oxford: Clarendon Press, 1889), 145.

28. Herald of Sir John Chandos, *Life of the Black Prince*, ed. Mildred Pope and Eleanor Lodge (1910; reprint, New York: AMS Press, 1974), lines 1395–97, my translation; see also Keen, *England in the Later Middle Ages*, 146.

29. Prestwich, *Armies and Warfare*, 104–6.

30. H. J. Hewitt, *The Black Prince's Expedition of 1355–1357* (Manchester: Manchester University Press, 1958), 156; for a discussion of ransoms, see 152–60.

31. Allmand, *The Hundred Years War*, 127.

32. McKisack, *The Fourteenth Century, 1307–1399*, 254.

33. Hewitt, *The Black Prince's Expedition of 1355–1357*, 160; the grants are identified on 160–63. Interestingly enough, Hewitt begins this discussed with an unattributed quotation from *Piers Plowman* A.III.197–98: "Not only was it the prince's nature to be lavish with gifts but also the spirit of the age made it politic 'to give meed to men who humbly serve him ... to honour them with gifts'" (160). See also Prestwich, *Armies and Warfare*, 101.

34. Hewitt, *The Black Prince's Expedition of 1355–1357*, 162–63.

35. Honoré Bonet, *The Tree of Battles*, trans. G. W. Coopland (Cambridge, Mass.: Harvard University Press, 1949), 150.

36. M. H. Keen, *The Laws of War in the Late Middle Ages* (London: Routledge & Kegan Paul, 1965), 146.

37. Keen, *Laws of War*, 139.

38. Ayton, *Knights and Warhorses*, 135; Prestwich, *Armies and Warfare*, 103, confirms this as the figure until 1360, stating that it was the portion of the booty that the Black Prince customarily demanded.

39. Keen, *Laws of War*, 146–48.

40. McFarlane, *The Nobility of Later Medieval England*, 28.

41. Huppé, "The A-Text of *Piers Plowman* and the Norman Wars," 44, refuses to interpret *Pere* in line 185 as a reference to Calais because he argues that it would mean that Conscience retreated from France but left the King and Meed behind. He does not recognize the change in chronology from the end to the beginning of the campaign that occurs here.

42. McFarlane, *The Nobility of Later Medieval England*, 38.

43. McKisack, *The Fourteenth Century, 1307–1399*, 147.

44. McKisack, *The Fourteenth Century, 1307–1399*, 147.

45. Huppé, "*Piers Plowman* and the Norman Wars," 42, contends that Langland could not be alluding to the campaign of 1359–1360 in these lines because "Edward had personal charge of the whole campaign which ended in the treaty of Bretigny as well as the negotiation of the treaty itself, so that to attack the conduct of the campaign leading up to the treaty was to attack Edward." Such a criticism of Edward's war policy is precisely what I argue Langland intends in this passage.

46. Skeat, ed., *Piers the Plowman*, 2:48–49; see also Kenneth Fowler, *The King's Lieutenant: Henry of Grosmont, First Duke of Lancaster, 1310–1361* (New York: Barnes & Noble, 1969), 208–9. Huppé, "The A-Text of *Piers Plowman* and the Norman Wars," 40, claims that the description of winter privations in A.III.176–79 does not fit the expedition of 1359–1360 and rejects Skeat's interpretation of "a dym cloud" as an allusion to the disastrous storm of 1360. Bennett, "The Date of the A-Text of *Piers Plowman*," 569, cites Froissart's account of the English suffering during this campaign to refute Huppé.

47. *Anonimalle Chronicle*, 46.

48. Gray, *Scalacronica*, 158.

49. *The Brut or the Chronicles of England*, ed. Friedrich W. D. Brie, Early English Text Society, o. s., 136 (London: Early English Text Society, 1908), 2:311, my translation.

50. Thomas Walsingham, *Historia Anglicana*, ed. H. T. Riley, Rolls Series, No. 28 (London, 1863–64), 1:287, also denies that Edward III was frightened by this storm.

51. *Chroniques de J. Froissart*, ed. Siméon Luce (Paris: Libraire de la Société de l'histoire de France, 1876), 6:4–5, my translation.

52. *Chroniques de J. Froissart*, 6:4.

53. *Chroniques de J. Froissart*, 6:4.

54. By assigning this defense of masculine militarism to a female personification, Langland indicates the misogyny of his own clerical ideology as David Aers explains in "Class, Gender, Medieval Criticism, and *Piers Plowman*," in *Class and Gender in Early English Literature: Intersections*, ed. Britton Harwood and Gillian Overing (Bloomington, Indiana: University of Indiana Press, 1994), 59–75; see also in the same volume, Clare Lees, "Gender and Exchange in *Piers Plowman*," 112–30.

55. Vale, *Edward III and Chivalry*, 76–91, argues that the foundation of the Order of the Garter in 1349 "was an integral part of Edward's Norman campaign from its inception, not merely a retrospective commemoration of its success" (77). See Prestwich, *The Three Edwards*, 203–9.

56. Allmand, *The Hundred Years War*, 48; see also Maurice Keen, "War, Peace and Chivalry," in *Nobles, Knights and Men-at-Arms in the Middle Ages* (London: Hambledon Press, 1996), 1–20; N. A. R. Wright, "The *Tree of Battles* of Honoré Bouvet (*sic*) and the Laws of War," in *War, Literature, and Politics in the Late Middle Ages*, ed. C. T. Allmand (New York: Barnes & Noble Books, 1976), 2–31.

CHAPTER 4

CHAUCER'S TALE OF MELIBEE

CONTRADICTIONS AND CONTEXT

JUDITH FERSTER

> Nothing is more necessary in arduous deliberations, and nothing, on the other hand more dangerous, than asking advice.
> —Guicciardini, *Storia d'Italia*

Chaucer's Tale of Melibee invites historicizing because it seems undeniably topical.[1] If we assume that the tale was written in the late 1380s (1386–1390),[2] it seems logical to historicize it by putting it into the context of the Hundred Years' War.[3] It is natural to want to connect the work of the premier poet of the age to England's most important war of the period, especially because, along with its companion, Sir Thopas, he tells it "in his own name" in the Canterbury book. But there are obstacles in the way of an easy settling on the French war as the true subject of the tale. For one thing, there were other conflicts that Chaucer could have been addressing, for instance Gaunt's war with Castile,[4] or the negotiations for a treaty with Flanders.[5] For another, some historicists think that the poem may not have targeted a specific conflict so much as the general topic of advice to the prince (with some special attention to advice from women).[6] Advice was a matter that was relevant to any war or peace but which would have had particular bite in the context of the revolt of the Appellant lords against Richard II in the middle to late 1380s. And another obstacle is the distinct interpretive tradition made up of critics who think the tale's irony and contradictions preclude its having any political message at all. Its many paradoxes shut down the advice genre, rendering it useless as a guide both to abstract issues of advice and to concrete historical events. Thus, either the tale is a pointed comment on some contemporary issue—we are not sure which one—or it implodes before it can reach its mark.

Although these two main groups of critics, the historicists and formalists, have not engaged each other directly, I believe that both approaches must be part of an interpretation of the tale. A serious attempt to historicize the tale, to show that it contributes to moral and political discourse in a particular time and place, must take account of the fact that it seems to trip over its own seriousness. In this essay, I will consider the Melibee and its critics, the political scene in England in the middle and late 1380s, and Chaucer's position during that time in order to ascertain what kind of work the tale might be doing in its society. I will then put this reading into the context of historicist approaches to Chaucer.

THE MELIBEE

The different historical events to which historicist critics want to connect the Melibee are all plausible referents for the allegory, because there was a common thread of war and peace and counsel among the events of the late fourteenth century and because the allegory is vague.[7] There was a good deal of war, and there were enough sentiments for peace that Chaucer might well have wished to contribute to the discussion. And it is likely that anyone who wanted to do so would see the wisdom of doing so in an oblique manner. But the multiple candidates that I mentioned above for the war and peace alluded to in the tale explain why many of the critics mention the importance of advice in the fourteenth century. If the tale is merely saying that advice is advisable, there is less need to pin down exactly what its particular advice was about.[8]

But the questions still remain: what in his own time made Chaucer think of the early fourteenth-century *Livre de Mellibée et de Dame Prudence*, which is itself a translation of the thirteenth-century *Liber consolationis et consilii* by Albertano of Brescia?[9] And for what purpose? Why did he want to insert it into the contemporary scene? How many, if any, relevant historical events did he mean to be drawing in? How current were they? For instance, did he mean for people reading a story about a woman who convinces a man to make peace with his enemies to think of the end of Edward III's reign when Alice Perrers was accused of destroying Edward's taste for the Hundred Years' War? Even if he didn't intend that association, could he prevent it?

Chaucer did give us one clear indication that he knew the tale could have political reverberations and that he wanted to control them: he left out the proverb in his French source on how troublesome it is to have a child as a king—"Et Salemon dit, 'Doulente la terre qui a enfant a seigneur.'"[10] This deletion shows that Chaucer knew that the tale could be taken as a reference to Richard II's accession to the throne when he was still a young boy. The deletion changes the French text to limit the interpretation of the tale.

Despite taking out the reference to youthful kings, Chaucer left in his source's reference to youthful counselors, which might have been almost as troublesome, because Richard was accused of paying too much heed to his young counselor, Robert de Vere.[11] In one case he removed the lines likely to cause offense; in the other he did not. Why the difference?

The formalist critics of the tale notice that it is occupied by the issues of war, peace, and advice that invite historicist readings. But by examining the way the issues are twisted and knotted, the formalists attack the notion that the tale straightforwardly comments on anything. They see the surface meaning of the tale as undermined by irony and paradox.[12] Some of them use post-structuralist theory, but despite post-structuralism's interest in contradictions not intended by the author, they all attribute these hermeneutical games to Chaucer the poet. They watch him pitting proverb against proverb and pulling morals out from under their *exempla*. As H. Marshall Leicester, Jr., says, Chaucer "decenters [the tale's] 'original' logocentric meaning as stable, timeless wisdom."[13] Or, as Daniel Kempton puts it in his equally deconstructive interpretation of the tale, in Chaucer's hands the "restless discourse of quotation undoes the idea of Holy Writ."[14]

According to the formalists, the Melibee calls into question the possibility of its own project, educating the ruler. Melibee's initial plan is to declare war on the enemies who wounded his wife and daughter (lines 1009, 1050), but Prudence wants him to eschew vengeance and be reconciled with his foes: "'Certes,' quod she, 'I conseille yow that ye accorde with youre adversaries and that ye have pees with hem.'"[15] After hundreds of lines of instruction and advice on peace-making, and even after Prudence has actually taken things out of Melibee's hands, making war unnecessary by winning the adversaries' acquiescence to her mediation of the conflict (1765–68), he resists her message. When she asks him what he intends to do, he replies that he will certainly exile and disinherit them all (1832–35). As Lee Patterson says, since "Prudence's task is to teach Melibee how to interpret," this is "an aporetic moment that subverts the pedagogical program the Melibee simultaneously espouses and enacts." According to Patterson, this moment reveals "a systematic contradiction that inhabits the text as a whole."[16] Melibee's scant progress reveals the contradictions at the heart of the tale.

The "pedagogical program" of the tale is sabotaged by the failings of both the student and the teacher. Melibee is obtuse, of course. Even when he accepts Prudence's reasonable advice to call a council to discuss his response to the attack of his enemies, he gets it wrong. Prudence had told him to summon his "trewe freendes alle" and his "lynage whiche that been wise," citing a maxim often included in the pseudo-Aristotelian advice manual *Secretum Secretorum*, "Werk alle thy thynges by conseil, and thou shalt never repente" (1002–3). Yet he summons "a greet congregacion of folk" who are neither true friends nor wise, including physicians and surgeons, flatterers and lawyers, old enemies to whom he was only superficially reconciled, and neighbors who fear him (1004–7). When he then ignores the advice of the few wise speakers and endorses the majority's call for war, Prudence has to start all over, critiquing his list of invited guests and reinterpreting their speeches, teaching him how to choose counselors (1115–26), and finally doing the peace-making herself.

Melibee is sometimes not merely obtuse, but illogical. For instance, after he has accepted the decision of his invited guests, he resists hearing Prudence's advice (1055–61). But his refusal to take her advice at this juncture is very peculiar because he has just done so: it was on her advice that he called the meeting that he now uses as a justification for not listening to any more advice (1056). As if to highlight this inconsistency, Chaucer adds a phrase to his source, saying that Melibee convened his meeting "by the conseil of his wyf Prudence" (1004). Melibee cannot refuse her advice now without impugning her earlier advice and himself: "I seye that alle wommen been wikke, and noon good of hem alle. For 'of a thousand men,' seith Salomon, 'I foond o good man, but certes, of alle wommen, good womman foond I nevere.' / And also, certes, if I governed me by thy conseil, it sholde seme that I hadde yeve to thee over me the maistrie, and God forbede that it so weere!" (1057–58). These are debatable though plausible reasons not to have taken her advice the first time she offered it, but not the second.

The quotation from Solomon notwithstanding, by bringing them up now he undermines his own authority.

Nor is Prudence's advice free of problems. Since we sometimes hear both her and Melibee's renditions of what others have said, we can compare their interpretations. At the initial council, for instance, the surgeons refuse to support the option of war against those who attacked Prudence and Sophie, paraphrasing the Hippocratic oath ("that we do no damage") and promising to try to heal Sophie's wounds (1011–15). Then the physicians speak: "Almoost right in the same wise the phisiciens answerden, save that they seyden a fewe woordes moore: / that right as maladies been cured by hir contraries, right so shul men warisshe werre by vengeaunce" (1016–17). Later, Prudence wants to know what Melibee thought of the surgeons' and physicians' advice, referring approvingly to the paraphrase of the Hippocratic oath and asking him particularly about his understanding of the physicians' extra words on the cure by contraries (1267–78). Melibee's version is "that right as [my enemies] han doon me a contrarie, right so sholde I doon hem another. / For right as they han venged hem on me and doon me wrong, right so shal I venge me upon hem and doon hem wrong; / and thanne have I cured oon contrarie by another" (1280–82).

Prudence exclaims about the self-interestedness of his interpretation: "Lo, lo ... how lightly is every man enclined to his owene desir and to his owene plesaunce!" Then she tries to correct his interpretation by redefining *contraries*. "Certes," she says,

> ... the wordes of the phisiciens ne sholde nat han been understonden in thys wise. / For certes, wikkednesse is nat contrarie to wikkednesse, ne vengeance to vengeaunce, ne wrong to wrong, but they been semblable. / And therfore o vengeaunce is nat warisshed by another vengeaunce, ne o wroong by another wroong, / but everich of hem encreesceth and aggreggeth oother, / But certes, the wordes of the phisiciens sholde been understonden in this wise: / for good and wikkednesse been two contraries, and pees and werre, vengeaunce and suffraunce, discord and accord, and manye othere thynges; / but certes, wikkednesse shal be warisshed by goodnesse, discord by accord, werre by pees, and so forth of othere thynges. (1283–90)

She goes on, adding an admonition from St. Paul.

The "fewe woordes moore" that the physicians add to the surgeons' sentiments transform them into their opposite, so that the narrator's judgment that the two groups are "almoost" the same seems comical or disingenuous. The issue—whether two things are opposite or alike—is exactly the issue raised by Prudence's interrogation of Melibee. After Melibee's fairly accurate reading of the physicians' advice, Prudence turns their meaning inside out by invoking a different sense of *contrarie*. While the word can mean, as she suggests, "opposite," it can also mean "opposed," which fits a retaliatory attack. Prudence is using a semantic switch, as well as her frequent interjections of "certes" and her hermeneutical lament, "Lo, lo . . . how lightly is every man enclined to his owene desir and to his owene plesaunce!," to take a contrary view of contraries and distort the physicians' intentions. Despite Melibee's slowness to accept Prudence's point of view, these interpretive difficulties are Prudence's: she is interpreting according to "desir" and "plesaunce." She does this again when she interprets Melibee's interpretation of the advice of the lawyers. They say, in essence, "Defend yourself" (1026–27); Melibee takes this advice to mean that he should defend himself by building towers (1333–34); and Prudence interprets the towers allegorically as pride (1335), but here there is no pretense of interpreting the lawyers' intentions.

Thus, since both Melibee and Prudence have faults as interpreters, it is no wonder that the whole project of educating Melibee is called into question. It is also called into question by a conflict at its heart. As Daniel Kempton points out, there is a contradiction between her early principle, "Make no felawshipe with thyne olde enemys" (1189), and her entire enterprise in the tale, producing a reconciliation between Melibee and his enemies.[17] Her ability to quote authorities on both sides of the question keeps her from justifying her choices between them at any given moment. The choices look pragmatic. When she wishes to displace Melibee's old enemies as advisers, she quotes one set of authorities. When she wishes to advocate peace, she quotes the other. Her wish to prevail overcomes her previous advice on the process of soliciting advice.

According to David Wallace, Prudence's contradictory positions are demanded by her rhetorical task, meeting whatever objections Melibee produces to resist her point of view. Wallace rejects the deconstructive view of the tale because, he contends, a monologic position is prohibited by her need to counter Melibee's thrusts and parries. She is demonstrating "just in time" manufacture of arguments, producing them as they are needed, whether or not they contradict the ones that went before.[18]

But Prudence's ability to jump from one maxim to its opposite stirs up another threat to the project: recognition of the dangers of advice itself. Taking these contradictions seriously challenges historicist readings of the tale as counseling peace to the king, but Wallace reads the tale as advice to advisors to kings, not to kings themselves. It is "not a *Fürstenspiegel*, but a handbook for go-betweens."[19] In this, he is like Carolyn Collette who speculates that the tale is an examination of women's roles as "a brake on the honor culture's tendency to self-destruction" through endless war.[20]

While she is trying to correct the damage done by the incorrectly constituted council that Melibee summoned at her behest, Prudence provides him with advice about advice, material that sounds some traditional themes from mirrors for princes like the *Secretum Secretorum*. In choosing counselors, she counsels, start with God: "Ye shul first in alle youre werkes mekely biseken to the heighe God that he wol be youre conseillour" (1115–16). Of course this is impossible because he has started with Prudence, both in calling the abortive council and now in letting her begin again by telling her, "I wol governe me by thy conseil in alle thyng" (1114). It is too late for him to start with God.

The next steps produce several additional problems: Melibee is to take counsel in himself and keep the results secret because secrecy is the only way to avoid being betrayed (1138–53). Neither friends nor foes are trustworthy (1141). Then he is to choose a few tested friends who are faithful, wise, and old to be counselors (1154–65). He must not consult all his friends, but just "a fewe" (1166). Yet he must not have just one counselor, he should have "manye" (1170). Not only is the recommended number of counselors unstable, but also it is not clear that it is a good idea to have counselors at all. This contradiction is fundamental. If one can safely tell secrets neither "to thy foo ne to thy frend" (1141), nor indeed to "any wight" (1145), then the whole project is compromised. Just in case we were tempted to think that wives might be a safe alternative to friends and foes, this last category ensures that they are eliminated, too. Like the liar's paradox, the tale is a self-consuming artifact. If Melibee takes Prudence's advice not to take the advice of other people, he has already done so. Advice, which a ruler must have, is a threat to him. Guicciardini's warning, which I use as the epigraph to this essay, is a nice expression of the double bind. Prudence admonishes that "whan thou biwreyest thy conseil to any wight, he holdeth thee in his snare" (1145). Needing advice makes the ruler vulnerable,[21] which produces a conundrum that not only seems to make Prudence inconsistent, but even jeopardizes her own goal of getting Melibee to do what she wants.

That the tale is riven with these contradictions threatens the historicists' claim that it addresses topical matters. A serious comment on getting good advice seems particularly unlikely. To make the connection between the tale and its time, we need more contextualizing information, particularly on relevant political events and on Chaucer's relationship to the court. These are the subjects of the next two sections.

ENGLAND IN THE LATE 1380s

The events between 1385 and 1389 that might have prompted Chaucer to write the Melibee bring together the issues of advice and military policy. Many of the historicists writing about the Melibee notice that the two issues are present, but they do not talk about their interrelations. These are crucial because the great promoters of advice—large land-holders who struggled with Richard II over control of the government and especially foreign policy[22]—were also promoters of war. Since they profited from war and wanted it vigorously pursued, they were offended by the king's attempts to make peace with France and offended that he tried to do it without consulting them. One chronicle reports that during the crisis of 1388, in which the Appellant lords tried a number of Richard's advisers for treason, they threatened to depose Richard "because it appeared that he preferred to govern through false traitors rather than through his most faithful friends the lords and nobles of the realm."[23] As magnates, they felt that their property gave them a right to advise the king that went back at least to the Magna Carta.

The Appellants' complaints about the king's inner circle, that it was too small and included the wrong people, were at least partly motivated by Richard's attempts to make peace with France. The appeals of treason they initiated against the king's counselors during the Merciless Parliament of 1388 included the peace negotiations with France, especially those involving Calais.[24] Thus the people who supported peace were not the same as those who spoke movingly of their rights to advise the king. According to Anthony Tuck, "the appellants' purpose was to remove the favourites from their positions of influence over the king, ensure their own access to patronage, and initiate a more militant policy towards France."[25] They accomplished all this, having purged the king's household and installed themselves on the council so that they controlled the government for the next year.

The Commons in Parliament did like peace, especially after the Rising of 1381, which ominously dramatized the domestic price of heavy taxes for war. They sometimes resisted appeals for money to prosecute the war, perhaps trying to avoid another outbreak of violence. In the years after the

Merciless Parliament, Richard's policy of seeking peace with France may well have been motivated by his wish to be less dependent on the Commons.[26] But the Commons sometimes joined with the Appellants in their opposition to the king because of his lack of success in procuring peace and what looked to them like financial mismanagement.[27] When the Appellants, too, succumbed to financial corruption, the Commons left the alliance.[28]

From 1386 to 1389, as the control of government shifted back and forth between the alliance of the Appellants and Parliament on the one hand and Richard and his advisers on the other, foreign policy changed from peace to war and back again. Finally, because the Appellants were as unsuccessful in waging war when they controlled the government in 1388 as Richard had been in waging peace in 1387, they were themselves forced to resume negotiations with France for a truce. When Richard regained power, he continued the negotiations that led to the peace that had long been his goal.

CHAUCER IN THE LATE 1380s

According to recent work on Chaucer's role in these turbulent years, although he had some connection to the family of one of the Appellants (Chaucer's friend Sir William Beauchamp was the brother of the Appellant Thomas Beauchamp, Earl of Warwick[29]), his affiliations were chiefly to royalists, including some of those killed by the Merciless Parliament (e.g., Tresilian, Thomas Usk, Brembre). According to Paul Strohm, of the eleven men convicted of treason by the Appellants, Chaucer was associated in some way with eight.[30]

In 1386, when the Wonderful Parliament impeached the king's favorite, Michael de la Pole, John of Gaunt, often a moderating influence, was out of England pursuing his interests in Castile. Chaucer may have felt vulnerable when the Parliament presented a petition requesting that all controllers given lifetime appointments by the king be removed because of their corruption.[31] Chaucer's was not a lifetime appointment, but in December of 1386, barely a month after the antiroyalist Wonderful Parliament, he resigned his two controllerships (wool and petty customs). He also left his house at Aldgate and gave up his annuities. He seems to have been taking himself out of the line of fire as the Appellants began to move against the beneficiaries of Richard's patronage.[32] According to Derek Pearsall, "There was no 'king's party' in the strict sense of the word, since all who were in government were the recipients of royal patronage in some measure. But insofar as there was one, Chaucer was of it."[33] Distancing himself from the bureaucracy may have felt like a prudent way to ride out the period that turned out to be dangerous for a number of his friends and associates who had connections with Richard, some of whom were merely deprived of their jobs, others of whom were executed.

But Chaucer did not go very far. When he spent 1385–1389 as a member of the Peace Commission for Kent and represented Kent in the Wonderful Parliament of 1386, he was probably still associated with Richard. As Lee Patterson points out, Chaucer's relationship with Kent may have been an example of "that meddling in local affairs of which men complained a decade later when they described Richard's tyranny."[34] Witnessing the Wonderful Parliament as a representative of Kent might have given Chaucer some vivid glimpses of the possible dangers to the king's friends in the erupting factional disputes.

THE MELIBEE IN THE LATE 1980s

The historical setting and Chaucer's place in it can help to reconcile the topicality of the tale with the contradictions that seem to destroy its ability to address contemporary issues. One possibility is that the elusiveness, its contradictions and paradoxes, are a cover for its political intent, since political speech was at least somewhat constrained.[35] The puzzles could be a disguise. Lynn Staley (Johnson) notes both that Prudence urges Melibee to take responsibility for his own actions and that Chaucer himself takes evasive action in order not to be held responsible for political comment (for instance, by presenting himself as a "mere" translator).[36] This contradiction may provide a link between the formalist and historicist readings. According to several commentators, the tale has to disguise its political commentary because it is so dangerous to take a side on the various conflicts. The historicists use this notion of political disguise when talking about the tale's *generality*, which makes it hard to connect it to specific historical events.[37] But the notion of disguise could also be used to explain the fact that the tale is a self-consuming artifact. What better disguise is there than to pretend not to be saying anything at all?[38]

But what is the political comment that Chaucer is trying to soften by making the tale a conundrum? If one takes a bipolar view of late-medieval English politics—the king versus everyone else—then advocating advice, as Prudence does most of the time, looks like advocacy on the side of the Appellants. But her calls for peace place her on Richard's side on the subject of the war with France. So the two issues had opposite valences. Those sympathetic to one were probably not sympathetic to the other.

Perhaps this split is the reason that Chaucer was willing to leave the criticism of young counselors in the tale just at the time Richard was criticized for having one among his favorites; Robert de Vere, although young, was not for the French war, as were the young counselors in the Melibee (1035–36). When the Merciless Parliament accused Richard's advisers, including de Vere, of treason, among the charges were treasonous dealings with France. That is, the Appellants were saying that attempts to create peace between the two countries were a betrayal of England.[39] Since de Vere was associated with Richard's peace policy, and two of Richard's Appellant antagonists, Thomas Mowbray and Henry Bolingbroke, were relatively young at this time, Richard would not have felt vulnerable to the charge that he was allowing inexperienced youths to drag him into war with France.

Since Chaucer was likely to have been on the king's side in the struggle with the Appellants, maybe his treatment of both issues supports the king: both Prudence's advocacy of peace and the deconstruction of Prudence's advice on advice could be ways of endorsing or comforting the king. Perhaps Chaucer was trying to make advice look ridiculous by showing that its bromides self-destruct. If Chaucer wrote the Melibee for Richard when he was feuding with the Parliament over who should choose his advisers, perhaps Richard was happy to be told that advice, praised though it was by his adversaries, produced its own problems. Maybe a deconstruction of the Appellants' ideology of advice was just what he wanted to hear.

In fact, the Appellants were rather like Prudence in that one of the reasons that they made such a fuss about advice was that they did not like the ruler's policy. Prudence disliked war and they disliked peace, but all of them used talk about the process of advice, especially the choice of advisers, to oppose its outcome. Prudence went from advising Melibee about how to get good advice to actually implementing her own plan. The Appellants and their supporters implemented their own plan by replacing Richard's hated favorites on the council. In some sense, Chaucer is using the tale to expose the ways in which those who talk about process are sometimes really trying to manipulate it. Prudence's advisory coup echoes the Appellants' takeover of the government in 1388.

The compartmentalization of the criticism of the Melibee, the separation of historicism from formalism, is unnecessary. The historicists can deal with the contradictions and paradoxes the formalists point out. And the formalists must understand that to point out contradictions and paradoxes is not to prevent the tale from having some political significance. The paradoxes and contradictions do not rule out politics; they merely make the tale's politics more complex.

In *A Theory of Literary Production*, Pierre Macherey considers the idea that literature can test ideology by finding and exploring its gaps and contradictions.[40] In the late fourteenth century, to expose the contradictions in the ideology of advice was to take sides in the conflict between the king and the Appellants. When the tale appears to be referring to contemporary politics, it probably is. And when it appears not to be referring to contemporary politics, it may still be.

CHAUCER IN THE 1990s

Since Chaucer is so rarely overtly topical, a number of critics have focused on ways in which, as David Aers says, "linguistic, social, and subjective processes" are "bound together in the structure and history of particular communities."[41] Examining Chaucer's themes and style, they argue that he attacks the dominant ideology by showing that it is not only not single, but also not "natural"—that the categories it presents are socially constructed. Their argument is that Chaucer understood culture as disenchanted, to use H. Marshall Leicester's word, that is, not God-given, but man-made.[42] For historicists like David Aers, Paul Strohm, David Wallace, and Peggy Knapp, Chaucer knew that ideas that benefitted a few were routinely presented as divinely ordered for the good of all, and he challenged the hegemony of a "top-down" social structure and the authority that justified it.[43] His response was to challenge ideology by deconstructing and multiplying it and thus toppling the hierarchy it supported. This approach is consonant with an earlier thread in Chaucer criticism in which Chaucer was seen as problematizing the verities of his culture.[44] When applied to the Melibee, this approach can emphasize the tale's antimilitarism, as David Aers does.[45] Or, it can emphasize the importance of horizontal rather than vertical relationships. As Paul Strohm reads it, the tale's promotion of counsel moderates "the ideology of the descending state ruled by a lord in the image of God."[46]

But the tale has also been read as more supportive of ruling-class ideology. Stephen Knight emphasizes the utility to rulers of reforming their use of wealth and of winning peace to maintain order. The Melibee is a "serious and thoughtful address to the powerful on how to save their power."[47] For Knight, it is the focus of Chaucer's conservatism in *The Canterbury Tales*.

According to Larry Scanlon, the Melibee's position on the power of rulers is paradoxical since Melibee must show he is worthy of sovereignty by giving it up (when he decides not to take vengeance on his enemies, who submit to him).[48] This paradox does not contradict Knight's view of the tale since the restraint is voluntary, but for Scanlon it has to do with the growing importance of statute law as adjudicatory process replaced the chivalric ideal of vengeance.[49]

As we have already seen, Lee Patterson provides another kind of historicist reading of the Melibee. Patterson argues that the tale's paradoxes and self-contradictions are Chaucer's way of rejecting the role of court poet. He refuses to give voice to "the traditional discourse of counsel" in favor of "a discourse that insists upon its autonomy from both ideological programs and social appropriations."[50] This view of the tale fits well with Patterson's approach to the rest of Chaucer's career in *Chaucer and the Subject of History*, where he argues that Chaucer is aware of the dynamic changes going on in his society but tries to withdraw from them. For instance, he reads the Miller's Tale as a response to the economic and political dynamism of the rural peasant class that registers the counter-hegemonic energy to be found in the countryside. For Patterson, the rest of *The Canterbury Tales* demonstrate "the extent to which the urgent social issues raised by the Miller's Tale have been disarmed."[51]

In my reading of the Melibee, I cross some of the categories I have set up here. I agree with the Chaucerians who affirm the ability of literature to perform a counter-hegemonic function. But in my reading of Chaucer's support for Richard II in the Melibee, I appear to be producing a conservative Chaucer like Stephen Knight's. However, I do not, as Knight seems to, accept that Prudence offers practical advice that could help a ruler rule better. I agree more with Patterson in his deconstructive reading of the tale, in which all advice collapses through its self-contradictions. But I do not find such deconstruction a block to topicality, for an attack on the efficacy of advice, along with the tale's ruminations on war and peace, would have had political valence in the middle of the 1380s. Thus deconstruction and historicism can work together. As Patterson points out in a later article, deconstruction's aim to bring to light "the suppressions and elisions" of ideology is a fundamentally historical project.[52]

In the shifting political circumstances in which Chaucer probably wrote the Tale of Melibee, the Appellants' successful displacement of Richard II may have made support of the king as risky as criticism of him might have been in another time. Perhaps in its context of the Appellants' struggles with Richard II over the Hundred Years' War, deconstruction of the ideology of advice has a strong political valence. The Melibee was a challenge, not to the king, but to the Appellants, the ruling elite who had challenged him.

NOTES

1. Guicciardini, *Storia d'Italia*, 1:16, quoted in Albert Cook, *History/Writing* (Cambridge: Cambridge University Press, 1988), 103. This essay is based on the more extensive discussion of The Tale of Melibee offered in chapter 6 of my book, *Fictions of Advice: The Literature and Politics of Counsel in Late Medieval England*, Middle Ages Series (Philadelphia: University of Pennsylvania Press, 1996), 89–107. Permission of the publisher to reprint this essay is gratefully acknowledged.

2. *The Riverside Chaucer*, ed. Larry D. Benson, 3rd ed. (Boston: Houghton Mifflin, 1987), 923. See J. S. P. Tatlock, *The Development and Chronology of Chaucer's Works*, Chaucer Society, 2d ser., vol. 37 (1907; reprint, Gloucester, Mass.: Peter Smith, 1963), 194–95; Dolores Palomo, "What Chaucer Really Did to *Le Livre de Mellibee*," *Philological Quarterly* 53 (1974): 313–14; Richard Firth Green, *Poets and Princepleasers: Literature and the English Court in the Late Middle Ages* (Toronto: University of Toronto Press, 1980), 143; Helen Cooper, *The Oxford Guides to Chaucer: The Canterbury Tales* (Oxford: Oxford University Press, 1989), 312; Lee Patterson, "'What Man Artow?': Authorial Self-Definition in *The Tale of Sir Thopas* and *The Tale of Melibee*," *Studies in the Age of Chaucer* 11 (1989): 139–40.

3. Gardiner Stillwell, "The Political Meaning of Chaucer's *Tale of Melibee*," *Speculum* 19 (1944): 433–44; William Askins, "The *Tale of Melibee* and the Crisis at Westminster, November, 1387," *Studies in the Age of Chaucer: Proceedings*, No. 2, 1986 (Knoxville, Tenn.: The New Chaucer Society [1987]), 103–12; Robert F. Yeager, "*Pax Poetica*: On the Pacifism of Chaucer and Gower," *Studies in the Age of Chaucer* 9 (1987): 97–121.

4. J. Leslie Hotson, "The *Tale of Melibeus* and John of Gaunt," *Studies in Philology* 18 (1921): 429–52.

5. V. J. Scattergood, "Chaucer and the French War: *Sir Thopas* and *Melibee*," in *Court and Poet*, ed. Glyn S. Burgess et al. (Liverpool: Francis Cairns, 1981), 287–96.

6. Stillwell, "The Political Meaning of Chaucer's *Tale of Melibee*"; Paul Olson, *The Canterbury Tales and the Good Society* (Princeton, N.J.: Princeton University Press, 1986), 119; Patterson, "'What Man Artow?'" 137. John Barnie, *War in Medieval English Society: Social Values in the Hundred Years War, 1337–99* (Ithaca, N.Y.: Cornell University Press, 1974); Green, *Poets and Princepleasers*; Paul Strohm, *Social Chaucer* (Cambridge, Mass.: Harvard University Press, 1989); Lynn Staley Johnson, "Inverse Counsel: Contexts for the *Melibee*," *Studies in Philology* 87 (1990): 137–55; David Aers and Lynn Staley, *The Powers of the Holy: Religion,*

Politics, and Gender in Late Medieval English Culture (University Park, Pa.: Pennsylvania State University Press, 1996), chapter 5.

7. Stillwell, "The Political Meaning in Chaucer's *Tale of Melibee;*" Olson, *The Canterbury Tales and the Good Society*, 119; Patterson, "'What Man Artow?'" 137.

8. Barnie, *War in Medieval English Society*; Green, *Poets and Princepleasers*, 143; Strohm, *Social Chaucer*; Johnson, "Inverse Counsel."

9. Renaud de Louens, *Le Livre de Mellibee et Prudence*, ed. J. Burke Severs, in *Sources and Analogues of Chaucer's Canterbury Tales*, ed. W. F. Bryan and Germaine Dempster (Chicago: University of Chicago Press, 1941), 568–614; Thor Sundby, ed., *Albertani Brixiensis. Liber consolationis et consilii, ex quo hausta est fabula de Melibeo et Prudentia* (Havniae: Fred. Host & Filium, 1873).

10. Renaud de Louens, *Le Livre de Mellibee et Prudence*, 581, lines 381–82.

11. Stillwell, "The Political Meaning of Chaucer's *Tale of Melibee*," 442.

12. See Donald McDonald, "Proverbs, *Sententiae*, and *Exempla* in Chaucer's Comic Tales: The Function of Comic Misapplication," *Speculum* 41 (1966): 453–65.

13. H. Marshall Leicester, Jr., "Oure Tonges *Différance*: Textuality and Deconstruction in Chaucer," in *Medieval Texts & Contemporary Readers*, ed. Laurie A. Finke and Martin B. Shichtman (Ithaca, N.Y.: Cornell University Press, 1987), 25.

14. Daniel Kempton, "Chaucer's *Tale of Melibee*:'A Litel Thyng in Prose,'" *Genre* 21 (1988): 274.

15. *The Riverside Chaucer*, ed. Benson, line 1675. All quotations are from this edition and are documented parenthetically by line number in the text.

16. Patterson, "'What Man Artow?'" 158, 157.

17. Kempton, "Chaucer's *Tale of Melibee*," 268.

18. David Wallace, *Chaucerian Polity: Absolutist Lineages and Associational Forms in England and Italy* (Stanford, Cal.: Stanford University Press, 1997), 233–34.

19. Wallace, *Chaucerian Polity*, 221.

20. Carolyn Collette, "Heeding the Counsel of Prudence: A Context for the Melibee," *Chaucer Review* 29 (1995): 428; Wallace, *Chaucerian Polity*, 245–46.

21. Ferster, *Fictions of Advice*, chapter 3.

22. Ferster, *Fictions of Advice*, 79–85.

23. Ranulf Higden, *Polychronicon Ranulfi Higden Monachi Cestrensis*, ed. Joseph Rawson Lumby (London: Longman & Co, Trübner & Co., 1886), 9: 103; this passage is translated in A. R. Myers, ed., *English Historical Documents 1327–1485*, vol. 4 of *English Historical Documents*, ed. David C. Douglas (New York: Oxford University Press, 1969), 155. Also see *The Westminster Chronicle 1381–1394*, ed. and trans. L. C. Hector and B. F. Harvey (Oxford: Clarendon Press, 1982), 218–19, 242–47.

24. Hector and Harvey, *Westminster Chronicle*, 204–5, 262–63.

25. Anthony Tuck, *Crown and Nobility, 1272–1461: Political Conflict in Late Medieval England* (Totowa, N.J.: Barnes and Noble Books, 1986 [first published, 1985]), 196.

26. Tuck, *Crown and Nobility, 1272–1461*, 199.

27. J. J. N. Palmer, *England, France and Christendom, 1377–99* (Chapel Hill: University of North Carolina Press, 1972), 82–85.

28. Palmer, *England, France and Christendom, 1377–99*, 137.

29. S. Sanderlin, "Chaucer and Richardian Politics," *Chaucer Review* 22 (1988): 173.

30. Strohm, *Social Chaucer*, 27; and "Politics and Poetics: Usk and Chaucer in the 1380s," in *Literary Practice and Social Change in Britain, 1380–1530*, ed. Lee Patterson (Berkeley: University of California Press, 1990), 94–95.

31. Strohm, *Social Chaucer*, 37.

32. Derek Pearsall, *The Life of Geoffrey Chaucer: A Critical Biography* (Oxford: Blackwell Publishers, 1992), 209. See also Strohm, *Social Chaucer*, 37; and "Politics and Poetics," 93. Lee Patterson, review of *Social Chaucer* in *Speculum* 67 (1992): 487.

33. Pearsall, *The Life of Geoffrey Chaucer*, 209.

34. Lee Patterson, *Chaucer and the Subject of History* (Madison, Wisc.: University of Wisconsin Press, 1991), 36.

35. Ferster, *Fictions of Advice*, chapter 2.

36. Johnson, "Inverse Counsel," 154.

37. Stillwell, "The Political Meaning of Chaucer's *Tale of Melibee*"; Green, *Poets and Princepleasers*, 164; and Barnie, *War in Medieval English Society*, 132.

38. David Lawton, "Dullness and the Fifteenth Century," *English Literary History* 54 (1987): 761–99.

39. Palmer, *England, France and Christendom, 1377–99*, 115.

40. Pierre Macherey, *A Theory of Literary Production*, trans. Geoffrey Wall (London: Routledge & Kegan Paul, 1978), 131–33.

41. David Aers, *Community, Gender, and Individual Identity: English Writing 1360–1430* (London and New York: Routledge, 1988), 3.

42. H. Marshall Leicester, Jr., *The Disenchanted Self: Representing the Subject in the Canterbury Tales* (Berkeley: University of California Press, 1990).

43. David Aers, *Chaucer, Langland and the Creative Imagination* (London: Routledge & Kegan Paul, 1980); and "The Parliament of Fowls: Authority, the Knower and the Known," *Chaucer Review* 16 (1981–82): 1–17; Strohm, *Social Chaucer*, "Politics and Poetics," and *Hochon's Arrow: The Social Imagination of Fourteenth-Century Texts* (Princeton, N.J.: Princeton University Press, 1992). See also Wallace, *Chaucerian Polity*; and Peggy Knapp, *Chaucer and the Social Contest* (New York: Routledge, 1990).

44. See, for example, Robert O. Payne, *The Key of Remembrance: A Study of Chaucer's Poetic* (New Haven, Conn.: Yale University Press for the University of Cincinnati, 1963); and two articles by Stewart Justman: "'Auctoritee' and the *Knight's Tale*," *Modern Language Quarterly* 39 (1978): 3–14; and "Medieval Monism and Abuse of Authority in Chaucer," *Chaucer Review* 11 (1976–77): 95–111.

45. David Aers, *Chaucer* (Atlantic Highlands, N.J.: Humanities Press International, 1986), 28–29.

46. Strohm, *Social Chaucer*, 163.

47. Stephen Knight, *Geoffrey Chaucer* (Oxford: Basil Blackwell, 1986), 139.

48. Larry Scanlon, *Narrative, Authority, and Power: The Medieval Exemplum and the Chaucerian Tradition* (Cambridge: Cambridge University Press, 1994), 213–15.

49. Scanlon, *Narrative, Authority, and Power*, 212–13.

50. Patterson, "'What Man Artow?'" 173.

51. Patterson, *Chaucer and the Subject of History*, 277; and "Making Identities in Fifteenth-Century England," in *New Historical Study: Essays on Reproducing Text, Representing History*, ed. Jeffrey N. Cox and Larry J. Reynolds (Princeton, N.J.: Princeton University Press, 1993), 69–107.

52. Patterson, "Making Identities in Fifteenth-Century England," 70, 71. For Patterson, when *The Siege of Thebes* deconstructs itself, it becomes a challenge to the ruler it addresses.

CHAPTER 5

Chaucer after Retters

The Wartime Origins of English Literature

JOHN M. BOWERS

TWO HISTORIES OF 1360

This account of the wartime origins of English literature takes as its starting point the year 1360. Two events occurred at this time, one of great contemporary notice described in all the major chronicles, the other of minor importance meriting only a tiny entry in a single royal record. The first was King Jean II's release from English custody guaranteed under the Treaty of Brétigny by the delivery of forty noble hostages into English hands. The second was the ransom of an English yeoman named Geoffrey Chaucer after he had been captured by the French near Retters (Réthel). Both events, however, can be seen to have far-reaching consequences for the beginnings of a true national scripture in England.

In 1360 King Jean II of France ended the first of two periods of English custody as a result of his capture at Poitiers four years earlier. Jean Froissart described a congenial captivity: "King John spent the rest of the winter there cheerfully and sociably. He was visited frequently by the King of England and his sons, the Dukes of Clarence and Lancaster and Lord

Edmund. They held several big entertainments and parties together, dinners, suppers and so forth, either at the Savoy or at the Palace of Westminster situated nearby, to which the King of France went privately whenever he liked by boat along the Thames."[1] The Treaty of Brétigny allowed his release on condition that his ransom of three million gold *écus* (£500,000) was guaranteed by the delivery of forty hostages, a group that was headed by his brother Duke Philippe of Orléans and his younger sons, Jean of Berry and Louis of Anjou.[2] When Louis later broke parole, King Jean took it as a point of honor to return to London, where he died in 1364, to be succeeded on the French throne by his son Charles V.[3]

Only after Agincourt was there again such a glittering array of French aristocrats concentrated about the English court. The Hainault native Froissart was ideally situated to report the extraordinary courtesy shown by Edward III and Queen Philippa, since he too migrated to England about 1360, probably as part of the teeming entourage accompanying the great men of France. Froissart tells in the Prologue to his *Chronicles* how he used a poetic account of the wars (now lost) to secure the patronage of Queen Philippa, who was also from Hainault, and he remained in England until about the time of her death in 1369.[4] With his way paved by Jean de le Mote, who had come from Hainault to the English court after Edward III's succession in 1327, Froissart's presence as clerk of the queen's chamber is the most conspicuous instance of what was a larger migration of French musicians, French painters such as Girard d'Orléans, and French poets such as Gace de la Buigne, who was the author of the *Roman des Deduits* commissioned by Jean II while in captivity.[5] These professionals joined with the aristocratic hostages themselves such as the Duke of Berry, who was destined to become the outstanding patron of the arts for the whole period as well as a contributor to Jean Boucicault's *Livre de cent ballades*, and altogether they infused the bilingual English court with an even more powerful and deeply pervasive sense of French cultural prestige.[6] Only after Poitiers, for instance, is the full weight of Guillaume de Machaut's work felt in England.[7]

Froissart's *Chronicles* suggests a great deal about French cultural incursion in its description of Enguerrand de Coucy, who later married Edward III's daughter Isabelle: "The young Lord de Coucy in particular took great pains to dance and sing well when his turn came. He was much applauded by both French and English" for singing songs in his native French.[8] In this sense, while the English had been victorious at Poitiers, they suffered a severe disadvantage in the arena of cultural competition. So total was French cultural dominance, it was a contest in which the English hardly realized that they were capable of competing. Probably not since the reign of Henry III was francophilia, not to mention francophonia, so rampant in and around the English court.[9] When Barbara Tuchman remarks that "England had turned the tables on William the Conqueror" with its military triumphs and territorial gains on the continent, too little regard is taken of the fact that English aristocratic culture was still subject to French dominance.[10] First the empire strikes back, and then, only later, the empire writes back to the center.[11]

In popular and even clerical discourse, however, contempt for the French was pervasive. Edward III's propaganda machinery was remarkably effective at denigrating the legality of the French cause, and the first decades of the conflict saw Ranulf Higden and Richard of Bury give clerical reinforcement to a chauvinistic disdain of Frenchmen as cowardly warriors, a disdain more crudely expressed by Laurence Minot in his English-language poems dated 1333 to 1352.[12] After the English victory at Crécy in 1346, Bradwardine's great ceremonial sermon played upon these national differences, concluding that the French defeat could be attributed to their loose moral standards as a people.[13]

The decade after Poitiers, however, does not bespeak much real cultural difference based upon any sense of ethnic distinctions at the highest levels of aristocratic society in England.[14] Captors and captives alike conversed in French, they sang the same French songs, and they danced the same fashionable dances in which the young Lord of Coucy had shown himself so admirable. While the English pursued their campaigns upon French territories as knights and brigands, the French came to England almost exclusively as high-born prisoners of war.[15] The continuation of military conflict would mean inscribing national differences invisible to Froissart during his service to Queen Philippa, indeed largely invisible to him throughout his long career as poet and chronicler.[16] Because the noblemen and knights who populate the *Chronicles* considered themselves members of a chivalric elite which transcended national boundaries, and book-catalogues indicate that the literary tastes of these insular aristocrats remained predominantly French,[17] it would fall to an English writer below the rank of nobility to assert these cultural differences, while staging other social antagonisms as well, and to make these literary advances in the English language.

The second significant event of 1360 is included inconspicuously in the account of William de Farley, Keeper of the King's Wardrobe: "Galfrido Chaucer capto per inimicos in partibus Francie in subsidium redempcionis sue de consimili dono regis die et anno supradictis xvi li."[18] That is, on

March 1, 1360, Edward III contributed £16 to the ransom of Geoffrey Chaucer, who had been captured by the enemy in French territories. Years later in 1386, Chaucer testified at the Scrope-Grosvenor trial that he had seen the Scropes armed before the town of Retters (Réthel) about twenty miles northeast of Rheims,[19] and therefore it has been concluded that the young Chaucer served under Prince Lionel in the division led by the Black Prince that took this route on the way to Rheims, which was then besieged from early December 1359 until January 1360. Speculation runs that Chaucer was taken prisoner during the siege of Rheims or during the unsteady advance of English forces into Burgundy that concluded with a truce in March 1360. The expeditionary force was the largest ever sent by the English, but the campaign itself was entirely lacking in battlefield glories. The Chandos Herald gave the whole episode the scantest notice in *The Life of the Black Prince*: "Both the king and the prince encamped there, ready for battle, but no battle took place."[20] Under what circumstances, then, did Chaucer fall into French hands if the English army fought no battle?

Though the English did not know it, they were encountering Charles V's new strategy of "guerrilla warfare" that called for avoiding all-out battles of the sort which the English tended to win. Instead, the English were forced to engage in expensive, time-consuming sieges upon fortified towns such as Rheims, while the French used their army at a distance to pick off stragglers and foragers.[21] Sir Thomas Gray, who accompanied the Black Prince's division, described how unarmed English esquires were taken prisoner while foraging for corn to feed the horses.[22] As one small casualty of this strategy, Chaucer's capture would have been as inglorious as the *chevauchée* itself. Thereafter the entire campaign was brought to a close by the peace of Brétigny, and Edward III and his sons embarked for England in the middle of May.[23] In all probability Chaucer went with them, at about the same time that Froissart and the forty French hostages were also gathering in Calais en route to England.[24]

The possibility that Chaucer was captured near Rheims has prompted speculation that the young would-be writer had the opportunity of meeting the great French poet Guillaume de Machaut, who was a canon of the cathedral and endured the siege inside the city walls. Donald Howard painted a very rosy picture of Chaucer's captivity as "a pleasant respite, a time to converse and read, hear songs and stories."[25] Fascinating as such musings may be, it is perhaps better to consider what is known for sure: the teenage English yeoman was captured by French soldiers on enemy territory. While Froissart was certainly correct in reporting that kings and princes were entertained with lavish courtesy, prisoners who ranked further down the social scale could not count on such congenial hospitality.[26]

Chaucer was in French hands for many weeks, maybe even months, before and after the ransom was agreed upon. Even though he was a *valettus*, or yeoman, to a royal prince, he had reason to fear the brutality of his captors, as well as the vengefulness of the civilian populace whose lands were being viciously devastated by his fellow Englishmen. Fourteenth-century warfare was largely a matter of inflicting *damnum* or destruction upon the general population.[27] Chaucer's Tale of Melibee would later recall the sufferings visited by war upon the common people: "ther is ful many a man that crieth 'Werre, werre!' that woot ful litel what werre amounteth.... For soothly, when that werre is ones bigonne, there is ful many a child unborn of his mooder that shal sterve yong by cause of thilke werre, or elles lyve in sorwe and dye in wrecchednesse."[28] In retaliation, peasants sometimes massacred English troops as well as the knightly prisoners of French noblemen. Jean de Venette, one of the prime witnesses to the 1359–1360 campaign, reported how a peasant force at Longeuil cut down a band of English knights without giving thought to possible ransom.[29] Indeed, some contemporary writers urged that the war's end would be hastened if captives were killed rather than ransomed.[30]

Besides these threats of violence, Chaucer shared in the widespread privations of the French region, especially if he were held inside the besieged city of Rheims where food rations ran dangerously low.[31] And the weather was appalling, with steady autumn rains turning to snow as the temperatures plummeted. The psychic trauma of the experience has sometimes been discerned in Chaucer's later reluctance to glorify warfare and give military encounters much heroic notice.[32] The description of Criseyde's fears when she is taken captive by the Greeks,[33] a passage without parallel in Boccaccio's *Filostrato*, may owe some of its intensity to Chaucer's remembrance of the fears he himself felt as a prisoner of the French.

There is every reason to suspect that Chaucer came away from this period of captivity with a deep dislike of the French. This point has never been properly considered. Even if he were not brutalized and physically mistreated, his pride surely had been wounded by his captive status. Since the young Chaucer in all likelihood sounded as provincial as the Prioress for whom "Frenssh of Parys" was unknown,[34] his captors had cause to mock his outlandish pronunciation of their language. They may even have insulted his very humanity. A ballade by Eustache Deschamps describing his encounter with English troops in Calais used as its refrain the phrase "Oil, je voy vo queue" [Yes, I see your tail]. This taunt played upon the long-standing French slander that Englishmen had tails in the manner of animals or demons, not men.[35] Chaucer's French captors could have ridiculed his mother-tongue as well, mocking him with English words pronounced like bestial grunts, such as those recorded by Deschamps.[36] The poet Jean Régnier left a moving account of an unlucky English prisoner who spoke no French at all, surrounded by Frenchmen who did not understand his cries for help in English.[37] These accounts suggest the range of humiliations that the young Chaucer endured during his captivity in 1360.

We know nothing about Chaucer's activities during the period immediately after his return to England. Though the years 1360–1366 offer a biographical blank that has invited a number of hypotheses,[38] we do know something about the England to which he returned. Noble French hostages were being accorded great courtesy, and French ballades and *dits* set the new standard for poetic accomplishment. Since Chaucer's surviving English lyrics appear to be late and are characterized by deeply philosophical turns, it has been suggested that the decade of the 1360s was the period when the young poet composed—in French—the "many a song and many a leccherous lay" which he recalls much later in his "Retraction." If he did compose verses like the fifteen "Ch" poems of the Pennsylvania manuscript,[39] his efforts put him in direct competition with this collection's identifiable poets—Machaut, Deschamps, Granson—whose native language was the enemy's language, as his wartime experiences had made painfully clear. Because all courtly performances were by nature competitions for attention, the youthful Chaucer would have savored the chance to best these performers in their own language, trying to beat them on their own turf as it were. And what he lacked in supreme quality, he compensated for in sheer volume. John Gower later recalled that the youthful Chaucer filled the whole country with his verses.[40] But for Chaucer to have continued writing in French would have meant reproducing the practices of the dominant culture in the very act of assaulting it. The disappearance of his early French lyrics may represent more than the vicissitudes of poetic survival in an essentially oral culture. Possibly Chaucer himself destroyed these early poems, or treated them with such neglect that they fell into oblivion, with only a few fortunate survivors ending up as anonymous filler in an omnibus collection such as the Pennsylvania manuscript.

This was also the period when an extraordinary psychological and artistic alchemy was taking place.[41] The young Chaucer was undergoing the inward metamorphosis that would transform him from a clever versifier of fashionable ditties into a poet who produced—in English—a minor masterpiece at his first assay with the *Book of the Duchess*. Chaucer's refusal to acknowledge Machaut as his principal source for this work, however, as well as his failure to mention this French poet anywhere amid the showy name-dropping of his later works, signals his resistance to the hermeneutic activity which granted authority to the object of translation. Never sardonic with anti-French passion, Chaucer had learned the lesson (perhaps from reading Langland's *Piers Plowman*) that frothy moral outrage was as unstylish as it was unproductive.[42] His dream-vision poems become flamboyant travesties of the "real things" composed by Machaut and Froissart, so that parody becomes the very condition of his artistic productions, as with other postcolonial writers with whom Chaucer might be valuably compared.[43]

Fourteenth-century England represents an early example of *absentee colonialism*, when a country is still dependent upon the culture of its previous rulers long after political independence has been fully realized. England was in most respects further advanced in becoming a unitary state than was France, and the early stages of the war accelerated this process. As Robin Neillands observes, "Edward III had turned his kingdom from a small, divided, offshore island into one of the greatest military powers in the western world."[44] Yet the precocious nation-state England trailed behind the "mosaic state" France in the creation of a true national culture.[45] The antagonisms of the Hundred Years' War caused a polarization that would render England's cultural dependence upon France less and less acceptable. It was not patriotic.[46] War virtually necessitated the idea of national difference and the alienation of the enemy.[47] Whether national self-consciousness was a result of the war or its cause has been hotly debated, but certainly the two developed in tandem.

Because literature belongs to the realm of civil culture, it lags behind the initiatives of military society represented by the chivalric orders who actually made war, as well as by the preachers who defended the national cause.[48] Just as Roman imperialist expansion preceded the creation of a national scripture under Augustan patronage, particularly Virgil's *Aeneid* with its argument for Rome's manifest destiny,[49] English expansionist ambitions in France were rewarded with military successes at Sluys, Crécy, and Poitiers before the emergence of a true national poetry in the

English language. War created a non-English antagonist, and only later did literature contribute to the formation of the Englishness of the protagonist.[50] Yet this assertion of Englishness did not come early or automatically to Chaucer.

What Chaucer seemed finally unable to effect was a complete alienation from the French. Common customs, a common aristocratic language, close alliances with French-speaking territories such as Hainault, and personal relationships with individuals among the French chivalric class seem to have made complete divorce impossible for a poet who was anxious to succeed on the fringes of England's royal court.[51] His writings remained always on the horizon of expectations of audiences steeped in French literary practices. To this day, "Chaucer and the French Tradition" remains one of the most durable approaches to his work, whether critics such as George Kane consider it a point of departure or others such as Charles Muscatine, James Wimsatt, and Lee Patterson insist upon the constant centrality of its formal and rhetorical means.[52] The postcolonial reading of Chaucer sees his struggles with the French tradition as something much more than an attempt to free himself from sterile literary conventions in a push toward greater psychological and colloquial realism.[53] It figures in a larger struggle toward the liberation of language, temperament, social character, and finally authorial subjectivity itself from what Terry Eagleton aptly describes on behalf of the colonial subject as "alien ways of experiencing."[54]

The following three sections of this paper describe how the well-known phases of Chaucer's career can be matched with the contours of England's shifting military and diplomatic relations with France during the last three decades of the fourteenth century. Chaucer's early works as a translator and adaptor of French sources become legible as acts of textual aggression designed to seize and bring home the spoils of a conquered culture. After Richard II's marriage to Anne of Bohemia in 1382, when England had sought allies elsewhere in Europe to encircle and contain the French, Chaucer himself turned to Italian sources as a maneuver for avoiding direct engagement with the francophone tradition. In the 1390s, however, when Richard II began pursuing a policy of rapprochement with France and wedded the French Princess Isabelle, Chaucer's creative activities responded by splitting into two unequal, incommensurable efforts. The *Legend of Good Women* was produced as a travesty parodying the poetry of French court culture to which official English culture had suddenly and unexpectedly reverted, whereas the *Canterbury Tales* fulfilled Chaucer's ongoing project of creating an entire library of English works in poetry and prose.

"GRANT TRANSLATEUR, NOBLE GEFFROY CHAUCIER"

Aside from the lost French lyrics which may have been his first compositions, Chaucer's earliest English works were the translations of the beginning of the *Roman de la Rose* and the "ABC to the Virgin" from Guillaume Deguileville's *Pelerinage de la vie humaine*. These exercises perpetuated rather than resisted French literary dominance. Caroline Eckhardt finds much to praise in Chaucer's vividness and colloquial elegance as well as his very high degree of fidelity in reproducing his source: "The *Roman* has thus been translated into an English near-equivalent that still carries with it the prestige, sophistication, and courtliness associated with its original."[55] Yet the very terms used to describe his English rendering, slavish and faithful, expose the subservience of the translator's efforts as well as the moral assessment: "good" if faithful, "bad" if free.

In many ways Chaucer's practice corresponds with the fourfold hermeneutic motion of translation described by George Steiner as the act of elicitation and transfer of meaning: trust in the value of the source text, extraction of semantic substance, incorporation into the target culture, and restoration of cultural balance.[56] Chaucer's early devotion to the artistic values of the *Roman de la Rose* had been so complete that his translation became subordinate, "subaltern" in the fullest sense, foreclosing the possibility of redressing any cultural imbalance. His only escape seems to have been dropping the assignment, or passing it off to the anonymous translators of Fragments B and C, while he moved forward with little regard for the survival of his part of the translation. While it still had sufficient currency to become the target of criticism in the Prologue to the *Legend of Good Women*, the God of Love's narrow focus upon the *Rose*'s harsh treatment of women excludes a much greater range of dissatisfaction that had been registered by the poet himself. Willful neglect may also account for the disappearance of "The Book of the Leoun" listed in his "Retraction" if this lost work was, as usually thought, a translation of Machaut's *Dit dou Lyon* or Deschamps's *Dit du Lyon*. It was one thing to translate an international classic such as the *Roman de la Rose*, something quite different to show too much homage to a living French "master."

We are so accustomed to the literary status which Chaucer has held for nearly six centuries that we are not likely to be impressed that his efforts as a translator gained the notice of his French contemporaries. This French response should not be so surprising, however, according to Fredric Jameson in his assessment of the postcolonial writer: "When the other speaks, he or she becomes another subject, which must be consciously registered as a problem by the imperial or metropolitan subject."[57] Eustache Deschamps's ballade of commendation to the English poet probably in the late 1380s has drawn consistent attention, and yet its famous refrain-line, "Grant translateur, noble Geffroy Chaucier," seems altogether extravagant, as does its odd comparisons of the English writer to Socrates, Seneca and Ovid. All of these gestures seem to form an exercise in hyperbole quite routine for this French poet. But what has been less fully appreciated is its subtle effort at demeaning Chaucer's enterprise as the mere importation of the French *Rose* for an English garden. Extravagant praise belies condescension in assuming that England would be poetically barren without such imports, just as there is a mild insult in offering to send his poems without asking Chaucer to return the favor by sending more samples of his own writings.[58] Elsewhere Deschamps's attitude was one of unmitigated ethnic hostility, as displayed in the ballade mocking English speech and ridiculing Englishmen for their tails.[59] It is a telling fact, therefore, that only the Prologue to the *Legend of Good Women* shows the faintest signs of indebtedness to Deschamps. This suggests that the English poet sensitively registered the condescension implicit in the French poet's lofty but contrived praise.

Chaucer's allusion to the *Roman de la Rose* in the *Book of the Duchess* signals his emergence from the subaltern position. His early translation was a necessary point of departure. Otherwise the *Rose* would have remained a formidable obstacle because, in addition to its classic status as a vernacular masterwork, it was also a powerful document in the creation of the French aristocratic subject: courtly, male, libidinous, aggressive, learned, articulate, acquisitive, and ultimately victorious. The *Rose* occults the tactics of feudal warfare in its account of a man journeying to an unfamiliar land, penetrating the walled defenses of the enclosure, neutralizing civilian resistance within, and seizing the most valuable treasure to satisfy his masculine desire. The *Book of the Duchess* reduces this potent text to "cultural wallpaper," as it were, forever present in the dreamer's bedroom, which was also his reading room, as wraparound stimulus to color the imagination and to suggest images for further thought: "And alle the walles with colours fyne / Were peynted, bothe text and glose, / Of al the Romaunce of the Rose" (*BD* 332–34). The poet awakes to these bright figures, but he is provoked to leave them behind as the enticements of aesthetic passivity. The bedroom is where a docile imitator would sleep away his career in admiration of the *Rose*'s lush beauties. Chaucer prefers to explore an unknown terrain of native possibilities, homely sights, and English voices. It is a moment of leave-taking that anticipates his descent into the realm of Rumor in *The House of Fame*. At the end of his career, Chaucer's most brilliant creations become his most successful assaults upon the aristocratic subject of the *Rose*: the female desires of the Wife of Bath, the stifled sexuality of the Prioress, and the parodic courtliness and nonheterosexual obsessions of the Pardoner. The one pilgrim who most closely resembles Amans is the Squire, whose performance is allowed to collapse in a shambles of wayward intentions and potentially incestuous desires, overwhelmed by the profusion of discursive models appropriated flamboyantly, and fatally, from the French courtly tradition.

When the political culture was altered by the reopening of all-out war in 1369, the poetic scene in England also changed. The death of Queen Philippa deprived Froissart of his patroness; and the death of Duchess Blanche of Lancaster, probably a year earlier, provided Chaucer with the occasion for his first original work.[60] The English poet who emerged was no longer a student intimidated by his French masters. As if to recuperate his failures as a young warrior taken prisoner, he started "plundering" French possessions and "taking hostages" from among the nobility of French poets, Guillaume de Lorris, Guillaume de Machaut, and Jean Froissart. "After trust comes aggression. The second move of the translator is incursive and extractive," says George Steiner; "the translator invades, extracts, and brings home."[61] For Chaucer, no less than ancient Roman writers such as Cicero, the translation of foreign texts meant looting foreign cultures for the enrichment of his own. Linguistic imperialism deprecated the alien text but annexed its materials in order to impose dominance through the translator's own language. St. Jerome declared his intentions with all the pride of a Roman general: "The translator considers thought-content a prisoner [quasi captivos sensus] which he translates into his own language with the prerogative of a conqueror [iure victoris]."[62] Nietzsche characterized all premodern practice in exactly these terms: "Indeed, translation was a form of conquest."[63]

Machaut wrote the *Dit de la Fonteinne Amoureuse* for the Duke of Berry on the occasion of his departure for England as a hostage in 1360, and it was from this work as well as *Le Jugement dou Roy de Behaingne* and *Remede de Fortune* that Chaucer extracted so many of the ingredients for his *Book of the Duchess*.[64] Another source was Froissart's *Paradys d'Amour*, a work actually composed in England during the 1360s and the only work by Froissart demonstrably known by Chaucer.[65] Yet the English dream-vision does much more than simply borrow from its French sources. It selects and excludes, it lays claim to images and themes, it usurps rhetorical intentions, and it trumps the seriousness of purpose by substituting an English duchess struck down in her prime for a French bride merely left behind, Berry's recently wedded wife, Jeanne of Armagnac. Its aggressiveness is most clearly exposed in the way the Duke of Lancaster supplants the Duke of Berry. Just as the French sounding "Blanche" becomes the plain English "faire White," the poem's determined Englishness is reflected in the fact that native vocabulary displaces many of the Romance alternatives offered by the sources.[66] Hybridity has functioned as camouflage for a whole other agenda. Not merely aiming at parity and restored balance, Chaucer's interpretive adaptation pushes toward a superior status for his writings. Lacking the showy virtuosity of a musical composition,[67] the *Book of the Duchess* suggests something more meditative, more intimate, more variable in tone, more challenging to interpretation, in short more readerly. Chaucer is already producing *literature*.[68]

Chaucer took direct aim at the dominant culture by adapting French poetic diction, the French *dit*, the French courtly manners of his characters, and then treating all of these appropriations as if they had been English all along. His translation project was more disruptive because it moved visibly on the horizon of expectations for those already familiar with the French traditions.[69] Like Edward III claiming the French throne while refusing to recognize the possibility of competing Valois claims, Chaucer's denial of prior sovereignty shows itself in his unwillingness to acknowledge his French sources.[70] The *Book of the Duchess* (332–34) treats the *Roman de la Rose* as if it were an anonymous cultural artifact without an author and hence, by definition, without authority.[71] Though later in his career he adapted Oton de Granson's *Cinq Balades Ensievans* in his own *Complaint of Venus*, his production is less a tribute than an act of sophisticated vandalism. Chaucer neglected two of the five original balades, he altered the gender of the speaker, and he added an envoi whose demanding rhyme-scheme was so expertly accomplished that it undercut the tongue-in-cheek apology "rym in Englissh hath such skarsete" (80).[72] The commendation in the last line of the *Complaint*, where Granson is praised as "flour of hem that make in Fraunce," in effect reinforced the national border which Chaucer had done so much to draw between himself and his French contemporaries.

CHAUCER'S ITALIAN STRATEGY

Chaucer's textual contest with his French contemporaries underwent radical redefinition as the politics of Anglo-French warfare became a messier business.⁷³ Rather than demobilizing after the Treaty of Brétigny, many English troops remained abroad to become *routiers* or mercenaries in the hire of non-English lords such as Charles of Navarre. As one means of dealing with surplus military manpower, John of Gaunt's campaign in Spain meant that the war was no longer a clear, two-sided conflict between England and France. Alliances became murky, and the loyalties of allies such as Jean of Armagnac were liable to shift. Other territories were involved as the English made diplomatic efforts to encircle the French. Chaucer himself played a direct role in these international maneuvers, beginning with his 1373 mission to Genoa and Florence, a mission that brought him as a writer in direct contact with the Italian culture of Petrarch and especially Boccaccio.⁷⁴

When hostilities began anew in 1369, the Tower of London was nearly empty of French aristocrats and all of the cultural baggage which they had brought with them. It would remain so for the next twenty years. A series of continental *chevauchée* led by Sir Robert Knolles (1370), John of Gaunt (1373–1374), and Thomas of Buckingham (1380–1381) took terrible tolls without gaining any real military advantage or realizing any financial gain. During Edward III's dotage and Richard II's minority, England's grand ambitions became bogged down and, some would say, waned into chivalric disenchantment and malaise.⁷⁵ Nearly every Parliament during this period sparked a political crisis because the Commons stubbornly refused to grant taxation to subsidize foreign adventures. The year 1381 saw the return of the last English army sent to France during the fourteenth century. Meanwhile Michael de la Pole's policy of appeasement fueled French ambitions to bring the war to English soil. Two invasions were planned, one in 1385 and the other in 1386. Although neither was executed, the threats emboldened the Appellants, especially Gloucester and Arundel, to take over the young king's foreign policy in an effort to launch new offensives.

This thumbnail sketch of the Hundred Years' War 1360–1387 suggests that the antagonisms felt earlier toward an external adversary, along with diplomatic efforts at encirclement, were replaced by concerns for England's internal stability and defense against invasion. Usually dated about 1378, *The House of Fame* reflects this unaccustomed sense of isolation and peril, first in its image of the Temple of Venus amid a vast expanse of wasteland, then in the terrifying abduction of the narrator by the eagle. Fame's "house" itself is figured as a castle perched upon a lofty rock, that is, as a bastion situated in an ideal position for defense against attackers.

This mountain-top citadel higher than any in Spain (1117)—another territory where Chaucer traveled on diplomatic mission,[76] incorporates in itself another architectural structure with unflinching political implications: it is a museum. Perhaps inspired in part by the Palais de Justice that Chaucer had seen in Paris in 1377, Fame's palace replaces the statues of the forty-seven French kings with the representations of classical writers.[77] Literary authorities displace royal authorities in an awesome display of the poetic past. "The museum and the museumizing imagination are both profoundly political," as Benedict Anderson points out, because only the powerful can assert the privilege to abstract and put upon display the relics of other cultures.[78]

Since a museum project deploys a canon of privileged authors and titles in a manner inseparable from the cultural definition of a nation,[79] the enshrinement of the great European tradition in the *House of Fame* has political implications in no small part because the French contribution has been silently but vigorously excluded. It is a work whose audience has been rigorously determined in linguistic terms: "Now herkeneth every maner man / That Englissh understonde can" (509–10). In the process of creating new works that might enter the line-up of epic masters listed at the end of *Troilus*—"Virgile, Ovide, Omer, Lucan, and Stace" (5.1792)—Chaucer went about the business of reading the cultural canon as an outsider. The results are so endearingly eccentric because they are truly ec-centric, off center, marginal to the continental mainstream that inspired their creation. He "made strange" the authorities that he rewrote: Virgil in Book I of the *House of Fame*, Homer in *Troilus*, Lucan in Book III of the *House of Fame*, and Statius in the Knight's Tale. His entire poetic career is bracketed by two zany retellings of Ovid: the nonmetamorphosis of Seys and Alcyone in the *Book of the Duchess*, and the manic digressiveness of the legend of Apollo and the crow in the Manciple's Tale at the end of the *Canterbury Tales*.

As the place of art and memory, Fame's museum deploys its array of frozen literary figures to construct a tradition so ordered and so scrupulously arranged as a pattern of succession that an author such as Chaucer, as an heir to this tradition, would have been compelled to enter a genealogical series that brought with it a whole host of weighty obligations. These cultural instrumentalities demanded obedience by making various threats, not least of all the threat of literary immortality, which the poem's dreamer explicitly rejects: "Sufficeth me, as I were ded, / That no wight have my name in honde" (1876–77). These genealogies of literary predecessors would otherwise have proved too intimidating as an arsenal of cultural discipline, one which could not be naturalized with any lasting assurance. As an escape from a burden of tradition that was as much continental as it was historical, the dreamer's comic descent into the House of Rumor announces the shift from high culture to low, from poetry as an epistemological object to poetry as a performative site, where the pleasure of "tidyings" evades the disciplinary hermeneutics of an official tradition imposed from outside. It is an evasion that is fully realized in the wayward, disruptive and competing voices of his Canterbury pilgrims. This relocation deprives the official culture of its exclusive material content and, perhaps more importantly, the privileged terms for constructing a singular human subject that excludes all other possibilities.

England's anxiety concerning its own national security is articulated as the theme of "commune profyt" announced by Chaucer at the beginning of *The Parliament of Fowls* (46–49).[80] In 1381 the English Rising had launched a violent assault upon the gentry classes and their administrative clergy, and in 1382 the Blackfriars Council contributed to the sense of alarmism by targeting Wycliffism (whose agents were also blamed as instigators of the revolt) as a serious threat to the sacerdotal orders and to Christian orthodoxy generally.[81] These internal insecurities, together with the difficulties of Richard II's rule, became the dominant themes of the religious chroniclers to the near exclusion of the war.[82] Chaucer's promotion of English over French, already under way in the 1370s, needed to be reinscribed within this scheme of domestic disruption and attempts at consolidation.[83]

Usually dated to the early 1380s, *The Parliament of Fowls* moves toward an allegorical account of the negotiations for a royal wedding that were concurrent with the last fourteenth-century campaign upon French soil.[84] Its invocation of the theme of "commune profyt" alludes to the justification of war according to Roman Law, as well as the royal rationale for huge expenditures for the national defense extracted by taxation.[85] Impatient over the endlessness of these financial requests, the Good Parliament of 1376 brushed aside the formulaic appeal for the defense of the realm—*pugna pro patria*—and began to question whether the enrichment of individuals was not taking precedent over national priorities.[86] International maneuvering, occulted in the courtship of the three male eagles, ends in nothing better than stalemate. On the other hand, the homely marriage alliances of the diverse native populace, represented by the various birds blowing hot and cold in vivid vernacular, refocuses attention on the "commune profyt" of an all-encompassing society.[87] "By drawing a bold relation between cultural and social conflict," Paul Strohm observes, "and by enriching his chosen form of avian debate or 'judgment' with the specifically social idea of the deliberative forum of parliament, Chaucer shifts from the amatory to the civic arena."[88] The question of war, however, never arises amid the petty squabbling. And for good reason.

War meant revenue gathering, the central and sorest subject of parliamentary debates during the 1370s and 1380s, and since increased revenue meant more royal spending generally, those functionaries who oversaw the gathering and dispensing of money could not fail to profit.[89] Such controversies touched Chaucer personally, since he was a royal servant acting as the controller of the wool custom and wool subsidy in the port of London, 1374–1386.[90] Though little noted by Chaucerians, the wool subsidy was the most profitable source of extraordinary revenue to the crown during the period, representing over half of all proceeds, and this income was intended to go directly and exclusively to the war effort.[91] *The Parliament of Fowls* takes keen notice of the conflicting interests of the crown, which were international and chivalric, and of the Commons, which were largely local and profit-driven.[92] Because three out of four Parliaments following the 1381 uprising refused to grant direct taxation, no royal army could be financed, and English military ambitions were stymied. But Chaucer sidesteps the real controversy over taxation and expenditure by translating these divergent desires into the allegory of aviary mate selection. The allegory discloses only in the most general terms the narrow self-interests which complicated the transformation of a true social cohesiveness beyond the mercenary aims of the chivalric classes.[93]

It has long been recognized that the Trojan background of *Troilus and Criseyde* had special relevance to Chaucer's audience because London had been aggrandized as the "Troynovaunt," or New Troy.[94] Benedict Anderson has observed that claims of cultural parity encoded in such toponyms—New England, New York, New Orleans—accomplish more than a diachronic gesture of inheritance. They occur "only when substantial groups of people were in a position to think of themselves as living lives *parallel* to those of other substantial groups of people—if never meeting, yet certainly proceeding along the same trajectory."[95] For Londoners to identify with Troy meant acknowledging, implicitly at least, a parallel destiny that ended in defeat and destruction. Whereas England's mythic founder was the Trojan Brutus, an ingredient in the nationalist mythology to which Chaucer alludes in his "Complaint" to Henry IV in 1399, France's foundation was credited to Antenor,[96] the arch-traitor whose exchange for Criseyde, by the fatal decision of the Parliament, spelled the double doom of Troilus and Troy itself.

Usually absent from critical discussions of *Troilus*, however, is consideration of its wartime context. The poem was composed during a period when the English had become aware of French plans for a full-scale invasion that would have brought the fighting onto English soil for the first time.[97] French naval raids had caused much damage to ports along the southern coast during 1377–1380, and in 1382 the Commons was anxious that the Scots, who were allies of the French, were preparing for an attack "that would be the strongest and most evil war that could befall us."[98] Michael de la Pole, the chancellor who had been the main architect of the peace policy toward France since 1383, fell victim to the rapid strengthening of the war party led by the earls of Buckingham and Arundel.

The escalation of national fears reached a climax in 1385–1386 when it was discovered that Charles VI, supported for the first time by the two great fiefs of Flanders and Brittany, planned a campaign which had as its goal nothing less than the destruction of the English kingdom. At a time when Gaunt's forces were committed in Spain, the French king in person, accompanied by his uncles and the ranking nobility, led what was the largest army raised by either side during the Hundred Years' War. One writer compared the armada with its 30,000 troops to the Greek fleet that attacked Troy[99]—a comparison that would not have been lost upon the author of *Troilus*.

When word reached London that the French were staging a massive build-up of men and materials at Sluys in Flanders, there was something like mass hysteria.[100] Walsingham reported how Londoners were thrown into such a panic that they desperately prepared for a siege by pulling down the houses nearest the city walls. This is exactly where Chaucer was living at the time in Aldgate.[101] Although the French invasion was never finally launched, London did suffer a siege of sorts. The government had responded to the emergency by raising an army of 11,000 men, who were mostly stationed around London. No doubt as a reaction to the violence of 1381, orders were given that the troops should not approach within fifty miles of the city's walls. When no French forces arrived and the defending troops were not paid, however, the soldiers turned predatory and behaved, according to Walsingham, exactly like an enemy in their own land.[102] For those inside the city of London, then, the fears of being surrounded by a hostile army had in fact been realized in 1386, exactly when Chaucer is thought to have been completing *Troilus*.[103]

RICHARD II's RAPPROCHEMENT WITH FRANCE

The years 1387–1388 marked an important juncture in Anglo-French relations. After seizing power from the young king, the Appellants had attempted to reopen hostilities without securing adequate tax revenues from the Commons to finance any effective military project. The fiasco of Gloucester's Breton campaign of 1388 was the last straw. The Cambridge Parliament later that same year earmarked its subsidy for defense against the Scots, but refused to approve any money for continental campaigns. Richard II's policy finally won out.[104] The years 1389–1394 were distinguished by continuous negotiations and uninterrupted peace. Amid increasingly cordial relations between the two kingdoms, a final settlement was achieved as a result of intense dealings throughout 1395–1396, with a twenty-eight-year truce cemented by an agreement for Richard to marry Princess Isabelle, the six-year-old daughter of Charles VI.[105]

To suppress the francophobia that had been officially sanctioned for decades, Richard II encouraged a high degree of fraternization between the two sides, beginning with the great peace tournament held at Smithfield in 1390, for which Chaucer constructed the scaffolds and lists as part of his duties as Clerk of the King's Works.[106] Frenchmen such as Jean Froissart and Jean Creton received warm welcomes in the royal household. By far the most notable sign of mutual cooperation was the fervor for a crusade stirred by Philippe de Mézières, who had been a tutor to the young Charles VI. His famous *Epistre au Roi Richart* (1395) pleaded for a peace between the two realms as prelude to a joint military venture to liberate the Holy Land,[107] and his Order of the Passion attracted over eighty new members between 1390 and 1395, including the dukes of Berry, Bourbon, and Orléans from France, and the dukes of Lancaster, Gloucester, and York from England. The disastrous defeat of Christian forces at Nicopolis in autumn 1396 would shatter this international unity by depriving the old enemies of their common cause. It would also deal a serious and ultimately fatal blow to the domestic prestige of Richard II, who had successfully used the idealism of the crusade to stifle criticism of his detente with France.[108]

This pro-French attitude in England's royal culture during the last decade of Richard II's reign clearly left Chaucer in the lurch. He had fashioned his entire career as a creative assault upon the French poetic tradition in concert with the nation's military hostilities toward the French. The king's official about-face induced a kind of "literary schizophrenia" that characterized the final phase of Chaucer's career, a "split poetic personality" most clearly symptomatized by what I believe to have been the simultaneous productions of *The Legend of Good Women* and *The Canterbury Tales*.

The *Legend* is almost universally reckoned to be an anomaly in Chaucer's career and an embarrassment for Chaucerian criticism. The courtly dream-vision does not fit into the discursive formation of a career that moved inexorably away from the artificiality of French practices and toward the solid home-grown realism of the *Canterbury Tales*. Scholars have therefore worked hard at dating the *Legend* well prior to the *Tales*, squeezing it between the completion of *Troilus* around 1386 and the start of the pilgrimage frame-narrative around 1388. It is commonly dismissed as an initial exercise in the use of iambic pentameter and a tinkering with the framed collection of shorter narratives, a valedictory to all that went before, a transitional experiment which was itself soon abandoned. Its incomplete status has been taken as an admission of frustration and failure, and Robert Burlin speaks for many readers when he characterizes the entire undertaking as "a colossal blunder."[109]

This view is complicated by the fact that the Prologue was revised at some later date, in all likelihood after Queen Anne's death in 1394, since it lacks lines commanding that the work be delivered to the queen at one of the royal residences: "And whan this book ys maad, yive it the queene / On my byhalf at Eltham or at Sheene" (*LGW* F, 496–97). Widely considered as an aberration on top of an aberration, this revised version (G) can be taken as proof positive that Chaucer conceived the work under royal duress, proceeded with a fitful obstinacy, reworked the Prologue when his arm was twisted by his royal patron, but finally left the collection incomplete when he felt no further social pressure to continue with his poetic penance. So vexing is the idea that Chaucer could have devoted his attentions to the *Legend* when he was supposed to be concentrating his mature genius on the *Tales* that one recent critic has taken pains to argue that the G Prologue is the earlier of the two, written as a tribute to the poet's wife Philippa after her death in 1386, and that the F Prologue was later revised from a defective copy as a "command performance" for Queen Anne with the addition of the references to Eltham and Sheen.[110]

These argumentative contortions are motivated by the implicit desire to create a neatly partitioned chronology which would safeguard the last dozen years of Chaucer's life as the exclusive preserve of the *Canterbury Tales* enterprise. To the contrary, Paul Strohm's study "Queens as Intercessors" clearly connects Alceste's efforts on behalf of the dreamer with Queen Anne's theatrical intercession on behalf of London during the royal entry of 1392,[111] a date which might therefore be posited for the original F version of the Prologue to the *Legend*. What is more, John Fisher has forcefully restated the case that Chaucer revised the G Prologue after Queen Anne's death in 1394 and that this revision occurred during 1395–1397 at the height of the poet's creative energies, not as a dubious effort at aesthetic improvement but quite cunningly as a social gesture in conjunction with Richard II's marriage to Isabelle of France.[112]

Clearly Chaucer was dividing his time, and I would propose that he created an even more radical division in the latter phase of his career as a writer. Robert Payne includes this challenge in his assessment of the G Prologue to the *Legend*: "why didn't Chaucer revise into it some indication, or even a mention, of the *Canterbury Tales*?"[113] The answer may be that the two works do not inhabit the same social space. What I have termed his "literary schizophrenia" meant a splitting of his career into the public and the private, the official and the closeted, the one designed for immediate courtly consumption, the other intended for a trusted coterie of fellow civil servants—and a posthumous readership. If the author's audience is always a fiction, Chaucer imagined two prestige audiences for these two very different kinds of textual production: the king for the *Legend* and posterity for the *Canterbury Tales*.

In this context of a pro-French royal culture, Chaucer undertook the writing and rewriting of the Prologue to the *Legend*. His uses of the framework of Machaut's *Jugement dou Roy de Navarre*, which had been written almost half a century earlier in 1349, returns to a negotiation with the highly conventional practices of French poetry that he had worked hard to transcend during the 1380s through his appropriation of Boccaccio's innovative narratives. The dreamer's histrionic worship of the daisy draws upon more recent French poems, such as Froissart's *Dit de la Marguerite* and Deschamps's *Lay de Franchise*, and initiates an elaborate and all-pervasive parody of Ricardian admiration of French cultural objects generally.[114] When the narrator kneels before the daisy, the scene becomes a cunning lampoon of the genuflecting before French courtly icons which had been made official at England's royal court. The surprise assault upon the dreamer by the God of Love fairly represents the temperamental rages for which Richard II was notorious, dramatizing, too, the sense of insecurity that must have been felt by those attending this volatile monarch.[115] Instead of receiving rewards for his work as a poet, Chaucer suddenly finds himself charged with a crime, and the entire dream turns into a Kafkaesque nightmare of trial, judgment, and threat of punishment.

By terming this crime a "heresy" against the God of Love, the poem makes recourse to a vocabulary fraught with heightened anxiety by suspicions of Wycliffite heresies in court circles, most notably among the group of "Lollard knights" that numbered several of Chaucer's most important connections. The prosecutorial momentum of the age would later overtake his friend Sir Lewis Clifford, who was forced in 1402, under circumstances not unlike those described in the Prologue to the *Legend*, to recant his theological errors and offer public penance.[116] Only the intercession of Queen Alceste rescues the dreamer by counseling an alternative penalty as an act of penance: the writing of a collection of "legends" honoring women martyred for the sake of love.

While Chaucerians have preferred to imagine that some of these individual narratives date from the early 1380s, prior to the composition of the Prologue itself, there is no external evidence to indicate that they are not late, perhaps very late, delivered separately as little command performances by Chaucer on the installment plan, so to speak, throughout the 1390s. Richard II's appreciation of classical tales may have been considerable, since he had been part of the audience for the Trojan story of *Troilus*, as the Prologue to the *Legend* testifies, and, in a move puzzling to historians, the king arranged in the mid-1390s to have himself eulogized with the phrase "prudent as Homer" on his tomb commissioned for Westminster Abbey.[117] Though the Man of Law refers to a "large volume" available for reading, his extensive catalogue of the "Seintes Legende of Cupide" (*CT* II, 60–76) contains some remarkable anomalies. Although some of the characters that he names do appear in the final work, eight of them do not; and the narratives of two of them, Cleopatra and Philomela, were written by Chaucer but are not mentioned by the Man of Law. These anomalies suggest the fluidity and open-ended ambitions of an ongoing assignment, that is, a work still very much in progress while Chaucer was working also on his *Tales*.

Chaucer never completed this assignment. While it has long been believed that he dropped the project around 1388 to devote himself completely to the *Canterbury Tales*, I would suggest that the *Legend* was unfinished because the reign of Richard II was cut short. The collapse of the king's crusading alliance with the French after the defeat at Nicopolis, his unpopular marriage in 1396 with the French child bride, Isabelle, and his relentless move toward autocratic rule after 1397 lost Richard II more and more adherents. This disappearance of support is eerily invoked in the revision of the G Prologue to the *Legend*. In the original Prologue, the God of Love had left the scene with a huge entourage while commending his

20,000 attendants to the dreamer as subjects for future books praising these courtly women's steadfastness in love (*LGW* F, 559–64). Because the G-revision of the Prologue omits these lines entirely, the dreamer is relieved of his obligation to compose 20,000 legends, but the God of Love (Richard II's alter ego) is also deprived of his vast retinue of loyal followers.

The God of Love has no grand exit. He vanishes as the figment of a troubled sleep. It was as if Chaucer, the shrewd observer of social currents, had foreseen the desertion of the monarch by his supporters throughout England, especially in London, that paved the way for Henry Bolingbrook to seize power in 1399. As a poem composed for the Ricardian court and embodying the style, temperament, and tyrannical posturings of the deposed king, the *Legend* had no ready-made audience during the early Lancastrian era. The outcast status of the revision to the Prologue made in the latter 1390s, during Richard II's most fervent embrace of French culture, is witnessed by the fact that its text survives in the single copy Cambridge Gg 4.27.

Never truly published during Chaucer's lifetime, on the other hand, the *Canterbury Tales* with its aggressive Englishness was available to become the prestige text for Lancastrian court culture when its agents, including the poet's son Thomas Chaucer, went about the business of legitimizing the status of the new dynasty and preparing to inaugurate a new era of warfare with the French. The road to Canterbury was also the road to France, and the production of the Ellesmere manuscript of the *Tales* was followed in a few short years by the English victory at Agincourt. I do not take these to be coincidental connections, but they belong to an entirely separate study of English poetry's agency in a revitalized and aggressive national culture during the first decades of the fifteenth century.[118]

The manufacture of a Chaucerian tradition, first by these Lancastrian promoters and now by modern literary historians, has been sustained by a myth of origins that is itself demonstrably arbitrary and contrived. To select the year 1360, or any other, as a starting point for an English national scripture largely means investing further validity to Derrida's claim that "the idea of writing—therefore also of the science of writing—is meaningful for us only in terms of origins."[119] I believe that Chaucer deserves full credit for consciously, deliberately, and persistently undertaking the business of producing a body of literature and indeed a precise *kind* of literature—narrative, comic, alive with vivid characters—designed to be read by posterity and to serve as the basis for subsequent vernacular practice. But just as he could not have predicted the course of that future practice when his life ended in 1400, he could not have predicted the contents and contours of his literary output before it had begun. It has been the purpose of this paper to suggest ways of revising somewhat the well-known account of Chaucer's career by fixing a different "origin," in the events attending the French wars in 1360, and then reading the record of his textual productions against the record of England's military and cultural contests with France during the final three decades of the fourteenth century.

NOTES

1. Jean Froissart, *Chronicles*, trans. Geoffrey Brereton (Harmondsworth: Penguin, 1978), 69. He later describes the traffic of French noblemen between Calais and London in the period from Poitiers in 1356 until Jean II's death in 1364 on 143–45 and 167–69.

2. See Dorothy M. Broome, *The Ransom of John II, King of France, 1360–1370*, Camden Miscellany 14 (London: Office of the Royal Historical Society, 1926).

3. The classic work by Edouard Perroy, *The Hundred Years War*, trans. David C. Douglas (1951; reprint. Bloomington: Indiana University Press, 1959), 132–42, offers a concise survey of this period.

4. Froissart, *Chronicles*, 37–38.

5. James I. Wimsatt, *Chaucer and His French Contemporaries* (Toronto: University of Toronto Press, 1991), 43–76.

6. Barbara W. Tuchman, *A Distant Mirror: The Calamitous 14th Century* (New York: Knopf, 1978), 185–203, devotes an entire chapter to the social, political and cultural consequences of so many important French noblemen residing in England for nearly a decade. Rossell Hope Robbins, "Geoffroi Chaucier, Poète Français, Father of English Poetry," *Chaucer Review* 13 (1978): 93–115, at 112 n78, offers this challenge: "One wonders what effect the captivity of forty French noblemen in England, as a result of the Treaty of Brétigny, in 1360, had on the diffusion of French literature among the English lords serving as their guardians." The challenge was brilliantly taken up by Elizabeth Salter, "Chaucer and Internationalism," *Studies in the Age of Chaucer* 2 (1980): 71–79. Lee Patterson, in his review of Paul Strohm's *Social Chaucer* (Cambridge, Mass.: Harvard University Press, 1989) in *Speculum* 67 (1992): 487, has criticized Strohm for focusing upon a single, class-defined social determinism for the production of literature "because it overrides secondary causes such as the importation of a French court literature in the later years of Edward III's reign."

7. Lynette R. Muir, *Literature and Society in Medieval France* (New York: St. Martin's, 1985), 210–19, suggests that war with England encouraged the emergence of named poets like Machaut who took as their subject the entire substance of French aristocratic culture.

8. Froissart, *Chronicles*, 168. See Nigel Wilkins, "Music and Poetry at Court: England and France in the Late Middle Ages," in *English Court Culture in the Later Middle Ages*, ed. V. J. Scattergood and J. W. Sherborne (London: Aldus, 1983), 183–204, esp. 190–97.

9. Ranulf Higden, who died in the 1360s, criticized Englishmen for being excessively devoted to foreign imports but scornful of their own native productions; see Antonia Gransden, *Historical Writing in England ii: c. 1307 to the Early Sixteenth Century* (Ithaca, N.Y.: Cornell University Press, 1982), 51–52. The twelfth-century ascendancy of French culture throughout Europe is examined by Joachim Bumke, *Courtly Culture: Literature and Society in the High Middle Ages*, trans. Thomas Dunlap (Berkeley: University of California Press, 1991), 61–101. Albert C. Baugh, *A History of the English Language*, 2nd ed. (New York: Appleton-Century-Crofts, 1957), 154–59, discusses Henry III's preference for Frenchmen, especially from Poitou. See also M.T. Clanchy, *From Memory to Written Record: England 1066–1307*, 2nd ed. (Oxford: Blackwell, 1993), 200–23.

10. Tuchman, *Distant Mirror*, 195. See John Tomlinson, *Cultural Imperialism* (Baltimore: Johns Hopkins University Press, 1991), 1–33.

11. Lifted from Salman Rushdie's statement "the Empire writes back to the Centre," this phrase serves as the title of the extremely useful study, *The Empire Writes Back: Theory and Practice in Post-Colonial Literatures*, ed. Bill Ashcroft, Gareth Griffiths and Helen Tiffin (London and New York: Routledge, 1989).

12. See *The Poems of Laurence Minot*, ed. Richard H. Osberg (Kalamazoo: Medieval Institute Publications, 1996). John Barnie, *War in Medieval English Society: Social Values in the Hundred Years War, 1337–99* (Ithaca, N.Y.: Cornell University Press, 1974), 45–49; and Christopher Allmand, *The Hundred Years War: England and France at War c. 1300–c. 1450* (Cambridge: Cambridge University Press, 1988), 136–50. Gransden, *Historical Writing*, 58–59 and 102, points to the patriotic fervor sparked by Edward III's early campaigns as an enabling condition for the monastic chronicles. Pro-English propaganda took several textual forms: the dispatch of letters to be read publicly from pulpits and market crosses; the publication of letters justifying a particular action; the request for bishops to order special prayers for success on the battlefield; and the production of tracts and pictorial genealogies asserting the legitimacy of dynastic claims.

13. "The *Sermo Epinicius* Ascribed to Thomas Bradwardine (1346)," ed. Heiko A. Oberman and James A. Weisheipl, *Archives d'historie doctrinale et littéraire du moyen âge* 25 (1958): 295–329, at 323–24.

14. Kenneth Fowler, introduction to *The Hundred Years War*, ed. Kenneth Fowler (London: Macmillan, 1971), 20–21, notes that extreme xenophobia and chauvinism were not evident in the upper echelons serving as the audience of Froissart and the Chandos Herald.

15. H. J. Hewitt, *The Organization of War under Edward III, 1338–62* (New York: Barnes & Noble, 1966), 177–78.

16. Antonia Gransden, "Propaganda in English Medieval Historiography," *Journal of Medieval History* 1 (1975): 363–82, and "The Uses Made of History by the Kings of Medieval England," in *Culture et Idéologie dans la Genèse de l'Etat Moderne*, ed. J.-P. Genet, Collection de l'Ecole française de Rome, no. 82 (Rome: Ecole française de Rome, 1985), 463–78, concludes that English monarchs never persistently or systematically enlisted chroniclers to the nationalist cause.

17. Jeanne E. Krochalis, "The Books and Reading of Henry V and His Circle," *Chaucer Review* 23 (1988): 50–77.

18. *Chaucer Life-Records*, ed. Martin M. Crow and Clair C. Olson (Oxford: Clarendon, 1966), 23–28.

19. Crow and Olson, eds., *Chaucer Life-Records*, 370. Derek Brewer, *Chaucer and His World*, 2nd ed. (Cambridge: Brewer, 1992), 56–61, offers an imaginative fleshing-out of these events.

20. The Chandos Herald, *The Life and Campaigns of the Black Prince*, ed. and trans. Richard Barber (New York: St. Martin's, 1986), 104. See Desmond Seward, *The Hundred Years War: The English in France 1337–1453* (New York: Atheneum, 1978), 97–101.

21. Barnie, *War in Medieval English Society*, 28–29. See also John Keegan, *The Face of War* (Harmondsworth: Penguin, 1978), 70–72.

22. Gransden, *Historical Writing*, 96, cites Gray's *Scalacronica*. Barnie, *War in Medieval English Society*, 91–95, has high praise for Gray's account of the campaign.

23. John Palmer, "The War Aims of the Protagonists and Negotiations for Peace," in *The Hundred Years War*, ed. Kenneth Fowler (London: Macmillan, 1971), 59–63, believes that the failure of the 1359–1360 campaign to realize a great victory such as Poitiers induced the English to sell short in the Treaty of Brétigny.

24. Chaucer was apparently in Calais again in October of 1360, since there is a record of payment to him for conveying letters back to England for Lionel, Earl of Ulster; see Crow and Olson, eds., *Chaucer Life-Records*, 19–22.

25. Donald R. Howard, *Chaucer: His Life, His Works, His World* (New York: E. P. Dutton, 1987), 72; he further speculated, 71–73, that the young Englishman might also have met Eustache Deschamps, who was probably with his uncle Machaut inside Rheims during the siege. See also Wimsatt, *Chaucer and His French Contemporaries*, 78–84.

26. Not many years later, Sir John Strother received a letter from his man Walter Ferrefort begging to be ransomed from a French prison where he was bound with iron fetters on his feet and hands; see Anthony Tuck, "Why Men Fought in the 100 Years War," *History Today* 33 (April 1988): 38. C. T. Allmand, *Society at War: The Experience of England and France during the Hundred Years War* (Edinburgh: Oliver & Boyd, 1973), 83–85, gathers contemporary statements on the proper treatment of prisoners.

27. Hewitt, *Organization of War under Edward III*, 93–139, and C. T. Allmand, "The War and the Non-combatant," in *The Hundred Years War*, ed. Kenneth Fowler (London: Macmillan, 1971), 163–83, make clear that this mode of warfare was principally intended to inflict suffering upon the enemy without distinction between combatants and civilians.

28. Tale of Melibee in *The Riverside Chaucer*, ed. Larry Benson, 3rd ed. (Boston: Houghton Mifflin, 1987), 219, lines 1038–42. See V. J. Scattergood, "Chaucer and the French War: *Sir Thopas* and *Melibee*," in *Court and Poet*, ed. Glyn S. Burgess et al. (Liverpool: Francis Cairns, 1981), 287–96; and R. F. Yeager, "*Pax Poetica*: On the Pacifism of Chaucer and Gower," *Studies in the Age of Chaucer* 9 (1987): 97–121.

29. *The Chronicle of Jean de Venette*, ed. Richard A. Newhall, trans. Jean Birdsall (New York: Columbia University Press, 1953), 92, and generally 87–107, describes the terrible misery of French civilians during 1359–1360.

30. Fowler, introduction to *The Hundred Years War*, 1–27, at 22. The Jacquerie of 1358 was largely a violent reaction against the nobility which made war by the rural civilians who endured war's hardships; see Richard Cazelles, "The Jacquerie," in *The English Rising of 1381*, ed. R. H. Hilton and T. H. Aston (Cambridge: Cambridge University Press, 1984), 74–83.

31. Hewitt, *Organization of War under Edward III*, 104, and Gransden, *Historical Writing*, 96, cite Sir Thomas Gray's *Scalacronica* on the widespread scarcity of victuals during the winter of 1359–1360.

32. J. A. Burrow, *Ricardian Poetry* (London: Routledge & Kegan Paul, 1971), 93–102, detects a persistently unheroic attitude even in the Knight's Tale. Derek Pearsall, *The Life of Geoffrey Chaucer* (Oxford: Blackwell, 1992), 40–46, admits that warfare did not provide Chaucer with his favorite subject, but rejects as unhistorical the trend among critics to view the poet as a pacifist. See also Elizabeth Porter, "Chaucer's Knight, the Alliterative *Morte Arthure*, and Medieval Laws of War: A Reconsideration," *Nottingham Medieval Studies* 27 (1983): 56–78.

33. *Troilus and Criseyde*, 5.701–707, in *Riverside Chaucer*, ed. Benson, 569.

34. *Canterbury Tales* I.126, in *Riverside Chaucer*, ed. Benson, 25; see Baugh, *History of the English Language*, 167–68, and two articles by W. Rothwell: "Stratford atte Bowe and Paris," *Modern Language Review* 80 (1985): 39–54, and "Chaucer and Stratford atte Bowe," *Bulletin of the John Rylands Library* 74 (1992): 3–28. The decline had an early beginning; Walter Map, *De Nugis Curialium*, ed. Montague Rhodes James (Oxford: Clarendon, 1914), 246–47, reported that in 1182 Henry II's son Geoffrey was ridiculed for "speaking the French of Malborough."

35. The ethnic slur about Englishmen having tails can be traced back as far as Wace's *Brut* in the twelfth century, and it was still being voiced in the seventeenth century; see George Neilson, *Anglicus Caudatus: A Medieval Slander* (Edinburgh: G. P. Johnson, 1896). In Chaucer's Shipman's Tale, it is the French wife who has a *taille*—and knows how to use it!

36. Wimsatt, *Chaucer and His French Contemporaries*, 239–40, cites this ballade with translation and commentary. The first stanza concludes with a mockery of harsh English speech: "L'un me dist *dogue*, l'autre *ride*; | Lors me devint la coulour bleue: | *Goday* fait l'un, l'autre *commidre*." Paul Meyvaert, "'Reinaldus est malus scriptor Francigenus':Voicing National Antipathy in the Middle Ages," *Speculum* 66 (1991): 743–63, notes that the terms of ethnic derision were always subject to particular historical circumstances.

37. Fowler, introduction to *The Hundred Years War*, 22.

38. The most imaginative speculations are those offered by John Gardner, *The Life and Times of Chaucer* (New York: Knopf, 1977), 127–67; see also Howard, *Chaucer*, 79–108. Pearsall, *Life of Geoffrey Chaucer*, 55–73, focuses sensibly on the powerful French influences at the English court which formed a dazzling background against which Chaucer moved invisibly during these years.

39. Issues of authorship are set forth in James I. Wimsatt, *Chaucer and the Poems of 'Ch' in University of Pennsylvania MS French 15* (Cambridge: Brewer, 1982), 1–8. Rossell Hope Robbins, "The Vintner's Son: French Wine in English Bottles," in *Eleanor of Aquitaine: Patron and Politician*, ed. William Kibler, Symposia in the Arts and the Humanities, no. 3 (Austin: University of Texas Press, 1976), 147–72, and "Geoffroi Chaucier, Poéte Français," construct a substantial case for Chaucer's lost early verses having been written in French.

40. See *Confessio Amantis*, 8:*2943–47, in *The English Works of John Gower*, ed. G. C. Macaulay, Early English Text Society, e. s., 81 and 82 (London: Oxford University Press, 1900–1901), 2:466: "For in the floures of his youth / In sondri wise, as he well couth, / Of Ditees and of songes glade, / The whiche he for mi sake made, / The lond fulfild is overal."

41. Edward W. Said, "Yeats and Decolonization," in *Nationalism, Colonialism, and Literature* (Minneapolis, Minn.: University of Minnesota Press, 1990), 79: "And along with these nationalistic adumbrations of the decolonized identity, there always goes an almost magically inspired, quasi-alchemical redevelopment of the native language."

42. Helen Cooper, "Langland's and Chaucer's Prologues," *Yearbook of Langland Studies* 1 (1987): 71–81, offers one of the more concrete arguments for Chaucer's having read *Piers Plowman*.

43. Terry Eagleton, "Nationalism: Irony and Commitment," in *Nationalism, Colonialism, and Literature* (Minneapolis, Minn.: University of Minnesota Press, 1990), 31–34, sees Oscar Wilde as a perfect example of this flamboyant artistry and self-mocking individualism.

44. Robin Neillands, *The Hundred Years War* (London and New York: Routledge, 1990), 171.

45. Joseph R. Strayer, *Medieval Statecraft and the Perspectives of History* (Princeton, N.J.: Princeton University Press, 1971), contains two essays pertinent to the

consolidation of the medieval state: "France: The Holy Land, the Chosen People, and the Most Christian King," 300–14, and "The Historical Experiences of Nation-Building in Europe," 341–48.

46. Baugh, *History of the English Language*, 168–69: "French was the language of an enemy country, and the Hundred Years' War is probably to be reckoned as one of the causes contributing to the disuse of French." See also Basil Cottle, *The Triumph of English 1350–1400* (London: Blandford, 1969), 51–88.

47. John Le Patourel, "The Origins of the War," in *The Hundred Years War*, ed. Kenneth Fowler (London: Macmillan, 1971), 37. Allmand, *Hundred Years War*, 7, takes the contrary position: "In France and England it was the breakdown of the historic feudal order, no longer able to meet the demands of changing times, and its gradual replacement by an order of nations increasingly aware of their growing national characteristics, which was the fundamental cause of the long conflict."

48. G. R. Owst, *Literature and Pulpit in Medieval England*, 2nd ed. rev. (Oxford: Blackwell, 1961), 131–36 and 215–25, describes the fierce immediacy of "the English pulpit as the mouthpiece of the new national spirit" (131).

49. David Quint, *Epic and Empire: Politics and Generic Form from Virgil to Milton* (Princeton, N.J.: Princeton University Press, 1993), 21–96.

50. Bernard Guenée, *States and Rulers in Later Medieval Europe*, trans. Juliet Vale (Oxford: Blackwell, 1985), 52–54.

51. True anti-French prejudice of this sort was possible for the Yorkshire soldier of fortune Laurence Minot during the years 1347–1352. See Cottle, *Triumph of English*, 61–66; and Derek Pearsall, *Old English and Middle English Poetry* (London: Routledge & Kegan Paul, 1977), 122–23. If Chaucer participated in any unguarded ethnic prejudice, he inherited a Londoner's dislike for the Flemings: he denigrated them as drunkards in the Pardoner's Tale; he mentioned them as the targets of Jack Straw's rebels in the Nun's Priest's Tale; and he made a Flemish native the mockery of knighthood in the Tale of Sir Thopas.

52. George Kane, "Chaucer and the Idea of a Poet" (1976), reprinted in *Chaucer and Langland* (Berkeley: University of California Press, 1989), 15–31; Charles Muscatine, *Chaucer and the French Tradition* (Berkeley: University of California Press, 1957); Wimsatt, *Chaucer and His French Contemporaries*; and Lee Patterson, "Feminine Rhetoric and the Politics of Subjectivity: La Vieille and the Wife of Bath," *Speculum* 65 (1990): 87–108, most recently reprinted in *Rethinking the "Romance of the Rose": Text, Image, Reception*, ed. Kevin Brownlee and Sylvia Huot (Philadelphia: University of Pennsylvania Press, 1992), 316–58.

53. D. S. Brewer, "The Relationship of Chaucer to the English and European Traditions," in *Chaucer and Chaucerians*, ed. D. S. Brewer (University, Ala.: University of Alabama Press, 1966), 1–38, esp. 1–15; E. Talbot Donaldson, "Idiom of Popular Poetry in The Miller's Tale," in *Speaking of Chaucer* (London: Athlone, 1970), 13–29; and P. M. Kean, *Chaucer and the Making of English Poetry* (London: Routledge &

Kegan Paul, 1972), 1:1–30, locate the poet's verbal directness and uncluttered narration in the tradition of English-language romances. The nationalist ideologies inherent in these pre-Chaucerian texts have been exposed by Susan Crane, *Insular Romance: Politics, Faith, and Culture in Anglo-Norman and Middle English Literature* (Berkeley: University of California Press, 1986).

54. Terry Eagleton, *Literary Theory: An Introduction* (Minneapolis, Minn.: University of Minnesota Press, 1983), 215: "Imperialism is not only the exploitation of cheap labor-power, raw materials and easy markets but the uprooting of languages and custom—not just the imposition of foreign armies, but of alien ways of experiencing."

55. Caroline D. Eckhardt, "The Art of Translation in *The Romaunt of the Rose*," *Studies in the Age of Chaucer* 6 (1984): 41–63, at 46 and 50.

56. George Steiner, *After Babel: Aspects of Language and Translation* (Oxford: Oxford University Press, 1975), 297–303.

57. Fredric Jameson, "Modernism and Imperialism," in *Nationalism, Colonialism, and Literature* (Minneapolis, Minn.: University of Minnesota Press, 1990), 49.

58. The text and translation are printed by J. A. Burrow, ed., *Geoffrey Chaucer: A Critical Anthology* (Baltimore: Penguin, 1969), 26–28. The French apparently had scant regard for English originality. Froissart's *Chronicles*, 132, records a moment on the eve of the battle of Poitiers in which Marshal Jean de Clermont berated Sir John Chandos for wearing the same device as himself: "You can never think of anything new yourselves, but when you see something good you just take it!"

59. Peter Rickard, *Britain in Medieval French Literature, 1100–1500* (Cambridge: Cambridge University Press, 1956), 193. It is no doubt important to know that Deschamps's birthplace, Vertu-en-Champagne, was burned to the ground by the English in 1380.

60. D. W. Robertson, Jr., *Chaucer's London* (New York: John Wiley & Sons, 1968), 130, links the resumption of the war with Chaucer's first serious efforts as an English-language poet.

61. Steiner, *After Babel*, 297–98.

62. Quoted by Hugo Friedrich, "On the Art of Translation," in *Theories of Translation*, ed. and trans. Rainer Schulte and John Biguenet (Chicago: University of Chicago Press, 1992), 12–13.

63. Friedrich Nietzsche, *The Gay Science*, trans. Walter Kaufmann (New York: Vintage, 1974), 137.

64. Wimsatt, *Chaucer and His French Contemporaries*, 109–40, makes clear that the young English poet had knowledge of works from every standard division of Machaut's output: short lyrics (ballades, virelays, and rondeaux), longer lyrics (lays, motets, and complaints), and *dits* of all lengths.

65. Wimsatt, *Chaucer and His French Contemporaries*, 174–209, identifies Froissart as Chaucer's natural rival in English court circles during the 1360s. Wimsatt,

"The *Dit dou Bleu Chevalier*: Froissart's Imitation of Chaucer," *Mediaeval Studies* 34 (1972): 388–400, argues that influence moved in both directions. This conclusion resists the French claims that Froissart could not possibly have been impressed by an English poet; see Normand Cartier, "*Le Bleu Chevalier* de Froissart et *Le Livre de la Duchesse* de Chaucer," *Romania* 88 (1967): 232–52. For Chaucer's indebtedness to both Machaut and Froissart in the *Book of the Duchess*, see B. A. Windeatt, *Chaucer's Dream Poetry: Sources and Analogues* (Cambridge: Brewer, 1982), 3–70.

66. Joseph Mersand, *Chaucer's Romance Vocabulary* (Brooklyn: Comet Press, 1939), 90–92. Mersand's conclusion is that Romance vocabulary increased in later texts when the poet worked from Italian sources (137–38). James I. Wimsatt, "Chaucer and French Poetry," *Writers and their Background: Geoffrey Chaucer*, ed. Derek Brewer (Athens: Ohio University Press, 1974), 126: "It is a paradox that the *Book of the Duchess*, pervasively informed with French antecedents, strongly sounds the English note."

67. *The Parliament of Fowls* ends with the disclaimer that the poet did not write the melody for the lyric: "The note, I trowe, imaked was in France; / The wordes were swiche as ye may heer fynde" (677–78). Robertson, *Chaucer's London*, 215–16, has suggested that these lines have two important implications: the English court preferred French tunes, and Chaucer himself was not a composer.

68. Since Le Mote and Machaut are routinely praised as composers, one wonders whether Chaucer lacked musical talent and was therefore forced from the beginning to redefine the terms of his poetic enterprise, replacing the lyric with the narrative, rejecting live performance in favor of the written word. The earliest Chaucer portraits show him always with a pen; only the *Troilus* frontispiece offers the romanticized vision of the poet reading before the Ricardian court. See Elizabeth Salter, "The *Troilus* Frontispiece" (1978), reprinted in *English and International: Studies in the Literature, Art and Patronage of Medieval England*, ed. Derek Pearsall and Nicolette Zeeman (Cambridge: Cambridge University Press, 1988), 267–71; David R. Carlson, "Thomas Hoccleve and the Chaucer Portrait," *Huntington Library Quarterly* 54 (1991): 283–300; and Pearsall, *Life of Geoffrey Chaucer*, 285–305.

69. Steiner, *After Babel*, 298–99, believes that translation does not happen in a vacuum and can be readily incorporated because the native semantic field is somehow already prepared, but he allows that "whatever the degree of 'naturalization,' the act of importation can potentially dislocate or relocate the whole of the native structure."

70. For cruder forms of artistic support in these land-grabbing contests, see Elizabeth Danbury, "English and French Artistic Propaganda during the Period of the Hundred Years War: Some Evidence from Royal Charters," in *Power, Culture, and Religion in France, c. 1350–c. 1550*, ed. Christopher Allmand (Woodbridge, Suffolk: Boydell, 1989), 75–97.

71. The Merchant's Tale mentions only vaguely "he that wroot the Romance of the Rose" (*CT* IV, 2032). The Cheshire author of *Cleanness* was much more forthright in citing Jean de Meun by his surname: "Clopyngnel in þe compas of his clene *Rose*" (line 1057); *The Poems of the "Pearl" Manuscript*, ed. Malcolm Andrew and Ronald Waldron, York Medieval Texts, 2nd series (Berkeley: University of California Press, 1993), 155. Pierre-Yves Badel, *Le "Roman de la Rose" au XIVe siècle: Etude de la réception de l'oeuvre* (Geneva: Droz, 1980), documents the text's universal spread among secular and clerical readers inside and outside France. Two recent books help gauge the extent of that textual omnipresence: *Rethinking the "Romance of the Rose": Text, Image, Reception*, ed. Brownlee and Huot, esp. 287–373, and Sylvia Huot, *The "Romance of the Rose" and its Medieval Readers: Interpretation, Reception, Manuscript Transmission* (Cambridge: Cambridge University Press, 1993).

72. *Riverside Chaucer*, ed. Benson, 648–49, 1081–82. Wimsatt, *Chaucer and His French Contemporaries*, 210–41, devotes an entire chapter to Chaucer's relations to Granson. See also Pearsall, *Life of Geoffrey Chaucer*, 71, on the mutuality of poetic indebtedness.

73. For a concise survey of the war from 1360 to 1396, see Allmand, *The Hundred Years War*, 20–26.

74. Howard, *Chaucer*, 169–303, makes a direct connection between the poet's diplomatic missions and his turn to the Italian models of Boccaccio.

75. Perroy, *Hundred Years War*, 178–86 and 196–206; and Barnie, *War in Medieval English Society*, 14–31. Anthony Goodman, *John of Gaunt* (Harlow: Longman, 1992), esp. 211–40, offers the Duke of Lancaster's career as a paradigm of distractions and disappointments. Johan Huizinga's celebration of chivalry has been undercut by more recent works: Maurice Keen, "Huizinga, Kilgour and the Decline of Chivalry," *Medievalia et Humanistica* 8 (1977): 1–20; Terry Jones, *Chaucer's Knight* (Baton Rouge: Louisiana State University Press, 1980); and Malcolm Vale, *War and Chivalry: Warfare and Aristocratic Culture in England, France and Burgundy at the End of the Middle Ages* (Athens: University of Georgia Press, 1981). Lee Patterson, *Chaucer and the Subject of History* (Madison, Wis.: University of Wisconsin Press, 1991), 165–230, reads the Knight's Tale as testimony to this chivalric disenchantment.

76. Crow and Olson, eds., *Chaucer Life-Records*, 64–66, print the record of a safe-conduct for Chaucer to travel in Spain in 1366, probably on business relating to English support of Pedro of Castile, whose tragic fate became the subject of a vignette in the Monk's Tale (*CT* VII, 2375–90).

77. Laura Kendrick, "Chaucer's *House of Fame* and the French Palais de Justice," *Studies in the Age of Chaucer* 6 (1984): 121–33.

78. Benedict Anderson, *Imagined Communities: Reflections on the Origin and Spread of Nationalism*, rev. ed. (London and New York: Verso, 1991), 178.

79. Eric Hobsbawn, *The Invention of Tradition* (Cambridge: Cambridge University Press, 1983), has a central concern with the ways in which literary traditions are implicated in nationalistic movements.

80. See Anne Middleton, "The Idea of Public Poetry in the Reign of Richard II," *Speculum* 53 (1978): 94–114; and Stephen Knight, *Geoffrey Chaucer* (Oxford: Blackwell, 1986), 23–31.

81. Anderson, *Imagined Communities*, 48, observes that early nationalisms in Latin America did not try to incorporate the lower classes and, to the contrary, feared the political mobilization of the native Indians and Negro slaves. The Wycliffite agenda deserves much fuller consideration than possible here because it possessed a steady antiwar component. See Anne Hudson, *The Premature Reformation: Wycliffite Texts and Lollard History* (Oxford: Clarendon Press, 1988), 367–70, on this pacifist strain.

82. Gransden, *Historical Writing*, 163.

83. Barnie, *War in Medieval English Society*, 97: "In the 1370s and 80s chroniclers and poets were clearly experimenting with language in an attempt to define their patriotism more exactly;" see 97–166.

84. Larry D. Benson, "The Occasion of *The Parliament of Fowls*," in *The Wisdom of Poetry*, ed. Larry D. Benson and Siegfried Wenzel (Kalamazoo: Medieval Institute Publications, 1982), 123–44, restates the durable argument that the "formel eagle" is Anne of Bohemia and the three suitors are Richard of England, Charles of France, and Friedrich of Meissen.

85. Ernst H. Kantorowicz, *The King's Two Bodies* (Princeton, N.J.: Princeton University Press, 1957), 232–72; and Gaines Post, "Two Notes on Nationalism in the Middle Ages," *Traditio* 9 (1953): 281–320, esp. 293–96.

86. Allmand, *Hundred Years War*, 23.

87. This is the conventional view of Paul A. Olson, "*The Parlement of Foules*: Aristotle's *Politics* and the Foundations of Human Society," *Studies in the Age of Chaucer* 2 (1980): 53–69.

88. Strohm, *Social Chaucer*, 129.

89. Allmand, *Hundred Years War*, 169.

90. Crow and Olson, eds., *Chaucer Life-Records*, 148–270.

91. S. W. Sherborne, "The Cost of English Warfare with France in the Later Fourteenth Century," *Bulletin of the Institute of Historical Research* 50 (1977): 135–50, esp. 141–46.

92. Janet Coleman, "A Political Analysis of Literary Works c. 1280–1400: Ideology and Perception of 'the State' in England," in *Culture et Idéologie dans la Genèse de l'Etat Moderne*, ed. J.-P. Genet, Collection de l'Ecole française de Rome, no. 82 (Rome: Ecole française de Rome, 1985), 433–62, esp. 433–35 and 455–57.

93. On the dream-vision of courtship as an allegory of assigning political allegiances, see Louise Olga Fradenburg, *City, Marriage, Tournament: Arts of Rule in Late Medieval Scotland* (Madison, Wis.: University of Wisconsin Press, 1991), 123–34.

94. John Clark, "Trinovantum—The Evolution of a Legend," *Journal of Medieval History* 7 (1981): 135–51; and generally Patterson, *Chaucer and the Subject of History*, 97–164.

95. Anderson, *Imagined Communities*, 188.

96. Gransden, "Uses Made of History," 467.

97. D. W. Robertson, Jr., "The Probable Date and Purpose of Chaucer's *Troilus*," *Medievalia et Humanistica* n.s. 13 (1985): 143–71, reconstructs a historical context: "Troy is under siege as Chaucer describes it, and a similar situation existed in England almost at any time between 1377 and the close of 1386" (154).

98. Sherborne, "Cost of English Warfare," 146–47, and Barnie, *War in Medieval English Society*, 42.

99. Barnie, *War in Medieval English Society*, 27; and J. J. N. Palmer, *England, France and Christendom, 1377–99* (London: Routledge & Kegan Paul, 1972), 67–87, with comparison to the Greek fleet sent against Troy on 74. For documents relating to the French preparations, see L. Mirot, "Une Tentative d'invasion en Angleterre pendant la guerre de Cents Ans, 1385–1386," *REH* 81 (1915): 249–87 and 417–66.

100. Barnie, *War in Medieval English Society*, 43–44.

101. Thomas Walsingham, *Chronica Monasterii S. Albani*, ed. Henry Thomas Riley, Rolls Series (London: Longman, Green, Longman, Roberts, and Green, 1863–64), 2:127 and 147–48. For the poet's Aldgate residence, see Crow and Olson, eds., *Chaucer Life-Records*, 144–47.

102. Barnie, *War in Medieval English Society*, 44. See Walsingham, *Chronica Monasterii S. Albani*, 2:146–48; and *Knighton's Chronicon, 1337–1396*, ed. and trans. G. H. Martin (Oxford: Clarendon, 1995), 348–51.

103. Robertson, *Chaucer's London*, 158.

104. Palmer, *England, France and Christendom*, 88–141.

105. Palmer, *England, France and Christendom*, 142–51 and 166–79.

106. Crow and Olson, eds., *Chaucer Life-Records*, 472–73.

107. Philippe de Mézières, *Letter to King Richard II*, ed. and trans. G. W. Coopland (Liverpool: Liverpool University Press, 1975).

108. Palmer, *England, France and Christendom*, 166–210. For the general shift in the Ricardian agenda, see J. J. N. Palmer, "English Foreign Policy 1388–99," in *The Reign of Richard II*, ed. F. R. H. Du Boulay and Caroline M. Barron (London: Athlone, 1971), 75–107. Allmand, *Hundred Years War*, 143, observes that the "religion of monarchy" in France no less than in Ricardian England was one clear feature of nation-building carried forward under the threat of renewed hostilities.

109. Robert B. Burlin, *Chaucerian Fiction* (Princeton, N.J.: Princeton University Press, 1977), 34. The 1386–1388 dating of the work as a transitional exercise has a long history: John L. Lowes, "The Prologue to the *Legend of Good Women* Considered in its Chronological Relations," *PMLA* 20 (1905): 749–864; Robert W. Frank, Jr., "The Legend of the *Legend of Good Women*," *Chaucer Review* 1 (1966): 110–33; and Michael D. Cherniss, "Chaucer's Last Dream Vision: The 'Prologue' to the *Legend of Good Women*," *Chaucer Review* 20 (1986): 183–99.

110. John Eadie, "The Author at Work: The Two Versions of the Prologue to the *Legend of Good Women*," *Neuphilologische Mitteilungen* 93 (1992): 135–43.

111. Paul Strohm, "Queens as Intercessors," in *Hochon's Arrow: The Social Imagination of Fourteenth-Century Texts* (Princeton, N.J.: Princeton University Press, 1992), 95–119, connects Alceste's intervention on behalf of the dreamer with Queen Anne's intervention on behalf of London in 1392.

112. John H. Fisher, "The Revision of the Prologue to the *Legend of Good Women*: An Occasional Explanation," *South Atlantic Bulletin* 43 (1978): 75–84.

113. Robert O. Payne, "Making His Own Myth: The Prologue to Chaucer's *Legend of Good Women*," *Chaucer Review* 9 (1975): 197–211, at 199.

114. H. C. Goddard, "Chaucer's *Legend of Good Women* II," *JEGP* 8 (1909): 47–111, inaugurated the view, now commonplace, that the work was designed to parody its French sources. Lisa Kiser, *Telling Classical Tales: Chaucer and the Legend of Good Women* (Ithaca, N.Y.: Cornell University Press, 1983), esp. 62–70, sees as the target of much of this parody the God of Love, the poem's fictive representation of Richard II. Derek Brewer, "Chaucer's Anti-Ricardian Poetry," in *The Living Middle Ages: Studies in Mediaeval English Literature and Its Traditions*, ed. Uwe Böker, Manfred Markus and Rainer Schöwerling (Stuttgart: Belser, 1989), 115–28, reads much of the poet's career as a reaction against the royal court.

115. James Simpson, "Ethics and Interpretation: Reading Wills in Chaucer's *Legend of Good Women*," *Studies in the Age of Chaucer* 20 (1998): 73–100, links the poetics of the work more securely with "the discursive environment of Richard II's court" (82) and specifically "the tyrannical reading of his patron" (74).

116. Walsingham, *Chronica*, 2:253. On Clifford as a heretic, see K. B. McFarlane, *Lancastrian Kings and Lollard Knights* (Oxford: Clarendon Press, 1972), 212; Hudson, *Premature Reformation*, 291–92; and Margaret Aston, "William White's Lollard Followers" (1982), reprinted in *Lollards and Reformers: Images and Literacy in Late Medieval Religion* (London: Hambledon Press, 1984), 71–100, at 98, n. 117.

117. Michael Bennett, "The Court of Richard II and the Promotion of Literature," in *Chaucer's England: Literature in Historical Context*, ed. Barbara Hanawalt, Medieval Studies at Minnesota 4 (Minneapolis, Minn.: University of Minnesota Press, 1992), 16: "It is hard to know what Richard II or his panegyrist intended to convey by likening him to Homer, '*animo prudens ut Homerus*'."

118. See a preliminary sketch of this account in John M. Bowers, "The House of Chaucer & Son: The Business of Lancastrian Canon-Formation," *Medieval Perspectives* 6 (1991): 135–43.

119. Jacques Derrida, *Of Grammatology*, trans. Gayatri Chakravorty Spivak (Baltimore and London: Johns Hopkins University Press, 1974), 4. Christopher Cannon, "The Myth of Origin and the Making of Chaucer's English," *Speculum* 71 (1996): 646–75, offers both a highly informed account of this language tradition and a sophisticated critique of tradition-making itself.

CHAPTER 6

Politics and the French Language in England during the Hundred Years' War

The Case of John Gower

R. F. YEAGER

Language is, by nature, political. We scarcely need George Orwell, or the ready army of psychologists (pop and not) with studies dedicated to the issue, to find this statement credible. In our own lives there are moments when we are keenly aware of the politics of language, as, for instance, when we choose our words carefully before a traffic court judge. At those times, everything seems to hang, not only upon *what* we say, but also (or perhaps especially) upon *how*. Yet occasions of such linguistic self-consciousness are relatively rare in modern life. Luckily for most of us, most of the time the political valences of language are expediently submerged. The traffic judge, or the equivalent, does not invade our lives that often. Even as we implicitly recognize, initiate, and respond to linguistic signals of power and authority in the daily round of communication, we have the luxury also to ignore their influence, speak and write more or less as we like, and suffer comparatively little by way of consequence.

Opportunity for this kind of blissful indecisiveness, it goes without saying, has not always been available, here or elsewhere. Times of tumult, of war and social unrest, of totalitarian threat enforce disclosure of the politics of language, often making of them the difference between life and death. It is to this urgency that Orwell responded when he traced what he called "the decline of a language" to "political and economic causes." His examples ("Defenseless villages are bombarded from the air, the inhabitants driven out into the countryside, the cattle machine-gunned, the huts set on fire with incendiary bullets: this is called *pacification*") leave little doubt about Orwell's sense of his times, or what he thought was put at risk by language carelessly or falsely rendered.[1]

Now, it is not common to include John Gower and Orwell in the same sentence—usually for very good reasons, I think. Yet there are several ways in which Orwell and Gower resemble each other: their uncompromising moral outrage at the state of the state, for example; their willingness to speak out boldly; their similar understanding that literature, and scrupulously crafted language, should serve as bulwarks against times they each viewed as increasingly twilit and barbarous. Orwell's familiar and frightening vision of Cold War Europe can help us imagine England and the continent as Gower knew them in the last quarter of the fourteenth century, when the Hundred Years' War in France dragged on from muddle to botch, and at home the doddering old king, then the hapless, arrogant young one and the rapacious lords and commons floundered on, apparently toward ruin. For it is against this background, dark and, *mutatis mutandis*, Orwellian, that Gower's writings must stand to be understood. There is a moral conservatism underlying Orwell's rage which, when provoked into utterance, sounds very like Gower flailing against the shadow enclosing his times. Hence my title, and hence also my argument that Gower's French poetry has much to tell us about the politics of language during the Hundred Years' War.

Of course, it is perhaps a little disingenuous to focus solely on Gower's French poetry, as if it alone illustrates his political directions. In fact all of his choices, whether to compose a particular piece in English, in Latin, or in French, reflect Gower's view of the political realities of his day in their squaring of language, subject, and audience. This is because Gower's poetry, like Orwell's prose, is quintessentially public writing. For Gower, the purpose of poetry was to effect change in society, and his work's introspection, its brooding, is invariably upon the fate of the commonweal, not upon the *sturm und drang* of an individual life. The selection of a language, then, is altogether rhetorical when Gower makes it, a thoughtful decision to facilitate persuasion.

His deliberation makes the problem of Gower's French (or more accurately, Anglo-Norman) poetry interesting, both on its own terms, and for what it suggests about English-French politics near the midpoint of the Hundred Years' War. Gower's extant French corpus consists of (1) the *Mirour de l'Omme*, a poem of 29,945 lines as we have it (though originally it was somewhat longer);[2] (2) a collection of fifty-one ballades, known nevertheless as the *Cinkante Balades*; and (3) a collection of eighteen ballades known as the *Traitié pour essampler les amantz marietz*, or simply, the *Traitié*. These poems have attracted scant attention as political statements. On first glance, this neglect seems appropriate. The ballades take love and marriage as their primary subject; and, while some notice has been accorded to the *Mirour* as social satire, it is the elaborate Christian *schema* of the *Mirour*, which retells the story of creation and the fall, describes a *psychomachia* of virtues and sins, and projects a possibility of redemption through devotion to the Virgin Mary, that has drawn most critical focus.[3]

Nonetheless, the overwhelmingly political design of Gower's poetic enterprise in English and Latin dictates a closer look at his French writings and their politics also. To see what Gower was up to, however, requires an argument which may appear meandering at first. For this I apologize in advance. Yet, if I am right, the problem warrants such scrutiny as can be applied best in this way. By its conclusion, I hope to have shown that Gower's decisions—to compose in French the works he did at a time in English history when the use of the native tongue was spreading, as Chaucer seemed to recognize, and when the nation itself was at war with France—were none of them casual. Each in its own way, Gower's French writings are *ipso facto* political, their language and content inextricably associated in their author's mind.

THE CHRONOLOGY OF GOWER'S FRENCH TEXTS

To begin, we must consider when Gower might have been at work on the *Mirour*, the *Cinkante Balades*, and the *Traitié*. Unfortunately, assigning precise dates to Gower's French texts is difficult. Our ground is firmest with the *Mirour*, since it refers to events, among them the Great Schism, which provide a *terminus*, of some kind, of 1378; in fact many have considered the poem a product of 1376–1379.[4] But harder evidence, to determine with certainty whether the *terminus* is *ad quem* or *a quo*, is lacking in the *Mirour*. The ballade sequences are knottier cases still, for they make no identifiable reference to datable events. Tradition designates the *Cinkante Balades* as early work, primarily because their lighter tone and amorous subject matter suggested to some readers the concerns of youth; and the *Traitié*, because it directly addresses married lovers, is thought to have been composed late, possibly as a wedding gift for Agnes Groundolf (apparently his nurse), whom Gower married as an elderly man in 1398.[5]

But the flimsiness of such chronologies is obvious. What we might call the "romantic Gower," the poet-lover lyrically expressing his own experience as it overtakes him, need not (and probably did not) exist outside of the poetry. If an old man can marry, he can write love poems in the voice of one younger; nor is it requisite to be married to create admonitory ballades for those who are. In principle, Gower could have made the poems assembled in his sequences one by one, over the full course of his career, a period spanning perhaps forty years. And he might have done so like Petrarch, inspired by a Laura more of the imagination than of flesh and blood. In the end, then, putting dates to the composition of Gower's French poems would be helpful for the light we might gain on how Gower worked during historically momentous times; but it must be admitted that we do not, and probably will not, know when Gower was writing what.

The picture nonetheless grows clearer, politically at least, if the manuscript evidence is taken into account. Although multiple copies of his English and Latin writings have come down to us, Gower's French legacy is sparser. Both the *Mirour de l'Omme* and the *Cinkante Balades* exist in single manuscripts—a uniqueness I believe to be revealing, as I hope to show below.[6] Of the *Traitié*, in contrast, we have ten copies; but in no manuscript is the *Traitié* found alone. In all ten manuscripts it appears combined with other poems, of which the *Confessio Amantis* is the most common, followed by the *Vox Clamantis* and the *Cronica Tripertita*. If we look at the probable transcription dates of these manuscripts (as opposed to when Gower might have written the poems), an interesting, even problematic, pattern suggests itself. MS Camb. Univ. Add. 3035, the unique copy of the *Mirour de l'Omme*, it is generally agreed, was transcribed early, perhaps before 1380; but whatever the case, it substantially antedates the coronation of Henry IV in 1399. All ten of the remaining manuscripts containing Gower's French poetry, that is, the unique version of the *Cinkante Balades* in MS Trentham and nine examples of the *Traitié*, are late copies produced after 1400. Until a complete survey of all Gower's manuscripts is available, it is impossible to be certain of the exact relationship of the copies, or more than to guess at how accurately what we have reflects Gower's hand in their assembling. If, however, for lack of better evidence, we take the extant record strictly at face value, discounting all but those manuscripts Gower himself might have seen or approved (those, that is, judged to have been rendered before his death in 1408), we are faced with what, were we bowlers, we would call a "bad split": French copied both early and late in Gower's career, but nothing in that language in between.

Perhaps not very much should be made of this, or at least, not very fast. The remaining manuscripts offer no clue as to what has been lost, and it is of course possible that, with everything before us, the manuscript record would show an unbroken output of French poetry written throughout Gower's career. MS Trentham, for example, containing the *Cinkante Balades*, might be a Henrican copy of an earlier Ricardian original now lost, and so on. Yet, short of the unforeseen discovery, such as a trove of manuscripts long locked in a trunk, we have only the record of the "bad split" to work with, and to that we must give our closest attention.

There is, in fact, more to think about in the manuscript record as we have it. In addition to the pattern of early and late manuscripts containing French, there is also the number and nature of those manuscripts to consider. As has been noted, the *Mirour de l'Omme* exists today in a single copy. Since MS Camb. Univ. Add. 3035 is not a holograph, at least one more copy must have been made, at a date earlier than MS Camb. Univ. Add. 3035, but the unique status of the manuscript suggests that at best there were never many copies of the *Mirour* in circulation. Why this might be, when such a deal of labor went into its composition—30,000 lines of twelve-line stanzas is no instant achievement—is curious. Did the *Mirour* not circulate because Gower grew to dislike it? Or was there no sustained audience for it shortly after its completion? The fact that Gower chose to claim the *Mirour*, along with the *Vox Clamantis* and the *Confessio Amantis*, as one of the three great books supporting the head of his effigy on his tomb (albeit with the Latin title, *Speculum Meditantis*, on which more below), suggests that if there were disenchantment with the *Mirour* it was not Gower's but his audience's.

The notion that before 1380 the *Mirour* might have lost its intended audience, and so was not extensively recopied either for presentation or general reading, is interesting in light of the similar singularity of the *Cinkante Balades* and the distribution of the manuscripts containing the *Traitié* as well. Whether Gower was at work on the *Cinkante Balades* early, late, or sporadically throughout his career, the fact is that they also have come down to us in one manuscript, Trentham, as noted above. Unlike Camb. Univ. Add. 3035, the cause of whose production (and hence its intended readership) we cannot know, MS Trentham seems very much a book created with a particular reader, and possibly a particular occasion, in mind. The contents of MS Trentham help make clearer who and when this might have been. Along with the *Cinkante Balades*, Trentham includes "To King Henry IV, In Praise of Peace," in English; "Rex celi deus," also addressed to Henry, in Latin; two French balades with Latin verses in between (Macaulay calls this "the Dedication") addressing Henry; the *Traitié*; and two Latin compositions (fragmentary because of a lost leaf), one beginning "Ecce patet tensus," the other "Henrici Quarti."

Whenever they were actually written, then, the focused contents of MS Trentham make it look as if it were prepared as a gift for Henry IV. One of its earliest known owners, Sir Thomas Fairfax, noted as much in 1656 on the first blank leaf: "Sr. John Gower's learned Poems the same booke by himself presented to king Henry ye fourth before his Coronation." Whether Fairfax was correct in his claim about MS Trentham itself, or what grounds he had to make it, remains obscure. Fairfax seems not always to have been certain if Henry received the manuscript before or on the occasion of his coronation; and Macaulay has warned that the relative plainness and other features of MS Trentham suggest against its ever having been "the actual presentation copy." For, "if such a copy there were, [it] would probably have been more elaborately ornamented."[7] MS Trentham is, in Macaulay's view, a version "written about the same time and left in the hands of the author."

Nevertheless, if Henry's ownership of MS Trentham itself is unlikely, general agreement exists that the manuscript at least replicates one prepared for the king.[8] This assumption, if correct, suggests Gower's sense of Henry's taste, and so may provide us with political insight of several kinds. With the exception of "To King Henry IV, In Praise of Peace," everything in MS Trentham is Latin or French, with the latter the predominant language. The contents of MS Trentham thus underscore what appears to be a movement, certainly in the *reproduction* of Gower's work, away from English and toward French and Latin in the final years of his life. Possibly this trend in manuscript copies reflects a similar turn in Gower's new compositions as well. In any case, based on the work we have extant, apart from "To King Henry IV, In Praise of Peace," Gower wrote no English poetry after 1390, when it is thought he made his final revisions of the *Confessio Amantis*. His non-English output was significant, however: perhaps the *Traitié* (if we follow the traditional chronology, which places its composition ca. 1398, contemporaneous with his marriage), perhaps the *Cinkante*

Balades (if we assume he wrote them for inclusion in MS Trentham), and certainly the *Cronica Tripertita* and most of the shorter Latin verse.

Describing just the *prima facie* record, then, Gower's *oeuvre* could be said to divide into three periods: an early French period, concluded about 1378 and consisting at least of the *Mirour de l'Omme* and possibly some or all of the *Cinkante Balades*; a middle period, when Gower wrote Books II–VII of the *Vox Clamantis*, added Book I (the so-called "Visio" c. 1381), and cast the *Confessio Amantis* in its first form (i.e., what Macaulay calls Recension I), but produced nothing identifiable in French; and, beginning perhaps as early as 1391, a later, "mixed" but mostly non-English period, during which Gower is known to have completed only "In Praise of Peace" in English, along with two sets of revisions to the *Confessio*, while he either wrote or revived the *Cinkante Balades* and the *Traitié*, and composed most of the Latin poems, including the shorter pieces and the *Cronica Tripertita*, and revised Book VI of the *Vox Clamantis* to accommodate the last days of Richard II.

GOWER'S CAREER AND THE HUNDRED YEARS' WAR

Admittedly, to so "periodize" Gower is to write both rough and large across the record, when more nuanced strokes may offer the truer representation, at least of the history of Gower's writing. But if the manuscript record can merely suggest when Gower was composing, it does nonetheless reveal more certainly when his works were "taken public"—when, that is, they were given a form which could be read outside the authorial presence. And of course it is exactly at that point—the public point, when a literary work's influence on others can begin, and not when it still lies safe (and subject to suppression or emendation) in its author's storage chest—that that work becomes political.

Let us consider, then, the political climates extant during Gower's long life to determine what sort of context and reception his works might have received, were they put into circulation at those moments the manuscript record seems to suggest. The traditional date accepted for Gower's birth is 1330; it is known that he died in 1408.[9] Assuming the former to be true, Gower lived almost exactly through the rising and falling of three very different English kings: Edward III, who, although crowned in 1327, did not establish his independent authority until 1330 (coincidentally, perhaps, the year Gower was born); Richard II, who reigned from 1377 to 1399; and Henry IV, Richard's deposer, who survived Gower by only five years, dying in 1413.

Stretched against the framework of the Hundred Years' War, Gower's life spans as well the primary events of the conflict. He was seven when hostilities began in 1337, sixteen and twenty-six when the English won their great victories at Crécy and Poitiers in, respectively, 1346 and 1356, on the latter occasion bringing back to London as prisoners the bloom of French chivalry, including King John II. In 1360, when Edward III signed the Treaty of Brétigny, relinquishing his claims to the French throne and to Normandy in exchange for formal recognition of his right to Poitou, Ponthieu, Guines, the Aquitaine, and Calais, and a ransom for John of three million *écus*, Gower was very likely thirty.[10] This makes him about forty when hostilities resumed in 1369, and close to fifty by 1379 when it has been suggested he ceased working on the *Mirour de l'Omme*. By 1389, when Richard, newly recovered in authority from the challenge of the Appellants, accepted the three-year French truce which the barons had initiated, Gower was nearly sixty and had moved his residence into the Priory of St. Mary Overys in Southwark. He was about seventy the year Richard married Isabella of France and negotiated what was expected to be a twenty-eight-year truce; by 1402, with Henry on the throne for three years, Isabella safely back in France after Richard's fall, and hostilities starting up again across the channel, Gower very likely was seventy-two. In the year of his death, 1408, Gower would have been between seventy-five and eighty. He had seen no more seasons of peace between England and France.

Comparing the events of the war with Gower's literary career is speculative but intriguing. No records are known to exist from his early years to indicate his education (which must have been substantial) or to establish when he began to write poetry. John Fisher, back-filling from Gower's statement in the *Mirour* that he wore "a garment with striped sleeves" (line 21,773) [vestu la raye mance], sees Gower attending the Inns of Court in the 1350s and practicing in the court of Chancery at least until 1368, when he had "made enough money to buy Kentwell Manor" in Suffolk.[11] Thereafter Gower presumably lived off his revenues and dealt in real estate. Such efforts would have afforded him the requisite leisure to engage in the serious composition of poetry, a taste for which, it is thought, he had acquired during his student days.

According to this scenario, then, Gower started writing in the 1370s, apparently in Anglo-Norman, apparently (based on what remains) with the *Mirour de l'Omme*. But on thoughtful reconsideration, this hardly seems likely as the beginning of a literary career. Does a poet, albeit in his forties and possessed of a moralizing inclination, create as his first-ever poem the *Mirour de l'Omme*? Or does he work his way up to it, making (perhaps as a law student, perhaps in exchange with another young poet of his acquaintance) what Chaucer described in his Retraction as his own juvenalia, "many a song and many a leccherous lay"?[12] The latter explanation appears the more logically sound, even if in comparison to Chaucer's we mentally reverse the ratio of Gower's fledgling songs to his "leccherous lays." That we do not have any of these early works should not trouble us; Chaucer's are lost, too. The point is, however, that to assume that the *Mirour de l'Omme*, in the form we have it, is a first work is absurd. While it may contain the oldest datable *reference* in Gower's remaining *oeuvre*, nothing about the *Mirour* confirms it as its author's initial work. Gower must have written other, less ambitious pieces before embarking on the *Mirour*.

That said, another and more germane point may be made. All the references to the Great Schism in the *Mirour* confirm for us only that Gower worked on the poem after 1377. It is reasonable to conclude that Gower composed the references at a moment close to the events he condemns, but there is no proof of this. He may have gone back to the poem much later, adding the lines in response to an inspiration of which we have no knowledge. In fact, revisitation was his practice. In both the *Vox* and the *Confessio* we have evidence that Gower emended passages years after their composition, indicating that for him a poem was continually present and subject to revision.[13] And of course it is even less clear when Gower might have begun the *Mirour*. Before 1377, yes, but how much before?

DATING THE *MIROUR DE L'OMME*

The question has bearing on the central concern of these pages: the politics of an Englishman choosing to write in French during the Hundred Years' War. English-French relations vary greatly over the period from 1350 to 1378 when Gower is thought, respectively, to have been nurturing his poetic talent while a student at the Inns of Court and putting the finishing touches on the *Mirour de l'Omme*. During these years the crown also passed, in 1377, from Edward III to the ten-year-old Richard II. And worthy of record as well is another event of signal importance, notable perhaps particularly by a lawyer with business in the courts of London and the king: the enactment of the Statute of Pleading by Parliament in 1362. This document has sufficient importance for us that it is worth quoting at some length:

> Because it is often shewed to the king [that] ... great mischiefs ... have happened to divers of the realm, because the laws, customs, and statutes of this realm be ... pleaded, shewed, and judged in the French tongue, which is much unknown in the said realm; so that the people which do implead ... in the king's court, and in the courts of others, have no knowledge or understanding of that which is said for them or against them ... and that reasonably the said laws and customs shall be most quickly learned and known, and better understood in the tongue used in the said realm ... ; and in divers regions and countries, where the king, the nobles, and others of the said realm have been, good governance and full right is done to every person, because that their laws and customs be learned and used in the tongue of the country; the king, desiring the good governance and tranquility of his people ... hath ordained and established ... that all pleas which shall be pleaded in his courts ... shall be pleaded ... in the English tongue, and that they be entered and enrolled in Latin.[14]

Although the Statute of Pleading was not the first act directing that court records no longer be kept in French (it was preceded by an order of the mayor and aldermen of London in 1356 that all records of the sheriff's court of London and Middlesex be in English), it is significant that it applied to the king's courts and that it took effect in 1362, two years after the Treaty of Brétigny.[15] Implicit in its text are notions of 'realm' and 'people' which clearly associate the boundaries of spoken English with the reach of English power.

But it was precisely this power which was reconfigured at Brétigny. In relinquishing his claim to the crown of France, in exchange for a heavy ransom for John II and consolidating his individual—as opposed to national—control over Calais, Ponthieu, Poitou, Guines, and the Aquitaine, Edward effectively denationalized the war, albeit for only a handful of years. If John was by that act recognized as king of France, Edward was king of England with continental holdings. The difference undoubtedly was not lost on the Commons, who had begrudgingly anted-up the second-largest campaign appropriation of Edward's reign in 1359, only to see it cast away in an ill-advised race for Rheims in the harsh winter of 1359–1360, which left Edward with heavy casualties and no victory to show for them.[16]

Against such a backdrop, the issue of a national language as a political instrument acquires sharper definition. Although there is no parliamentary record linking the passage of the Statute of Pleading with the apparently permanent separation of France and England as sovereign states, the timing and language of the statute itself seem too coincidentally related to the

Treaty of Brétigny to be wholly independent developments. Between 1360, when Edward's crown became exclusively English, and 1369, when in response to Charles V's provocations he simultaneously renewed formal hostilities and his claim to the kingship of France, there could only have been a national inward refocusing, of which the Statute of Pleading is but an isolated evidentiary scrap.

That this shift in national focus was, however, both slow and inconsistent is indicated as well by the statute. Whether by force of habit or because it represented an initial step in a direction not altogether clear, the statute requiring that English be used in the courts of England was nonetheless entered into the parliamentary rolls in French. Parliament was opened, however, by the chancellor speaking in English in 1362.[17] But while this seems ironic from a modern perspective, the French of the statute merely echoes the linguistic reality of the times. As William Calin has most recently noted, "For three hundred years after the Conquest French was the language of the upper classes in England," and it retained both a propriety and a cultural prestige throughout Edward's reign.[18] Only in the Ricardian years does the vernacular assert itself in English letters—unhesitatingly in the work of Chaucer, Langland, the poet of *Pearl*, and in the English writings of Gower.[19]

Before turning to this period, however, let us bring together the disparate lines of argument we have been following concerning Gower's early French poetry and the war. We have suggested, first, that to assume Gower began his poetic enterprise in his late 40s with the *Mirour de l'Omme*, regardless of whatever new leisure his improved financial status may have afforded him, seems unreasonable at best. Much more plausible is the assumption that, like most poets then and now, he started writing as a young man, perhaps while a student. That his initial ideal for the well-made poem should have been in French is probable, given the cultural milieu of the court and nobility, and given Gower's demonstrated affinities with the landed classes (e.g., his purchasing of the manors of Kentwell and Aldington) and especially with the king.[20] Further, although there is internal evidence to indicate Gower worked on the *Mirour* as late as 1378, there is no proof at all to establish when he began it; indeed, given what better hints we have of Gower's work habits discoverable in the *Vox Clamantis* and the *Confessio Amantis*, both of which he revisited and reshaped over ten or fifteen years, it seems prudent to assume an earlier date for the beginning of the *Mirour* than is commonly assigned.

Were this *terminus a quo* postable as early as 1356–1360, following the great English victory at Poitiers and before Edward's renunciation of the

French crown at Brétigny, it would explain much. At that time Gower was between twenty-six and thirty years old, clearly mature enough to commence a major work like the *Mirour*. That he should have chosen then to compose his most ambitious project to date in French, when France and England seemed about to become one kingdom under a single crown, has a likelihood about it which is not diminished by the nature of the French itself: Anglo-Norman, the dialect of Edward and his Parliament, soon to be (as Gower and others must have believed) the speech of government and power in Paris and beyond. Even Gower's self-deprecations, that he knew little Latin or French ("Poy sai latin, poy sai romance," *MO* 21775) have to be qualified, not only as a transparent manipulation of the humility *topos*, but also as a political flourish. It is "romance" that he doesn't know—a term Gower extended beyond linguistic boundaries to encompass the world of Gallic ideation, the most of which he found morally suspect.[21] And in any case, *romance* must be Gower's word for a dialect other than the Anglo-Norman which he employs to voice his denial of any capacity to write in French. Conceivably, when he began using it to compose the *Mirour*, "homespun" Anglo-Norman could well have seemed to Gower, and to some of his countrymen before 1360, the conqueror's (that is, Edward's) particular French.

What may be true of Gower's "French period," then, is that it began and was shaped in significant ways in reaction to the course and politics of the Hundred Years' War. If Gower commenced the *Mirour* as early as 1356–1360, he undoubtedly did so with some expectation of a "greater England" encompassing France. Perhaps he slowed work on it after Brétigny, picking it up again in earnest after 1368, when Edward again styled himself king of France; perhaps he merely completed it as he could, bit by bit, until he acquired leisure along with financial independence in the late 1370s.

GOWER'S "MIDDLE" PERIOD

We have, of course, no sure way to confirm such speculation, and the facts may be altogether different. But at least these possibilities square well the career stages of most poets with what we know of Gower's own work habits and the major events of the times. It does seem likely, furthermore, that Gower put the *Mirour* aside not long after Edward III died in 1377 and at that time entered what I have called his "middle" period, when English and Latin, but not French, seem to have occupied his thoughts. There are no identifiable references to events datable later than 1378 in the *Mirour*, and Gower's descriptions of the Peasants' Revolt and his hortatory urgings of the young Richard to emulate the battlefield ferocity of his father the Black Prince occur in the Latin of the *Vox Clamantis*, not the *Mirour*'s French. These latter passages allude to the war, and we can benefit from looking at excerpts:

> It is also your concern, O king, to be your people's defender in arms. And in order to defend justice with valor, remember your father's deeds as a model for this. . . . France felt the effects of him; and Spain, in contemplating the powers with which he stoutly subjected her, was fearful of him. Throwing his foes into disorder, he hurled his troops into the midst of his enemies and broke up their course of march like a lion. . . . O king, remember your father's deeds, so that the praise which he earned may be bestowed upon you. Fortune favors the brave and brings to fulfillment what courage wishes, and furnishes it strength. Peace excels over every good, but when our tried and tested rights call for war, it should be waged.[22]

The open-ended, even hopeful, tone of advice here suggests that Gower wrote these lines while Richard was quite young, with intent to influence him. Since Gower evidently revised the *Vox Clamantis* at several points in his career, it is difficult to date passages with certainty. Elsewhere in Book VI, Gower also described Richard as an "undisciplined boy" who "neglects the moral behavior by which a man might grow up from a boy."[23] This sounds more like a description of a teen-ager who has frustrated his councillors by refusing good advice over time. Combined with other revisions to Book VI, rendered perhaps as late as 1393, these lines indicate a span of years between the first and final versions of the *Vox*, with the poet's changed assessment of Richard's rule intervening.[24]

Whenever Gower composed the passages above, however, they are clearly addressed to Richard. What is interesting and important for our present purposes is the shift in language chosen to address the sovereigns, from Anglo-Norman, which Gower apparently believed would accommodate Edward III, to Latin for Richard. For it is clear from all of its three titles (*Mirour de l'Omme, Speculum Hominis, Speculum Meditantis*, on which subject more below) that Gower conceived of his major French poem as in many ways a mirror for princes, toward which special hermeneutic purpose he would have thoughtfully selected the language to suit the reigning Edward. I think it quite likely that in the beginning he considered the Latin work *Vox Clamantis* a similar project, designed to influence Richard, a different king in different times. That the *Vox* ultimately was transformed into something else altogether by the addition of a new Book I (i.e., the "Visio" allegorically describing the Revolt of 1381 in progress) and revisions to Book VI by the time of its completion says much about the roiled political years prior to Richard's majority in 1388, but nothing at all about Gower's initial decision to write his next major poem after the *Mirour* in Latin rather than French, and to construct it around a detailed schooling of the young king. But why Latin, which Gower must have deemed more effective than French to advise the just-crowned Richard about the French war, as in the passage above, and other matters?

Before fully turning from Edward's reign and Gower's "French period" to Richard and his "middle," however, two further observations should be noted regarding the *Mirour*. The first can serve to summarize one line of argument presented thus far. I suggested earlier that perhaps we now possess but a solitary manuscript of the *Mirour de l'Omme* because Gower, feeling he had scant audience left for the poem, had few copies made. If that is correct, and Gower was influenced to select Anglo-Norman for his first major poem by expectations of an English victory (by an Anglo-Norman–speaking king) in the war against the French—expectations which sputtered in 1360 only to rekindle eight years later and linger in rudimentary form until Edward's death—then the dearth of *Mirour* manuscripts is no longer mysterious. Although at least one other copy of the *Mirour* must have existed, as exemplar for MS Camb. Univ. Add. 3035, the poem simply did not circulate, either because Gower kept it by him or because any readership familiar with the poem and able to commission copies independently felt with its author that the *Mirour* was a work whose affective moment—and whose effective tongue and idiom—had passed along with Edward III.

The second observation is that, lost audience or no, Gower obviously did not want the *Mirour de l'Omme* forgotten. Thus in his final years Gower returned to the *Mirour*, changing its name from French to the Latin *Speculum Hominis*, or, as it appears on his tomb on the spine of one of the three great tomes supporting his effigy's head, *Speculum Meditantis*. Gower clearly wished the statement of his tomb to convey that his life's achievement included three major poems, all with Latin titles. That Gower altered the language of his title in response to changing conditions after Henry's coronation, and so acted politically rather than aesthetically, I shall argue further on. Here it is important to note that the relative unfamiliarity of the *Mirour* could only have eased the process, and possibly Gower's mind, as he contemplated shifting his title from French to Latin to accommodate the language preferences of yet another audience in an England ruled by yet another king.

GOWER'S ADVICE TO RICHARD II

Beginning with the *Vox Clamantis*, then, Gower set out to advise a new, unfamiliar king who was, not incidentally, still a boy. When Richard succeeded Edward, the securest thing Gower probably knew about the new king was that he was underage. As May McKisack has noted, "Little is known of Richard of Bordeaux until he steps to the forefront of the political scene during the Peasants' Revolt. Born . . . in 1367, he had been brought to England at the age of four, shortly after the death of his elder brother Edward of Angouleme, and his early childhood was passed . . . in the care of his mother, the princess Joan, and of the *magistri* chosen for him by his father."[25] From his own wide reading of didactic literatures, Gower would have known and expected that the accepted tutelage of a prince included equivalent exposures to "noriture and letture"—roughly, manners and letters—and so Gower would have taken into account those *magistri*, whose opinions and values the boy would hear most authoritatively, according to the Black Prince's plan.[26]

Perhaps Gower had some acquaintance, at least by reputation, with Richard's guardians, Guichard d'Angle, Richard Abberbury, and Simon Burley. All were prominent, Guichard d'Angle most as a model of the old knightly class (such would have been his "noriture" value to Richard), and Burley in broader ways. Companion to the Black Prince in France and at the battle of Najera, Burley became Richard's acting chamberlain with full control over the knights of the chamber. A splendid dresser, liberal in his gifts, Burley seems altogether likely to have drawn public attention.[27]

What might have interested Gower most was Burley's "taste for books" (McKisack's phrase); an inventory of the goods from his two London houses lists nineteen volumes, mostly in French, but ranging in content from romances to the *Brut* to a traveller's dictionary in several languages to philosophy to Henri de Gauchi's translation of the *De Regimine Principum* of Egidio Colonna.[28] Taken together, Burley's is not a large library (though we cannot say how complete the inventory might be), but it is enough to indicate that here was an inquiring mind and a man whom contemporaries might assume figured in Richard's life not only as a noble exemplar but as a learned one also. Indeed, Burley might well have been the most bookish of the Black Prince's acquaintances who also possessed impeccable credentials on the battlefields of France and Spain. On the face of it, in Guichard, Abberbury, and Burley it would appear that Richard's father had found tutors to provide "noriture and letture" for his royal son.

To such a prince, apparently so well schooled according to current wisdom, a Latin poem of advice of the kind contained in the first version of Books II–VII of the *Vox Clamantis* is an altogether appropriate gift from a poet and loyal subject who sought to start a project with little assurance of his recipient's preferences or capacities. There are hints, however slight, that Gower got it right. What we can surmise of Richard's Latin tends to corroborate a poetic gamble of Gower's kind. Only four titles survive from Richard's own library, but among these books is a *Libellus Geomancie* bound together (as MS Bodley 581) with a *Philosophia Visionis* and a *Rosarium*. The book is the more interesting because Richard seems to have commissioned it himself in 1391.[29] The Latin is technical and by no means easy. Had not Richard felt at home with it, however, he assuredly could have got the text translated into English or French. That he asked for, seemingly, and received it in Latin may be an important clue to the breadth of Richard's linguistic capacities.

Yet, whatever these capacities might have been at full extension, it is clear from the larger record that learning was not in fact Richard II's special interest. Gower may have believed so through 1381, although shortly thereafter his vision of Richard abruptly changed, and along with it his plan for the *Vox Clamantis*. At Mile End and at Smithfield the fourteen-year-old king exhibited surprising qualities of courage and resourcefulness in handling the Peasants' Revolt.[30] For Richard and those who watched him, the events of Mile End and Smithfield were defining, albeit briefly. The rebellion was a determining moment for Gower as well, for it is this rupture in the social order which apparently transformed the *Vox Clamantis* from the *speculum principis* it might have become into a condemnation of a society which, having glimpsed what lay beyond the brink, seemed to Gower to lack the strength of leadership and moral character necessary to avoid chaos.

Concomitantly, the revolt also marks a change in Gower's attitudes toward the French war. In the work Gower produced prior to 1381, the *Mirour* and early portions of the *Vox*, references to fighting in France follow the line generally adopted by Edward and the barons, that is, that overseas conquest was both noble and an appropriate use of English resources. After 1381, however, Gower's concerns are increasingly to heal what, in the *Confessio Amantis*, he terms "divisioun" in England and abroad. In the process he trades his belligerent patriotism for an international pacifism and a search for harmonious resolution of the disorder he found so frightening at home.[31] Looking ahead historically, we can see that this position generally parallels, for a variety of reasons, the war policies of Richard and Henry IV.

That Gower's attention should have turned inward, away from the continent, is hardly surprising. The years between 1381 and 1389, when Richard asserted his majority and royal independence from his *magistri* and baronial interests generally, were dominated in England by struggles for political hegemony of increasing bitterness. In these the Commons, wielding the fiscal authority of Parliament, played a significant role, as did the court parties loyal to various magnates (e.g., the Lancastrians, headed by Gaunt; the Mowbrays; the Percys; the factions of Mortimer and Arundel) and the small group of favorites (especially Michael de la Pole and Robert de Vere) close to the king. The demands of the French conflict were continual during these years and fighting took place on the seas, in Flanders (the ill-advised raid on Ypres by Henry Despenser), in Scotland, and in Castile (the latter campaigns waged to deter threatened French-Scottish and French-Castilian invasions which never came).

The full significance of this activity is multileveled, some self-evident and some not. The pursuit of "national interests" abroad was, like the tip of the iceberg, driven by subsurficial forces, larger and altogether personal, whose aim was to consolidate and advance positions of the several important constituencies. Inevitably at the center were the tax monies Parliament could levy to support programs against the French espoused by the factions: the so-called "way of Flanders" (under which banner Despenser crossed the Channel), the "way of Portugal" (Gaunt's attack on Castile), and even the invasion of Scotland led by Richard himself in 1385. Because of this the Commons themselves emerged as yet another special interest, equally factionalized and similarly self-protective in their attempts to avoid assuming the full financial burden of the magnates' adventurism while themselves seeking opportunities for profit and trade.[32]

The results of so much maneuvering between 1381 and 1388, ostensibly over foreign affairs but in the end about English money and domestic power, were two. First came inevitable implosion; the ascendancy of the Appellants and the Merciless Parliament of 1388 revealed clearly and prophetically how insular politics had been and would be, under both Richard and Henry IV. The second was the transformation of Richard of Bordeaux (as he was known as a boy) into an Englishman whose focus was perforce upon his own countrymen and country. Perforce in part because, after the brief, terrible reign of the Appellants, Richard had little choice but to look to his nearest and dearest to renew his power base, lest he be swept away; but also because, for all that has been written about his supranational idealization of kingship, the Richard who emerges from the chroniclers reveals infrequently but consistently a domesticity of concern and a lack of interest in overseas conflict not shared by any of his Plantagenet elders.

Consider the following: that it is Richard's unmediated engagement with the peasants in 1381, encounters that could only have transpired in the vernacular exchange, which serves as his seminal act of individuation; that his unusual solution, albeit for sound reasons, to the marrow-deep antipathy of the magnates was to retreat from Windsor far into his own country, to the provinces, notably Cheshire and the west; that the companions with whom he apparently felt comfortable (apart from such as de Vere) were his archer bodyguards who felt free to banter in Cheshire dialect with him, addressing him as "Dycum"; that his mature interest in the French war is confined to establishing peace and national extrication; and that, in another turn away from France, as he established the character of his court Richard extended his patronage increasingly to local artists and subjects of particularly English importance.[33] Into this latter category are to be included works as diverse in direction and medium as, on the one hand, the Wilton Diptych, and on the other the vernacularization of poetry preferred at court, a body of writings as inclusive as Chaucer's work; *Pearl*, which John Bowers has argued persuasively was composed by a West Country poet familiar with Richard's interests[34]; and John Gower's *Confessio Amantis*, the earliest version of which claims as its *raison d'etre* a direct commission from Richard.

None of this activity, apart significantly from his efforts to sign a peace, indicates a focus on France or on the war. Clearly, Richard II's interests were at home, in England. Such, then, is the proper context to examine Gower's report of the "commission" he received from Richard, presumably in English, for political content as well as charm. These lines describing the "commission" are worth pausing to consider briefly. Out on the Thames rowing in a small boat, Gower says he encountered the royal barge and was asked onto it by the king who, after some talk, further requested of the poet "som newe thing" for Richard himself to read (*CA* 24–78★). This charge, despite his infirmity, Gower accepted, and (assuming the meeting ever took place as described) he seemingly finished the poem anticipating Richard's readership. He concludes it, in any case, with a prayer for the king, 144 lines of encomia, and fictively incorporates the presentation of his poem to Richard, a loyal retainer completing his master's task.

It is, of course, the particular carrying out of that task which interests us. On its face, the *Confessio Amantis* scarcely resembles any known earlier work of Gower's, except perhaps in the scale of its design. By claiming, as he does in the Prologue, that he will write a poem containing "wisdom to the wise / And pley to hem that lust to pley" (*CA* 84–85★) Gower proffers a criterion—"pley"—for his new poem which has been present only in the most abstract of senses in either the *Mirour* or the *Vox*. Moreover, the *Confessio*, despite its Latin title, Latin prose glosses, and headnotes in Latin verse, is overwhelmingly a poem in English, a language in which Gower had shown no interest as far as we know until this moment. Why now, one has to ask? The true reason is necessarily irrecoverable, but it must be admitted, no matter how the question is shaped, that by the later 1380s English had become an option for poetry as serious as French or Latin for Gower, in whose mind apparently it had never been before.

We have to infer that it had so become for Richard as well. Did the meeting Gower describes in the Prologue occur on the Thames, and did King Richard specify his wishes about subject matter and about the vernacular? Perhaps, but in any case it seems unlikely Gower would have included Richard so prominently at both ends of so major a poem if he had not expected the king's approval of both its content and its languages, should the *Confessio* come into royal hands, authorially presented or no. (It is worth noting here that, if we are correct about Richard's Latin skills and his growing commitment to English, the presence of both in the *Confessio* suggests a heretofore unnoticed gesture of Gower's to please and flatter the king.)

This expectation becomes more evident the more closely we compare the probable calendar of Gower's writing with Richard's activities. This "English moment" in Gower's literary career, which the *Confessio Amantis* represents, correlates fully, in both rumor and actuality, with Richard's distancing himself from the French war and his plunge into Englishness. To finish the first, or "Ricardian," version of the *Confessio* by 1390, Gower had to have been at work on it for some time, possibly as early as Richard's progress through the Midlands and Wales, which occupied ten months of 1387 and culminated in his return to London, where the overwhelming warmth of his greeting by his English subjects must have seemed real enough and a vindication of his strategy of domesticity and separation from the barons and "their" war in France.[35] But Richard's triumph was short-lived, and again the war was at the center of the about-face. Indeed, it has been suggested that it was the rumor that Richard was on the verge of peace terms with the French which finally precipitated the action of the Appellants at the end of the year, and in the charges of misleading the king laid against Burley, Beauchamp, Berners, and especially Salisbury, as the presumed instigator of the peace with France, Richard's turning away from the war figured prominently. In Salisbury's case, it meant the difference between the "favor" of beheading accorded the others and a traitor's rope, as a betrayer of his country in his dealings with the French enemy.[36]

Where did this turn of events leave Gower, hard at work on the *Confessio*, written in English professedly to satisfy his king? Much depends on the nature of Gower's political loyalties between 1387 and 1389. These have proven—not accidentally, perhaps—difficult to pin down, and have stirred a variety of speculations.[37] What seems to be the case is that Gower adopted a modified version of the Appellants' official position regarding Richard, that is, that the king was victim to (unnamed) worthless advisors, which could include de Vere and the others for those inclined to think so, but also, as Judith Ferster has recently argued, would not rule out the Appellants themselves, were one of another mind.[38] As substitute for his failed counselors, Richard is urged by Gower in the *Confessio* to listen to the *vox populi*, personified not by the peasantry but by the gentry, whose support Richard so critically failed to muster in 1399.[39] This is, of course, the class whose needs the Statute of Pleading was designed to accommodate. There is some evidence that these incipiently middle-class property owners and merchants may have formed part of Gower's early readership, perhaps even constituting a new intended audience as his views changed and Richard faltered.[40] If so, such readers could be counted on to seek out books in English rather than in French or (exclusively) Latin, like the *Vox Clamantis*, and their opposition to the war in France was strong. Thus, whether or not Gower began the *Confessio Amantis* with a royal commission and Richard II as his expected first reader, he would seem to have brought the first version of his poem to a close with powerful political directives influencing his choice of English as his language of composition. French, at the time and for this audience, certainly was not in order; nor perhaps was Latin, if circumstances by 1390 had drawn what Gower calls "the people" near the center of his targeted readership.

GOWER'S THIRD PERIOD

Sometime between 1390 and 1393 Gower's opinion of Richard II clearly altered further. For this transition there are two bodies of evidence, one derived primarily from the historical record and the other based upon revisions Gower made of his existing work. In turning to examine them, we leave behind what might be termed Gower's "middle period" of Latin and most important English composition and enter his third, or "mixed" period, in which French reappears and English figures but scantly.

Again, the pattern of these linguistic shifts resembles the character of England's kings and their attitudes toward the war in France. In certain ways it would seem that Richard's behavior between 1390 and 1393 was such that Gower must have felt supportive.[41] The king appeared to have turned over a new leaf in 1389, promising to follow conciliar advice and to seek the opinions of the Commons.[42] Both were stances Gower had urged in the *Confessio*. However, as George B. Stow has recently demonstrated, in an attempt to pinpoint Gower's change of allegiance, Richard's concessions may have been well intentioned, but they were rendered empty almost immediately by his actions.[43] These included reappointment of ousted key supporters, enlarging the royal affinity by a substantial number of knights retained for life, and, most importantly, in Stow's view, Richard's flagrant violation of the Ordinance of 1390.[44] With the Ordinance, Commons sought to curtail the lawlessness of baronial retainers who claimed immunity from prosecution because of their livery. The conditions under which such livery could be granted by anyone, including the king, were restricted. At the 1390 Smithfield Tournament, Richard openly distributed his White Hart livery to a variety of new life-retainers, as if to demonstrate royal superiority to the Ordinance. Stow argues that this arrogance awakened the country, and Gower as well, to Richard's autocratic intentions, many of which, by 1393, were rapidly being implemented. Thus Stow finds "the year 1390–91 ... the most likely year for Gower's alienation from Richard II."[45]

If so, Gower put his new opinion directly into his work, revising both the *Vox Clamantis* and the *Confessio Amantis* by 1393. The changes Gower made to the *Vox* occur in Book VI, lines 545–80 and 1159–1200. The original of the first passage defends the youthful king against charges of decay in the realm, placing the blame on bad advice from corrupt advisors, as we have seen above; in the original second passage, Gower offers a hymn of praise and a prayer that God guide the royal boy Richard in needful times. The revised passages are dramatically different. In the new version of the first, Gower maintains his criticism of the advisors, but nonetheless holds Richard chiefly accountable for the country's malaise. The second passage he rewrites to demand that the king reform his rule and himself, to bring both them and the nation into accord with justice and the law.[46]

At the same time, apparently, Gower was remaking the *Confessio Amantis* in ways reflecting similar disenchantment with Richard. Manuscripts of the poem produced after 1390 show changes to Books V, VI, and VII which, depending upon how one reads the added narrative material, may or may not have been intentionally political. Altogether striking, however, is the removal of references to Richard. The Prologue is entirely rewritten so that, instead of taking his direction from the king on his barge in the Thames, Gower now claims inspiration by the state of the nation itself (for which reason, he says, he composes in English); the praise offered Richard in Book VIII is deleted; and the dedication of the project to Richard, implicit in the royal charge, is canceled by the addition of a new, formal dedication to Henry of Lancaster, then Earl of Derby.[47] Gower's third, "mixed" period had begun.

Gower's early allegiance to Henry, seven years before Richard's deposition, has provoked the full range of scholarly description, from sycophancy to clairvoyance.[48] Very likely Gower (who seems to have had a relationship with the Lancasters both long and close) was motivated a little by each, if not by significant luck, in his call. But what matters here are the unencumbered facts themselves that by 1393 Gower had altered his two best-known major works, either to criticize or exclude Richard and (in the case of the *Confessio*) to focus attention on Henry of Lancaster. For present purposes, Gower's new allegiance requires a comparable refocusing, as it would seem that along with his rejection of Richard came not a rejection of English as a poetic medium, certainly, but nonetheless a re-evaluation of it in relation to French and Latin as media for reaching the king and for commenting on political events, including the then-suspended hostilities with France.

GOWER AND HENRY IV

It is Gower's "mixed" period which produces many of the broad lineaments of my case, as sketched above: the attachment of the *Traitié pour essampler les amantz marietz* only to manuscripts of the *Vox Clamantis* in its post-1393 form, to manuscripts of the *Cronica Tripertita* (ca. 1400, Gower's most powerful rebuke of Richard), and to versions of the *Confessio Amantis* dedicated to Henry; the inclusion of the single known copy of the *Cinkante Balades* in the Trentham MS, along with "To King Henry IV, In Praise of Peace" and a variety of shorter poems in Latin, most directly addressing Henry; the apparent preponderance of new work composed in French (*Traitié*, perhaps the *Cinkante Balades*) and in Latin (the *Cronica*, the shorter poems) over English ("In Praise of Peace" alone seems to have been original to the period); and finally the reclamation of the *Mirour de l'Omme* (albeit with a Latin title) to appear on Gower's tomb, as anchor to his posthumous self-presentation.

Examined closely and in context, this body of work is revealing, beginning with Gower's relationship to Henry IV, which differs significantly from, even as in many ways it resembles, Gower's relationship to Edward III and Richard. Again we see the poet in familiar stance, writing as king's counselor, composing mirrors of advice, including "Rex Celi Deus," "In Praise of Peace," and other Latin pieces. Nevertheless, if these are *specula*, they are strikingly shorter than his earlier efforts aimed at Henry's predecessors. The difference may, of course, indicate a flagging of Gower's energies, aged and blind as he says he was by 1400, but other factors are worth our notice as well.

There is, for one, the unavoidable fact that Gower was closer to Henry and knew him better than he did Henry's predecessors. Charmed moment on the Thames aside, Gower's access to Richard or Edward can only have been extremely indirect, if it existed at all. Whatever Gower's original intentions were for the *Mirour*, for example, that Edward ever saw it seems unlikely, and the same should be said for Richard's reading of the *Vox*, and perhaps even the *Confessio*. With Henry, however, Gower went back some distance. His connections with the Lancastrian house are currently under examination in a variety of quarters, but even the little which has turned up so far is suggestive of a relationship with Gaunt and his family which would have brought Gower into Henry's presence early, and which, parenthetically, helps make sense of Gower's "clairvoyant" support of Henry as the man to right England in 1393, when the latter was still Earl of Derby.[49] And there are the various tangible instances of Henry's connection and favor: the collar of "S" pattern, present on the tomb effigy and shown in the portrait in MS Fairfax, Henry awarded Gower in 1393; the annual gift of two pipes of Gascon wine Henry established for Gower in 1399.[50] The advantage this foreknowledge gave Gower as advisor to the new king was simple but essential. Probably it is behind the different poetry Gower selected for Henry. To be taken seriously by Henry, Gower did not have to establish his credentials in a poem of epic length, but could cut to the chase, presenting his arguments point-by-point in shorter form.

Moreover, knowing him better undoubtedly guided Gower in all those formal choices concerning work designed for Henry's reading. Again it is relevant to consider what little record history has left us of Henry's preferences and character in order to "read" Gower's product in relation to the war. A man of action, named in the chronicles as a paragon of chivalric virtue frequently tested in the lists and on crusade, Henry was also commended for his piety and chastity (he apparently remained celibate for three years, from the death of his wife Mary Bohun in 1394 until he remarried Joan of Navarre in 1397, no small feat, as the chroniclers noted, given the temptations for a man in his position). Henry was something of a scholar and a reader, as well.[51] Gower himself alludes to this in "In Praise of Peace" when he remarks: "Thus tellen thei whiche olde bookes conne, / Wherof, my lord, y wot wel thow art lerned" (24–25). The allusion could be idle flattery, of course, but corroborative scraps appear in the record: letters exist, in French, Latin, and English from Henry's own hand, composed in a clear, direct style; there are reports of Henry's close attendance to lectures at the University of Paris, and of a visit to Bardney Abbey, where he took stock of the library and read there quietly for a time; and, if it is true that the father's example is visible in the children, it is significant that all three of Henry's son, Henry V, John, and Humphrey, were well educated by design, exhibiting (Humphrey especially) a love of learning throughout their lives.

Such a man as Henry helps to explain, perhaps, the shape of Gower's work in his latter years. The comparative brevity and tone of the pieces may reflect Gower's understanding of Henry's tastes as a man proud and respectful of education but direct of manner and lacking time or inclination for rhetorical roundabout. The appearance of the two balade sequences in French—the *Cinkante Balades*, in a manuscript possibly prepared as a gift for Henry, and especially the attachment of the *Traitié por essampler les amantz marietz*, with its rejection of all love affairs save those leading to marriage, to the manuscripts of the *Confessio Amantis* produced after Henry's accession—seem likely enough to have been geared toward Henry's pleasure. There is some suggestion that Henry valued French poetry of a polished but thoughtful kind; he is reported, for example, to have attempted to bring Christine de Pizan to England.[52] In a realm governed by this Henry, the writing of French balades of Gower's moral sort, and even the recuperation of the *Mirour de l'Omme*, seem increasingly of a piece and sensible. So also the Latin, which Gower could direct not only to Henry but also to his learned (and religiously conservative) lord chancellor Thomas Arundel, recipient apparently of MS All Souls Col., Oxf. 98, an all-Latin collection including the virulently anti-Ricardian *Cronica Tripertita*.[53] Henry, as well as the Archbishop, potentially had the skills and perhaps the inclination to read it.

And what of the English poetry? Why did Gower opt to use his native vernacular less under Henry than Richard, apparently producing only "In Praise of Peace" for Henry's eyes primarily? The answer lies, I think, in the problematic status English writing and English books held in the period precisely between Henry's accession and Gower's death, brought about by English literacy as a sign of Lollardy and the vicious suppression of the sect by Arundel, especially, and Henry as well. Perhaps at this moment Gower had second thoughts about the readership of English merchants the *Confessio* seems to have interested. In essence, Gower may have felt vulnerable that sections of the *Confessio*, if not the entire poem, being in English, could be misconstrued in a witch hunt and so backed away from English poetry except for the single piece safely addressed to Henry. In such a climate, Latin was safer, a sign very clearly, even (or perhaps especially) to those who could not decipher it, of its author's conventional allegiance and scholastic theologies.

But such an argument is too extensive to include here; doing that would take us far from Gower's poetic and political responses to the French war after 1399.[54] As important as Henry's trilingual proclivities were and as familiar with them and with the man as Gower likely was, the most significant factor influencing English-French relations during Gower's last years (and so the languages of Gower's poetry) was the question of Henry's right to the English throne and so to any claims in France. Any active French policy depended on settling this issue, first in Henry's mind and then publicly. The situation was delicate, for despite his blood-claims to both crowns (variously through both paternal and maternal lines, though difficulties existed with each), as a usurper Henry should not rule England, much less France.[55] This problem was not lost on the French, who never officially acknowledged Henry's government, sent aid to Henry's enemies in Wales between 1404 and 1406, and raided the English coast.[56] That the French were unable to capitalize further on England's weakness during Henry's struggle to establish control of the country was, from the English perspective, the result of near-incredible luck: Charles VI's growing madness and inability to lead; swelling internecine friction between the factions of Orléans and Burgundy (which erupted into civil war in 1410); and until 1402, the presence in England of Richard II's widow, the French princess Isabella, whose safe return it has been suggested motivated Charles VI to confirm the truce signed by Richard with Henry's representatives in 1400.[57]

Put briefly, Henry's position with regard to the French war reflected the situation's complexity. He claimed kingship in France as well as England in 1399, but because of his clouded right by so doing he vitiated the blood connection that had been Edward's and Richard's strongest argument and demoted possession of France to one of several entitlements which came with England's crown.[58] Perhaps in consequence, the lack of assertion

Henry showed in regard to the greater issue of Franco-English rule is understandable. On the questions of Calais and Gascony, however, he acted forcefully if rather ineffectively, given the constraints of unrest at home and a bare treasury. Adopting the view that the Treaty of Brétigny remained in force, Henry's policy was that all the lands named therein were sovereign to the English crown. Hence he named his son Henry duke of Aquitaine in 1399, and opposed as thoroughly as he could all French incursions into Gascony. In 1410 and 1412, after Gower's death but significantly illustrating English attitudes, including Henry's, Parliament reaffirmed the crown's possession of the French territories delineated as English at Brétigny.[59]

Clearly circumstances in France were less Henry's concern during Gower's last years than the terrible unrest at home, even exacerbated as they were by French assistance in Scotland and especially to the Welsh rebels.[60] Hence, to a poet like Gower, looking to advise his king on important issues, Henry's lack of an established French policy would have been obvious though ultimately diminished by distance. Far more pressing for both king and subject were the problems at home. Consider the events of 1400–1401: the Epiphany Rising and the execution of its leaders, several of whose heads were mounted on London Bridge; risings in Devonshire and Chester; the news of Richard's death; Henry's two invasions of Scotland; Glendower's revolt in Wales; the burning of William Sawtre for heresy, the first such death in England, but not the last; under compulsion by Parliament, the sacking of Henry's chancellor and three other close advisors; tax riots around the country, at Dartmouth, Bristol, and Norton St. Philip; the price of wheat driven up beyond most commoners' reach. Truly, such times as these achieved an Orwellian darkness.

In these circumstances, Gower composed "In Praise of Peace" which, Frank Grady has recently argued, was intended at once to create a "legitimating discourse" for Henry's rule by incorporating "the language of the 'Record and Process,' the 'official' Lancastrian account of the usurpation" and more subtly to "expose both the difficulties inherent in imagining a pacific Lancastrian monarchy and the problem at the heart of [Gower's] own historical method."[61]

The Gower Grady offers us is thus helpful in bringing the present argument to a close by reminding us once more of the poet in his historical moment. At the end of Gower's life the times were parlous for everyone, especially perhaps for moralists like Gower who saw himself dutybound to speak out with advice to king and nation. Grady finds an ironic self-awareness in "In Praise of Peace" which, if it is there in fact, may result from Gower's closer acquaintance with Henry IV than with Edward or Richard, and so may reflect an irony which Henry could share. At the very least, such a reading of Gower's last English poem provides an attitude to view the entirety of his carefully managed linguistic enterprise, particularly as it applies to his handling of French in the changing context of three monarchs' involvements with the war in France. For by the end of his life Gower, like Henry IV, could not have seen the fighting overseas as productive, neither of great threat nor great profit. Risk, to be sure, existed for Henry across the channel, but it was significantly less by comparison than the dangers to life and limb at home.

True to pattern, Gower's resuscitation of French with Henry's accession follows the broad curve of the war in France, and in the case of the poems of his closing years, his perception of Henry's mixed attitude towards France. Showing himself to be the master of his last sovereign's three languages, while committing himself to none except, perhaps, to Latin as the most enduring idiom in which to speak out, even should events at home close in upon him dangerously, Gower demonstrates an Orwellian tenacity, as well as a certain historical detachment—one might call it irony—born undoubtedly of his years in the business of jeremiad, choosing and speaking in the appropriate tongue. When French poetry issues again from Gower's quill, it appears balanced by profoundly partisan Latin composition and a single significant and specifically directed English poem. Old, sick, and blind, as he portrays himself in his last years, Gower was concerned in part to hedge his linguistic bets but not to remain quiet despite the dangers and his handicaps.

In a sense, the political realities of language in the England Gower knew—a nation shaped by an ever-changing foreign war and, at the time of his death, domestic religious and political struggle turned increasingly violent—are present to be read between the figures on his tomb. Undoubtedly Gower designed his effigy with one eye firmly on his place in history and another on the murky present. There we see the poet in repose, his head at rest upon his three great books, one French, one English, and one Latin, proof positive that, despite the dangers, he had spoken out profoundly for the moment and for all time. But all the titles are in Latin, the most learned, the most lasting, and perhaps the safest tongue of all.

NOTES

1. George Orwell, "Politics and the English Language," in *Shooting an Elephant and Other Essays* (New York: Harcourt, 1945), 67.

2. On the question of the *Mirour's* lost leaves, see G. C. Macaulay, ed., *The Complete Works of John Gower*, 4 vols. (Oxford: Clarendon, 1899–1902), 1:lxix. All quotations from Gower's poetry are from this edition and documented parenthetically in the text by book and/or line number. Macaulay's volume 1 includes the French works; 2 and 3, the English; and 4, the Latin.

3. See, most recently, Thomas H. Bestul, "Gower's *Mirror de l'Omme* and the Meditative Tradition," *Mediaevalia* 16 (1993, for 1990): 307–28.

4. See, for example, John H. Fisher, *John Gower: Moral Philosopher and Friend of Chaucer* (New York: New York University Press, 1964), 99; and John S. P. Tatlock, *The Development and Chronology of Chaucer's Works*, Chaucer Society, 2nd ser., vol. 37 (1907; reprint. Gloucester, Mass.: Peter Smith, 1963), Appendix A.

5. On Gower's marriage, see Fisher, *John Gower*, 57–58.

6. Fisher, *John Gower*, 303–7, remains the most inclusive study of the Gower manuscripts.

7. Macaulay, *Works*, 1:lxxxi.

8. See Macaulay, *Works*, 1:lxxxi; Fisher, *John Gower*, 71–72, concurs that "the nature and purpose of its contents are clear."

9. Gower's will was recorded August 15, 1408, and proved on October 24 of the same year; see Macaulay, *Works*, 4:xvii. While no evidence exists firmly establishing Gower's date of birth, circumstances point to 1330; see the discussion of Fisher, *John Gower*, 41–69, esp. 46.

10. On the terms of the Treaty of Brétigny, see May McKisack, *The Fourteenth Century, 1307–1399*, Oxford History of England 5 (Oxford: Clarendon Press, 1959), 140–41.

11. Fisher, *John Gower*, 46, 54–56.

12. *The Canterbury Tales*, X:1087, in *The Riverside Chaucer*, ed. Larry D. Benson, 3rd. ed. (Boston: Houghton Mifflin, 1987), 328.

13. See Macaulay, *Works*, 2:xxi–xxviii.

14. *Statutes of the Realm*, 1:375–76, trans. Albert C. Baugh, in *A History of the English Language*, ed. A. C. Baugh and Thomas Cable, 3rd ed. (Englewood Cliffs, N.J.: Prentice-Hall, 1978), 148–49. The original statute is in French.

15. *Calendar of Letter-Books . . . of the City of London*, ed. R. R. Sharpe, Letter-Book G (London, 1905), 73.

16. On the events of 1359–1360 and the Commons' appropriations, see Anne Curry, *The Hundred Years War* (New York: Macmillan, 1993), 65–67.

17. English was also used to open Parliament in the following year; see *Rotuli parliamentorum*, vol. 2 (1363) (n.p., n.d.), 268, 275.

18. William Calin, *The French Tradition and the Literature of Medieval England* (Toronto: University of Toronto Press, 1994), ix.

19. Another kind of evidence is offered by acts of towns and guilds, which begin to appear infrequently in English after 1362. By 1388, however, when Parliament required foundation reports from all guild organizations, most complied in Latin, but more (49) were in English than in French. See *English Gilds*, ed. Toulmin Smith et al., Early English Text Society, o.s. 40 (1870; reprint. London: Oxford University Press for the Early English Text Society, 1963).

20. See Fisher, *John Gower*, 51–58, and 97.

21. I have discussed this issue in some length in the second chapter of my *John Gower's Poetic: The Search for a New Arion* (Woodbridge, Suffolk: D. S. Brewer, 1990), esp. 67 ff.

22. *Vox Clamantis*, Book VI, chapter 13; the English translation is that of Eric W. Stockton, *The Major Latin Works of John Gower* (Seattle, Wash.: University of Washington Press, 1962), 242.

23. *Vox Clamantis*, Book VI, chapter 7; Stockton, *Major Latin Works*, 232.

24. See Stockton, *Major Latin Works*, 232 ff., for versions of Gower on Richard.

25. McKisack, *Fourteenth Century*, 424.

26. See Richard Firth Green's discussion of the royal education, with special reference to Richard II's, in *Poets and Princepleasers: Literature and the English Court in the Late Middle Ages* (Toronto: University of Toronto Press, 1980), 74–78.

27. On Guichard, Abberbury, and Burley, see *Dictionary of National Biography*.

28. See McKisack, *Fourteenth Century*, 424. On Burley's books, see Maude Violet Clarke, *Fourteenth Century Studies*, ed. L. S. Sutherland and May McKisack (Oxford: Clarendon Press, 1937), 120–21.

29. On this book and Richard's commission of it, see Gervase Mathew, *The Court of Richard II* (New York: Norton, 1968), 40–41.

30. On Richard's behavior see Anthony Tuck, *Richard II and the English Nobility* (New York: St. Martin's, 1974), 51 ff.

31. I have argued the case for Gower's pacifism in "*Pax poetica*: On the Pacifism of Chaucer and Gower," *Studies in the Age of Chaucer* 9 (1987): 97–121.

32. See Anthony Steel, *Richard II* (Cambridge: Cambridge University Press, 1962) 108 ff.

33. On Richard's Cheshire nickname, see Clarke, *Fourteenth Century Studies*, 98 (citing the Kenilworth chronicler—BL Add. 35295, fol. 260r-v); on Richard's patronage to English artists, see John M. Bowers, "*Pearl* in Its Royal Setting: Ricardian Poetry Revisited," *Studies in the Age of Chaucer* 17 (1995): 111–55.

34. Bowers, "Pearl in Its Royal Setting," passim.

35. See McKisack, *Fourteenth Century*, 447 ff.

36. McKisack, *Fourteenth Century*, 458–59.

37. See for example Mathew, *Court of Richard II*, 81; Stockton, *Major Latin Works*, 19; Fisher, *John Gower*, 133, 178; and most recently, Judith Ferster, *Fictions of Advice: The Literature and Politics of Counsel in Late Medieval England*, Middle Ages Series (Philadelphia: University of Pennsylvania Press, 1996), 108–36.

38. Ferster, *Fictions of Advice*, 126.

39. Ferster's argument is very persuasive here; see *Fictions of Advice*, 126–32.

40. See Fisher, *John Gower*, 117; A. I. Doyle, "English Books in and out of Court from Edward III to Henry VII," in *English Court Culture in the Later Middle Ages*, ed. V. J. Scattergood and J. W. Sherborne (New York: St. Martin's, 1983), 162–81; and A. I. Doyle and M. B. Parkes, "The Production of Copies of the *Canterbury Tales* and the *Confessio Amantis* in the Early Fifteenth Century," in *Medieval Scribes, Manuscripts & Libraries: Essays Presented to N. R. Ker*, ed. M. B. Parkes and Andrew G. Watson (London: Scolar, 1978), 163–210.

41. See for example Fisher, *John Gower*, 117–18.

42. On this whole matter of conciliar advice to Richard, see Tuck, *Richard II*, 139 ff.

43. See George B. Stow, "Richard II in John Gower's *Confessio Amantis*: Some Historical Perspectives," *Mediaevalia* 16 (1993, for 1990): 3–31.

44. On these points see Stow, "Richard II in John Gower's *Confessio Amantis*," 18–19; and Chris Given-Wilson, *The Royal Household and the King's Affinity: Service, Politics and Finance in England, 1360–1413* (New Haven: Yale University Press, 1986) 214–15, who argues the same case in greater detail.

45. Stow, "Richard II in John Gower's *Confessio Amantis*," 33.

46. Macaulay prints both versions of both passages; see *Works*, 1:245–47 and 264–67, respectively.

47. For a full account of the revisions, see Macaulay, *Works*, 2:cxxvii–clxx; see further Fisher, *John Gower*, 116–27, for historical analysis.

48. Fisher takes the harshest line in *John Gower*, 113; for "clairvoyant," see Russell Peck, ed., *Confessio Amantis*, Medieval Academy Reprints for Teaching 9 (1966; reprint. Toronto: University of Toronto Press, 1980), 495.

49. On Gower's extended relations to the Lancastrian house, see for example Paul Strohm, "Saving the Appearances: Chaucer's *Purse* and the Fabrication of the Lancastrian Claim," in *Chaucer's England: Literature in Historical Context*, ed. Barbara Hanawalt, Medieval Studies at Minnesota 4 (Minneapolis, Minn.: University of Minnesota Press, 1992), esp. 33–34; Sylvia Wright, "The Author Portraits in the Bedford Psalter-Hours: Gower, Chaucer and Hoccleve," *British Library Journal* 18 (1992): 190–201; and my own forthcoming "John Gower and the Iberian Connection: The Portuguese and Spanish Translations of the *Confessio Amantis*."

50. On both see Fisher, *John Gower*, 68.

51. On Henry's character, see James Hamilton Wylie, *History of England under Henry IV*, 4 vols. (London: Longmans, 1884–98), esp. 2:487, 3:325, 4:128–37, 160–61, 223–24; J. L. Kirby, *Henry IV of England* (London: Constable, 1970), 250–57.

52. See Wylie, *Henry IV*, 4:136–37.

53. For a description of MS All Souls Col., Oxf. 98, see Macaulay, *Works*, 4:lx–lxi.

54. Currently I am examining this issue in an essay tentatively titled "Lollardy and Language: John Gower's Later Poems."

55. For a summary of the problems of blood-claims, see Curry, *Hundred Years War*, 91–93.

56. On French raids on English coastal towns, see E. F. Jacob, *The Fifteenth Century*, Oxford History of England 6 (Oxford: Clarendon Press, 1961), 73.

57. On this point see S. S. Pistono, "Henry IV and Charles VI; the Confirmation of the Twenty-eight Year Truce," *Journal of Medieval History* 3 (1977): 357.

58. The situation has prompted Edouard Perroy to call the French crown "one of England's stage properties" at this time; see *The Hundred Years War*, trans. David C. Douglas (1951; reprint. New York: Capricorn, 1965), 213.

59. *Rotuli parliamentorum* vol. 3, 427, 656–57.

60. On French aid to Henry's enemies see Jacob, *The Fifteenth Century*, 54–58, 73–74.

61. Frank Grady, "The Lancastrian Gower and the Limits of Exemplarity," *Speculum* 70 (1995): 555 and 558; see also Paul Strohm, "Saving the Appearances," 21–40, which serves Grady as a starting point.

CHAPTER 7

THE UNCERTAINTY IN DEFINING FRANCE AS A NATION IN THE WORKS OF EUSTACHE DESCHAMPS

EARL JEFFREY RICHARDS

During the Hundred Years' War, medieval French writers took wide ranging and often contradictory positions on France and England. Deschamps's representation of England and France, in some forty works written between 1385 and 1405, shows these contradictions most clearly.[1] On the one hand, he relies on an ancient rhetorical tradition of national epithets[2] in which national differences were transitory and accidental, a tradition that denies metaphysical status to national identity, and hence in contemporary terms is anti-essentialist; on the other, his poetry can be considered the beginning of a "patriotic" literature in French, adapting the position that France was divinely elect among the nations, a position that assigns metaphysical privilege to a historical community, and thus, again in contemporary terms, amounts to an essentialist endorsement of one nation over another. This latter position was hardly new in the late fourteenth century: it had been a stock element of French royal propaganda,[3] but prior to Deschamps it had found, at best, only sporadic acceptance among vernacular writers.

A review of Deschamps's image or literary representation of France and England demonstrates a fundamental uncertainty in defining exactly what constituted France as a nation, and this in the midst of the Hundred Years' War when one would logically most expect a clearly defined sense of nation. Hitherto, this ambiguity has largely escaped scholarly notice.[4] The only unambiguous sense of *nation* for Deschamps is that of "birth": when he praises the inhabitants of cities (*Balades*, no. 1472, 8:174–75) he speaks of "François ou Allemans, /Anglès, autres nativitez / Bourgoingnons, Bretons et Normans" [French or German, English or other nations, Burgundians, Bretons and Normans], using the term *nativitez* (birth) to designate not only such traditional nations as France, Germany, or England, but also well-defined regions such as Burgundy, Brittany and Normandy.

This indeterminacy corresponds to the historicity and relativity of the concept of France as a nation, even as late as the end of the fourteenth century, and thus casts serious doubt on the well-entrenched claims that France has the strongest and oldest tradition of national identity in Europe or that the late Middle Ages witnessed the "birth" of national consciousness. The remark by the chronicler Michel Pintoin, monk of Saint-Denis, bears repeating: "il y a la France qui est un royaume et ne saurait être un pays. Et il y a dans le royaume des pays, dont aucun ne doit être appelé la France"[5] [there is France which is a kingdom and cannot be a homeland. And there are homelands in this kingdom, none of which ought to be called France]. One of the best-known medieval statements on nationality, made only ten years after Deschamps's death, was the claim by the English delegation at the Council of Constance in 1415 that there were three plausible definitions for *nation*: "sive sumatur natio ut gens secundum cognationem et collectionem ab alia distincta, sive secundum diversitatem linguarum . . . sive etiam sumatur natio pro provincia aequali"[6] [either nation is taken as a group of people related by blood, a collection distinct from others, or as linguistic difference . . . or even as a political unit (literally, "for a congruent province")]. This "pick-and-choose" attitude should caution us from looking for a well-established sense of the very concept of 'nation,' and it should also prompt us to examine the uncertainty of French national identity in Deschamps more closely.

This uncertainty stemmed as well from the fact that medieval authors were torn between the traditional belief that nationality was a mark of the sin of pride—dating from the confusion of Adamic speech after the Tower of Babel, and at best transitory (even the names of the "seventy-two nations" after Babel fluctuate wildly throughout the Middle Ages[7])—and an inchoate sense of national superiority that began to emerge in the middle of the thirteenth century as a result of the investiture crisis[8] and which in turn was strengthened during the mid-fourteenth century as part of the crisis over papal succession. This uncertainty was also reinforced by conventional loyalties to estates that blur national distinctions. Aristocratic and ecclesiastical writers, with their cosmopolitan orientation, were hardly inclined to view national differences as ultimately incompatible. The new claim that, with the decline of imperial prestige in Italy and Germany during the investiture crisis of the thirteenth century, the French nation had assumed a special position within the divine plan of history, following the motto, coined by Guibert de Nogent, "gesta Dei per Francos" [the works of God by the French], gained currency and poignancy during the course of the Hundred Years' War. As Peter Rickard noted in his wonderfully erudite *Britain in Medieval French Literature*, the end of the Anglo-French struggle resulted in "a growing conviction that God was on the French side and would not allow the rebels to win. Numerous French victories and English setbacks were said to be due to divine intervention."[9]

Of course the way to this privileged position for "France" in the plan of salvation history had been carefully prepared. French claims of cultural superiority, first articulated in the late twelfth century by Chrétien de Troyes in the Prologue to *Cligés*, directly contradicted the spirit of humanism, as Ernst Robert Curtius long ago noted.[10] Chrétien's prayer to God that "*l'onors*" (line 37) [the honor] that France enjoy should reside there forever is a far cry from claiming French culture was divinely sanctioned, but it marks a first step. Prior to Deschamps, the belief that France exercised a special mission within the plan of salvation can be detected in Fulcher of Chartres, Guibert de Nogent, Jean de Joinville, and especially the *Grandes Chroniques de France*.[11] These late thirteenth-century chronicles, compiled by the monks of Saint-Denis, not only cultivate the "strongest sense of a national heritage"[12] but also claim a special, divinely instituted prerogative for the French kingdom: "Et lui a nostre sire donné, par sa grace, une prerogative et un avantage sur toutes autres terres et sur toutes autres nascions"[13] [And to it Our Lord has given, by His grace, a prerogative and an advantage over all other lands and over all other nations]. The French "nation" assumes a transcendental, metaphysical status that it had not enjoyed before. From a late medieval political perspective, this concept of a nation encompassing and transcending all social estates—characteristic in secularized form of the concept of nation in France since the French Revolution, a concept that replaced Louis XIV's claim that "la nation réside dans la personne du Roi" [the nation resided in the person of the King]—was troubling on two counts: first, because it competed with traditional

Christian universalism, and second, because it subverted traditional estatist hierarchy in the name of a higher national unity.

Writing in the *City of God* (Book 18, chapter 29), Augustine sounds an unambiguous warning against national cultural pride. In rejecting the superiority of ancient Egyptian lore over the revelations of the Hebrew prophets, he admonishes his readers: "Nulla igitur gens de antiquitate suae sapientiae super patriarchas et prophetas nostros, quibus divina inerat sapientia, ulla se vanitate iactaverit, quando nec Aegyptus invenitur, quae solet falso et inaniter de suarum doctrinarum antiquitate gloriari, qualicumque sapientia sua patriarcharum nostrorum tempore praevenisse sapientiam."[14] [Therefore let no people boast with any vanity about the antiquity of their wisdom surpassing our patriarchs and prophets in whom divine wisdom resides, since not even Egypt, which customarily glories falsely and vainly in the ancientness of its learning, is found to have preceded in time with its wisdom, of what quality soever, the wisdom of our patriarchs.] Yet rather than appealing to this tradition of Augustinian universalism, Deschamps connected the future of France with the prophecy of the Sibyl in the *City of God* (Book 10, chapter 27). In *Balades de moralitez*, no. 284, he writes:

> Sebile, tu de qui Saint Augustin,
> En son livre de la Cité de Dieu,
> Parle et conclut en tenant ceste fin
> Qu'en la Cité as et doiz avoir lieu,
> Car esperit de vraie prophecie
> Eus, et des dix fus plus auctorisie,
> Et qui parlas plus veritablement
> Du Fil de Dieu, de sa mort, de sa vie,
> Du cours du monde et du definement;
> . . .
> Du regne aux Gaulx, de leur foy, de leur lin,
> Parlas a droit, et de leur fin t'ensieu:
> Quant ilz lairont de Dieu le droit chemin,
> . . .
> La vient leur mort . . . (2:137–38).

[O Sibyl, you about whom Saint Augustine speaks / in his book *The City of God* / and concludes, maintaining this point that you have, / and must have, a place in the City, / for you had the spirit of true prophecy, / and were the most authoritative of the ten [Sibyls], / and spoke most truly / of the Son of God, of his death, of his life, / of the course of the world and its end . . . of the rule of the Gauls, of their faith, of their lineage, / you spoke truly, and I follow you concerning their end, / that when they leave the straight path of God, / . . . then their death would come].

The credibility of the Sibyl extends for Deschamps from the coming of Christ to the rise of the French nation, of the "Senonian Gaul" (the Latin term *Senones* refers to a province of Cisalpine Gaul near the modern city of Sens; Augustine uses the phrase which Deschamps takes as a reference to contemporary France). This succession is potentially far more radical than a simple adherence to the topos of the *translatio studii* from Greece to Rome to France, since it appears to confuse cultural and spiritual legitimacy at the same time it confuses sacred and pagan history as in the earlier work, *Balades de moralitez*, no. 185, "Déploration des maux de la France" (2:1–2), where Deschamps lists biblical prophets, pagan sages, and Christian apostles who together all deplore the evils "that must come to the kingdom of the Gauls."

This assigning of a metaphysical legitimacy to the French nation is somewhat at odds with Deschamps's traditional estatist loyalties. The moralizing and pessimistic tone of his work, written admittedly under the impact of the earlier phases of the Hundred Years' War—the French defeats at Crécy (1346) and Poitiers (1356), the social unrest as manifested in the Jacquerie (1357–1358)—is most acutely expressed in his many *complaintes* whose form recalls the medieval Latin *planctus*. In *Balades de moralitez*, no. 255, "Complainte du pays de France" [Lament of the land of France], (2:93–94), he has France speaks in the first person, lamenting the loss of

> Vaillance, Honeur, Sens et Chevalerie,
> Congnoissance, Force, Bonté, Vertu,
> Largesce, Amour, doulz Maintien, Courtoisie,
> Humilité, Deduit, joieuse Vie,
> Et le bon nom que je souloie avoir (2.93).[15]

[valor, honor, sense, and knighthood, / knowledge, strength, goodness, virtue / generosity, love, fair behavior, courtliness / humility, joy, happy living / and the good name that I used to have].

Following a similar approach, his sixth *lay*, "Ci commence le lay des douze estas du monde" [Here begins the lai of the twelve estates of the world], (2:226–35), carefully describes the estates of society. He praises the past—a typical example of the nostalgic topos of the *laudatio temporis acti*—when the position of the estates was stable.

Accepting or submitting to this traditional hierarchy was a matter of course for Deschamps, or as he says in the refrain to balade no. 23 of the *Balades de moralitez*, "riens ne vault tant comme obeissance" [nothing is worth as much as obedience] (1:101–3). He rails elsewhere against the corrosive or subversive force of capital: in *Balades de moralitez*, no. 53, "Sur les financiers" [On the financiers] (1:143–44), the poem's envoi hammers home the point:

> Prince, pou vault estre homme de paraige,
> Saiges, prodoms, n'avoir grant diligence;
> Pour le jour d'ui vault trop pou vassellaige :
> Nulz n'a estat que sur fait de finance (1:144).
>
> [Prince, it is hardly worth anything being a man of high lineage, / wise, upright, nor to have great diligence, / for nowadays vassalage hardly counts, / no one has social status based on anything but money.]

Deschamps criticizes the divisions within France caused by pride, lust, hatred in *Chançons royaulx*, no. 378 (3:137–38), as though division within the body politic were a struggle between the virtues and vices. He condemns unequivocally the uprising of the Maillotins in Paris on March 1, 1381, in *Chançons royaulx*, no. 379, "Fuiez, fuiez pour les maillès de plonc" [Flee, flee, because of the leaden hammers] (3:139–40). Deschamps considers the bourgeois who revolted against the new taxes in support of the war to be worse than the Saracens, "Car pis ont fait que ne font Sarrazins" [For they have done worse than the Saracens] and believes that the Prince should rightly punish these miscreants. This poem, by equating estatist difference (the bourgeois rebels) with religious difference (the Saracens), reveals the uncertainties surrounding the category of difference itself.

Deschamps's traditional allegiance to estatist hierarchy is reflected as well in his almost instinctive aversion to the social upheavals contemporaneous to the first phases of the Hundred Years' War, such as the uprising (1356–1358) organized by the provost of the merchants, Étienne Marcel and the subsequent uprising of the peasants, called the Jacquerie. In *Balades de moralitez*, no. 163 (1:306–7), Deschamps lists three things that God should protect us from: a popular revolt, an angry lord, and sudden death. Deschamps comments the most on the first: "L'en ne porroit peuple esmeu retarder / Qu'il n'ait avant sa folour assevie; / Je le puis bien en pluseurs lieux prouver" [one can hardly restrain the people in revolt before it has satisfied its folly—I can prove it in many places]. Stability, an ordered social hierarchy and a wise king underlie all of his political musings. In one of his many dream visions of the "body" of France—and, as Liliane Dulac has noted, Deschamps was the first to use this metaphor to describe France—Deschamps appeals for strong political leadership (not hard to understand in light of the crisis in royal authority arising from the minority and subsequent madness of Charles VI), for a "good head" for the nation; the envoi of his *Chançons royaulx*, no. 387, (3:155–57) has a personified France repeat, "Riens ne me fault, mais que j'aye bon chief" [I lack for nothing but for a good head].

The German Romanist Franz Walther Müller, writing in what I believe is a classic and unjustly neglected article on the history of the word and concept of *nation* in French literature, claimed that Deschamps's conception of nation in general and of France in particular reflected a nostalgia for an earlier harmony.[16] Although Müller does not specifically indicate this, Deschamps's nostalgia, prompted by his horror of social unrest, focused, not surprisingly, on the figure of Charlemagne. For example, in *Balades de moralitez*, no. 140, "Cause des maux de la France" [Cause of the evils befalling France] (1:265–66), Deschamps returns to his moralist approach to political unrest and argues that pride, envy, hatred, indifference ("petit Confort"), great riches, lust, presumption ("Oultrecuidance") have nearly killed what he calls in the refrain "Le noble royaume de France" [the noble kingdom of France]. The answer to these evils comes in an appeal to Charlemagne articulated in the following balade, no. 141, (1:266–67), "Plaintes de France." Its refrain emphasizes: "Preux Charlemaine, se tu feusse [sic] en France, / Encore y fust Rolans, ce m'est advis" [Valiant Charlemagne, if you were in France, / Roland would still be there, it seems to me]. The persistence of the myth of Charlemagne in France hardly ended with Deschamps; at his coronation on December 2, 1804, Napoleon informed Pius VII, "Je n'ai pas succédé à Louis XVI, mais à Charlemagne" [I have not succeeded Louis XVI, but Charlamagne]. But Deschamps did not stop with Charlemagne; he dates the divine election of France from Clovis. In *Balades de moralitez*, no. 263, "Sur quelz poins doit durer ce royaume" [In what direction should this kingdom remain] (2:104–5), Deschamps argues that the French monarchy had "commencez par divine ordenance" [begun through divine command], with a direct "declaracion" from God to Clovis, sending "la saincte unction" from heaven. In *Balade*, no. 980, "Autre balade touchant le royaume des Français" [Another ballad concerning the kingdom of the French] (5:222–24), Deschamps again invokes the divine election of France.

Just as Deschamps still adheres to an estatist order endangered by war and internal unrest, he still takes the term *nation* in its equally traditional meaning of "birth," as was seen above in *Balades*, no. 1472, (8:174–75). As such, *nation* did not and could not reflect a larger unity transcending estatist differences. To this extent, as Müller claims, Deschamps's application of the term is both traditional and conventional. Yet the nascent sense of a privileged position for France within salvation history announces a break with the otherwise conventional aspects of Deschamps's understanding of French identity. The test for this newly developing sense of French cultural identity is Deschamps's image of England, since French identity in his lyric seems to depend on English alterity, and the two constructions, not surprisingly, go hand in hand. Deschamps, however, stays close to traditional epithets describing the national traits of the two countries. National epithets were an integral part of medieval rhetoric, and it is no surprise that a rhetorical authority like Deschamps was well versed in them: he was, after all, the author of an *Art de dictier* or poetic handbook.

This rhetorical orientation is also present in Deschamps's use of the term *debat* to describe the conflict between France and England. For Deschamps, the medieval French word *debat* has both its full literal force of "physical conflict" or "struggle" (preserved in the English word *battle*) and its rhetorical sense of "debate" (Latin *altercatio*). This "debat" results from the moral failings and sins of all parties. In *Balades*, no. 1124 (6:40–42), he uses the terms *conflis* ("conflict") and *debat* ("struggle, debate") synonymously when he laments that in his fifty years he has seen tribulations and "vengeance soudaine, / Conflis de roys en France et en Espaigne / Pour nos pechiez, et universel guerre / Pour le debat de France et d'Angleterre" [sudden vengeance, / the conflicts of kings in France and Spain, / for our sins, and universal war / because of the conflict of France and England]. The reference to "nos pechiez" [our sins] is also important, since it points to the moral shortcomings of mortals rather than positing the superiority of one nation over another. The term *debat* occurs again with the same force in *Balades*, no. 1148 (6:77–79): tracing human misfortune since biblical times, Deschamps notes "puis ne fut veu en terre / Tant de doleurs et de male meschance / Qu'on a veu partout courir et querre / Pour le debat d'Angleterre et de France" [there was never seen on earth / so much suffering and misfortune / as one has seen occurring and striking everywhere / because of the struggle of England and France].

Generally, in depicting France, Deschamps alludes to traditional French preeminence in *studium*. In *Chançons royaulx*, no. 324 (3:20–21), with the memorable refrain, "Tournez toudis le bec pardevers France" [always turned toward France, i.e., with the snout (*bec*) turned to France], he repeats the standard commonplace stemming from the topos of *translatio studii*, "L'estude y est plus qu'ailleurs honourée" (line 29) [study has always been honored there more than elsewhere]. The entire poem sings the praises of an idyllic France seen as a country of harmony and culture, a country whose past harmony now lies shattered as a result of war and civil strife. The kingdom of France will endure, he writes in *Rondeau*, no. 1113 (6:23), "tant qu'il vouldra garder / Bonne justice" [as long as it maintains justice]. The obverse side of France's adherence to study is that the French are so lost in thought that they are unable to act quickly enough against real threats: in *Balades de moralitez*, no. 253 (2:90–91), Deschamps's own title announces this recurrent topic in his lyric, "Comment les consaulx des Françoys sont trop longs et mal executez selon leur sens" [How the deliberations of the French are too lengthy and poorly executed according to their intentions]. In the poem he explains how Julius Caesar conquered Gaul because the French wasted their time in consultation ("François perdent leur temps a conseillier"), with the implication being that the English were about to do the same to France as Caesar had done to Gaul. He sounds exactly the same note again in *Rondeau*, no. 673, devoted to the difference between England and France: the English are quick to act, the French waste their time on deliberations (4:132). This image seems to anticipate a much later stereotype of France as the land of ratiocination that the German Romantics were so quick to criticize.

Of course, Deschamps sides with the French against the English,[17] but when he makes several of his impassioned pleas for peace, he is remarkably evenhanded, almost as though he can forget for a moment that God is on France's side. In a poem dated to 1385, *Balades de moralitez*, no. 48, he uses the refrain, "Sanz paix avoir, nous auron guerre, guerre" [Without peace, we will have war, war] in order to distribute the blame for the conflict on all combatants. He begins with the desperate observation, "Quarante ans a chanté de *Requiem* / Nostre curé, sanz faire porter paix" (1:136–37) [Our priest has sung the *requiem* for forty years without making peace come]. In *Chançons royaulx*, no. 394 (3:170–72), he addresses a request for peace to the kings of France and England. It is fairly blunt and plays on the traditional estatist conceptions of the duty between sovereign and subject:

> Qui a vous ont esté obeissans,
> Corps et ames mis a perdicion
> Pour assouvir voz .ii. cuers convoitans
> De terre avoir et de possession.
> Voz ancesseurs en ceste affliccion

> Sont trespassez, et de leur entreprise
> N'ont que .vii. piez de la terre conquise
> Pour leur tombel : plus n'en aront jamais;
> Se bien pensez a ce que je devise
> A voz subgiez soit donné bonne paix (3:171).

[Whoever has been obedient to you / has destroyed body and soul / to satisfy your two hearts lusting / for lands and possessions. / Your ancestors died in this affliction, / and have only conquered seven feet of ground / for their graves: they will have nothing more. / So if you reflect well on what I am saying, / may peace be granted to your subjects.]

This last line is, significantly, the refrain that is repeated throughout the poem. Deschamps plays no favorite between England and France: both kings have abused their office and their subjects. The following poem, *Chançons royaulx*, no. 395 (3:173–75), gives the kings' rhetorical answer, with its obligatory refrain: "Et pour ce a tous bonne paix octroyons" [And for this reason we grant good peace to all]. In *Balades*, no. 1171 (6:115–17), Deschamps makes the simple appeal, "laissez aler guerre, querez concorde" [stop going to war, seek peace]. For a modern age used to seeing wars as inevitable products of economic struggles, there is a certain poignancy to Deschamps's belief that the warring factions could be somehow brought together by a simple act of marriage: in *Balades*, no. 1181 (6:133–34), on the 1395 marriage of Richard II and Isabelle of France, his refrain expresses the hope, "Toute paix vint par un saint mariaige" [Every peace comes from a holy marriage].

After all, Deschamps will argue, Christians should not be warring among themselves, but instead fighting the Saracens: "Querons ailleurs guerre qui nous afiere, / Sur Sarrazins levons nostre banniere" (*Balades*, no. 883, 5.68) [Let us seek war elsewhere that concerns us, let us lift our banner against the Saracen]. Although Deschamps urges the princes of Christendom to unite against Islam—and may have inspired Christine de Pizan to make the same claim in her *Ditié de Jehanne d'Arc*,[18] I suspect that Deschamps's conception of France was not as heavily influenced by the categories of salvation history as was Christine's because his use of biblical metaphors, while considerably more extensive than Christine's, seems more decorative than theological. In part this conclusion stems from the fact that Deschamps phrased his many allegorical prophecies obscurely, avoiding the kind of unambiguous theological position taken by Christine.[19]

The longest work that Deschamps wrote that is devoted to the image of France is his visionary beast allegory, *La Fiction du lyon* (8:247–338). This long and rambling fictional "treatise" of 2954 lines ends with the "death" of its author who left it "unfinished" ("imparfaicte"). Near the end the fiction tells how the fox plotted to cause a war between the lion Noble, king of the beasts of Gaul, and the leopard "qui estoit grans / Sire de l'Isle des Geans" (lines 2853–54) [who was the great lord of the Island of Giants]; the leopard is still used in the arms of England, and the term "Island of Giants" was first used in the twelfth-century *Roman de Brut* to designate England. The work breaks off one hundred lines later before it can begin to develop the Anglo-French rivalry in the given framework of a beast allegory, a challenge that proved impossible.

The obscurity of Deschamps's allegorical prophetic visions (comparable to Dante's prophecy of the Veltro in *Inferno*, I) stems in part from the fact that the allegorical tradition of medieval philosophical epic, with its roots in Prudentius's *Psychomachia*, was well adapted to portray the struggle of virtues and vices but not the historical conflict of nations. Not only his millenarian bent,[20] but also the strong influence exerted on him by the rhetorical tradition of national epithets prevented him from writing in a concretely referential way about France and England. Several of his poems are indebted to the tradition of the *anglicus caudatus*, the Englishman with a tail: in *Rondeau*, no. 671 (4: 130), he speaks of this "queue"; and in *Balades*, no. 868 (5:48–49), he exclaims to the English, "Soit en France ou en Limosin, / Levez vostre queue, levez!" [Whether in France or Limousin, hold up your tail, hold it up!]. In *Balades*, no. 893 (5:79–80), "Récit d'une aventure à Calais" [Tale of an adventure at Calais], Deschamps narrates an encounter with two Englishmen during which he claims to see their "tails." Deschamps cannot tear himself away from a literary tradition divorced from historical reality.

To assess the significance of these examples, one might recall briefly the history of the "Englishman with a tail."[21] According to an old legend, when the Benedictine missionary Augustine of Canterbury (died 604) preached in Rochester, he was mocked by the locals who attached fish tails to the back of his vestments during a sermon. Incensed, Augustine prayed that his detractors be punished by having children born with tails. The story of this curse spread throughout Europe. To demonstrate the prevalence of this epithet in Europe, one might recall that the Provençal poet, Pierre d'Auvergne, referred disparagingly in 1155 to the "Engles coutz." Jacques de Vitry recounts in his *Historia occidentalis* (1223–1225) that rival "nationes" of the

University of Paris referred to English students as *caudati* ("having tails"). Matthew of Paris, writing in the late fourteenth century about the earlier Third Crusade (1289–1292), reports that the French under Philippe Auguste frequently used the phrase as an invective against the English led by Richard the Lionhearted. The Italian poet Fazio degli Uberti records it in his *Dittamondo* from 1370.

The other traditional national epithet that finds a place in Deschamps's work is that of "perfidious Albion," (Napoleon's well-known epithet for England). Apparently the first recorded reference to "anglica perfidia" comes in the chronicle of Otto of Saint Blasien, composed in 1209/10, describing Richard the Lionhearted's behavior at the siege of Akkon in 1191.[22] It is difficult to determine how old the tradition is, but its pan-European popularity can be seen in the fact that by 1561 when Scaliger wrote his *Poetices libri septem*, a compendium of many earlier works, he also refers to "Angli perfidi."[23] In *Chançons royaulx*, no. 337 (3:47), Deschamps claims: "Nous sommes bien trompé, / Aux Anglois n'avons paix n'alongne" [We have been well deceived, we have no peace nor truce with the English]. In *Chançons royaulx*, no. 344 (3:62–64), he notes as well, "Englès y pensent mal engin . . . ilz pensent barat" [The English are plotting evil / . . . thinking of treachery]. In his poem on the death of Richard II, *Balades*, no. 1200 (6:184–85), "De la mort du roy Richart d'Angleterre," the *plainte / planctus* quickly turns from mourning the death of Richard to commenting on the treason in terms typical of the legal interpretation of treason as an offense to the king's person, *lèse-majesté*. Richard, Deschamps writes, had been murdered "par traiteurs consaulx / De majesté blecée" [by treasonous counsels / of wounded majesty], but this treachery serves Deschamps as a springboard to a meditation on England:

> Angleterre, sur toutes nascions
> Et au jour d'ui haie pour tes maulx,
> Et cilz qui tant a fait d'occisions
> Des innocens pour regner comme faulx
>
> [England, above all nations / hated today for your evils, / and who has committed so many murders / of innocent people in order to rule falsely].

The balade ends with the envoi, "Plourez, Anglois, les tribulations / Qui vous viennent, et voz destructions" [Lament, English, the tribulations / that will come to you and your destruction]. Deschamps also wrote a balade on the various names of England (no. 1154, 6:87–88), further evidence of his familiarity with the longstanding tradition of national epithets. Deschamps's knowledge of traditional rhetorical epithets on France seems equally well founded; he employs the traditional epithet of "Douce France" in *Balades*, no. 1142 (6:69), and no. 1317 (7:79–80); and he composed a Latin poem on France, no. 1331, "Commemoracio hystorie Senonum Gallorum" (7:93–102), in which the designation of the French as the Senonian Gauls can be traced back to classical Latin sources, as was noted above. When he speaks of Flanders, on the other hand, he only notes that the land is accursed, without reference to traditional epithets.[24]

Nevertheless, despite all his hostility to the English cause, Deschamps can still celebrate a poet of the English language. The modern equation of language, culture, and nation had little meaning for the French poet, and this salutary fact points out once again his traditional approach to national identity. In his frequently cited balade no. 285 to Geoffrey Chaucer, "Grant translateur, noble Geffroy Chaucier" (2:139) [Great translator, noble Geoffrey Chaucer], Deschamps serves up lavish praise for Chaucer's eloquence in the English language. His *laudatio* is couched in complicated, rhetorically intricate clauses, as though to stress that the literary republic is still undivided. He writes to Chaucer:

> Tu es d'amours mondains Dieux en Albie:
> Et de la *Rose*, en la terre Angelique,
> Qui d'Angela saxonne, [et] puis flourie
> Angleterre, d'elle ce nom s'applique
> Le derrenier en l'ethimologique;
> En bon anglès le livre translatas;
> Et un vergier ou du plant demandas
> De ceuls qui font pour eulx auctorisier,
> A ja longtemps que tu edifias
> Grand translateur, noble Geffroy Chaucier (2:139–40).

[You are the God of earthly love in Albion, / and you translated into good English the book of the *Rose* / in the angelic / English land which takes its name from the Saxon Angela, / which then flowered into England; / and for a long time / you have built a garden where you asked for a sapling / from those who act to legitimize themselves, / great translator, noble Geoffrey Chaucer].

All of the bucolic imagery of a courtly *locus amoenus* is invoked in order to praise the English poet. Regardless how much Deschamps knew about Chaucer's works,[25] there was no room here for national hatreds or prejudices.

In the end, what is the significance of the uncertainty of the meaning of *nation* in Deschamps? It is not a question here of cataloguing his different positions in order to "deconstruct" or to "destablize" the concept of a nation, but to show instead that Deschamps himself had trouble "constructing" an identity for France in the first place. Deschamps's gradual abandonment of the older universalist and moralist position and his concomitant hesitating cultivation of the tradition of France's divine election shows how the very concept of nation was in massive flux at the end of the fourteenth century and beginning of the fifteenth century, just as the remarks of the English delegation to the Council of Constance in 1415 show. France the nation could be Noble, the lion-king in a visionary beast allegory, or a female personification in a lyrical lament, or the "doulx pays" celebrated in the *Chanson de Roland*, or the land of study and reason where justice reigns, or the divinely elected kingdom founded by Clovis. England could be perfidious, warlike, inhabited by men with tails, personified by a leopard. Colette Beaune is entirely correct to point out the various stages in the formation of a national consciousness during the Middle Ages.[26] What this close examination of Deschamps's understanding of what France was as a nation shows is that the process creating such a national consciousness had no inner logic but was an expedient, imperfectly cobbled and illogical improvisation.

NOTES

1. All quotations from Deschamps's works are from his *Oeuvres complètes*, ed. Queux de Saint-Hilaire and G. Raynaud, SATF (Paris: Didot, 1878–1904), 11 v. All translations are my own. French titles given in parentheses were supplied by these two nineteenth-century editors. Other rubrics were either supplied by Deschamps himself or by Raoul Tainguy, the scribe who assembled his works in BnF f. fr. 804.

2. Hans Walther, "Scherz und Ernst in der Völker-und Stämme-Charakteristik mittellateinischer Verse," *Archiv für Kulturgeschichte* 41 (1959): 263–301.

3. The bibliography on this topic is immense. See, for instance, Helene Wieruszowski, *Vom Imperium zum nationalen Königtum, Vergleichende Studien über die publizistischen Kämpfe Kaiser Friedrichs II. und König Philipps des Schönen mit der Kurie* (Munich: Oldenbourg, 1933); and Joseph R. Strayer, "France: the Holy Land, the Chosen People, and the Most Christian King," in his *Medieval Statecraft and the Perspectives of History* (Princeton: Princeton University Press, 1971).

4. A recent and very useful anthology of Deschamps's poetry with commentary, *Eustache Deschamps en son temps*, ed. Jean-Patrice Boudet and Hélène Millet (Paris: Publications de la Sorbonne, 1997), presents nine lyrical works as represen-

tative of Deschamps's attitudes toward "Pays, nation, clocher" [Homeland, nation, parish]. The combination of these topics (to describe only nine poems!) reveals immediately the difficulty in reconstructing the meaning of France in Deschamps's work, a difficulty which is compounded when one expands the sample of poems. See also Liliane Dulac's "La représentation de la France chez Deschamps et Christine de Pizan," in *Colloque "Autour d'Eustache Deschamps," (November 1998, Amiens)*, ed. Danielle Buschinger (Amiens: Presse de l'UFR de Langues, Université de Picardie, 1999); my thanks to the author for providing me with a copy of her essay in manuscript.

5. Cited in *Eustache Deschamps en son temps*, 158.

6. *Magnum oecumenicum Constantiense Consilium*, V (Frankfurt, 1700), 92.

7. See Arno Borst, *Der Turm von Babel: Geschichte der Meinungen über Ursprung und Vielfalt der Sprachen und Völker*, 4 vols. (Stuttgart: Hiersemann, 1957–1963).

8. The situation within the Holy Roman Empire was described by Frantisek Graus, "Funktionen der spätmittelalterlichen Geschichtsschreibung," *Geschichtsschreibung und Geschichtsbewußtsein im späten Mittelalter* (Sigmaringen: Jan Thorbecke Verlag, 1987), 45, 47: "The actual situation in the empire [during the fourteenth and fifteenth centuries] substantially complicated any kind of historical national stylization of the empire . . . while historical writing was not susceptible to the trend that I characterize as 'nationalizing' here . . . only historical writing was able to draw a codified and thus truly obligatory picture of the total development which was necessarily perceived as being historical. Footnote: this process had already begun in many countries during the twelfth century (cf., for example, Geoffrey of Monmouth, Suger, Cosmas, Kadlubek)." [Die faktische Lage im Reich [im 14. und 15. Jh.] erschwerte jede historische nationale Hochstilisierung des Imperiums ungemein . . . für den Trend, der hier als 'Nationalisierung' bezeichnet wird, ist nicht nur die Geschichtsschreibung anfällig gewesen . . . aber nur die Historiographie konnte ein kodifiziertes und damit wirklich verpflichtendes Bild der zwangsläufig als historisch empfundenen Gesamtentwicklung zeichnen. Anmerkung: Dieser Prozeß setzte in vielen Ländern bereits im 12. Jh. ein (vgl. z.B. Geoffrey of Monmouth, Suger, Kosmas, Kadlubek).]

9. Peter Rickard, *Britain in Medieval French Literature, 1100–1500* (Cambridge: Cambridge University Press, 1956), 190–91, cites as examples the *Mistère du siège d'Orléans*, Charles d'Orléans, the chronicle of Bertrand du Guesclin, the chronicle of Mont St. Michel, the *Chronique de la Pucelle*, Jean Chartier's *Chronique de Charles VII*, and Olivier de la Marche's *Mémoires*.

10. Curtius terms Chrétien's claims as the opposite of a commitment to humanism: "Das ist das Gegenteil eines humanistischen Bekenntnisses;" see *Europäische Literatur und Lateinisches Mittelalter* (Berne: Franke, 1984), 389.

11. See my "Christine de Pizan and Sacred History," in *The City of Scholars: New Approaches to Christine de Pizan*, ed. Margarete Zimmermann and Dina De

Rentiis (Berlin: de Gruyter, 1994), 18: "In describing the Crusader troops from various European lands arriving together near Nicaea to form a greater Christian host under French leadership Fulcher compares this modern army to the crowds assembled from different nations in Jerusalem on the feast of Pentecost united typologically into a single supranational church. Guibert explicitly isolates a special role for the French in defending the Apostolic Throne itself whereas Jean de Joinville combines royal history and hagiography as part of his clear purpose to present the king as a saint." See also my discussion of the importance for Christine of categories based on sacred history in Fulcher and Guibert in "French Cultural Nationalism and Christian Universalism," in *Politics, Gender and Genre: The Political Thought of Christine de Pizan*, ed. Margaret Brabant (Boulder, Colorado: Westview Press, 1992), 75–94.

12. Roger Ray, "Historiography, European," in *Dictionary of the Middle Ages*, Joseph Strayer, editor in chief (New York: Scribner, 1985), 6: 264.

13. *Les Grandes Chroniques de France*, ed. Jules Viard (Paris: Société de l'histoire de France, 1920–53), 1:4.

14. Saint Augustine, *The City of God Against the Pagans*, trans. George E. McCracken et al., The Loeb Classical Library, no. 411 (Cambridge, Mass.: Harvard University Press, 1957–72), 6:12, my translation.

15. He takes a similar approach in *Balades de moralitez*, no. 159, "France dégénérée" (1:288–89), in which the envoi laments the loss of France's radiance, "la lumiere de France."

16. Franz Walther Müller, "Zur Geschichte des Wortes und Begriffes 'Nation' im französischem Schrifttum," *Romanische Forschungen* 58/59 (1947): 247–321. Müller's reflections on the changing concept of the nation in France were intended as an answer to Nazi propaganda; the publication of his work immediately following the defeat of the Nazis deserves more attention than has been the case.

17. In *Chançons royaulx*, no. 344 (3:62–64), the refrain argues that "Paix n'arez ja s'ilz ne rendent Calays" [you will not have peace until they surrender Calais]. Throughout this poem Deschamps stresses that the French desire peace and that the English are recalcitrant. The same theme is found in *Chançons royaulx*, no. 359 (3:93–95), "Nous n'arons paix aux Anglois de l'année" [We will not have peace with the English this year].

18. See the exhaustive survey of Joan of Arc's reception in Nadia Margolis, *Joan of Arc in History, Literature and Film* (New York: Garland Publishing, 1990).

19. Deschamps's allegorical visions include *Balades de moralitez*, no. 26, (1:106–7), where Deschamps compares himself with two Biblical prophets, Jeremiah in the Old Testament and Simeon in the New; *Balades de moralitez*, no. 67, (1:164–65), an obscure prophecy regarding Charles VI; *Balades de moralitez*, no. 81 (1:183–84), "Sur ce qui doit advenir" [On what must come], obscure prophetic visions invoking prophets and Sibyls; *Balades de moralitez*, no. 180, (1:315–16),

"Vision prophétique de l'Angleterre" [Prophetic vision of England]; *Balades de moralitez*, no. 182, (1:317–18), "Prédiction contre l'Angleterre" [Prediction against England]; *Balades de moralitez*, no. 211 (2:33–34), with the rubric "De la prophecie Merlin sur la destruction d'Angleterre qui doit brief advenir" [On Merlin's prophecy of the destruction of England which must soon occur]; *Balades de moralitez*, no. 229, (2:57–58), "Prophétie politique sur Charles VI," another visionary beast allegory whose meaning is not clear; and *Chançons royaulx*, no. 327 (3:26–28), "Guerre aux Anglais," a visionary beast allegory whose meaning is obscure.

20. Deborah Fraioli has carefully studied the influence of the so-called Second Charlemagne Prophecy on Deschamps in "The Literary Image of Joan of Arc: Prior Influences," *Speculum* 56 (1981): 811–30, especially 827.

21. The discussion here is indebted to the documentation assembled by Günther Blaicher, "Zur Entstehung und Verbreitung nationaler Stereotypen in und über England," *Deutsche Vierteljahrsschrift*, 51 (1977): 549–74. See also Peter Rickard, "*Anglois coué* and *l'Anglois qui couve*," *French Studies* 8 (1953): 48–55.

22. A. Cartellieri, "Perfides Albion," *Preußische Jahrbücher* 168 (1917) : 468–69.

23. Giulio Cesare Scaligero, *Poetices libri septem* (Genevae: Apud Ioannem Crispinum, 1561): 257–58.

24. *Balades de moralitez*, no. 16, (1:92–93) "Contre la Flandre," claims that Flanders descends from a biblical lineage of accursed people (Cain, Sodom and Gomorrah, Judas). The following balade, no. 17 (1:94–95) has the refrain, "Mais ne me plaing fors du pais de Flandres" [But I lament nothing but the country of Flanders]. See also the balade against the city of Ghent, "fausse ville de Gand," no. 94 (1:201–2), and the invective against Flanders in *Chançons royaulx*, no. 334, (3:41–42) "Contre les Flamands," and *Balades*, no. 812 (4:329–30).

25. See the most recent discussion of this work, William Calin, "Deschamps's 'Ballade to Chaucer' Again, or the Dangers of Intertextual Medieval Comparatism," in *Eustache Deschamps, French Courtier-Poet, His Work and His World*, ed. Deborah Sinnreich-Levi (New York: AMS Press, 1998), 73–83.

26. Colette Beaune, *Naissance de la nation française* (Paris: Gallimard, 1985).

CHAPTER 8

THE POLITICAL POETICS OF THE *DITIÉ DE JEHANNE D'ARC*

ANNE D. LUTKUS
and
JULIA M. WALKER

For the English, at least for Shakespeare, the defining moment of the Hundred Years' War may well have been the battle of Agincourt. In popular French recollections of the conflict, on the other hand, a key focus is the crowning of Charles VII as the rightful king of France. That this crowning displeased a significant number of French-speakers at least as much as it did their English allies, headed by the duke of Bedford as regent for the infant Henry VI, is all too easily overlooked, especially when the bright light of celebrity radiating from Joan of Arc floods the political/historical arena. Joan of Arc drove the English from France, so says popular history. While we know that this is not literally true, we do tend to gloss over the multiplicity of problems which Joan's intervention did *not* solve. More particularly, by a sort of historical alchemy we assume that the saving of Orléans led to the crowning of Charles at Rheims and both somehow directly resulted in Joan's death at the hands of the retributive English. It is easy to forget that Charles himself had problems with Joan, that the new king and his popular woman warrior were openly hostile over a key political issue only hours after the coronation. Christine de Pizan's poem *Ditié de Jehanne d'Arc* (*The Tale of Joan of Arc*), however, provides evidence of that hostility, for the poet herself takes a very strong position on what was evidently a serious and historically immediate political debate: whether Charles should take Paris by force in August of 1429 or choose to believe that the duke of Bedford and the Burgundians would hand over the city after a truce. The 489 lines of the poem not only foreground this specific political issue but also articulate a profound critique of current events by a writer who had long identified her voice as one raised in the best interests of France.[1]

Critics have spoken of Christine de Pizan's *Ditié de Jehanne d'Arc* as everything from a hymn of thanksgiving to a justification of feminism;[2] we, however, read it as active political propaganda presented as poetic prophetic history. In the last stanza of the *Ditié de Jehanne d'Arc*, Christine de Pizan dates the poem "the last day of July" 1429. The literal acceptance of this date[3] unfortunately has blinded scholars to the possibilities of the poem as active political propaganda. We question the date as a way of interrogating Christine de Pizan's perception of the relations between Joan and Charles following the coronation at Rheims.

The historical narrative in the poem mentions the lifting of the siege of Orléans in May, the coronation on July 17, the progress of Joan and Charles toward Paris on July 23, and their arrival at the outskirts of Paris on July 29, only two days before the poem is dated. In their edition of the text, Kennedy and Varty try to explain the apparent speed of composition by suggesting that Christine de Pizan must have begun the poem in May.[4] We disagree, placing our argument at the crux of a twofold question: how soon after the coronation at Rheims did Joan herself realize that her goal of taking Paris was at odds with the immediate plans of Charles, and how soon did this dissent among the king's supporters and the king himself become public knowledge? We maintain that the answer to the latter question could not possibly be two days; nor are there any firm grounds on which to argue that this political issue was clearly articulated at any time between the crowning of Charles on July 17 and the expiration of the truce with Burgundy in early August. For Christine de Pizan to see the taking of Paris as a point of contention, her poem must have been written more than two days after July 29. Nor is this argument merely a textual exercise in the dating of a piece of literature. Until now, Christine de Pizan's poem has been read as a work praising Joan but not as a work criticizing Charles. It is this revisionist reading that we here present. If Christine de Pizan wrote this poem in late August or early September, then what we have is a well-informed and strongly argued piece of propaganda for Joan and implicitly against the king of France on the issue of taking Paris. Of course Charles should let—must let—Joan take Paris, "for [the king] will enter Paris, no matter who may grumble about it!—the Maid has given her word that he will," says the voice of her advocate Christine de Pizan in stanza 54.

That Christine de Pizan spent most of her professional life writing for royal and noble patrons makes her decision to speak on behalf of Joan, "no matter whom it may displease," all the more telling. That she was nearing the end of her own life adds the weight of final speech to the already empowering strategy of prophecy within the poem. An element of negative evidence which supports this dating and reading of the poem is the fact that, even as he sponsored the rehabilitation of Joan's reputation in the 1450s, neither Charles nor any of the participants produced this document, although its references to the Second Charlemagne Prophecy would have made it a natural choice for public attention. Charles could hardly have been unaware of a poem by a woman who had written of and for his grandfather, father, mother, and uncles, and who, moreover, authored the document in question while living in the convent of his sister, Marie. *Ditié de Jehanne d'Arc* is therefore not merely an interesting literary footnote, as it is often cited for being the only poem in French to praise Joan during her lifetime, it is also evidence of an element of educated, royalist public opinion which identified Joan of Arc's goals and actions as better for France than the goals and actions of France's king, Charles VII.

If we consider the possibility that Christine de Pizan was fighting her own battle, opening another front as it were, on the side of Joan of Arc, then the date of the poem becomes a matter for careful consideration, for the later she wrote it, the more powerful and daring a political document it becomes. Other than "the last day of July," itself inscribed within the bounds of the poem, not in the line of prose following the verse, we have no documentation supporting any specific date for the poem. The Berne manuscript, one of the two surviving fifteenth-century manuscripts of the poem, is bound (nonchronologically) with documents dated from 1428 into the 1430s. Willard opines that after writing the last line, "Christine de Pizan laid down her pen forever, insofar as is known."[5] This may well be true, but it does not follow that she laid that pen to rest on the last day of July 1429. We do not know the date of her death; indeed, this poem has always been used as an argument for her having died before things went seriously wrong for Joan in 1430. The other date cited for Christine de Pizan's death, however, is late 1431, when her daughter-in-law was granted permission to return from Poissy to Paris. Since there is no reason to believe that Christine de Pizan died long before this date, she might have been alive through Joan's trial and execution, and the poem theoretically could have been written at any time in 1429 or 1430.

The poet's inclusion of the date has been read as an unproblematically historical gesture; we suggest that by dating the poem earlier than she wrote it, Christine de Pizan is able to employ the construct of prophetic history all the more effectively because her poem shows a knowledge of acts and situations which did not exist on the last day of July in 1429. We want to examine the limens of poetry and history, evaluating Christine de Pizan's poem in relation to the historical events of July, August, and September of 1429, and arguing for the poet's power to construct herself as the sibylline voice of past, present, and future French history. Unlike the plays of Shakespeare, which could comment upon England's historical past, shape his audience's perceptions of that past, and influence the nationalist enthusiasm of his own historical present, Christine de Pizan has an opportunity to speak of history in the present tense moment that the events are occurring. Her poem, read as constructed history and historical prophecy, could arguably have some effect upon the events of her time. In any case, what we see here is rare in literary and historical writings: a present-tense voice speaking of present-tense conflicts. Like Shakespeare or Thucydides or Virgil, Christine de Pizan may have hoped to shape the opinions of generations to come; unlike those writers, she addresses a conflict which is not yet resolved as her ink dries. Much of the power of this literary response to the conflict lies in its immediacy.

When Charles was crowned on July 17, 1429, he immediately entered into a treaty with the duke of Burgundy. The terms of the treaty included a two-week truce, after which the duke would cede Paris to the new king. While historical scholars debate the attitude of Charles toward the terms of this truce,[6] we are more concerned with what Joan knew and said about the agreement. Régine Pernoud prefaces her chapter entitled "From Rheims to Compiègne" with a letter from Joan herself to the duke of Burgundy asking him to "make a good firm peace" and saying, "I beg and require you with clasped hands that you make no battle nor war against us."[7] Pernoud, however, distinguishes the "good firm peace" for which Joan pleads from the two-week truce which actually was negotiated. Indeed, Pernoud makes the point that "Joan was carefully excluded"[8] from any knowledge of this treaty, further stating that the route which Charles took after leaving Rheims included "sudden changes of direction which were a torment to Joan and her followers, whose one idea was to make straight for Paris."[9] Making the issue of what Joan knew even more complex, Pernoud cites the testimony of Dunois, given at the Trial of Rehabilitation, who quoted Joan as saying to the Bishop of Rheims while on that supposedly tormenting journey from his city: "please God, my Maker, that I may now withdraw myself, leave off arms, and go and serve my father and my mother by keeping the sheep with my sister and my brothers who will rejoice so greatly to see me again."[10]

Did Joan know about the truce with the duke of Burgundy? Did she construe it as contrary to the goals behind her own plea that he "make no battle nor war against us," or did she welcome it at face value as a chance to stop fighting? Marina Warner cites a letter from Joan to the people of Rheims written during these two weeks: "it is true," she acknowledges, "that the King has made a fifteen-day truce with the Duke of Burgundy by which he should render him the city of Paris peacefully at the end of the fortnight. However do not be surprised if I do not enter it as quickly; for a truce made in this way is so little to my liking, that I do not know if I shall keep it; but if I keep it, it will only be to safeguard the honour of the king."[11] In the face of this letter, it is difficult to believe that Joan knew nothing of the truce. There is nothing questionable about the authenticity of the document; we must conclude that Pernoud simply ignores it because it contradicts her reading of events.

But it is equally difficult to draw conclusions about Joan's ultimate intentions—either her intentions regarding Paris or the more immediate intentions raised by this letter. The letter itself suggests not only that Joan was unhappy with the truce, but that her dissatisfaction was shared by the people of Rheims and that these citizens may have expected some action from the Maid. Perhaps we can cite with certainty only the judgment of Charles T. Wood: "Human expectations far exceeded Joan's capacity to deliver."[12] In a letter to Queen Marie and her mother Yolande, written while Charles was in Rheims for the coronation, David de Brimeu explicitly acknowledges the varied agendas of Charles and Joan relative to the possibility of a treaty with Burgundy. De Brimeu, according to Pernoud and Clin,

> expressed the hope that the king will conclude "good treaty"... before he leaves. The same letter alluded to Joan: "She leaves no doubt that she will put Paris in her power [or make Paris obey]." That was to indicate clearly the preoccupations of each one. Joan thought only about pursuing an offensive that had been shown as profitable, while the king thought only about negotiating and, as to the matter of the "good treaty," was going to conclude a truce ... of two weeks! After a day of triumph at Rheims, there is once more total misunderstanding.[13]

More specifically, Colonel de Liocourt, in his *La mission de Jeanne d'Arc*, states that Joan actually got Charles to agree to march on Paris, and to that end "the necessary orders were given" to put an army on the road; on the next day, however, other forces prevailed with Charles.[14]

No matter how we patch together the somewhat contradictory contemporary documents, one conclusion does emerge: in the two weeks or fifteen days after the crowning of Charles on July 17, there is no evidence that Joan was actively trying to take Paris on her own. Additionally, there are strong grounds for arguing that she was at least hopeful that Paris would come into Charles's hands as promised. The importance of the truce in the context of our argument lies in its foregrounding of Paris as the specific issue over which Charles and Joan would ultimately disagree. Christine de Pizan, living in a convent where the king's sister was also residing, could have been aware of the nuances of the truce or the perceptions of the truce by citizens such as those of Rheims; obviously she was aware of the issues at stake. While she never mentions the truce in her poem, Christine de Pizan does address the varied interests represented by the factions among the king's supporters. Moreover, the mere fact of the existence of the truce on the fictive date of the poem makes the problem of actively taking Paris, which the poet constructs as central, an anachronism.

Whatever Joan may have known or hoped, she did not actively try to capture Paris until September of 1429. The letter which she sent to the count of Armagnac on August 22 makes her priorities plain: "when you hear that I am in Paris, send me a message and I will tell you in whom you should rightly believe, and what I shall know by the counsel of my just and sovereign Lord, the King of all the world, and as far as I can, what you should do. I commend you to God: May He keep you. Written at Compiègne the 22 day of August."[15] Here, unlike the letter sent to the people of Rheims during the two-week truce, Joan cites God, not Charles, as the power to whom she is immediately answerable. As she attacked the Saint-Denis and Saint-Honoré gates of Paris on September 7 and 8, all accounts suggest that she was acting "for Jesus' sake," as the Burgundian Bourgeois of Paris records her words,[16] for Saint-Denis, "because that is the [war]-cry of France," as she said at her trial,[17] and even, as she also said at her trial, "at the request of noblemen at arms who wanted to make a skirmish or some valliance in arms against Paris."[18] Of Charles she says only that she went "against La Charité at the request of my king."[19] Charles T. Wood makes the point that part of Charles's newly constructed identity as king was that he was to be closely identified with God, indeed "as the regent of God, His lieutenant for the

Kingdom."[20] Charles's claim does not mean, however, that Joan conflated the two in all her discourse; her testimony about the attack on Paris suggests that it was more Joan's undertaking than that of her king, although it would have been done for Charles, even if it displeased him at that moment.

The conflict over the taking of Paris is the historical and political paradigm to which Christine de Pizan's poem speaks. Its imperatives would have been meaningless hyperbole if actually composed on the last day of July during the two-week truce when even Joan's rhetoric on the subject of Paris was couched in the subjunctive. Written during late August or early September, however, the verses would have the force of political immediacy. In that case, the poem draws upon the construct of historical prophecy by being dated in July. Christine de Pizan, like the oracles she cites, constructs herself as knowing what must happen in the future. And again, in either case, she sets herself not on the side of the king but with Joan and Joan's plans for Charles and for Paris. This position is certainly a radical revision for a writer who has so consistently championed the cause of Charles.

While we can limit the direct implications of her argument to the disagreement over the taking of Paris, we must not underestimate the courage required for Christine de Pizan to oppose Charles on any topic. Supporting Charles's claim to the throne had cost Christine de Pizan much in the decade before this poem; that she is now willing to challenge his authority is significant. Of course, there is the standard political argument that a firmly established power, even if new, can tolerate dissent. But not only was Charles far from firmly established (for all that he had been crowned), but what we know of his personality does not suggest that he would have tolerated much dissent on individual issues from subjects who wished to be viewed as loyal to the crown. Indeed, his treatment of Joan herself, to whom he owed so much, supports this political reading of Charles's view of dissent; for not only did he attempt to distance himself from her as the agency of his coronation, but he became completely intolerant of any support for her among his nobles. This climate of political crisis and the intolerance it generated make the tone and message of Christine de Pizan's poem all the more remarkable. Whether she was sufficiently well informed of the current political conditions to realize that support for Joan would be read as opposition to Charles, or whether she simply decided to speak her mind without weighing the consequences, we cannot know, although Poissy was hardly a politically naive community. Without trying to reconstruct intentionality, let us look at the words of the poet as she speaks to the particular political situation near Paris in the late summer and early fall of 1429.

As Maureen Quilligan points out, in the context of Christine de Pizan's existing work, the "Maid was living, incontrovertible proof of what Christine had been arguing all along."[21] In her earlier historical writing, Christine de Pizan "appeals to a humanist ideal more usually associated with masculinist enterprises—historical fame and personal glory," to borrow the words of Quilligan.[22] In the *Ditié de Jehanne d'Arc* Christine de Pizan moves away from models of personal fame to images of relatively humble female saviors as she invokes Esther, Judith, and Deborah, asserting, as Deborah Fraioli suggests, that "the Maid's accomplishments surpass even the accomplishments of these illustrious women."[23] In a return to her own strategies of sibylline speech, Christine de Pizan foregrounds the element of prophecy as she writes of the woman warrior.

The authority Christine de Pizan invokes at the poem's very personal opening is her own and God's. Christine de Pizan identifies herself without the humility topos so common in her other works, identifies the life she has led for the past eleven years, and reminds her readers that Charles VII is the rightful king of France, all in the first stanza of the poem. Beginning "Je Christine," as one would begin a will or a legal testament, Christine de Pizan invokes the authority of no muse or patron saint; she claims her own authority to speak as coming directly from God. Even here she is a claimant rather than a supplicant, asking God for neither permission nor inspiration, but simply for a good memory, speaking of, rather than to, the Deity: "But now I wish to relate how God, to whom I pray for guidance lest I omit anything, accomplished all this through His grace. May it be told everywhere, for it is worthy of being remembered, and may it be written down—no matter whom it may displease—in many a chronicle and history-book!" (stanza 7). The restoration of Charles "the rejected child of the rightful King of France" (stanza 5) is what has been accomplished through God's grace; the matter of the poem, which will serve as a model for future chronicles and histories, is as the author describes it in its closing line, "a very beautiful poem composed by Christine."

Before that self-consciously literary line, however, comes the historical device of the date: the last day of July 1429. Christine de Pizan blurs the boundary here, slipping between the historical and the literary in an effort to control the first paradigm within the second. Having inscribed her identity and generative poetic authority at the beginning and end of the poem, Christine de Pizan devotes the body of the work to Joan: Joan's effect on Charles, on the French loyal to Charles, on the English, on the French allied with the English, and (most significantly) Joan's effect on the reader. In this version of events, Joan does not derive her authority from having put Charles back on the throne; Charles is empowered through Joan. If anything, Charles is described as a victim in terms which cast his actions in a somewhat dubious, if not shameful, light: "Charles (how strange this is!) the King's son—dare I say it?—fled in haste from Paris" (stanza 1). That Charles had to flee is a source of sorrow for the poet/speaker, but that Charles is able to stop fleeing is figured both as a natural phenomenon, linked to the seasons in the second through third stanzas, and as a political operation accomplished "through a young virgin" (stanza 11). Indeed, "all this [the restoration of Charles] has been brought about by the intelligence of the Maid," says her historian in stanza 13. In marked contrast to Joan's accomplishments through her own intelligence, Charles is empowered by Joan through the intervention of God, "And what honor for the French crown, this proof of divine intervention" (stanza 12), while Joan's actions are empowered by God and made famous to French people by her historian, "Je, Christine," just as Aeneas is empowered by the historical voice of the Sibyl, constructed by Virgil, who speaks of the Trojan past, the Roman future, and the present-tense warfare. Joan is, in this equation, perhaps more important than Charles; the poet gets to have it both ways, taking power from her subject, but also giving the power of fame through historical narrative.

We can obtain a clearer sense of Christine de Pizan's priorities by calculating the number and types of address within the stanzas of the poem. In eighteen stanzas the poet empowers her own voice by the emphatic use of the first person. In addition to these stanzas, there are twenty-four more in which the *je* is implicit in the imperative constructions for and questions to those who must heed her voice.[24] When not employing these most personal strategies, the poet joins herself to the people of France, speaking in the first person plural in seven stanzas. The stanzas of the poem which are unmarked by the constructed personal voice of the poet, although they are framed by such constructions, significantly include both the references to the Second Charlemagne Prophecy and to the historical events of Charles's crowning. These stanzas, we will argue, are set apart by Christine de Pizan as she attempts to differentiate between types of history within her poem.

We are led to this recognition of narrative manipulation by the shifting objects of address within the *Ditié*. The ultimate audience for this poem is the people of France, while the immediate subject is the relationship between Joan and Charles, with the former being figured as the most important. Charles is directly addressed by the voice of the poet in only six stanzas and only once by name; Joan is directly addressed even less frequently, in only four stanzas and only once by name. Christine's apostrophe to Charles is far from the words of the humble subject: she tells him in stanzas 13–16 that his honor has been "exalted by the Maid" (13) and not by his own actions; while he may be destined for greatness, he has not yet achieved it on his own. On the other hand, the poet never speaks of Joan by name, only to her (in stanza 22), while Charles is spoken of by name in four stanzas. By style or title, however, the poet signals her primary subject as she speaks of the king in fourteen stanzas and of the Maid in twenty-seven.[25] That this poem is about Joan the Maid, not Charles the king—indeed, about constructing Joan the Maid as both immediately and ultimately more important to France than Charles the king—is borne out by a reading of the passages of prophetic and actual history. Both initially and ultimately, of course, Charles is the primary historic figure. But in the historical moment of August or September of 1429, the historical moment created within the imaginative boundaries of Christine de Pizan's poem, Joan is the key figure for the fate of France.

In this poem, Christine de Pizan constructs four paradigms of historical narrative: the factual present, the factual past, the prophetic subjunctive, and the prophetic declarative. The factual present is framed by the life of the poet as set forth in the opening stanza of the poem. In the lifetime of "Je, Christine," Charles "the King's son" has "fled in haste from Paris" eleven years before, but now "exactly on the 17th day of July 1429 that Charles was, without any doubt, safely crowned at Rheims" (stanza 49) and "returns through his country" (stanza 50). Separating these two events, we find the narrative of Joan's early battles in stanzas 33–36: "A little girl of sixteen ... drives her enemies out of France, recapturing castles and towns." Interestingly, only Joan's actions are presented in the present tense, even though the coronation at Rheims came after the lifting of the siege of Orléans. The agency for present-tense history, then, is Joan.

The factual past is figured first as historical narratives which exist independent of the circumstances of fifteenth-century France. For example, the histories of Moses, Joshua, Gideon, Esther, Judith, Deborah, Achilles, and Hector are mentioned in relation to Joan, but the relationship is not one of causation. The biblical figures may be seen as types of the Maid, but the poet does not claim that they foretold or caused her coming. Yet this catalogue sets up the paradigm within which the generation of the Second Charlemagne Prophecy can be constructed as the factual, rather than the fictive past. Linking the biblical references to the mythic by mention of divine inspiration in stanzas 29 and 30, Christine de Pizan canonizes the fictive by eliding it with the biblical through the common comparison of Joan herself. Joan is like these historical figures: these figures were divinely inspired as Joan is divinely inspired; Joan is also the fulfillment of historical prophecies, so those prophecies are therefore history. As the poet presents it, biblical history and mythic Second Charlemagne Prophecy constitute a seamless whole. The prophecies of Merlin, the Sibyl, and Bede, foregrounded in stanza 31, are "found in history" (line 239) and are the words of those writers who "made prophecies about her, saying that she would carry the banner in the French wars and describing all that she would achieve" (lines 245–48). The past and the present meet in Joan. All that seems to be in question is the future.

Having so carefully erected the construct of prophecy as the key to history, Christine de Pizan is now in a powerful position to locate her words within the protocols of myth, fact, and gender suggested by her ordering of Merlin, the Sibyl, and Bede. Between the mythic Merlin and the factual Bede, she places the feminine Sibyl—a style, not a name, but a style always given to a woman. Within this poem, Christine de Pizan usurps the style of Sibyl to produce two types of prophecy: subjunctive and declarative. The poet narrator speaks to Charles in the former, weaker mode of discourse. In stanza 13 she begins her apostrophe to Charles; in stanza 16 she states that "there will be a king of France called Charles, son of Charles, who will be supreme ruler over all kings"; but in stanza 17 she concludes that she can only hope Charles VII to be this "supreme ruler": "I pray to God that you may be the person I have described." By phrasing this identification so tentatively in the subjunctive, Christine de Pizan usurps the power of unconditional historical prophecy for herself; she grants that power unequivocally only to Joan, not to Charles. Charles *may* or *should* be the fulfillment of a prophecy, but Joan *is*: "the beauty of her life *proves* that she has been blessed with God's grace . . . whatever she does, she always has her eyes fixed on God. . . . It *is* my belief that no miracle was ever more evident" (stanzas 32–33, emphasis ours). Even Charles is included in the flat statement that no "more can be said of any other person" (23), for God "has given to her a heart greater than that of any man" (26). The emphasis on Joan's gender is more than Christine de Pizan's protofeminism coming to the surface of this poem; the Second Charlemagne Prophecy speaks of a woman being the person who will restore France. The king must, of course, be named Charles, but royal males with that name are much more common than women warriors. Again, we see that Joan is the central figure in this political paradigm.

As a number of scholars have pointed out,[26] Christine de Pizan first mentions Merlin, the Sibyl, and Bede (and thus implicitly the Second Charlemagne Prophecy[27]) in stanza 31, the exact midpoint of the poem: "for more than 500 years ago, Merlin, the Sibyl and Bede foresaw her coming, entered her in their writings as someone who would put an end to France's troubles, made prophecies about her, saying that she would carry the banner of the French in wars and describing all that she would achieve" (stanza 31). Not content with merely invoking the prophecies of others, Christine de Pizan articulates her own by constructing Joan as the generative force by which these things would be accomplished. In stanzas 42 and 43 she speaks of Joan leading Charles to the Holy Land where they will both gain glory. As Virgil creates a mythic past for his historical hero, Augustus Caesar, Christine de Pizan creates a mythic future for her hero, Joan of Arc. The voices of Bede, Merlin, and the Sibyl speak from the past as the voice of "Je, Christine" speaks of the future. And what of the present? Of course Charles should let—must let—Joan take Paris: "for [the king] will enter Paris, no matter who may grumble about it!—the Maid has given her word that he will," says the voice of "Je, Christine" in stanza 54.

In stanzas 41–43 the poet sets up a series of statements about Joan's future accomplishments. Joan "will cast down the English for good . . . will restore harmony in Christendom and the Church . . . will destroy the unbelievers . . . will destroy the Saracens . . . will lead Charles" to the Holy Land, which he will conquer. Only here does Charles figure in declarative future history, and again the agency of his participation is Joan. The French construction *par elle* (translated by Kennedy and Varty as the active "she will") places Joan's actions above even her person, although her agency is therefore figured as divinely inspired; these deeds ordained by God for France and for Charles will be accomplished by and through Joan. These stanzas stress the relation between God's will and Joan's actions; Charles's actions are subordinated within this construction. As this prophetic section of the poem draws to a close, Charles disappears completely.

> Therefore, in preference to all the brave men of times past, this woman must wear the crown, for her deeds show clearly enough already that God bestows more courage upon her than upon all those men about whom people speak. And she has not yet accomplished her whole mission! I believe that God bestows her here below so that peace may be brought about through her deeds.
>
> And yet destroying the English race is not her main concern for her aspirations lie more elsewhere; it is her concern to ensure the survival

of the Faith. As for the English, whether it be a matter for joy or sorrow, they are done for. In days to come scorn will be heaped upon them. They have been cast down! (stanzas 44–45)

Surely those last lines, if nothing else in the poem, might have been cherished by the chroniclers of the 1450s, had they not been so firmly enmeshed in a narrative which constructs Joan, not Charles, as both a national and virtually apocalyptic leader. Christine de Pizan's strategy of differentiating historical discourse allows her to privilege Joan over Charles by both the formation and the content of her poetry. Without closing the door on the possibility that Charles could participate in this triumph and claim his own place in this prophetic history, as she had always hoped he would, Christine de Pizan makes it clear that he has yet to accomplish as much as had the Maid. The rebels to whom the poet speaks in stanzas 46 through 48 are defined by their failure to recognize the power of the Maid. While the strong language of these stanzas would not be addressed overtly to the king himself, the warning explicit in these lines speaks just as well to Charles and those of his nobles who made the truce which Joan opposed: "Oh, all you blind people, can't you detect God's hand in this? . . . Has she not led the King with her own hand to his coronation?" (stanza 47). It is difficult to imagine a more direct and immediate response to present-tense history and a warning to other French people about how this divine intervention should be read.

Again, the parallel to Shakespeare comes to mind. But the parallel is outweighed by the contrast, for the famous St. Crispin's Day speech which he writes for Henry V is a work of art crafted over a century later, suggested by Holinshed's observation (also noncontemporary) that Henry noted the battle was fought on this day. The voice of Christine de Pizan the poet is here very different, stronger even than the voices which bring us immediate information over CNN, for hers is not simply the voice of an observer but of a partisan participant in the struggle within and over France. It is significant that Christine de Pizan never presumes to speak for Joan. Again, the voice is that of historical realism—the poet can speak of Joan and for herself—representing a political reality, not a work of political art. This poem is a document aimed not at reconstructing history but at shaping the political present.

As we look at the last twelve stanzas of the poem, we return to the argument with which we opened the essay. Christine de Pizan marks these last stanzas with a clear reference to Charles in the historical present, his coronation in stanza 49. But immediately before this, in stanza 48, the poet presents Joan as the agent of that coronation. And after the specific reference to Charles in 49, the coronation stanza, the person of the king begins to fade from the poem. In the following eleven stanzas, the king is represented only by pronoun, by implication, by the words *prince*[28] and *lord* and by that phrase so close to the status which Charles was not quite granted earlier in the poem, *supreme ruler* (stanza 60).[29] Although Charles does not vanish as completely as he does in the earlier prophetic passage, here we find his presence carefully problematized. Indeed, there is no reference to the king at all in stanza 54, where Kennedy and Varty emend the text to read "for [the King] will enter Paris, no matter who may grumble about it!"[30] Joan, on the other hand, is still the Maid in stanzas 50, 51, 52, 53, 54, and 59.

The issue, of course, is Paris. On the last day of July 1429, Paris was not actively an issue. The terms of the truce with the duke of Burgundy were still in effect, and there would be no reason for Christine de Pizan to write, "I don't know if Paris will hold out" (stanza 53). The next statement, "if it decides to see her as an enemy, I fear that she will subject it to a fierce attack, as she had done elsewhere," is also more reasonably understood if it was written in mid-to-late August or even September. The poet would have known about the truce, as did the concerned people of Rheims whom Joan addresses in her letter. Furthermore, this entire passage about the taking of Paris sits oddly in a poem which is simply one of celebration. Why would a simple poem of celebration conclude as does this one? "But I believe that some people will be displeased by its contents, for a person whose head is bowed and whose eyes are heavy cannot look at the light" (stanza 61). These people who will be displeased by this version of history—the same people the poet scorns with the statement in stanza 7 that she will write "no matter whom it may displease"—could be only those people who did not see the agenda of Joan as the best plan for France. If these displeased people were merely the defeated minority within the new kingdom of Charles VII, there is no reason for them to be thus privileged at both the beginning and the end of this poem. That the displeased people included not just Burgundians, but Charles himself, is the logical conclusion.[31]

Whether she wrote this poem in August or September of 1429 or even later, Christine de Pizan uses the power of prophetic history to place herself clearly on the side of Joan the Maid and against the actions, if not the person, of Charles VII. Nor does she mean this political propaganda to be read as an anonymous act, for she signs every stanza of the document which both begins and ends with her own name. Finally, the tone of the poem suggest that there is still a serious matter to be decided. Whether this is literally the taking of Paris or the imprisonment or even the trial of Joan, we cannot know. But whatever the issue, it called forth the strongest rhetorical strategies of a writer known for expressing her personal views. Quite self-consciously, Christine de Pizan built her own structures of authority upon the authority of Joan so that she might argue for the goals of the Maid, thus linking her fate to that of Joan in a truly self-consuming literary artifact. That her poem must now be resurrected into the canon of her work by the use of many of the same documents employed in the so-called rehabilitation of Joan is surely a "tresbel"[32] example of poetic justice. In a sense, this poem is more than a response to the Hundred Years' War; it is itself an artifact of that conflict.

NOTES

1. This essay is a revised version of "PR pas PC: Christine de Pizan's Pro-Joan Propaganda," in *Fresh Verdicts on Joan of Arc*, ed. Bonnie Wheeler and Charles Wood, The New Middle Ages 2 (New York: Garland Publishing, 1996), 146–60. Permission of the publisher to reprint this essay is gratefully acknowledged.

2. Maureen Quilligan, *The Allegory of Female Authority: Christine de Pizan's Cité des dames* (Ithaca, N.Y.: Cornell University Press, 1991), argues that Joan constitutes a justification for Christine de Pizan's work, contending: "It cannot be entirely an accident then that the unique and singular female writer in late medieval France should so overlap the advent of the unique and singular female warrior; although it is not possible to prove such things, it does make sense to suppose that Christine's arguments, so highly visible to all court members, may have helped prepare them to accept a woman's authority. Her constant retelling of the Amazon myth, arguing for their legitimate domain in the martial realm of their own in text after text, could very well have prepared the culture at court to see a woman warrior as something other than a monster" (280). This statement, we believe, is radically overstating the case.

3. Charity Cannon Willard, *Christine de Pizan: Her Life and Works* (New York: Persea, 1984), 207, concludes her chapter on Joan in Christine's biography with the sentimental hope that the writer died before things began going wrong for the Maid. In "PR pas PC," as in this essay, we argue that Christine de Pizan's use of July 31, 1429, is fictive. At the Third International Christine de Pizan Symposium in July 1998 at Lausanne, Switzerland, Professor Angus Kennedy, in his paper "La date du *Ditié de Jehanne d'Arc*: un résponse à Anne D. Lutkus et Julia M. Walker," took issue with this assertion. Kennedy argued that because Christine de Pizan's other dated works included real rather than fictive dates, we should read "the last day of July" as also literal. He further argued that the medieval writer (in which category he

included Christine de Pizan) would not have imagined a fictive date. During the discussion session, Walker rebutted this last point by reminding the audience that Dante's date of 1300 was fictive.

    4. Christine de Pizan, *Ditié de Jehanne d'Arc*, ed. and trans. Angus J. Kennedy and Kenneth Varty, Medium Aevum Monographs, n.s., 9 (Oxford: Society for the Study of Medieval Languages and Literature, 1977), 2; unless otherwise stated, all references to the poem are to this translation and are documented parenthetically in the text.

    5. Willard, *Christine de Pizan*, 207.

    6. Régine Pernoud, *Joan of Arc: By Herself and Her Witnesses*, trans. Edward Hyams (New York: Stein and Day, 1966; reprint, New York: Scarborough House, 1982) dismisses the political reality of the truce: "This truce condemned the royal army to inaction; and in exchange the Duke made Charles the fantastic promise that he would hand over Paris to the King. In fact he, and Bedford with him, was simply seeking to gain time: Bedford had called for reinforcements from England immediately after the battle of Patay, and early in July three thousand five hundred knights and archers disembarked at Calais.... This army left Calais on July 15th for Paris where it arrived on the 25th" (128–29, page citations are to the reprint edition).

    7. Original deposited in the Archives Départementales du Nord; cited in Pernoud, *Joan of Arc: By Herself*, 128.

    8. Pernoud, *Joan of Arc: By Herself*, 128.

    9. Pernoud, *Joan of Arc: By Herself*, 130. Of course, Paris had always been one of Joan's goals, as her letter to the English on March 22 indicates.

    10. Pernoud, *Joan of Arc: By Herself*, 131. In Régine Pernoud and Marie-Véronique Clin, *Jeanne D'Arc* (Paris: Fayard, 1986), Joan's words are analyzed as follows: "Ce ton de regret, si inhabituel chez elle, la révèle désarmée devant ce qu'il lui faut combattre à présent: la trahison, insaisissable, qu'elle sent toute proche et qui, àchaque pas, la précéde" (116). [This tone of regret, so unusual in her, shows her disarmed before what she now has to combat: treachery, incomprehensible, that she feels quite close which, at every step, precedes her.] Pernoud modifies, but does not retract, her earlier judgment that Joan knew nothing of the treaty with Burgundy. She and Clin state, "Elle voudrait se porter sur Paris et elle ne sait pas que d'avance Charles VII s'est engagé à y renoncer" (116). [She would like to go to Paris and she does not know that in advance Charles VII had engaged himself to renounce it.] The question "in advance of what or when?" remains unanswered.

    11. Cited from *Les Lettres de Jeanne d'Arc et la prétendue adjuration de St. Ouen*, Le Comte C. de Maleissye (Paris, 1911), 6–8, in Marina Warner, *Joan of Arc: The Image of Female Heroism* (New York: Vintage Books, 1981), 73. If Joan did know of the treaty, was she ready to honor it by going home to her sheep or was she just waiting for it to fall apart before she marched on Paris?

12. Charles T. Wood, *Joan of Arc and Richard III: Sex, Saints, and Government in the Middle Ages* (Oxford: Oxford University Press, 1988), 143

13. Pernoud and Clin, *Jeanne D'Arc*, 115: "s'exprimait l'espoir que le roi concluera 'a bon traité.' Avant qu'il parte. La même lettre faisait allusion à Jeanne: Elle ne fait doute qu'ele ne mette Paris en son obéissance. C'était indiquer clairement les préoccupations de chacun. Jeanne ne pensait qu'à poursuivre une offensive qui s'était révélée si féconde, tandis que le roi ne songeait qu'à négocier et, en fait de 'bon traité', allait conclure une trêve . . . de quinze jours! Ainsi, après une journée triomphale vécue à Rheims, on se retrouve en plein malentendu."

14. Colonel de Liocourt, *La mission de Jeanne d'Arc*, Tome II (Paris: Nouvelles Editions Latines, 1981), 197: "Forte du prestige qu'elle [Jeanne] avait alors, elle obtint facilement l'assentiment du roi. Incontinent, la décision fut prise de partir pour Paris le lendemain 18, et les ordres nécessaires furent donnés pour la mise en route de l'armée." While one might argue that this initial order was Christine de Pizan's source of information, one must also concede that if she heard of that decision, she was even more likely to hear of the other, more lasting order.

15. From *The Trial of Jeanne d'Arc*, ed. and trans. W. P. Barrett (New York, 1932) 180, cited in Wood, *Joan of Arc and Richard III*, 128.

16. Cited in Pernoud, *Joan of Arc: By Herself*, 135.

17. Cited in Pernoud, *Joan of Arc: By Herself*, 139.

18. Cited in Pernoud, *Joan of Arc: By Herself*, 134.

19. Cited in Pernoud, *Joan of Arc: By Herself*, 134.

20. Wood, *Joan of Arc and Richard III*, 150.

21. Quilligan, *Allegory of Female Authority*, 270.

22. Quilligan, *Allegory of Female Authority*, 250.

23. Deborah Fraioli, "The Literary Image of Joan of Arc: Prior Influences," *Speculum* 56 (1981): 815. Fraioli stresses the Deborah image was the most important of these for Christine, although unlike Jean Gerson she did not consider the image of a woman warrior unseemly. According to Fraioli, "Christine believed that Joan of Arc's appearance was prophesied five hundred years earlier not only by Bede but also by Merlin and the sibyls. Furthermore, her understanding of the ultimate goal of the Maid's mission comes to her through knowledge of a prophecy popular in France from 1382, called the Second Charlemagne Prophecy" (826).

24. In some of these stanzas the parallel constructions carry on the mode of personal address. For example, in the apostrophe to the English, which begins in stanza 39 ("And so, you English") and continues through 40 ("You thought") into 41 ("And know that she will"), the *she will* in 42 and 43 extends the mode of address.

25. The count would be twenty-eight if we included the very last line, with its direct reference to the poem itself, the poem titled with Joan's name.

26. See especially Kevin Brownlee's structural analysis in "Structures of Authority in Christine de Pizan's *Ditié de Jehanne d'Arc*," in *Discourses of Authority in Medieval and Renaissance Literature*, ed. Kevin Brownlee and Walter Stephens (Hanover, N.H.: Published for Dartmouth College by University Press of New England, 1989), 131–50. See also Therese Ballet Lynn, "The *Ditié de Jeanne d'Arc*: Its Political, Feminist and Aesthetic Significance," *Fifteenth Century Studies* 1 (1978): 149–56, to which Brownlee owes perhaps a somewhat greater debt than he acknowledges. For a comparison between Christine de Pizan's poem and Martin le Franc's 1440 verse *De Dame Jehanne la Pucelle*, see Harry F. Williams, "Joan of Arc, Christine de Pizan, and Martin le Franc," *Fifteenth Century Studies* 16 (1990): 233–37.

27. For a discussion of the Second Charlemagne Prophecy, see Marjorie Reeves, *The Influence of Prophecy in the Later Middle Ages: A Study in Joachimism* (Oxford: Oxford University Press, 1969), 320–31. Reeves remarks rather dryly that such prophecies "seem to be indestructible . . . [as] the Second Charlemagne survived the madness of Charles VI" (341). Added to the power of the Second Charlemagne Prophecy with its insistence upon a king named Charles, was the commonplace axiom of the second and third decades of the fifteenth century: France was lost by a woman (Isabeau) and would be restored by a woman (arguably Joan).

28. Stanza 60 is addressed to the citizens of Paris, who acknowledged the English Henry as their official prince and the duke of Burgundy as their practical overlord. While "your prince" almost certainly does refer to Charles, Christine de Pizan could easily have chosen a less problematic phrase if her only concern was to privilege Charles as the person to whom Paris should yield.

29. Although Kennedy and Varty translate both the stanza 16 title and the stanza 60 style as "supreme ruler," the words in stanza 16 are "Qui sur tous rois sera grant maistre" while the phrase in stanza 60 is "vostre chief greigneur."

30. If anything, the French makes Joan the subject of this phrase: "Car ens entrera, qui qu'en groigne! /—La Pucelle lui a promis."

31. This is, perhaps, putting things a bit too simply. Christine de Pizan questioned Queen Isabeau also because her alliance with Burgundy and general influence which resulted in the Treaty of Troyes; this treaty, supported by Burgundy, deprived Charles of the throne.

32. After stanza 61 of the poem appears this line: "Explicit ung tresbel Ditié par Christine."

CHAPTER 9

CLOTHING AND GENDER DEFINITION

JOAN OF ARC

SUSAN CRANE

Joan of Arc wore men's clothes almost continuously from her first attempts to reach the Dauphin, later crowned Charles VII, until her execution twenty-eight months later. In court, on campaigns, in church, and in the street she crossdressed, and she refused to stop doing so during long months of her trial for heresy. Joan's contemporary supporters and adversaries comment extensively on her clothing, and the records of her trial provide commentary of her own, making her by far the best-documented transvestite of the later Middle Ages.

Because Joan's use of men's clothes partakes of her self-proclaimed identity as "la Pucelle," the maiden sent by God to save France from the English, scholars have generally considered her transvestism to be an attribute of her military and religious mission, a strategically useful behavior without implications for sexuality. But isolating transvestism from sexual identity risks assuming both that heterosexuality is the only possible position for Joan and that self-presentation has nothing to do with sexuality, that is, sexuality is innate and prior to choices about gendered behavior. I would like to reconsider Joan's crossdressing from the position that gender encompasses both the exterior, social interpretation of sexual practices and the more diffused generation, expression, and organization of desire that makes up sexuality itself. Locating sexuality within the complex of interpretive articulations that constitute gendered identity urges the possibility that Joan's transvestism refers to her sexuality as well as to her campaign to save France.

During her trial Joan articulates a gender position in conditions that directly shape the performance of gender. Michel Foucault's crucial insight concerning the institutional regulation of sexuality was that regulation is not primarily repressive but productive, and productive not only of normative repetitions of sexuality in new subjects but also of the conditions for revising and resisting those norms: "At issue is not a movement bent on pushing rude sex back into some obscure and inaccessible region, but on the contrary, a process that spreads it over the surface of things and bodies, arouses it, draws it out and bids it speak, implants it in reality and enjoins it to tell the truth: an entire glittering sexual array, reflected in a myriad of discourses, the obstination of powers, and the interplay of knowledge and pleasure."[1] Foucault's well-known tendency is to define the medieval as the time before competing discourses on sexuality developed and before power diffused itself so completely throughout the social fabric, but recent work brings into question his view of a "markedly unitary" medieval discourse on sexuality that was fully encompassed in penitential doctrine and that conceived homoerotic acts but not homosexual identity.[2] These reconsiderations of the medieval/modern dichotomy do not license treating the medieval as if it were modern, but rather predict that medieval discourses of sexuality will be multiple, even contradictory, as are modern ones. Discourses of sexuality such as *fine amor* and mystical marriage with God may be less visible now than penitential doctrine, but their effects on subjectivity deserve the greater efforts of recovery.

Joan's judges ask her to defend the self-presentation she is in the process of developing in part through adopting masculine dress. As the institution most concerned with regulating sexuality, the Church in varied manifestations—its authoritative texts, its sacraments, its courts of inquisition—encourages and enforces gender's "performativity," in Judith Butler's terminology, its reproduction in specific persons through their ongoing repetitions of its norms.[3] Yet, as Butler emphasizes, the repetition of sexuality's laws is a process during which a revisionary performance might be developed. In the case of Joan of Arc, I will argue, an intensified relation to the law produces not her acquiescence in self-correction but instead her persistent effort to distinguish herself from the category of womanhood as she understands it.

In writing of Joan's identity and Joan's statements, I am of course making a number of decisions about "Joan." First, I use her name to stand for her documentary traces, partial and uneven as they are, and for my interpretation of those traces. This documentary "Joan" is an appropriate subject for an analysis that takes gender to be constituted in its performance rather than derived from a pre-existing true self. Second, I choose to attribute recorded actions and statements to "Joan" while recognizing that her self-construction is heavily coerced, her will conditioned by her culture, and her responses circumscribed by her interlocutors's preoccupations. It is her ongoing enactment of constraints and resistances alike that articulates her identity (as best she can) and that deserves a name. Third, I recognize that the testimony of "Joan" about her past deeds and words is not always true to other records or testimony; I am concerned primarily with her self-articulation under the pressure of the trial itself. For example, I am not concerned to determine if God told her to crossdress or if she did so at the suggestion of Jean de Nouillompont, but rather to clarify how her stated motives fit with each other and with her wider self-defense, and what place she makes for crossdressing in her self-conception. Finally, in dropping the scare quotes from the name of "Joan," I am resisting what seems to me a misguided tendency among medievalists to claim that (other) medievalists believe that the past is fully recoverable, that "the making of texts is, severely and always, the making of meaning," or that history is "foundational and primary, the thingly origin" for language that itself eludes linguistic indeterminacy.[4] This naive version of the past's accessibility is no more tenable (and, I would argue, no more practiced) than the inverse claim that the past is an untranscendable horizon. To write of the past while claiming it is simply irrecoverable would be a futile contradiction; to assert the past's full identity with the present would equally eradicate it. Any writer about the past is caught paradoxically between what goes on from it—Nietzsche's and Gadamer's "effective past," *wirkliche Historie* or *Wirkungsgeschichte*—and all that language fails to mean or to convey.[5] There is no escape into the simplicity of either position, access or loss, in isolation from the other. To cite "Joan" without scare quotes is to recognize that she is a remnant but also a remain, a vestigial text that still has a few things to say for itself.

Joan was captured in May of 1430 by Burgundian forces, sold to the English in November, and tried for heresy in Rouen during the following February, March, and April by the Bishop of Beauvais, Pierre Cauchon, and the Papal Deputy Inquisitor, Jean le Maistre, and well over a hundred assistants. She was convicted of heresy in May of 1431, abjured during a public exhortation in the cemetery of St. Ouen, but relapsed a few days later, reassuming the men's clothes she had agreed to stop wearing and reporting that she heard her voices reproaching her for having abjured them. The next day, the episcopal court declared her a relapsed heretic, and she was burned by the secular authorities on the following day, May 30.[6] This was not, however, her only trial; when Charles VII at last took control of Rouen eighteen years later, he initiated an investigation into the findings of her "procès de condamnation" which culminated in a "procès en nullité" that declared her conviction for heresy to have been invalid.[7] Evidence collected at this second trial seeks to validate the records from the first: despite its obvious bias toward a martyred supporter of Charles VII, the "procès en nullité" received much testimony sustaining the accuracy of the record of Joan's words in the "procès de condamnation."[8] The original trial's procedures and conclusions, rather than the evidence taken from Joan, were the basis for nullification.

Testimony from the nullification trial traces in fascinating detail how records from the first trial were generated. To summarize briefly, two official notaries and occasionally some other recorders kept running notes in French during the interrogations. The notaries compared their texts each day after dinner and drew up the minutes of the trial, still in French. One of the notaries, Guillaume Manchon, submitted his minutes to the authorities in charge of the nullification trial, and two copies deriving from those minutes have survived.[9] Remarkable as it is to have a French record of Joan's interrogation, it is yet more remarkable that Joan seems to have considered herself its coproducer. The surviving copies of the minutes record, and testimony at the nullification trial recalls, numerous occasions on which Joan demanded that her responses be corrected in the record, admonished the notaries to be more careful, asked for a copy of the work to be sent to Paris if she was to be interrogated again there, and refused to answer questions she felt she had already answered. Instead she replies "luisés bien vostre livre et vous le trouverés" [read your book carefully and you will find it], or "vous estes respondus de ce que vous en aurez de moi" [you already have as much of an answer as you will get from me].[10] The French minutes were read aloud to Joan at the end of the weeks of interrogation for her corrections.[11] After the minutes' completion, according to the Orléans manuscript, when a herald at the cemetery of St. Ouen cried out that she was a heretic, Joan retorted "qu'il n'estoit pas vray, ainsy qu'il est escript ailleurs" [that it was not true, as was written down elsewhere].[12] Although Joan's voice is in several ways constrained in the French minutes—by the questions her many inquisitors choose to ask, by certain omissions from the minutes that were noted during the nullification trial, and by the notaries' collating tendency to group responses to several questions together—it appears that, in Joan's opinion as well as that of the notaries and other witnesses, the French record of her statements is fairly accurate.

Throughout the trial, Joan refused to change from men's into women's clothing. Her dress was a continual source of friction with her inquisitors, for whom it was the visible sign of Joan's questionable spiritual status. In my view, the responses of Joan's contemporaries to her dress, from her inquisitors' hostility to her supporters' justifications, are more at odds than in consonance with Joan's testimony. In the best learned tradition, Joan's contemporaries refer her dress to one or more precedents. For her defenders, she is reminiscent of Camilla and the Amazons, the transvestite saints of the early Church, and the biblical Deborah and Esther.[13] Her detractors cite the prohibition against crossdressing in Deuteronomy and the Pauline text that women's hair is the veil of their modesty.[14] Invoking textual authority is not a strategy Joan uses (and of course is not a strategy fully available to one of her background), nor do her statements about her dress coincide very well with the authorities her supporters invoke. Given the unusual care with which the records of this trial were made and the validation they received at the nullification trial, I have found Joan's own statements to be a more compelling subject for discussion than those of her contemporaries. Joan's explanations move beyond the more recognizable genealogies for crossdressing provided by her contemporaries into a gender revision that is unique to Joan's practice and could count as one of her most significant acts.

JOAN'S TESTIMONY

Early in the trial and at several later points as well, Joan explains her male dress as a merely instrumental gesture without moral or gendered significance. In her testimony she refuses to charge anyone with advising her to change clothes, stating instead that "il falloit necessairement qu'elle changeast son habit" [it was necessary that she change her clothes].[15] Several of her early statements dismiss her dress as a minor issue: "de veste parum est, et est de minori" [dress is a small thing, among the littlest]; she cannot recall if Charles, or his wife, or the ecclesiastical body that interrogated her for several days in Poitiers asked her anything about her dress.[16] These dismissive statements imply that crossdressing has no significance beyond a merely functional convenience. Indeed, when offered women's clothes she responds that if she were allowed to leave prison in them, she would wear them gladly: under those circumstances women's clothes, like men's in other circumstances, would serve her purpose of resisting the English.[17] In a telling formulation she links men's clothes directly to armed opposition: she "ne feroit pour rien le serement qu'elle ne se armast et meist en abit d'omme" [would never for anything swear not to arm herself and wear men's clothes].[18]

Associating transvestism with military goals and with the exigencies of travel characterizes her contemporaries' justifications as well. Typically they mention her clothing only in relation to her arming for battle: in Percival de Cagny's chronicle, "elle print et se mist en habit d'homme et requist au roy qu'il luy fist faire armures pour soy armer" [she put on men's clothes and asked the king to have armor made with which to arm herself]; the *Chronique de la Pucelle* has her explain at Poitiers, "il fault, pour ce que je me doibs armer et servir le gentil Daulphin en armes, que je prenne les habillemens propices et nécessaires à ce" [because I must arm myself and serve the gentle Dauphin in arms, I must take the clothing that is suited and necessary for the purpose].[19]

In fact, however, there is much about Joan's dress that escapes instrumental explanations, both before and during her imprisonment. Joan crossdresses at all times, not just for battle but in court, in prison, even to receive Communion. Her persistent transvestism requires an explanation that goes beyond mere instrumentality. How can it further her opposition to the English to refuse to wear a dress in church? This framing of the issue is concrete, not merely hypothetical, as the judges deny Joan's many requests for access to the sacraments until she has agreed to give up male attire.

Here Joan's self-justification takes a turn that is intriguingly different from that of her contemporary allies. She supplements the argument from instrumentality with the assertion that her crossdressing pleases God, and later that she took it by God's command: "il plaist a Dieu que je le porte"; "je le fais par le commandement de nostre Sire et en son service" [it pleases God that I wear it; I do it on the command of our Lord and in his service].[20] She links her civilian attire to her military purpose in the assertion that "l'abit et les armes qu'elle a portés, c'est par le congié de Dieu; et tant de l'abit d'omme que des armes" [the clothing and the arms she has worn have been by the permission of God, and just as much the men's clothing as the arms].[21] God's will becomes her standard explanation for why she will not leave off her male dress, even in order to hear Mass and take Communion at Easter. In the week before Palm Sunday she asserts that "quant a l'abit de femme, elle ne le prandra pas encore, tant qu'il plaira a nostre Sire" [as for women's clothes, she will not take them yet, until it pleases our Lord]. In the week before Easter she replies concerning her clothes "qu'elle ayme plus chier mourir que revoquer ce qu'elle a fait du commandement de nostre Sire" [that she preferred to die rather than to abjure what she had done at the command of our Lord].[22] Her insistence that she cannot leave off men's clothing in order to gain access to the sacraments is especially striking given her urgent pleas for access.

Joan's insistence on God's command that she crossdress even in prison contrasts with the explanations generated during the nullification trial around threats to her chastity. The conditions of Joan's imprisonment were harsh. Rather than being held in an ecclesiastical prison with women attendants as was normal in heresy cases, Joan was guarded by English soldiers and kept in fetters day and night. A witness at the nullification trial recalled that one of her guards had threatened to rape her and that the Earl of Warwick had replaced two guards and admonished the others; a number of witnesses explained her resumption of male clothing after her abjuration with accounts that her guards had removed her women's clothes from her room during the night, or had harassed her, or that an English lord had raped her.[23] Other supporters linked her crossdressing throughout her mission with her commitment to chastity.[24]

Joan's male attire may have had some symbolic meaning for her guards, but it is important not to exaggerate the degree to which it could have protected her chastity from forcible rape. She continued to be identifiably female, and she apparently slept undressed both in the field and in prison.[25] Only after her abjuration and relapse, when she rejected the woman's dress provided for her at her abjuration, did Joan herself attribute her clothing (somewhat obliquely) to the conditions of her imprisonment. At this point she stated both that she preferred men's clothes to women's and "qu'il luy estoit plus licite de le reprendre et avoir habit d'omme, estant entre les hommes" [that it was more suitable for her to retake and have men's clothes, since she was among men].[26] Here Joan incorporates her defense of crossdressing into her long-standing argument with the court that she should be in an ecclesiastical rather than a secular prison. She continues, on this final day of interrogation, that she resumed male attire because she was not allowed to hear Mass as promised and was not taken out of her fetters, but that if she were allowed to hear Mass and were transferred to a better prison, she would obey the Church.[27] The implication that her male guards constitute a sexual threat is strong and renders the more striking that during many weeks of interrogation, Joan, in contrast to her supporters before and after the trial, does not use that threat to explain her clothes. Indeed, even when her interrogators refer to her imprisonment, she refers to God's will: admonished as late as May 2 that she is wearing men's clothes "sans neccessité, et en especial qu'elle est en prison" [without cause, and especially since she is in prison], she answers, "quant je auray fait ce pourquoy je suis envoyee de par Dieu, je prendray habit de femme" [when I have done what I was sent to do by God, I will take women's clothes].[28]

Where is the place for self-definition within the Christian visionary's assertion of divine command? Many women mystics of the later Middle Ages attribute their behavior to God's will, evading (with limited success) institutional attempts to regulate their behavior by presenting themselves as merely the channel for divine messages and interventions in the contemporary scene. That "merely" has the character of litotes, however, in claiming direct contact with God in place of the more mediated spirituality available to most Christians through the institutional Church. The visionary risks appearing not to be the selfless vessel of the Lord but an ambitious self-promoter.[29] Joan's judges regard her claim to hear God's commands in this light, attending closely to aspects of her conduct such as her transvestism that might betray worldly aspirations. But Joan does not endorse their version of an exclusive relation between divine command and self-promotion. Her proverb "Aide toy, Dieu te aidera" [Help yourself and God will help you] expresses her refusal to dichotomize divine and human agency; indeed, her tendency is to foreground the role of her own initiative in acting on God's will.[30] In the struggle over whether to give up crossdressing in exchange for access to the sacraments, Joan takes initiative by omitting to ask her voices if she may do so in the days before Easter, asking for delays in responding to questions about her dress, and insisting to her judges that crossdressing should not be an impediment to taking Communion. Joan does not simply accede to what she understands as God's will but shapes and supplements it through her strategic resistances to the court.[31]

In the weeks of her testimony, to summarize, Joan moves from the position that her crossdressing is instrumental to her cause and of little significance to the position that it is a crucial sign of her identity regardless of her circumstances at any particular moment. This surplus to its practical use is where transvestism most clearly shapes Joan's sexuality. Attributed directly to God, it instantiates the relation of sexual and religious identity; as Simon Gaunt notes in his study of transvestite saints, "sexuality is central to the construction of sanctity in the Middle Ages."[32] Vows of chastity, mystical marriage with God, martyrdom in sexually suggestive contexts, and transvestism do not simply remove holy men and women from sexuality but continue to define them through reference to sexual identities they have reshaped and redirected. Gaunt's important perception can also be read the other way around to say that sanctity is central to the construction of sexuality in this period. Joan draws on God's authority to face down her judges; in other contexts she draws less contentiously on Christian values to present herself. But she refers as well to secular standards and values that have been less noticed in her self-presentation than the religious motivations for which she has become celebrated.

Three contexts provided for crossdressing in the interrogation records are Joan's commitment to virginity, her claim to military and social authority, and her relations with women and their conventional tasks. In each context Joan's testimony imbricates secular and sacred meanings to develop and defend a gender position distinct both from conventional femininity and from the biblical, Amazonian, and saintly models suggested for her by her defenders.

Virginity has powerful secular and religious merit in women, protecting their value in the economy of heterosexuality until such time as they marry and enacting their rejection of the sexual economy in favor of a spiritual life within religious practice. These two roles of virginity are to some degree at odds, the former presuming a sexuality to be engaged at marriage and the latter evading marriage definitively. In calling herself "Jeanne la Pucelle" instead of "Jeanne la Vierge," Joan aligns herself with the secular pattern of virginity, in which the stages of a woman's maidenhood, wifehood, and widowhood succeed one another.[33] The pattern is implicit as well in her account of committing her virginity to her voices at the age of thirteen "tant qu'il plairoit a Dieu" [for as long as it may please God].[34] Similarly, she often says that her crossdressing will have a terminus, although she defers it when specific moments of choice are presented to her.[35]

Like her uncloistered vocation of leading troops against the English, Joan's conception that her men's clothes and her virginity may be put off at some future time calls into question the many contemporary and modern analogies drawn between Joan and several transvestite saints of the early Church.[36] If Joan knew the stories of these saints, for example the version of St. Margaret's legend in which she evades marriage by cropping her hair and living in disguise as "Brother Pelagius," they may have influenced her own refusal to marry and her pledge of chastity.[37] However, Joan's transvestism contrasts with the saints' in important respects. Thecla, Marina, and

Margaret/Pelagius adopt ascetic dress that minimizes sexual difference and rejects the sex-marked position of the feminine. John Anson labels such stories a "monastic fantasy" designed to appease sexual longing by imagining a woman in the monastery who is unpolluting and need not inspire guilt; Gaunt points out that the sexual longing so appeased is complexly gendered by the apparent masculinity of its crossdressed object.[38] Although I am arguing that Joan's crossdressing does complicate her gender, it does not do so by submerging her sex in a male disguise. Nor does Joan's testimony suggest that she regards her sex as a hinderance to her spirituality. And she does not retreat from the world but rather enters it more fully by crossdressing. Her virginity amounts to a mobilization of her sex: as a "Pucelle" she lays claim to the status of innocence and purity associated with secular women's virginity, rather than repudiating her womanhood in the manner of the transvestite saints, who often supplement their crossdress with the ability to grow facial hair, perform extraordinary penances, and hide their sex from everyone until their deaths.

In conjunction with her secular transvestism, then, Joan's maidenhood works less to signal abnegation and rejection of the world than to claim status within its hierarchies. Kirsten Hastrup has argued that Joan would not have been able to lead men if she had not had the status of "Pucelle," unpolluted by sex and uncontained as yet by marriage.[39] Maidenhood also has strong religious meaning for Joan; she indeed states that it is the single condition necessary for her salvation.[40] The spiritual merit assigned to virginity within the Church endorses Joan's maidenhood, but can it temper the transgressiveness of her crossdressing? As noted above, her contemporary allies tend not to mention her dress except as a necessity of military campaigning; her adversaries call her "femme monstrueuse," "femme desordonnée et diffamée, estant en habit d'homme et de gouvernement dissolut" [monstrous woman, disorderly and notorious woman who dresses in men's clothes, whose conduct is dissolute].[41] Joan's testimony responds to the charge that her crossdressing is immoral by aligning it with her vow of chastity; she pledged her virginity to God "tant qu'il plairoit a Dieu" [for as long as it pleased God], and God commanded her to crossdress "tant qu'il plaira a nostre Sire" [for as long as it pleases our Lord].[42] Attributing her transvestism directly to God associates it with her vow of chastity to God, claims for both the highest moral status, and assigns to both a central importance in her identity.

Despite her alignment of transvestism with maidenhood, there is much evidence that during the trial Joan felt extraordinary pressure concerning her transvestism. She first anticipates execution when refusing to wear a dress made up to her specifications, asking that if she is to be undressed at her sentencing she be given a long woman's dress and a kerchief to wear at execution.[43] Late in the trial she begins to avoid attributing her crossdressing to God, using formulas for evasion such as "donnez moy dilacion" [grant me a delay] and "vous en estes assés respondu" [you have been sufficiently answered about this]. She concludes enigmatically that "elle sçait bien qui luy a fait prandre l'abit, mais ne sçait point comme elle le doit reveler" [she well knows who made her take (men's) clothes, but she does not know at all how she should reveal it].[44] Does her refusal to give up crossdressing come to appear so transgressive to her that she hesitates to ascribe it to God's will? Still later, when asked how she prays, she gives this example: "tres doulz Dieu . . . je sçay bien, quant a l'abit, le commandement comme je l'ay prins; mais je ne sçay point par quelle maniere je le doy laisser. Pour ce, plaise vous a moy l'anseigner" [very sweet God, I well know concerning my dress by what command I took it, but I do not know at all in what way I should give it up. So may it please you to teach me that].[45] This formulation again suppresses the source of crossdressing and might even be read as Joan's request for aid in giving it up, as if her own will to crossdress were the impediment. Her will also intrudes, though asserted only hypothetically, when she testifies on Palm Sunday that if it were in her power to change to women's clothes, she would do so; and contradictorily, that if it were up to her, she would not change her clothes in order to receive Communion.[46] Again, since Joan understands her will to be contiguous with God's, I believe her testimony is less relevant to her judges' dichotomized view of wilfulness versus submission to the Church than to Joan's evolving self-presentation. In these later interrogations, the parallel between maidenhood and transvestism slips from view. Joan's sense of trouble around crossdressing becomes salient, while her virginity apparently remains unproblematic.

Much earlier in the trial, Joan was asked "se elle eust bien voullu estre homme" [if she really would have liked to be a man] when she set out on her mission. Joan responds with an evasive formula, "dit que autresfoys y avoit respondu" [she said she had answered this elsewhere], though no answer can be found in the record.[47] Since Joan's evasions tend to appear where a question does not allow for a response accurate to her convictions, it is possible that Joan did not believe that either "yes" or "no" would properly represent her position. Crossdress itself, according to Marjorie Garber, confuses categories; "this interruption, this disruptive act of putting into question, is ... precisely the place, and the role, of the transvestite."[48] Taken in isolation, Joan's virginity could represent the highly orthodox spiritual retreat of a heterosexual from marriage. But her continued engagement in secular affairs and her noninstrumental, secular crossdressing queer her virginity, that is, they move her virginity beyond its canonical meanings in ways that suggest a revision of heterosexual identity.

JOAN'S PRACTICE

Joan's secular role and her claim to high social status involve her in persistent and even flamboyant crossdressing during the two years between her departure from Vaucouleurs and her capture at Compiegne. When she set out from home to find the Dauphin Charles, she was in women's dress; some townspeople in Vaucouleurs presented her with a set of men's clothes in which she completed her journey to Charles (a contemporary witness details a black doublet, a short black tunic, and a black cap on her now shorn black hair).[49] There is a slight possibility that Joan continued to wear a dress on some occasions for the first few months of her mission. She gave a red garment, probably the red dress in which she had left home, to her godfather five months later; the 1429 treatise *De quadam puella* relates that Joan is as capable as an experienced war leader when on horseback "vestibus et armis virilibus induta" [clothed in male attire and armor]; "ubi autem de equo descendit, solitum habitum reassumens, fit simplicissima, negotiorum saecularium quasi innocens agnus imperita" [but when she descends from her horse, and assumes her usual clothes, she becomes completely naive, as inexperienced in the ways of the world as an innocent lamb].[50] This equation of femininity with ignorance and innocence might seem to restrict Joan's authority to the battlefield, but the mediating role the treatise assigns to clothing implies that masculine capability is as easy to acquire as masculine garments. If Joan's crossdressing was indeed only occasional during the early months of 1429, this passage suggests what was to be gained by giving up female attire altogether: part of the attraction of male attire was surely its associations with masculine authority.

The authority Joan claims through crossdressing violates class as well as gender lines: Joan soon abandoned the sobriety of her black Vaucouleurs clothing and began to dress as a knight and courtier. The *Chronique des cordeliers* mentions in addition to her armor "très noble habis de draps d'or et de soie bien fourrés" [very noble clothes of cloth-of-gold and silk well trimmed with fur]. Other records note a hat of blue silk or velvet with gold embroidery and a brim divided into four parts, a robe of scarlet Brussels cloth and a dark green tunic ordered for her by Charles d'Orléans, decorations of embroidered nettle leaves to represent the house of Orléans, and a slashed tunic of cloth-of-gold.[51] These records tally with the trial's charge that she dressed in clothes "curtis, brevibus, et dissolutis" [short, small, and dissolute], in "sumptuosis et pomposis vestibus de pannis preciosis et aureis ac eciam foderaturis" [sumptuous and magnificent clothes of precious fabrics and gold and also of furs].[52] Joan is caught between two semiotics: the tailoring and luxury that express high status in secular circles are susceptible to moral objections from the clergy.

I will slight the relations between crossdressing and social authority to focus on sexuality. For some scholars my omission covers the whole field of female transvestism, which in their view has social meaning only. Vern Bullough argues that whereas medieval sources attribute male crossdressing to lust for women or effeminacy, female crossdressing is motivated by desire for the social advantages of men: protection from sexual assault, mobility, access to arms, and so on.[53] Caroline Bynum makes a similar point in generalizing from the case of Joan of Arc: "cross-dressing was for women primarily a practical device.... Perhaps exactly *because* cross-dressing was a radical yet practical social step for women, it was not finally their most powerful symbol of self."[54] The practical advantages of taking the role of a knight rather than a peasant, and a man rather than a woman, are evident in Joan's case, but to consider her crossdress only in terms of social advantage elides her damaging refusals to give it up in prison and oversimplifies the gender identity Joan articulates during her trial.

Joan's testimony about her conduct in war is one context for considering that identity. Bynum argues that religious women who crossdress continue to see themselves "in female images ... not as warriors for Christ but as brides, as pregnant virgins, as housewives, as mothers of God."[55] Joan in contrast sees herself most accurately as a warrior, never drawing on imagery of pregnancy, motherhood, or nurturing, but she is a warrior with a difference: asked which she loved better, her standard or her sword, she replies that she loved the standard forty times better, and that she carried the standard herself in battle "pro evitando ne interficeret aliquem; et dicit quod nunquam interfecit hominem" [in order to avoid killing anyone; and she added that she had never killed anyone].[56] She does approve her sword, "quia erat bonus ensis guerre et bonus ad dandum bonas alapas et bonos ictus, gallice *de bonnes buffes et de bons torchons*" [because it was a good sword for war and good for giving good slaps and good blows, in French "good whacks and good wallops"].⁵⁷ The French phrase testifies not only to Joan's colloquial vocabulary but again to her curious restraint about killing. Her sword seems less to threaten life than to punish and chastise in the manner of her weapon of choice, a heavy stick or *martin* by which she was known to swear ("par mon martin") and which she sometimes used on her own disobedient soldiers and their camp followers.⁵⁸ This diffidence about killing may also motivate Joan's discomfort with the term *chief de guerre*, which she used in a letter of warning to the king of England but repudiated during her interrogation, later explaining that "s'elle estoit chief de guerre, s'estoit pour batre les Angloys" [if she was a war leader, it was to fight the English].⁵⁹ Her letter indicates that she would rather the English simply left at her warning, though if they do not, "je les feray tous occire" [I will have them all killed]; again she distances herself from the killing by however small a margin.⁶⁰ She sees herself as a fighter, then, not a mother or a bride, but the modifications she brings to war leadership by carrying her own standard, refraining from killing, and preferring her stick and her standard to her sword constitute her refusal to succumb uncritically to the conventional model of the masculine warrior.

JOAN'S RELATIONS WITH WOMEN

Joan's testimony about women's roles and her relations to women both defers to femininity and departs significantly from it. The trial's focus on clothing can present this range of evidence succinctly. Following Deuteronomy's prohibition, Joan's judges consider crossdressing to be a reprehensible violation of the feminine category, "contra honestatem sexus muliebris et in lege divina prohibita ac eciam Deo et hominibus abhominabilia et per ecclesiasticas sancciones sub pena anathematis interdicta" [against the uprightness of the female sex and prohibited by divine law, equally abominable to God and to men, and forbidden by ecclesiastical law under pain of anathema].⁶¹ The faculty of the University of Paris sustains the connection between crossdressing and crossgendering in their opinion that "relicto habitu muliebri, virorum habitum imitata est" [having given up women's way of dressing, she imitated the comportment of men]; the recurrence of *habitus* in its literal and figurative senses reinforces the argument that clothing expresses gender.⁶² As detailed above, Joan counters during the trial that her clothing is insignificant to the state of her soul and (quite differently) that her clothing signifies her mission rather than her gender alignment. Both positions become less tenable as the struggle over access to the sacraments reveals her deep commitment to crossdressing and as pressure from the court calls into question for her whether her crossdressing should be attributed to God's command. The explanation she gives after her relapse, that "elle ayme mieulx l'abit d'omme que de femme" [she likes men's clothes better than women's] gains credit from earlier testimony revealing the ease with which she adapted to them from the beginning; when asked what reverence she showed to St. Michael at the Dauphin's court, she replied that she "se agenoulla et oulta son chaperon" [knelt and took off her cap].[63] Here again Joan's identity as "Pucelle" appears complexly gendered; she inhabits the masculine gesture as well as men's clothing. Joan's masculine *habitus* helps account for doubts about her sexuality when she presented herself to the Dauphin. Jean Pasquerel testifies that Joan was twice visited by women to determine "si esset vir vel mulier, et an esset corrupta vel virgo; et inventa fuit mulier, virgo tamen et puella" [if she were a man or a woman, and if she were deflowered or a virgin; and she was found to be a woman, but a girl and a virgin].[64] That women were chosen to make this determination suggests Joan's female sex was not in much doubt; male physicians would have been more appropriate investigators of sexual anomaly had it seemed likely that Joan was male. However, that the sex determination needed to be made at all indicates that Joan's crossdressing and crossbehavior were perceived to complicate her sexuality and move it beyond the normative.

Joan rejects feminine roles while continuing to identify herself as a woman. Of women's occupations ("oeuvres de femme") she declares "que il y a assés autres femmes pour ce faire" [that there are enough other women to do them].[65] When she determines that Katherine de la Rochelle is not a true visionary, she admonishes her "que elle retournast a son mary faire son mesnaige et nourrir ses enfans" [that she should return to her husband to keep house and raise her children], opposing women's conventional tasks to the visionary's way of life.[66] Marie Delcourt concludes that Joan is hostile to her family and to the lot of women which she has escaped, but I would argue on the contrary that Joan testifies to strong identifications with her mother and other women.[67] For example, Joan dismisses the men who have tried to convince her to give up crossdressing, but notes her allegiance to the women who have done so, even to women aligned against Charles VII: "s'elle le deust avoir fait, elle l'eust plustost fait a la requeste de ces deux dames que d'autres dames qui soient en France, exceptee sa royne" [if she had been able (to give up men's clothes), she would rather have done so at the request of these two ladies (Jeanne de Luxembourg and Jeanne de

Béthune) than of any other ladies in France, except for her queen].[68] When asked at the end of interrogation for her corrections to the minutes, Joan repeats that she would wear a dress to escape imprisonment, but she substitutes her mother for her earlier references to her mission: "tradatis michi unam tunicam muliebrem pro eundo ad domum matris et ego accipiam" [give me a woman's dress to go to my mother's house and I will accept it].[69] This fascinating revision seems to deny the dichotomy Joan has articulated between other women's lives and her own by equating her mother's domestic space with the public space she claims in opposing the English. In the revised escape scenario, Joan complicates her mission with a certain nostalgia for normalcy, a wish that her life could be brought into consonance with her mother's again through so simple a gesture as returning home in a dress.

The Latin record of the trial prepared after Joan's death by Thomas de Courcelles tends to suppress Joan's expressions of allegiance to women. In early testimony as to whether she knew any art or trade, "dist que ouy; et que sa mere luy avoit apprins a coustre; et qu'elle ne cuidoyt point qu'il y eust femme dedens Rouen qui luy en sceust apprendre aulcune chose" [she said yes, that her mother had taught her to sew; and that she did not think there was any woman in Rouen who could teach her more about it].[70] One of the most visible distortions of the French minutes occurs at this juncture in the Latin record; the mother vanishes, and the teaching relation with other women is replaced by competition: "Dixit quod sic, ad suendum pannos lineos et nendum; nec timebat mulierem Rothomagensem de nendo et suendo" [She said yes, to sew and stitch cloth, and she feared no woman in Rouen for sewing and stitching].[71] Courcelles' Latin record deletes altogether her testimony that during her captivity in Burgundy, Jeanne de Luxembourg interceded for Joan with her nephew, asking him not to turn her over to the English.[72] Courcelles also edits out Joan's request for a female servant after her abjuration.[73] These alterations to the French record sustain the court's accusation that Joan's crossdressing indicates a loss of feminine traits in general. But it is more accurate to Joan's testimony to note the persistence of positive relations with women even as she rejects women's tasks for herself, dressing and acting in masculine modes.

JOAN'S SEXUALITY

In what terms were Joan and her contemporaries able to perceive her redefined sexuality? There is little contemporary evidence for a medieval discourse of bisexuality or lesbianism, although as noted above the evidence is somewhat stronger for male homosexual consciousness.[74] Instead, the sexual binary dominates, and Joan's identity is perceived in terms of its poles, as a construction vacillating between them. *De quadam puella*, cited above, imagines this vacillation as a series of temporal shifts from one pole to the other, a shifting that respects Deuteronomy's enforcement of categories: Joan is alternately a clever leader when in armor and an ignorant maiden in a dress.[75] Unfortunately for Joan, her practice did not observe this purifying polarity. A final discrepancy between the Latin and French records brings out the transgressive potential in Joan's mixed position. The fifth of twelve articles drawn up at the end of the trial for deliberation by the court and other advisers charges that Joan crossdressed and cut her hair like a man's, "nichil super corpus suum relinquendo quod sexum femineum approbet aut demonstret" [leaving nothing on her body that proves or reveals her female sex]; the Orléans manuscript stops at that while the Latin record continues "preter ea que natura eidem femine contulit ad feminei sexus discrecionem" [except for what nature has provided her to distinguish the female sex].[76] The full Latin accusation suggests that Joan's fault is the greater in that she has not crossed over entirely (like the transvestite saints perhaps) into a masculine position. Her body is the more visible and shameful for its imperfect containment in crossdress. She occupies neither position in the gender binary, but contaminates both by combining them; hence Jean d'Estivet, one of the major figures in her trial, is said to have called her "putana" and "paillarda" [whore, wanton], although her physical virginity is unquestioned.[77]

Among her contemporaries, only Christine de Pisan imagines positively a Joan who conflates masculinity and femininity in one persona. The *Ditié de Jehanne d'Arc* (1429) uses the masculine form *preux* for Joan while maintaining *preuses* to modify other heroic women. This grammatical cross-gendering reinforces Christine's mixed imagery for Joan, "le champion et celle / Qui donne à France la mamelle / De paix et doulce norriture, / Et ruer jus la gent rebelle" [the champion, she who gives France the breast of peace and sweet nourishment, and who casts down the rebel host].[78] The simultaneity of feminine and masculine attributes contrasts to *De quadam puella*'s version of pure sequentiality. To be sure, Christine finds nothing normal in this simultaneity. "Véez bien chose oultre nature!" [Here truly is something beyond nature!] concludes this stanza, and a similar passage rhymes the doubly gendered adjectives for Joan, "fort [m.] et dure [f.]" with "fors nature" [outside nature].[79] But Christine's "Pucelle de Dieu" is miraculous, supernatural rather than unnatural. She is elevated beyond sex by dedication to God yet also a credit to the feminine sex in general: "Hee! quel honneur au femenin / Sexe!"[80] Of all her contemporaries, Joan might have found Christine her most congenial advocate. The poet's urgently prophetic voice parallels Joan's, and the *Ditié*'s crossgendered persona recalls the trial's evidence that Joan felt strongly allied with women even as she distinguished herself from them. Yet Christine's version of crossgendering, in its poetic and miraculous harmony, floats at some remove above the conflicted and shifting self-presentation that Joan attempts under the pressure of interrogation.

Marina Warner invokes the androgyne, an idealized nonsexual status, to describe Joan: "she was usurping a man's function but shaking off the trammels of his sex altogether to occupy a different, third order, neither male nor female, but unearthly, like the angels whose company she loved."[81] But gender theorists have argued compellingly that the concept of the androgyne, in its unconflicted wholeness, evades the issue of sexuality by idealizing it away.[82] Androgyny's prior sexuality, moreover, is conceived only in bipolar terms: only conventional masculinity and femininity come before androgyny, doing away with the possibility of any other sexuality. Androgyny evades sexuality while reasserting that it is binary; Joan's testimony, in contrast, draws on femininity and masculinity to present a *habitus* that matches neither. Joan's commitment to virginity frees her from genital sex, but her commitment itself, and her masculine dress and way of life, continue to shape her sexuality in the construction of "la Pucelle." At the very least, Joan's choice of the secular category of "Pucelle," her vocation to arms rather than prayer, and her strong relations with women leave open the possibility that she rejects heterosexual identity; at most, Joan's abstinence may have made it more possible for her to revise her gender, if one consequence of her new position would have been either unclarity about its implications for physical desire or a transgressive desire for women. Joan's virginity shields her self-construction from its most radical implications, but virginity is a crucial part of her sexuality, not an escape from it. Her transvestism, I have argued, shapes and expresses that sexuality in the interpretive register of gender.

The court's final expression of control over Joan was to surrender her to the secular authorities in a dress.[83] This dress expresses one last time the court's conviction that Joan's transvestism had moral implications for her sexuality as well as political significance for her resistance to the English. It may (ironically) have expressed as well Joan's longing to be accepted by the Church as a devout Christian. In either case, the dress Joan wore to execution is so belated a revision of her practice that it throws retrospective emphasis on the long resistance and the complex self-defense Joan constructed around transvestism during her trial.

NOTES

1. Michel Foucault, *The History of Sexuality*, vol. 1, *An Introduction*, trans. Robert Hurley (New York: Random, 1978), 72. This essay first appeared in the *Journal of Medieval and Early Modern Studies* 26 (1996): 297–320. Permission of the publisher to reprint this essay is gratefully acknowledged.

2. Foucault, *An Introduction*, 33; John Boswell's *Christianity, Social Tolerance, and Homosexuality: Gay People in Western Europe from the Beginning of the Christian Era to the Fourteenth Century* (Chicago: University of Chicago Press, 1980) opened the argument for homosexual identity in the Middle Ages. See also the essays by Boswell, David M. Halperin, and Robert Padgug in *Hidden from History: Reclaiming the Gay and Lesbian Past*, ed. Martin Bauml Duberman, Martha Vicinus, and George Chauncey, Jr. (New York: NAL Books, 1989); Simon Gaunt's reassessment of the issue, "Straight Minds / 'Queer' Wishes in Old French Hagiography: *La Vie de Sainte Euphrosine*," *GLQ: A Journal of Lesbian and Gay Studies* 1 (1995): 439–57; and in the same issue Louise O. Fradenberg and Carla Freccero, "Introduction: The Pleasures of History," 375–78.

3. Judith Butler, *Bodies that Matter: On the Discursive Limits of 'Sex'* (New York and London: Routledge, 1993), esp. 93–119; see also my *Gender and Romance in Chaucer's "Canterbury Tales"* (Princeton: Princeton University Press, 1994), 4–7, 31–33.

4. Quotations are from Steven Justice, "Inquisition, Speech, and Writing: A Case from Late-Medieval Norwich," *Representations* 48 (1994): 10; Gayle Margherita, *The Romance of Origins: Language and Sexual Difference in Middle English Literature* (Philadelphia: University of Pennsylvania Press, 1994), xi.

5. See *Post-Structuralism and the Question of History*, ed. Derek Attridge, Geoff Bennington, and Robert Young (Cambridge: Cambridge University Press, 1987); Michel Foucault, *Language, Counter-Memory, Practice*, ed. and trans. Donald F. Bouchard and Sherry Simon (Ithaca, N.Y.: Cornell University Press, 1977), 139–64; and Fradenberg and Freccero, "The Pleasures of History," on histories of sexuality in particular.

6. The best edition of the records of this trial is *Procès de condamnation de Jeanne d'Arc*, ed. Pierre Tisset with the assistance of Yvonne Lanhers, 3 vols. (Paris: Klincksieck, 1960–1971), hereafter cited as *Procès de condamnation*. Still useful for both trials with supplementary material is *Procès de condamnation et de réhabilitation de Jeanne d'Arc, dite la Pucelle*, ed. Jules Quicherat, 5 vols. (Paris: Renouard, 1841–1849), hereafter cited as *Procès de condamnation et de réhabilitation*.

7. The best edition of records from this trial is *Procès en nullité de la condamnation de Jeanne d'Arc*, ed. Pierre Duparc, 5 vols. (Paris: Klincksieck, 1977–1988). Some extracts are available in English in Régine Pernoud, *The Retrial of Joan of Arc*, trans. J. M. Cohen (New York: Harcourt, Brace, 1955).

8. On the scope and accuracy of the first trial's records see also *Procès de condamnation*, 3.17–41. On irregularities in the trial's procedures, see Henry Ansgar Kelly, "The Right to Remain Silent: Before and After Joan of Arc," *Speculum* 68 (1993): 992–1026; and Edward Peters, *Inquisition* (New York: Macmillan, 1988), 69, 73.

9. The *Procès de condamnation* edits the two manuscripts deriving from the French minutes—Urfé (Bibliothèque Nationale, lat. 8838) and Orléans (Bibliothèque Municipale d'Orléans, no. 518)—alongside the capacious Latin record established by Thomas de Courcelles, who assisted at Joan's trial, and the notary Guillaume Manchon. This latter document collects letters, charges, records of interrogation and deliberation, votes, and sentences for the entire proceeding, drawn up a few years after Joan's death. Another complete and heavily annotated edition of the two French manuscripts is *La minute française des interrogatoires de Jeanne la Pucelle*, ed. Paul Doncoeur (Melun: Argences, 1952). An English translation of the Orléans manuscript is *The Trial of Joan of Arc, Being the Verbatim Report of the Proceedings from the Orleans Manuscript*, trans. W. S. Scott (Westport, Conn.: Associated Booksellers, 1956). Latin acts were also produced during and just after the trial: a *procès-verbal* based on the French minutes and an *Instrumentum sententiae* summarizing the trial, Joan's abjuration, and her sentencing. Later copies of the latter survive: see *Documents et recherches relatifs a Jeanne la Pucelle*, vol. 2, *Instrument public des sentences* ..., ed. Paul Doncoeur and Yvonne Lanhers (Paris: Argences, 1954). For evidence during the nullification trial about the generation and accuracy of the French minutes, see *Procès en nullité*, 1.67–68, 181–83, 207, 214–18, 222–23, 243, 245–46, 414–28, 436.

10. Examples from among many are *Procès de condamnation*, 1.160, 169, 205, 208, 337 (Joan refers to the record), 1.147, 154 (Joan asks that the book be sent to Paris and read by clerics); *Procès en nullité*, 1.360 (Joan said to have corrected the notaries). Translations in brackets are mine.

11. *Procès de condamnation*, 1.181–82.

12. *Minute française*, 273.

13. Stephen G. Nichols observes of such comparisons that "each ... provides Joan with a different identity and genealogy;" see "Prophetic Discourse: St. Augustine to Christine de Pizan," in *The Bible in the Middle Ages: Its Influence on Literature and Art*, ed. Bernard S. Levy (Binghamton: Medieval and Renaissance Texts and Studies, 1992), 67. For a comprehensive discussion of literary responses in Joan's lifetime, see Deborah Fraioli, "The Literary Image of Joan of Arc: Prior Influences," *Speculum* 56 (1981): 811–30; see also *Procès de condamnation et de réhabilitation*, vols. 3–5.

14. *Procès de condamnation*, 1.14, 339, 377; Deuteronomy 22.5; 1 Corinthians 11.5–6, 13.

15. *Procès de condamnation*, 1.51. The minutes usually record Joan's statements in the third person.

16. *Procès de condamnation*, 1.75, 93–94. Where there are gaps in the French minutes, I quote from the Latin record of Thomas de Courcelles.

17. *Procès de condamnation*, 1.168: "se on luy donnoit congié en abit de femme, elle se mectroit tantoust en abit d'omme et feroit ce qui luy est commandé par nostre Seigneur" [if they let her go in a woman's dress, she would resume men's dress immediately and do what is commanded of her by our Lord]; see also 1.67, 181, 209–10.

18. *Procès de condamnation*, 1.168–69.

19. *Chroniques de Perceval de Cagny*, ed. H. Moranvillé (Paris: Renouard, 1902), 140; Guillaume Cousinot, *Chronique de la Pucelle*, ed. Vallet de Viriville (Paris: Delahays, 1864), 276.

20. *Procès de condamnation*, 1.67, 153.

21. *Procès de condamnation*, 1.227.

22. *Procès de condamnation*, 1.167, 210; see also 1.227, 344.

23. *Procès en nullité*, 1.181–82, 186–88; *Procès de condamnation*, 3.151–59; *Documents et recherches relatifs a Jeanne la Pucelle*, vol. 3, *La réhabilitation de Jeanne la Pucelle: l'enquête ordonnée par Charles VII* . . . , ed. Paul Doncoeur and Yvonne Lanhers (Paris: Argences, 1956), 36–37, 40–45, 51, 54. Jean Toutmouillé recalls Joan saying she was virginal at her death, 40–41.

24. For example, Cousinot, *Chronique*, 276–77: "quand je seroie entre les hommes, estant en habit d'homme, ils n'auront pas concupiscence charnelle de moi; et me semble qu'en cest estat je conserveray mieulx ma virginié de pensée et de faict" [when I am among men, dressed as a man, they will not have carnal desire for me; and it seems to me that in this manner I will better maintain my virginity in thought and deed].

25. *Procès en nullité*, 1.350, 387, in testimony friendly to her cause; Joan testifies, in contrast, that she slept "vestue et armee" [dressed and in armor] when in the field (*Procès de condamnation*, 1.263).

26. *Procès en nullité*, 1.396.

27. *Procès en nullité*, 1.396–97.

28. *Procès en nullité*, 1.344.

29. On the expression of holiness through clothing, see Dyan Elliott, "Dress as Mediator Between Inner and Outer Self: The Pious Matron of the High and Later Middle Ages," *Mediaeval Studies* 53 (1991): 279–308; and Gábor Klaniczay, "Fashionable Beards and Heretic Rags," chap. 4 in *The Uses of Supernatural Power: The*

Transformation of Popular Religion in Medieval and Early-Modern Europe, trans. Susan Singerman, ed. Karen Margolis (Princeton: Princeton University Press, 1990), 51–78.

30. *Procès de condamnation*, 1.156; for contrasting conclusions about Joan's agency see the interesting discussion by Karen Sullivan, "Inquiry and Inquisition in Late Medieval Culture: The Questioning of Joan of Arc and Christine de Pizan" (Ph.D. diss., University of California at Berkeley, 1993), 16–41.

31. *Procès de condamnation*, 1.156–58, 182–83, 208.

32. Gaunt, "Straight Minds / 'Queer' Wishes," 439.

33. Marina Warner, *Joan of Arc: The Image of Female Heroism* (New York: Knopf, 1981), 22–24; Sullivan, "Inquiry and Inquisition," 22–23. Joan testifies that her voices call her "Jehanne la Pucelle" in *Procès de condamnation*, 1.126.

34. *Minute française*, 157, from the Orléans manuscript; Urfé has "tout qu'il plairoit a Dieu," but Courcelles has "tamdiu quamdiu placeret Deo" at *Procès de condamnation*, 1.123; see also "quamdiu placeret Deo," 1.250.

35. *Procès de condamnation*, e.g. 1.95, 153–54, 344.

36. Warner, *Joan of Arc*, 135, 151–55; Marie Delcourt, "Le complexe de Diane dans l'hagiographie chrétienne," *Revue de l'histoire des religions* 153:1 (1958): 1–33.

37. Only two lives of transvestite saints are extant in Old French (see Gaunt, "Straight Minds / 'Queer' Wishes"), but Joan could have known saints' stories from sermons and feast-day celebrations.

38. John Anson, "The Female Transvestite in Early Monasticism: The Origin and Development of a Motif," *Viator* 5 (1974): 1–32; Gaunt, "Straight Minds / 'Queer' Wishes."

39. Kirsten Hastrup, "The Semantics of Biology: Virginity," in *Defining Females: The Nature of Women in Society*, ed. Shirley Ardener (New York: Wiley, 1978), 58–59.

40. *Procès de condamnation*, 1.149, 244; see also 1.174–75 where Joan is asked if she would still hear her voices if she were married or were not a virgin.

41. *Procès de condamnation et de réhabilitation*, 4.382, 406.

42. *Procès de condamnation*, 1.123, 167.

43. *Procès de condamnation*, 1.167–68; Courcelles obscures Joan's statement by deleting the phrase "se ainsi est ... qu'il la faile desvestir en jugement" [if it is necessary to strip her in judgment], which imagines that the court may tolerate physical coercion to change her way of dressing. See also 1.210, 227 where Joan again refers to death in relation to her crossdressing. Testimony at the nullification trial (e.g., *Procès en nullité*, 1.184) discredited the original sentence by declaring that Joan was executed for wearing men's clothing, an offense not grave enough to warrant death. Penances of one to three years are prescribed for crossdressing in contemporary manuals: Vern L. Bullough and Bonnie Bullough, *Cross Dressing, Sex, and Gender* (Philadelphia: University of Pennsylvania Press, 1993), 61; *Procès de condamnation*,

3.87. Modern scholars also occasionally attribute Joan's execution to crossdressing, but the first emphasis throughout the trial is on the validity of Joan's claim to hear voices; at the interview following her relapse, Joan's declaration that she continues to hear her voices carries in the Courcelles trial record the marginal annotation "responsio mortifera" [the fatal reply] (*Procès de condamnation*, 1.397 n. 1).

44. *Procès de condamnation*, 1.208.

45. *Procès de condamnation*, 1.252.

46. *Procès de condamnation*, 1.183.

47. *Procès de condamnation*, 1.64, 3.31 n. 1.

48. Marjorie Garber, *Vested Interests: Cross-Dressing and Cultural Anxiety* (New York and London: Routledge, 1992), 13.

49. In the account of the Greffier de la Rochelle, "elle avoit pourpoint noir, chausses estachées, robbe courte de gros gris noir, cheveux ronds et noirs, et un chappeau noir sur la teste;" cited in Jules Quicherat, "Relation inédite sur Jeanne d'Arc," *Revue historique* 4 (1877): 336. Jean de Nouillompont testifies in *Procès en nullité*, 1.290, that Joan crossdressed slightly earlier in clothes of a member of his household.

50. *De quadam puella*, in *Procès de condamnation et de réhabilitation*, 3.411–21 (quotation at 412). This treatise is sometimes attributed to Henri de Gorcum, sometimes to Jean Gerson: see Georges Peyronnet, "Gerson, Charles VII et Jeanne d'Arc: La propagande au service de la guerre," *Revue d'histoire ecclésiastique* 84 (1989): 334–70. Anne Llewellyn Barstow translates *De quadam puella* into English in *Joan of Arc: Heretic, Mystic, Shaman* (Lewiston: Edwin Mellen, 1986), 133–41. Jean Morel testifies that in mid-July of 1429 he received from Joan "unam vestem rubeam quam habebat ipsa indutam" [a red garment she had worn]; several witnesses recalled that when Joan arrived in Vaucouleurs "erat induta veste mulieris rubea" [she was wearing a red woman's garment]; see *Procès en nullité*, 1.255, 299.

51. Adrien Harmand, *Jeanne d'Arc: ses costumes, son armure* (Paris: Leroux, 1929), esp. 261–71, 320, 361–63; *Procès de condamnation et de réhabilitation*, 5.112–13.

52. *Procès de condamnation*, 1.207.

53. Vern L. Bullough, "Transvestism in the Middle Ages," in *Sexual Practices and the Medieval Church*, ed. Vern L. Bullough and James Brundage (Buffalo: Prometheus, 1982), 43–54; see also Bullough and Bullough, *Cross Dressing, Sex, and Gender*; and Michèle Perret, "Travesties et transsexuelles: Yde, Silence, Grisandole, Blanchandine," *Romance Notes* 25 (1984–85): 328–40.

54. Caroline Walker Bynum, *Holy Feast and Holy Fast: The Religious Significance of Food to Medieval Women* (Berkeley: University of California Press, 1987), 291 (her italics). Jonathan Goldberg makes a case for not ruling sexuality out of discussions of crossdressing in *Sodometries: Renaissance Texts, Modern Sexualities* (Stanford: Stanford University Press, 1992), 105–16.

55. Bynum, *Holy Feast and Holy Fast*, 291.

56. *Procès de condamnation*, 1.78.

57. *Procès de condamnation*, 1.78. The vernacular intrusions in the Latin record deserve an article of their own. Justice, "Inquisition, Speech, and Writing," provides a lively one for heresy trials in Norwich, but his explanation that vernacular intrusions should be attributed to the notary's boredom because they "possessed no evidentiary advantage *as* vernacular phrases—no more than they would in Latin" (3, his italics)—is belied by two of the three examples he cites, which make their arguments in verbal puns—every Friday is *fre* day and the stinging *bee* of oaths *by* God—that would be lost if translated into Latin (2–3). These puns would have been more evident before long *i* diphthongized in the later fifteenth century.

58. See *Procès de condamnation et de réhabilitation*, 4.4 n. 1; Cagny, *Chroniques*, 141.

59. *Procès de condamnation*, 1.82, 221, 262.

60. *Procès de condamnation*, 1.221.

61. *Procès de condamnation*, 1.207.

62. *Procès de condamnation*, 1.363; *habitus* is also the pivotal term in the passage quoted above from *De quadam puella* on Joan's shifting dress and behavior. See Sullivan, "Inquiry and Inquisition," 32 and 35, on the language the court chooses for Joan's transvestism.

63. *Procès de condamnation*, 1.396, 118.

64. *Procès en nullité*, 1.389.

65. *Procès de condamnation*, 1.213.

66. *Procès de condamnation*, 1.104.

67. Delcourt, "Complexe de Diane," 18–28.

68. *Procès de condamnation*, 1.95.

69. *Procès de condamnation*, 1.181; see note 17 above for Joan's earlier references to wearing a dress in order to leave prison.

70. *Procès de condamnation*, 1.46.

71. *Procès de condamnation*, 1.46.

72. *Procès de condamnation*, 1.94.

73. "Se on la veult laisser aler a la messe et oster hors de fers et meictre en prison gracieuse *et qu'elle eust une femme*, elle sera bonne et fera ce que l'Eglise vouldra" [If they would let her go to Mass and take off her fetters and place her in an appropriate prison *and give her a woman servant*, she would be good and do as the Church wished] (*Procès de condamnation*, 1.396–97; 2.345 n. 1; italicized phrase omitted in Courcelles' text). In some cases, such as his omission of his vote in favor of torturing Joan, Courcelles may be striving to protect himself or the court from discredit, but many of his changes seem to distort Joan's statements in order to discredit her. Doncoeur's notes in *Minute française* are particularly attentive to Courcelles' changes.

74. But see Rudolf M. Dekker and Lotte C. van de Pol, *The Tradition of Female Transvestism in Early Modern Europe* (New York: St. Martin's, 1989), which finds traces of transvestite practices in the fifteenth century; and Judith C. Brown, *Immodest Acts: The Life of a Lesbian Nun in Renaissance Italy* (New York: Oxford University Press, 1986).

75. Attempting to reassert the categories of male versus female clothing in the face of their disruption makes sense only if transvestism has substantial meaning (rather than being merely circumstantial). Kirsten Hastrup applies Mary Douglas's concept of purity and danger to sexuality and transvestism in two articles, "The Sexual Boundary—Purity: Heterosexuality and Virginity," and "The Sexual Boundary—Danger: Transvestism and Homosexuality," *Journal of the Anthropological Society of Oxford* 5 (1974): 137–47, and 6 (1975): 42–56.

76. *Procès de condamnation*, 1.293; *Minute française*, 257. Here the collator of the Orléans manuscript is translating from the Latin record, and the omission is consistent with earlier expressions of support for Joan in this manuscript.

77. *Procès en nullité*, 1.349, 351.

78. Christine de Pisan, *Ditié de Jehanne d'Arc*, ed. and trans. Angus J. Kennedy and Kenneth Varty, Medium Aevum Monographs, n.s. 9 (Oxford: Society for the Study of Mediaeval Languages and Literature, 1977), lines 199, 222, 188–91.

79. Pisan, *Ditié de Jehanne d'Arc*, lines 192, 274, 277. Although we reach different conclusions, my discussion is indebted to Sullivan, "Inquiry and Inquisition," 235–39.

80. Pisan, *Ditié de Jehanne d'Arc*, lines 265–66.

81. Warner, "Ideal Androgyne," chap. 7 in *Joan of Arc*, 139–58 (quotation at 146).

82. See Marjorie Garber, *Vice Versa: Bisexuality and the Eroticism of Everyday Life* (New York: Simon and Schuster, 1995), esp. 214–19.

83. Harmand, *Jeanne d'Arc: ses costumes*, 381–400.

CHAPTER 10

A Pacifist Utopia

Cleriadus et Meliadice

MICHELLE SZKILNIK

The fifteenth-century French romance *Cleriadus et Meliadice* recounts the social climbing of a young Spanish knight, Cleriadus. The knight's father, the Count of Esture (Asturias), rules England in the name of King Philippon, who is too old to travel through his lands. Brought to the court of England by his father, Cleriadus falls in love with the king's only child, his daughter Meliadice, and after many adventures, allowing him to display his numerous and extraordinary qualities, he marries Meliadice and becomes king of England.

As this brief summary indicates, *Cleriadus et Meliadice* raises some puzzling questions. Why would a fifteenth-century author, presumably French, write a story celebrating the king of England? France and England had been at war, at least on and off, for almost a century. France herself was dramatically divided among many factions, some of which supported the English claims. Could the author be writing at the court of England? Was he an English supporter? We know nothing about him except what the text itself leads us to deduce. Cleriadus accedes to the English throne through marriage to the daughter and only heiress of the king; is this an indirect rejection of Salic law? If Cleriadus, who is not related to the king and moreover has no royal blood in his veins, can rightly rule England, thanks to his superior qualities, and displace the king's own brother, shall we infer that the claims of English kings on the French crown have some grounds, and that inheriting a kingdom through the mother (which will be the case for Meliadice's children), as long as one has the qualities required for governing, is legitimate? In this case, the romance would indirectly take sides with England in the quarrel between the two belligerents.[1] However, the very positive portrayal of the king of France does not fit with this interpretation. Shall we conclude that the author had no intention of reflecting on the contemporary situation and chose his characters and setting merely because they were available in the common literary stock? The romance starts with this rather innocuous sentence: "Après le temps du roy Artus et des compaignons de la Table Ronde, il fut en Angleterre, laquelle estoit appellee pour le temps la Grant Bretaigne, ung roy que on appelloit Phelipons."[2] [After the time of King Arthur and the companions of the Round Table, there was in England, which was then called Great Britain, a king named Philippon.] Is *Cleriadus et Meliadice* another interminable Arthurian romance?[3] And is not Arthur beyond the petty quarrels of the fifteenth century? As we shall see, however, the romance is not Arthurian and does have contemporary resonances, even if the echoes of the Hundred Years' War seem distant.

What surprises most at first reading is that the romance, while clearly describing a fifteenth-century society, does not allude to the actual political situation of France and England. The only passing and indirect allusion has been noted by the romance's editor, Gaston Zink: "En ce temps là, le roy de France et cellui d'Angleterre si estoient tout ung et bons amis ensemble et les deux royaumes bien en paix" (321). [At this time, the kings of France and England were of one disposition and good friends, and the two kingdoms were at peace.] Zink rightly observes that although the Hundred Years' War is still going on at the time the romance is composed, the author, so it seems, is not interested in commenting on the present.[4] However, this allusion to peace between France and England also supports the opposite conclusion. By offering an attractive depiction of Europe at peace, of general happiness, social harmony, comfortable prosperity, is the author not in fact throwing into relief the sad reality? If *Cleriadus et Meliadice* is indeed a kind of *bildungsroman* and illustrates the amazing career of a young, gifted knight, as Zink demonstrates in his introduction, it is also an implicit reflection on the actual state of the world.[5] Moreover, it seeks to provide solutions to the chaos caused by poor government.

In his introduction, Zink suggests that the date at which the romance was composed might also explain its mood. *Cleriadus et Meliadice* was written around 1440–1444, at a time when truces were being negotiated.[6] The Treaty of Tours, signed on May 28, 1444, was to offer a yearlong peace (officially broken on July 17, 1445, by the king of France but already violated by the English in Normandy as early as March)[7] and was apparently welcomed with relief by both parties. The date of composition would thus account for the pacifism so striking in the romance, and especially for the numerous episodes dramatizing French and English friendship. Although this date, supported as it is by other evidence, seems very likely, it still fails to fully solve the problem. People at the time might have been enthusiastic at the prospect of peace—even temporary peace—and full of goodwill towards their enemies, yet *Cleriadus et Meliadice* reflects much more than a fleeting hope; the message of peace it brings, however simplistic it might sound, was probably appealing throughout the long war.

I contend that *Cleriadus et Meliadice* is in a certain way a response to Froissart's *Chroniques*, his monumental work on the first part of the Hundred Years' War. On the one hand, its idyllic presentation of kingdoms at peace is an antidote to Froissart's description of war. On the other hand, Froissart and the author of *Cleriadus et Meliadice* share the same chivalrous ideal. In the alleged realism of Froissart's chronicle, kings and noblemen strive towards lofty goals but, overcome by Fortune, do not always succeed in behaving according to their ideals; in the fictive world of our romance, these ideals are fully embodied not only in the hero, Cleriadus, but also in many secondary characters. The noble society Froissart dreams of (while painting, despite himself, a much harsher one) is thus described at length in *Cleriadus et Meliadice*. One can read this romance as a pacifist utopia, a fable according to which one good man can change the face of the world and usher in an age of harmony and unity.

Cleriadus et Meliadice obviously differs from Froissart's work in that it is not a chronicle and does not purport to convey historical truth. As we have seen, the beginning of the story even proclaims its relation with the world of Arthurian fiction. Froissart himself, however, does not hesitate to invoke King Arthur in his *Chroniques*, comparing, for instance, Philippa de Hainault, King Edward III's wife, to Queen Guinevere and underlining the relation between the Round Table and the Order of the Garter.[8] By the time Froissart composes his *Chroniques*, the legendary king has acquired an historical dimension. Referring to him in any work dealing with Great

Britain, whether fiction or history, lends prestige to the text, connects its characters to a respected, admired, and uncontroversial figure of the past.

The characterization rather than the Arthurian allusion indicates the romance genre of *Cleriadus et Meliadice*. The two main characters and numerous others, endowed with the best qualities to the highest degree, clearly do not belong to reality. Their exotic, sometimes allegorical names betray their fictional origin: Porrus le Fayé, Brun l'Amoureux, Bon Vouloir, Diligence, Bonne Encontre, Felon sans Pitié. Some of the places mentioned also bear names with symbolic meanings: Passaige de la Claire Fontaine, Isle Perdue, Joyeuse Maison, Ville Joyeuse; these are places that one will be at a loss to locate.

However, next to these names, there are others more familiar to readers of history and possibly to Froissart's readers. If we look at toponyms, we find two kinds: common ones, likely to appear in fiction and in historical texts, and more specific ones that are rarer in romances, especially in Arthurian romances. Among the first ones, let us list Angleterre, Alemaigne, Danemarche, Turquie, Grande Bretaigne, Yrlande, Escoce, France, Galles, Castelle (Castile), Espaigne, Paris, Londres.[9] What surprises here is not that the romance alludes to these well-known places but rather the sheer number of countries or cities mentioned. The second set of names comprises Anjou, Berry, Gascongne (Gascony), Provence, Champaigne, Lombardie, Vindesoze (Windsor), Iort (York), Duraine (Durham?), Valence (in Spain), Milan, Nappelles (Naples), Gennes (Genoa), Saint Denis, Vincennes, Calays (Calais), Estampes, and others. Striking here are both the number and the specificity of the places. True, they are often only names mentioned in passing, but they still endow the romance with realism. *Cleriadus et Meliadice* fits the trend of "realistic" romances started in the thirteenth century by Jean Renart with his *Guillaume de Dole*.[10] But it also echoes Froissart's *Chroniques*, replete with toponyms for obvious reasons.

We can draw a similar conclusion in analyzing characters' names. All characters are fictitious and their names invented; some, however, ring familiar. The Count of Eu, for instance, a relative to the king of France in our romance, recalls Raoul d'Eu, constable of France, who appears in Froissart's *Chroniques*.[11] Messire Lianor (or Lyonnet) de Mortimer recalls Messire Rogier de Mortimer who is also an historical figure. The same can be said of Tristan de Beaufort (Baudoin de Biaufort in the *Chroniques*), Messire Gorins de Grant Pré (the Count of Grantpret in the *Chroniques*). Other names, though slightly different, sound close to those of historical characters: Henry de la Cardinille (Messire Benedic de la Cornille),[12] Gault de l'Espine

(Seigneur d'Espinoit), Guion d'Ormal (Count of Ormant), Doreux de la Roche (Pierre Count of Dreux, with an involuntary play on words). I do not contend that the author of *Cleriadice et Meliadice* was consciously using names of historical persons to write some kind of *roman à clef*, only that he chose names with contemporary resonances in order to base his romance on reality, and that, by doing so, he trod on Froissart's ground.

There is another way in which *Cleriadus et Meliadice* conveys verisimilitude: the care it takes to record information faithfully and to indicate how news is transmitted. In this respect the role of messengers is essential. Messengers scour countries and cities throughout the romance. They deliver orders and news but also bring back impressions about the persons they have seen and are thus a good source of information. At the beginning of the romance, King Philippon sends a messenger to the Count of Esture, inviting him to come to court. The second chapter is devoted to the messenger's mission. Back in England, the messenger not only testifies that he has accomplished his task but also comments on the count's qualities: "j'ay trouvé le plus noble conte, large et courtois qui soit aujourdui et, sire, je vous mercye, car il m'a tant donné du sien que je en suis riche à tousjours" (8). [I found the noblest count, most generous and courteous that lives nowadays, and, sir, I thank you, for he gave me so much of his wealth that I am rich forever.] Kings and noblemen highly reward messengers for their services, thus buying their faithfulness and eagerness to collect information. Heralds also enjoy a prestigious status for similar reasons. Their official function is to shout their lords' mottoes and to proclaim winners during tournaments (659, 662), but they do much more: they spread news and make reputations. That is why they also receive splendid gifts. Cleriadus gives out magnificent robes and gold; ten heralds subsequently go running through the palace shouting: "Largesse! Largesse! Largesse au roy Cleriadus" (674). [Generosity, generosity, generosity from King Cleriadus!] Froissart recalls that King Edward at his wedding also handsomely rewarded *hiraut et menestrel* [heralds and minstrels].[13] The role played by messengers and heralds in our romance thus parallels the function they serve in Froissart's work: they are excellent informants because they share the life of the actors of the great drama both authors are recording.

None of the analogies I have so far suggested between *Cleriadus et Meliadice* and Froissart's *Chroniques* means that the author of the romance had been directly influenced by the *Chroniques*. That both the romance and the chronicle assign the same strategic role to heralds, squires, and messengers only testifies that in real life these persons were indeed valued as good sources of information. As for the names of places and persons, they are common enough to have come to the author's mind without supposing Froissart's mediation. Yet the similarities remain pertinent in that they reveal a common interest in the contemporary situation, an interest that leads Froissart to chronicle the war and the author of *Cleriadus et Meliadice* to depict a world at peace. This world retains many features of the real one and exhibits others that might look ideal to us but, for the author, are within reach if only people pay attention to his advice.

This peaceful world, like the real one, does unfortunately experience violence. But violence is contained and all its manifestations quickly resorbed to give room to what is most important: the bright picture of joyful and friendly entertainments.

Let us first analyze how the main hero, Cleriadus, deals with violence. The portrait of Cleriadus is as stereotypical as one could wish: handsome, of an uncommon strength since his childhood, brave, generous, humble, unselfish, loyal, fair, and an excellent manager of his lands. One can barely list all his qualities, which, of course, he possesses in the highest degree. Though idealized, Cleriadus has a counterpart in reality: Gaston Phebus, Count of Foix. The image of the perfect knight and lord, he was, according to Froissart, handsome, generous, merciful, fair, wise, educated, and also a good manager of his fortune.[14] As Froissart says of him in the *Voyage en Béarn:* "De toutes choses il estoit si tres parfait que on ne le pourroit trop louer."[15] [In every regard, he was so perfect that one could not praise him too much.]

Among Cleriadus's qualities, the one which is most interesting for our purpose is his generosity; not only does he lavish marvelous gifts on everyone around him (as *largesse* is one of the qualities expected from a king)[16] but he also treats his worst enemies with mercy. He seldom kills anybody.[17] Most often, his opponent, unable to sustain the fight any longer, asks for mercy; Cleriadus grants it and sends the vanquished foe to his lady. The only time he kills (and even makes mincemeat of) his enemies is in Cyprus where the English and the French, who have come to the rescue of the king of Cyprus, defeat an army of Saracens, thanks mainly to Cleriadus's deeds (321–25). But violence against Saracens is justified, and Cleriadus cannot be accused of cruelty for killing the great khan. The pagans being fundamentally evil, there is no point in showing mercy to them.[18] As we shall see with another example, true evil cannot be redeemed and must be extirpated, that is, exterminated. Cleriadus thus appears to be like the perfect Christian knight: merciful with people of his kind but justly merciless with God's foes.

This episode, which shows French and English united in their fight against Saracens, recalls the actual crusades of Mahdia and Nicopolis at the end of the fourteenth century. The first one (1390), proposed by the Genoese to King Charles VI of France, was comprised mainly of French knights and Genoese soldiers, but crusaders also came from England and Spain. The second one, finally launched in 1394, was directed against the Turks who had occupied the Balkans since 1370. It had been a topic of discussion between the French and the English since 1392. The kings of France and England even thought of enrolling. In France, many noblemen took part in the adventure, including the Count of Eu, a cousin of the king.[19] This Count of Eu is not the Constable Raoul de Brienne, dead at the time of the crusade. Yet it is worth noticing that in *Cleriadus et Meliadice* the French constable (who does not have a proper name) is sent to Cyprus, against "ung des plus grans cans de Turquie" (271) [one of the most powerful khans of Turkey];[20] a Count of Eu, distinct from the constable, appears later in the story; and in Froissart there is a Count of Eu, constable of France. Dim memories of the past have perhaps worked their way into *Cleriadus et Meliadice*. By celebrating a crusading episode (successful in the romance but disastrous in reality), the romance's author "rightly" redirects violence: war should not erupt among Christians. The only justified violence is aimed at pagans. Moreover, success will surely be achieved if Christians, whether French, English, or of any other nationality, are united and guided by worthy leaders.[21]

If we now consider Cleriadus's enemies within the boundaries of the Occidental world, his generosity seems wise and judiciously granted. For far from being fundamentally evil, most of them are, at the bottom, good people driven to bad deeds by unfair circumstances. Porrus le Fayé, for example, was changed into a cruel lion by vindictive fairies. Under his wild shape, he was condemned to kill many knights until the day when the best knight in the world would injure him and thus put an end to the spell (123–28). Returned at last to his normal shape, Porrus confesses all his bad deeds to Cleriadus and thanks him. Thereafter, he lives a happy and peaceful life. Similar is the fate of Felon sans Pitié [Merciless Villain]: betrayed by his wife, who has run away with her lover, driven to madness by despair, he attacks everyone passing on his lands in hopes of avenging himself. Cleriadus defeats him and convinces him to renounce his anger. Felon accepts and during a parodic baptism changes his name into Fortuné d'Amour [Lucky in Love]. He then becomes so valiant and courteous that people celebrate his worth as much as they used to complain about his misbehavior

(180). Examples of this kind abound. The author himself underlines the similarities by concluding the episodes with almost the same sentence: "depuis furent bons amys ensemble" (87, 176, 622) [since then they became very good friends] or "autant que ilz avoient fait de maulx, depuis ilz firent... de bien" (102, 622, 633) [they since did as much good as they had done evil]. All that is needed to enact this total conversion of the wickedest is a positive role model, a part played by Cleriadus. This easy transformation suggests that evil is most often ignorance of good and a lack of opportunity to develop the positive qualities latent in everyone. But as soon as bad knights are shown the right path, they readily become mere shadows of Cleriadus, accomplishing the same benevolent deeds, displaying the same honorable qualities, only at a lower degree.

This optimistic view of human nature, however, is challenged by one fully evil character in the romance: the king of England's own brother, Sir Thomas. From the outset of the romance, the narrator warns the reader that Sir Thomas embodies evil: "cellui seigneur estoit plain de deshonnestes taches comme estre fel et orgueilleux, plain de ire, cruel en toutes choses et irraisonnable" (2) [this lord was full of terrible defects: he was wicked and arrogant, full of anger, cruel in every circumstance and unreasonable]. Although the information explains why the king did not choose his brother as his representative, it also sets an expectation which will only be met much later and, in some way, even disappointed. The reader is naturally convinced that Sir Thomas will contest the king's choice up front and try immediately to eliminate his rival, the Count of Esture. However, he readily agrees with the king's decision, and there is no hint at this point that he might be concocting a revenge. Only three hundred pages later does Sir Thomas finally act in character. But instead of directing his anger at the Count of Esture, he plots Meliadice's death and Cleriadus's downfall (291–97). It makes sense narratively that he should attack the protagonists rather than a secondary character, and there is also a psychological explanation: one can easily understand how Thomas might have become jealous of Cleriadus's prestige. Yet the best justification for this somewhat unexpected change is that it emphasizes the striking contrast between the supreme goodness personified in Meliadice and the vilest wickedness embodied by her uncle. Plotting the death of his own niece (who unites in herself all perfections) and waiting so patiently for the best moment (when Cleriadus and his father are away from court) show the depth of Thomas's slyness and malevolence. This Manichean presentation of the character allows a simplistic solution: kill Thomas and his ilk and the question of evil is solved. That is precisely what the romance proposes. Cleriadus comes back, finds out about Thomas's misdeeds, unmasks him in front of King Philippon, and has him and his partners in crime put to death (343–63). Evil is thus fully uprooted from the kingdom in the same manner it had been eradicated from Cyprus when Cleriadus killed the khan and his followers. Could readers of the time apply this solution to their own situation, to the state of war between France and England? Could they ascribe all their miseries to the misbehaviors of a handful of bad people whose deaths would rid the two kingdoms of their woes?

Of course King Philippon does share some of the responsibility, and the romance stresses his part, though involuntary, in his daughter's terrible ordeal. He is blamed for being weak and too eager to believe any negative report brought to him; when Thomas produces a forged letter supposedly addressed by Cleriadus to Meliadice and discloses their plan to kill the king, Philippon does not question its authenticity (292). His credulity in this instance is surprising since, at the beginning of the romance, he distrusts his brother so much that he does not want to let him rule the kingdom. King Philippon is, overall, a positive character; the romance often enumerates his qualities. So how can we account for his sudden failure? This portrayal of the king of England can be read in parallel—or perhaps in contrast—with that of the king of France. Though the king of France does not play a major role in the story, he is nonetheless a model typifying the ideal monarch, which the king of England may approximate but not attain. Does this suggest a contrast between the real fifteenth-century monarchs of France and England? Not only does the king of England allow at his court people whose perfidy is well known, he is crippled by defects unbearable in a king. Such is the meaning of the narrator's comment: "Ceste condicion de croire assez de legier ... est ung grant dangier et peril à ung roy ou à ung prince d'avoir ceste condicion, et se doit on bien informer des choses avant que on face jugement hatif, car moult grans inconveniens si en peuent venir" (292–93). [This disposition of gullibility ... is very dangerous and perilous for a king or a prince. One must be well informed before judging hastily, for serious problems can arise from it.] If King Philippon could have avoided his awful mistake with a sound judgment, could the same tool not be used by any prince or king in any situation, and, more precisely, in the present situation?

Although, as we have already stated, the romance does not seem to deal with contemporary reality, its advice for kings and powerful lords renders it a *miroir des princes*. This lesson in good management of oneself and one's lands takes two forms: an illustrated one with the description of Cleriadus's qualities presented in action[22] (and thus fitting another literary genre very popular in the fifteenth century, the *biographie héroïque*) and a plainly didactic one with numerous comments from the narrator himself. For instance, he stresses how important it is for a ruler to make himself loved by his subjects: "et, pour ce, c'est belle chose à ung seigneur ou à ung gentilhome de se faire aymer de chascun" (284) [for this reason it is good that a lord or a noble man try to be loved by everyone]. They are then sorry when he leaves and happy when he returns. We have seen already how the author disapproves of credulity. He underscores his opinion with a second statement when King Philippon discovers the truth about his brother's perfidy and is crushed by sorrow. None of his subjects pity him: "et pour ce, a icy bonne exemple comment nul roy ne prince ne doit croire legerement pour quelque rapport que on lui face, et aussi de faire hastivement justice s'il veult ouvrer sagement" (359) [here is a good example that no king nor prince should readily believe any report made to him and judge hastily if he wants to act wisely]. Retelling how Cleriadus always keeps his word, the narrator adds: "je vouldroye bien que la coustume en fust telle maintenant et les princes la tenissent aussi, car nul ne nulle ne doit parjurer sa foy et en seroit le monde meilleur et plus en l'amour de Dieu se ainsi on le faisoit" (362) [I would like the same habit to be followed nowadays and princes to hold it, too, for no one, man or woman, should betray his/her faith; the world would be better and more in God's love if people behaved like that]. Later, he builds on this idea and condemns lies. Here again he opposes Cleriadus's proper practice to those of his contemporaries: "pour nulle chose du monde, [Cleriadus] n'eust voulu mentir. Se la coustume fust maintenant itelle es seigneurs, chascun en vaulsist mieulx" (468) [Cleriadus would not have told lies for anything in the world. If nowadays lords behaved in the same way, everybody would be better off.] The narrator, obsessed with the notion of faithfulness, insists on it a third time: "C'est belle chose à ung prince que d'estre loyal et à ung homme, de quelque estat que il soit, de tenir sa foy où il l'a promise . . . et, pour ce, qui sera entachié de bonne loyaulté garde la bien et le bien lui en viendra et qui ne le sera si mecte paine de l'estre, car tous biens en peuent venir" (547). [It is a good thing for a prince to be loyal and for a man, whatever his social status might be, to keep his word. . . . And so, whoever is endowed with good loyalty must keep it with care, for good things will come to him from it; and whoever is not, must strive to be, for all good might come from it.][23] At a time when alliances between the powerful are constantly being reversed, when betrayals of all kinds are common practice, this plea for loyalty rings like a condemnation of contemporary practice and a desperate appeal to present leaders.[24] Thus *Cleriadus et Meliadice* offers good advice to the rulers and solutions to the miseries of the time; it also passes (albeit indirectly) severe judgments on behaviors that are held responsible for the war.

From this perspective, the episode at the court of France, which at first seems superfluous, becomes a necessary piece in the author's political agenda. On their way back from Spain to England, Cleriadus and Meliadice stop at the king of France's court for over a month. This long delay—Meliadice's parents cannot wait to see their daughter alive—is hardly justified by the French king's desire to meet Cleriadus. And Cleriadus does not need to accomplish any more stunning deeds to convince his fellows (or the reader) of his superior qualities. Indeed, his victory over six French knights and the demonstration of his hunting skills are redundant. However, as Zink has rightly noted, by welcoming Cleriadus and Meliadice like a royal couple, the king of France acknowledges Cleriadus's social success. In treating him like a peer, the king shows his discrimination. Whereas Philippon lent credence to his brother's false accusation and did not recognize Cleriadus's worth despite all the evidence, the king of France needs only one meeting with Cleriadus to confirm the truth of his opinion. He thus exhibits sound judgment, a quality needed in a king but dearly lacking in Philippon. Also worth noting is the fact that the king of France does not possess a proper name (neither does the constable) while the king of England does. Of course, one is a real actor in the drama; the other does not have a role in the narrative. But this generic title opposed to a proper name might also suggest that kings of France generally possess all the regal qualities while kings of England may or may not, depending on each individual. The main function of the episode, however, is to present the court of France and its head, the king, in the most positive light: "de coustume, c'estoit belle chose que de estre à la court du roy de France, en tous temps.... En ce temps là, on pouoit aller, de jour et de nuyt, comme vous avez ouy cy devant, sans nul dangier et mesmement les bonnes villes ne se fermient point si bien estoit le royaume uny et en paix, car le roy faisoit bien gouverner son royaume et en toute justice tant que il estoit craint et aymé sur tous autres" (475–77) [habitually, it was a great thing to be at the court of the king of France at anytime.... At this time, one could travel by day and by night, as you just heard, with no danger and also the good cities did not lock their gates such was the state of peace and unity in the kingdom. For the king ruled his kingdom so well and so fairly that he was feared and loved more than any other]. Later in the romance, Cleriadus says of the king of France: "Tout bien et honneur sont en lui. C'est le prince de cest monde qui, sur tous, doit estre loué et prisé" (616). [He possesses every good and honorable quality. Among the princes of the world, he is the one who should be most praised and exalted.]

The description of the extraordinary festivities with which the king of France welcomes the couple (dances, banquets, hunting party, tournament, vows to a peacock) on the one hand reflects the fifteenth-century taste for ostentation and theatricality, especially developed at the famous court of Burgundy.[25] By so representing the court of France, *Cleriadus et Meliadice* lends prestige to a court which at the time was in fact poor and troubled compared to others. Even though this blessed period of splendor belongs to a remote past, the possibility of its renewal exists. On the other hand, the episode at the court of France foreshadows Cleriadus's and Meliadice's wedding, during which the same magnificence will be deployed. The king of France and the future king of England thus share the same values and indulge in the same taste for luxury, parade, and pomp.

Mirroring each other, Cleriadus and the king of France represent the ideal leaders the present days are desperately lacking. Their joyous meeting, long prepared by the king's curiosity and desire, far from being superfluous, is a culmination. It describes at length what the reality should be, could be, if only the actual leaders displayed qualities similar to the characters. But, and this is the message of hope, these qualities can be acquired. One must strive to be loyal and fair; thus will one be loved and feared and be able to govern one's land properly. Such a leader will inspire admiration and others will emulate him. At last, the reign of peace, justice, and prosperity will come. Here is the meaning of the romance's last part, which, as Zink rightly points out, former scholars often ignored or dismissed as long and meaningless.[26] It realizes the dream of a united Europe managed by a handful of enlightened princes, all interrelated by marriage, all equally competent and caring about their subjects, a dream Froissart offered glimpses of in his *Chroniques* and fully developed in *Meliador*.

To our modern taste, *Cleriadus et Meliadice*, with its overwhelmingly good characters and predictable happy ending, seems dull. Comparing it to Froissart's fascinating *Chroniques* might seem incongruous and irrelevant. How dare we compare a master work with a tepid romance? But let us first remember that fifteenth and sixteenth-century readers enjoyed *Cleriadus et Meliadice* much more than modern scholars: the text is preserved in nine manuscripts and five printed editions (dated 1495 to 1529). So much for our hasty judgments, rightly condemned by the author himself. Indeed, had Froissart been able to read the romance, would he not have liked it tremendously? After all, is not the ideology at work in *Cleriadus et Meliadice* the same chivalric one propagated by Froissart's romance, *Meliador*?[27] No doubt that Froissart would have admired the chivalrous qualities embodied in Cleriadus. He would have appreciated the description of magnificent parties, elegant emprises, and elaborate tournaments.[28] He would have approved the final plan for managing Europe. He might have objected to some of the simplistic solutions offered by the romance, but he would have agreed that worthy lords such as the Count of Foix should become role models for other leaders. And overall, like the author of *Cleriadus et Meliadice*, Froissart believed that literature had the capacity to influence reality. However paradoxical it may sound, the *Chroniques* and *Cleriadus et Meliadice* present a similar response to the dramatic events of the fourteenth and fifteenth centuries.

NOTES

1. On fifteenth-century propaganda literature, particularly dealing with Salic law, see P. S. Lewis, "War Propaganda and Historiography in Fifteenth-Century France and England," *Transactions of the Royal Historical Society*, 5th ser., 15 (1965): 1–21.

2. *Cleriadus et Meliadice, roman en prose du XVe siècle*, ed. Gaston Zink (Paris-Genève: Droz, 1984), 1. Quotations from this edition are documented parenthetically in the text by page number.

3. Many scholars have reacted to *Cleriadus et Meliadice* in this way, classifying it among Arthurian romances. Gaston Zink, its modern editor, suspects that some of them never read past this first sentence; see his "*Cleriadus et Meliadice*, Histoire d'une élévation sociale," *Mélanges offerts à Alice Planche*, Annales de la Faculté des Lettres et des Sciences de Nice, 48 (Paris: Belles Lettres, 1984), 497–504, esp. 501.

4. Zink, *Cleriadus et Meliadice*, xxxiv.

5. Zink, *Cleriadus et Meliadice*, xlvii–lii; see also his "*Cleriadus et Meliadice*, Histoire d'une élévation sociale."

6. Zink, *Cleriadus et Meliadice*, xxxv.

7. See Jean Favier, *La guerre de Cent ans* (Paris: Fayard, 1980), 573 ff.

8. Jean Froissart, *Chroniques, dernière rédaction du premier livre, édition du manuscrit de Rome Reg. Lat. 869*, ed. George T. Diller (Geneva: Droz, 1972), 159 and 595 ff.

9. Also Chippre (Cyprus), Portingal (Portugal), Poulaine (Pologne), Tartarie, Damas.

10. See Anthime Fourrier, *Le courant réaliste dans le roman courtois en France au Moyen Age* (Paris: A. G. Nizet, 1960).

11. At the end of his edition, Diller adds two very convenient indexes: a toponymic one and an onomastic one. For precise references to the role of the characters to whom I will allude, see these indexes.

12. See also the index of proper names in Jean Froissart, *Voyage en Béarn*, edited by A. H. Diverres, French Classics (Manchester: Manchester University Press, 1953).

13. Froissart, *Chroniques*, 161.

14. On Froissart's chivalrous ideal, see George T. Diller, *Attitudes chevaleresques et réalités politiques chez Froissart, Microlectures du premier livre des Chroniques* (Geneva: Droz, 1984); Peter Dembowski, "Chivalry, Ideal and Real, in the Narrative Poetry of Jean Froissart," *Mediaevalia et Humanistica* 14 (1986): 1–15; Peter F. Ainsworth, *Jean Froissart and the Fabric of History: Truth, Myth and Fiction in the Chroniques* (Oxford: Oxford University Press, 1990).

15. Froissart, *Voyage en Béarn*, 66–67.

16. One wonders where all these riches come from, at the beginning at least, since Cleriadus, though a noble man is only the son of a count. However, after his success in Cyprus, he takes hold of the fabulous treasures of the great khan (325), thus becoming handsomely rich.

17. While rescuing a lady kidnapped by four knights, Cleriadus accidentally kills one of them: the poor knight breaks his neck when falling from his horse. Nonetheless, the dead body is well taken care of (84, 94).

18. In an almost contemporary romance, *Valentin et Orson*, the magician dwarf Pacolet is shown using all kinds of dubious tricks to allow his Christian friends a total victory over the Saracens, who are even stabbed in their sleep; see Arthur Dickson, *Valentin et Orson, a Study in Late Medieval Romance* (New York: Columbia University Press, 1929).

19. See Jonathan Riley-Smith, *The Crusades, a Short History* (New Haven: Yale University Press, 1987), 230–32.

20. This great khan is later referred to as *le grant Can de Tartarie* (274); his troops are usually referred to as *sarrazins*.

21. See Dembowski, "Chivalry, Ideal and Real," 13.

22. See Zink, *Cleriadus et Meliadice*, xlviii–lix.

23. Although men, being in command, are more often the targets of the narrator's comments, he also dictates rules of proper conduct for ladies, future wives, and future queens. Meliadice is, of course, hailed as the perfect model of female virtues and the narrator's interventions emphasize her good behavior even more than Cleriadus's: "Nul temps ne alloit la teste levee ne n'estoit baude ne effrayee en quelque maniere, mais tousjours simple et de moult belle contenance et bien atempree, qui est une belle chose et qui bien affiert à une pucelle qui est à marier" (317).

[Never would she go with her head raised, never was she bold nor animated in anyway, but always simple, nicely composed, and quiet, which is a good thing, well befitting a young girl not yet married.] For another example, see Zink, *Cleriadus et Meliadice*, 607–8.

24. See Favier, *La guerre de Cent ans*, 402 ff., 450 ff. for the different parties that try to take advantage of Charles VI's madness, the opposition between Armagnacs and Bourguignons, and in 1419 the murder of Duke Jean Sans Peur who had come for a meeting with the dauphin.

25. See Danielle Régnier-Bohler, ed., introduction to *Splendeurs de la cour de Bourgogne, Récits et Chroniques* (Paris: Laffont [coll. Bouquins], 1995).

26. Zink, "*Cleriadus et Meliadice*, Histoire d'une élévation sociale," 502.

27. See Dembowski, "Chivalry, Ideal and Real," 9–13.

28. Froissart was fond of depicting heroic enterprises such as the Battle of the Thirties (1351). On the fashion for absurdly heroic challenges at the end of the Middle Ages, see Cedric E. Pickford, *L'Evolution du roman arthurien en prose vers la fin du Moyen Age, d'après le manuscrit 112 du fonds français de la Bibliothèque nationale* (Paris: A. G. Nizet, 1959), 238–63. Also see Régnier-Bohler, *Splendeurs de la cour de Bourgogne*, xvii–xix.

CHAPTER 11

THE HUNDRED YEARS' WAR AND NATIONAL IDENTITY

ELLEN C. CALDWELL

The sequence of invasions and expulsions known since the nineteenth century as the Hundred Years' War may be read in such divergent historical narratives today as to question whether those narratives refer to the same events. Their differences depend largely on the historian's nationality or national alliance, beliefs about the legitimacy or necessity of that war or of war in general, and historical circumstances. Popular representations of that war in art and literature are no less divergent, and at this remove from the events, it is clear that the popular and professional representations have become dependent on one another in complex ways. Further, whether their provenance is from the historical or popular arena, representations of the Hundred Years' War have become intertwined with constructions of nationalism both by the English and the French. To underline the extent of nationalistic influence on those representations and the commentaries they prompt, I should like first to consider some refigurations of that war across the centuries. Each is based on a textual account or inscribes the Hundred Years' War in accordance with written tradition. I shall then turn to the literary inscriptions of the Hundred Years' War in *Henry VI, Part 2*, at the moment of emergent English nationalism. Since that time, the temptation has persisted to use this war to write "analogue history" of one's own time.

Once some of the nationalistic trappings of these representations have been discussed, it may be possible to acknowledge some of the broader social costs such foreign wars exacted. Focusing first on some French versions may move us away from the language of the invaders; focusing on Shakespeare's early plays may help us see the English view from below.

FRENCH REPRESENTATIONS OF THE WAR

Around 1373, Louis I, duc d'Anjou, commissioned a series of tapestries depicting the vision of John as described in the book of Revelation. Completed in about seven years, these immense *Apocalypse* tapestries are exhibited today in a modern gallery designed for their display in the château fortified by St. Louis at Angers. They comprise one among several *tapisseries historiées* [narrative tapestries] on different subjects, commissioned first by the young duc d'Anjou and then by his brother, Philippe le Hardi, duc de Bourgogne.[1] The designs for these tapestries were created by Charles V's painter, Hennequin de Bruges, who used as his inspiration thirteenth-century illuminated manuscripts of the Apocalypse; according to a note appended to the inventory of his library, Charles V "a baillée a mons. D'Anjou pour faire son beau tapis" [gave to Monsieur D'Anjou, for the making of his fine tapestry] a manuscript of the "Apocalipse en françois toute figurée et ystoriée" [Apocalypse in French, fully embellished and illuminated].[2] Two panels clearly reminiscent of those illuminations are of interest here. Panel 24 (21), that of the *sauterelles* [locusts], represents the fifth blast of the trumpet, or the appearance of fantastic grasshoppers that arise from the abyss to torment men for their sins. The passage from Revelation compares the *sauterelles* to horses ready for combat, and the designer of the tapestry has drawn them as such: they have the faces of men, heads crowned; the hair of women; cuirasses of iron; bodies of horses; tails like scorpions. Their king, the Angel of the Abyss, in Hebrew *Abaddon*, in Greek *Apollyon*, the Exterminator, is mounted on one of them. Behind him, emerging from the earth, are five more of the composite animals. Their crowned human heads and upper equine bodies alone are visible. In the tapestry the bearded Abaddon has the wings of a bat, as in the miniature tradition, and is therefore, in the iconography of the Middle Ages, satanic. Panel 26 (23) represents the sixth blast of the trumpet, in which the thousands of horsemen unleashed from hell punish a third of humanity for its sins and its idolatry. On the tapestry the horsemen appear as six armed soldiers riding horses equipped with the tails of serpents and the heads of leopards that issue smoke and sulfur from their mouths. With their lances these soldiers do violence to unarmed men.[3] There is a tradition, currently relayed to those visiting the tapestries at Angers, that in panel 24, the figure of the demonic Exterminator is intended to represent Edward III, followed by his five sons. In panel 26, the primary horseman is meant to represent the Black Prince in battle. I would further add that on other panels of the tapestry, the seven-headed beast is represented much as a seven-headed lion rampant, the heraldic symbol under which, quartered with the *fleur de lys*, Edward III claimed France.[4]

Why the young Valois prince would have commissioned an enormous series of tapestries of the Apocalypse remains unclear. From the insertion of his arms and secret symbols, however, one can assume he was in general responsible for the subject. What is often vaguely noted is Louis d'Anjou's acknowledgment of the catastrophic experiences of the French during the fourteenth century, including the war with the English and the visitations of the black plague.[5] Is it possible to be more specific? Louis I, duc d'Anjou (born July 23, 1339), second son of Jean II (called le Bon), was present at the battle of Poitiers, but was sent from the field or, as some chroniclers believe, fled before his father and his younger brother Philippe were captured by the soldiers of the Black Prince. The consequences of this defeat for the French must have seemed apocalyptic; it was followed by a popular uprising, as well as direct threats to the dauphin Charles by a Parisian mob. One of the conditions of King Jean's 1361 release from captivity in London was his replacement by royal hostages; Louis d'Anjou was foremost among them. In 1362 these hostages were removed to Calais after they concluded a second treaty with Edward III. In 1363, at a shaky moment in the negotiations, when the dauphin and the Estates refused to ratify this second treaty, the hostages were detained. Louis had had enough. He escaped from captivity to join his wife, Marie de Blois (daughter of the duc de Bretagne), whom he had not seen in thirty months. Although his elder brother Charles, the dauphin, tried to convince him to return as a hostage, Louis refused. Edward III wrote castigating him with these words: "vous avez moult blémi l'honneur de votre lignage" [you have gravely offended the honor of your ancestors].[6] Jean le Bon, mortified by his son's lapse of chivalry, and perhaps also not too unhappy to revisit his cousin Edward III, returned to London to stand hostage for Louis. Jean le Bon died there in captivity in 1364, a disastrous turn of events, for the ransom still had to be paid.[7]

In 1373, when Louis d'Anjou commissioned these tapestries, he was thirty-five years old, powerful and ambitious. By the time they were

completed, he and his brothers had effected the reconquest of most of
the disputed territories and had outlived both Edward III and his deadly
son the Black Prince. Of all the sons of Jean le Bon, Louis d'Anjou was
most instrumental in the French recovery of strongholds held by the
English, especially in the south of France, where he was lieutenant and
governor of Languedoc, but also in Normandy and Bretagne. While
Charles V reformed currency, the army, his internal administration, and
dictated policy and strategy, his brothers Louis, Jean, and Philippe, most
ably assisted by the constable Bertrand du Guesclin, methodically recaptured citadel after citadel. Thus, when Louis d'Anjou came to commission these tapestries, he had experienced firsthand and to his great personal distress the turbulence and military humiliation of the Hundred
Years' War, captivity in enemy territory, and eventually victory. Would
Louis d'Anjou have so honored, commemorated, or condemned the
English king and his sons by having them woven into his costly tapestry?
Later his brother Philippe would commission an *Apocalypse* tapestry as
well as one on the Battle of Roosebeke (which took place November 27,
1382, and at which he defeated the bourgeois rebels of Ghent).[8]

Historical subjects and the exploits of the commissioners were not
unknown in the representations on these tapestries. If the horsemen do represent Edward III and his sons, then those men Jean le Bon considered his
princely cousins are here revealed as figures made bestial by their dynastic
symbology of the lion or leopard, and their war is rendered monstrous, a
virulent plague sent by the heavens to punish mankind. These assumptions
are consistent with those of many contemporary writers, who viewed the
war with England, particularly the captivity of Jean le Bon, as the scourge
of God, punishment for the sins of the French people. In particular,
Françoise Autrand notes the Benedictine monk François de Montebelluna,
who claimed the captivity was divine punishment and who compared
Edward III to "le prince des sauterelles paré de fleurs étrangères" [the prince
of locusts adorned with foreign flowers].[9] This exegetical tradition seems
the most likely origin for any legends about Edward III and his sons as blasts
of the trumpet. The biblical authority implied in the awe, the impending
doom, and the occultic sentence of Revelation may thus be the final word
on what this war meant for the French, and no amount of admiration for
the prowess of a feudal enemy could efface the indictment of the tapestries:
the war was demonic punishment delivered by the English in their many
invasions and pillagings of France in the fourteenth century. And this was
before the more sustained encroachments of the fifteenth century had been

conceived. Further, the tapestries suggest that despite their extrahuman powers, the forces of the English, like those of Abaddon and his crew, will eventually be defeated.

The second phase of the war ended in 1453; by the late fifteenth and early sixteenth centuries, chroniclers building on the earlier coverage of Froissart and the monastic compilations had transformed these accounts through their own views of the war's aftermath. By the 1590s, during Elizabethan investment in an emergent nationalism, Shakespeare would turn their narratives into his own elaborately staged versions of this second phase: the invasion by Henry V, the extermination of Joan la Pucelle, and the "loss" of Normandy, as I shall discuss below.

It is not until the nineteenth-century crystallization of French and English national identities that the revival of medievalism and "historical realism" sparked further memorable representations of the events of the war. During 1829–1830, before his Moroccan journey and in the months preceding his *La Liberté guidante le peuple*, Delacroix completed a commission from the duchesse de Berry to paint *La Bataille de Poitiers*, a work she neglected to accept.[10] The English remember the battle as that in which the Black Prince captured Jean le Bon and his fourteen-year-old son Philippe on September 19, 1356.[11] In Delacroix's painting, the son shields his father, whose horse has fallen, as fighting men surround them; red pennons, presumably those of the English army, fly above the central figures as soldiers in variously emblazoned arms engage in combat in the foreground. Although it is perhaps possible that the event chosen for the canvas is intentionally ironic—the foolhardy king exposes his person in battle—the primary reminder seems to be that the French were steadfast, not that the English pummeled the French army, with lingering consequences for the populace. Michel Mollat du Jourdin notes that the defense of Jean and Philippe, based on the accounts of those who saw it, became legendary: "Nous devons au Florentin Matteo Villani [d. 1363] le récit du difficile combat soutenu dans un pays coupé de haies contre un ennemi embusqué dans les chemins creux, et celui, devenu légendaire, de la défense personnelle de Jean le bon, assisté de son fils Philippe, le futur duc de Bourgogne: 'Père. Gardez-vous à droite ... à gauche'."[12] [We owe to the Florentine Matteo Villani (d. 1363) the story of the difficult battle, fought in a countryside riddled with hedges, against an enemy hiding in ditches. We owe to him as well the story, now legendary, of the personal defense of Jean le Bon, assisted by his son Philippe, the future duke of Burgundy, "Father—look to your right ... to your left."] Delacroix's painting clearly recalls Villani's account or a later elaboration of it, with emphasis on bravery in the face of terrible odds, the pathos of the defense, and filial piety. This painting does not figure large in Delacroix's reputation, but along with his more celebrated *Bataille de Nancy*, it follows the tradition of battle painting revived by Napoleon. Although Delacroix's revolutionary impulses might seem at odds with the subject of royal bravery, the painting is in keeping with the militarism of the early nineteenth century, and its prominence in the Louvre assures its continued place in an expression of French nationalism rendered thus: soldiers should sacrifice themselves in the defense of the fatherland, even in the face of certain defeat.

There is a similar response to this first phase of the war in Rodin's extraordinary statuary group, *Les Bourgeois de Calais*. In 1884 the city of Calais decided to honor its medieval hero Eustache de Saint-Pierre, and when in 1885 Rodin received the commission to construct the monument, he chose to represent all six burghers of Calais as they prepare to surrender the keys of the city to Edward III. After a devastating eleven-month siege ending in 1347, Edward was convinced by Walter Manny to spare the lives of the citizens, whom he then expelled, repeopling Calais with English colonists.[13] In return for such clemency, Edward ordered Manny to bring before him the six richest burghers of Calais: "alez vous en arriere et leur dittes que pour l'amour de vous tous je les recheveray voulentiers tous comme prisonniers, sauf que j'en vueil avoir VI des plus gros de la ville, lesquelx venront par devant moy en pures et simples chemises, la hart au col, et m'aporteront les clefs de la ville, et feray d'eulx ma pure volenté"[14] [go back and tell them that for love of all of you I will willingly release them to you as prisoners; but I want six of them, the most important in the city, to come before me, dressed only in shirts, their necks in halters, and to bring me the keys of the city, and I shall do with them exactly as I please]. Led by Eustache de Saint-Pierre, the burghers surrendered. The description by the chronicler Jean le Bel seems indeed the moment Rodin represents, and it is known that he followed Froissart's more literary elaboration of the event from the earlier chronicler. When the Calaisiens viewed Rodin's *maquette*, they objected, claiming the sculptor had chosen the moment of the burghers' most desperate and degrading submission. Rodin defended his vision by saying that "Far from humbling himself before the king of England, the burgher was 'leaving the city to descend toward the camp. It is this that gives the group the feeling of march, of movement'."[15] By rendering intense suffering in the immense hands, bodies, and faces of the burghers, old or grown old from their trial, Rodin does convey that the effects of the siege were brutal and inhumane. Like Delacroix's painting, Rodin's correspondence indicates that he was "eager to declare a personal vision of French history, of patriotism and sacrifice."[16]

At the beginning of World War I, this vision was carried across the Channel and made fully, if ironically, analogical. The National Art Collections Fund acquired a casting of *Les Bourgeois* to be implanted in the gardens of London's Parliament in honor of Edward's queen, Philippa of Hainault. According to Jean le Bel, the reasoning, tears, and pleas of his commanders had failed to move the hard-hearted king to pity the burghers; Edward commanded that they be decapitated immediately. Then Philippa, who was heavily pregnant, fell to her knees and begged him to spare the burghers:

> "Ha! Gentil sire, depuis que j'ay passé la mer en grand peril ainsy que vous sçavez, je ne vous ay riens demandé, si vous prye et requier a jointes mains, que pour l'amour du filz de Nostre Dame, vous vueilliez avoir mercy d'eulx." Le gentil roy arresta un poy de parler et regarda la royne devant luy, à genoulx, amerement plourant; si luy commença ung petit le cueur à amollier, et luy dist: "Dame, j'amasse mielx que vous fussez aultre part, vous me priez si tendrement que je ne le vous ose escondire; et combien que je le face envis, neantmains prenez les, je les vous donne." Si prist les VI bourgoys par les chevestres et les livra à la royne, et quitta de mort tous ceulx de Calais pour l'amour d'elle, et la bonne dame fist revestir et aisier lesdis VI bourgoys.[17]
>
> ["Ah! Noble lord, from the moment I crossed the sea in great peril, as you know, I have asked you for nothing. So I beg and beseech you with clasped hands, for the love of the Son of Our Lady, to have mercy on them." The noble king ceased speaking an instant and looked at the queen before him, on her knees, weeping bitterly. His heart began to soften somewhat and he said to her: "Lady, I would prefer that you were somewhere else; however, you ask me so passionately that I dare not refuse you. And as much as I regret it, nevertheless, take them, I give them to you." Thus he took the six burghers by the halters and delivered them to the queen, saving all the citizens of Calais from death, for love of her. And the good Lady had the six burghers reclothed and did them ease.]

Duplicating the statuary group in London borders on the ironic; the moment of representation is that in which the burghers surrender to Edward III rather than the reprieve granted at Philippa's request, which in any event did not prevent the Calaisiens from being driven from their city. In October of 1914, Rodin gave a large number of sculptures to England "as a gift honoring the unified effort of England and France to stop the German menace." *Les Bourgeois* would also have been unveiled at this time, but the secretary of the fund postponed it for fear the reference to Calais's submission some five hundred years earlier would be untimely at the moment when "the German armies are making desperate attempts to reach Calais and again compel its surrender!"[18] Even during this era, the events of the Hundred Years' War were intentionally made the point of reference for patriotic self-sacrifice and were perceived as such by contemporaries.

The similarity between these two nineteenth-century popular, supremely nationalistic representations, Delacroix's *La Bataille de Poitiers* and Rodin's *Les Bourgeois de Calais*, lies in their concentration on the victims of the war. Doomed defense or complete self-sacrifice for what will be a losing proposition, perhaps with the hope of eventual deliverance, are the nineteenth-century visions of France deriving from the Hundred Years' War.[19] Differences between the painting and monument lie first in the choice of subject: the capture and imprisonment of the king must have been humiliating, but unlike the loss of Calais, it did not last two hundred years and did not represent so viscerally as the expulsion from Calais the suffering inflicted on noncombatants. Each work follows the written tradition to represent effectively moments particularly unhappy for the French during the Hundred Years' War. Neither, unlike most revisions created by the English, is designed to show those events from the point of view of the victor, either the Black Prince or Edward III.

But they are strangely in keeping with themes treated in the response of the written tradition of the fourteenth century recorded in the *Apocalypse* tapestries: the endurance and eventual defeat of the demonic invaders. If one can tentatively consider the *Apocalypse* tapestries as very early artistic and popular or even official representations of the war, then perhaps one should keep in mind what they mean for *all* representations of this war, contemporary and later. From the illuminated manuscripts of Froissart (himself sponsored by Philippa of Hainault, queen of Edward III) and other chroniclers; to propagandistic images produced during the fifteenth century, such as the Jesse trees of Henry VI in various manuscripts now in the British library, including one in which St. Louis presents Henry VI to the Virgin and Child;[20] to the window sponsored by "Foulques eyto[n]" in the church at Caudebec; to Shakespeare's *Henry VI* , *Henry V*, and perhaps *Edward III*;[21] to Nicolas-Guy Brenet's *La Mort de du Guesclin* (1777) and J. E.

Lenepveu's painting of Jeanne d'Arc, now in the Panthéon; to Rossellini's *Jeanne d'Arc*;[22] despite the English invaders' efforts to contain resistance, they were very early on despised by those whom they invaded, even if at that moment one can speak only conditionally of a unified "France."[23]

Between England and France, and within both England and France, competing versions of the war continue to be constructed. Between the two nations, France presents victimization, self-sacrifice, and endurance against England's tale of glory in conquest. As late as 1989 Kenneth Branagh's film version of Shakespeare's *Henry V* managed to exalt the English monarch's invasion of France, while there is yet another film version of the war, this one in two parts, *Jeanne la Pucelle: Les Batailles* and *Les Prisons*, starring Sandrine Bonnaire and directed by Jacques Rivette.[24] By the starkness of their imagery and the absence of glorified battle scenes, these two films, unlike Branagh's *Henry V*, convey a sense of the tragedy of the war. Within England itself, differing versions of this war have long existed, but because of later nationalistic agendas, they are more difficult to delineate. I shall present first what one would normally expect to see here, Shakespeare's *Henry V* and its continued role in English nationalism, and then his much earlier and less well-known staging of the contraction from the Hundred Years'War in 1450–1453, *Henry VI, Part 2*.

SHAKESPEARE'S *HENRY V* AND ANALOGUE HISTORY

It is difficult to overestimate the importance of the Hundred Years'War in England's conception of itself as a nation. Edward III and his son the Black Prince are remembered as warrior king and prince. The colonization of Calais by Edward III is considered one of the most important military achievements of his reign. Similarly, the battles of Poitiers and Agincourt and Henry V's siege of Rouen are spoken of in terms of their superior English military strategy. With the subtitle of his book on the Hundred Years' War, *The English in France, 1337–1453*, at least one popular historian, Desmond Seward, acknowledges that the war was an invasion and describes the horrors of the English *chevauchées*. Although sympathetic to the French, even he cannot resist saying:"It is arguable that the Hundred Years'War was medieval England's greatest achievement."[25]

Repeatedly the life of Henry V, his invasion, and the battle of Agincourt are represented on the stage and screen, often from some version of Shakespeare's *Henry V*, written most likely in 1599 and entered in the Stationers' Register in 1600. Andrew Gurr's stage history in his recent

Cambridge edition of the play notes the correlation between revivals of the play and national crises: it was restaged during the Jacobite rebellion of 1745, the French Revolution, the Napoleonic wars, the Boer War, World War I, the Battle of Britain, and D-Day.[26] Quite beyond what the king may have meant to Shakespeare in the very last years of Elizabeth's reign, he has continued to inspire analogue history; what that has meant to the English in the wars of this century is difficult to untangle. Jonathan Dollimore and Alan Sinfield describe Shakespeare's *disruptions* to an ideology of national identity in *Henry V*; like Spenser's *A View of the Present State of Ireland*, it reveals too much "the human cost."[27] Chris Fitter, in a critique of Branagh's film version of *Henry V*, claims, "Shakespeare's play, however, satiric, ambiguating and interrogative, is clearly an exposé of imperialist rhetoric and a critique of the institution of monarchy.... Monarchical interests, Shakespeare repeatedly shows, are inimical to those of the common people, whose support must thus be ideologically reinforced through oratorical inductions of false consciousness."[28]

The most important production of *Henry V* during World War II is Laurence Olivier's film version (released November 22, 1944), which opens with the dedication "to the Commandos and Airborne Troops of Great Britain—'the spirits of whose ancestors it has humbly attempted to recapture.'"[29] Olivier and those who supported him all appear to have recognized the nationalistic propaganda value of a film version of *Henry V* and to have received encouragement and support from the British government, particularly the Ministry of Information.[30] It is not possible to divorce Olivier's film production of *Henry V* from British war efforts or to ignore the propaganda at work on several levels in the film, from decisions about cuts in the text to decisions about particular shots or techniques.

Olivier excises from the play lines and scenes that render Henry V less than heroic; thus, there is no Cambridge conspiracy; no threatening of virgins, infants, and old people before the walls of Harfleur; no talk of putting to death the French soldiers captured at Agincourt.[31] According to Harry M. Geduld, "Henry's scene with the conspirators was probably eliminated not only because, as James Phillips maintains, 'it developed Elizabethan political ideas that are unfamiliar and even objectionable to modern audiences,' but also because, in 1944, it would have been interpreted as an allusion to the existence of a well-organized fifth column."[32] Those "unfamiliar" and "objectionable" ideas include, on the one hand, the historical tradition of the nobility's open and secret liaisons with the French and, on the other, Henry's deceitfulness in exposing the conspiracy and his ruthlessness in executing his cousins.

Further cuts were made to accommodate the time Olivier chose to spend re-enacting the battle of Agincourt. Although Graham Holderness claims that inordinate attention has been paid to Olivier's Agincourt scene, it in fact merits even further analysis.³³ A significant piece of footage, the first to be shot, it is the most informative segment of the film.³⁴ As Olivier himself admitted and as many critics have noted since, this Agincourt imitates the celebrated "Battle on the Ice" in Eisenstein's *Alexandr Nevskii* (released November 23, 1938), a comparison worth pursuing.³⁵ The visual and emotional power of Olivier's Agincourt is attributable to the compositional intricacies of its model. In Eisenstein's film, the legendary Alexander Nevsky and his soldiers fight Teutonic Knights, armored as metallic automatons, for a clearly nationalistic cause: to defend the motherland from its invaders.³⁶ In his essay "My Subject is Patriotism," Eisenstein explains that through this thirteenth-century subject the film was made to address the barbarism of contemporary German fascists, both in their treatment of the Jews and as they attacked the sanctity and integrity of Soviet nationalism.

> This is the subject of our film. We have taken a historic episode from the thirteenth century, when the Teutonic and Livonian knights, the ancestors of the contemporary fascists, undertook a systematic advance eastward in order to subjugate the Slavonic and other peoples, in precisely the same spirit as contemporary fascist Germany is trying to do, with the same frenzied slogans and the same fanaticism.... This is why the picture, though it deals with a specific historic epoch, with specific historic events, seems like a modern picture, according to the testimony of those who have seen it. The feelings which inflamed the Russian people in the thirteenth century when they repelled the foe are quite close to those which the Soviet peoples feel at the present time. Undoubtedly the same feelings fire those upon whom the predatory paws of Hitlerite aggression have already been laid.³⁷

It is always possible that Eisenstein writes here as prompted; other Soviet films from 1938 and 1939 are even more explicitly anti-Nazi. By the middle of 1939, the Nazi-Soviet pact sent all these films, *Nevskii* included, into recall.³⁸

Eisenstein considered the Battle on the Ice one of his three most successful sequences (with the "Odessa steps" and the "meeting the squadron" in *Potemkin*), and speaks of it frequently in other essays, especially in reference to the compositional methods by which he attempted to achieve emotional effect. He claims that all elements of the sequence were structured to parallel the beating of a terrified heart.³⁹ He credits D. W. Griffith, whom he met, as the progenitor of such scenes as his own in the development of Soviet *montage*. The charge of the knights thus must owe something in its conception to the charge of the Klansmen in *Birth of a Nation*; however, while admiring his technique, Eisenstein found Griffith's politics "repellent."[40]

In creating his 1944 *Henry V*, Olivier is clearly influenced by the *montage* and tracking shots of the attack by the "German wedge" and the subsequent battle on Lake Chedskoe. Aware of the emotional power attainable through the imitation of Eisenstein's techniques, Olivier transfers the charge of the knights, the precarious condition of the ice, Alexander's tactical brilliance and his rousing speeches about fighting for one's land to the charge of the French, the unforeseen natural phenomenon of the fields near Agincourt, Henry's speeches, and the defensive position assumed by the English. He further combines from Eisenstein an overstated nationalism with the notion that those who trust to their war machine instead of the heroic spirits of their soldiers become vulnerable in battle. Rather, those who face terrible odds will, by relying on their personal sacrifice, skills, stoutheartedness, spirit of brotherhood, and inspired leadership, outface their better-equipped enemies. Olivier easily appropriates Eisenstein's *montage* and the building to a pitch of emotion through the horses' hooves; the anxiety of the soldiers as they face the oncoming army and the flight of arrows from the German crossbowmen inspired specific shots in the Agincourt scene. Olivier makes much of the English bowmen who slaughter French soldiers as they become mired in the recently ploughed and muddy fields near Agincourt. Riding a white horse, his Henry V, like Nevsky, never flags before the effete, completely superficial, grandiosely armored and thus overconfident French commanders and soldiers.

The ways in which *Henry V* became a tempting vehicle for British propaganda as the D-Day landings grew imminent are easy to list and have been thoroughly discussed by Holderness. However, it has not been made clear how the play, matched against *Alexandr Nevskii*, provides a particularly aggressive and complicated vision of nationalism. As Gurr notes, there is no battle scene in the play besides the encounter between Pistol and Le Fer.[41] Olivier detaches a moment of defensive posturing from a campaign which is otherwise construable only as an invasion, and therefore presents the soldiers as prepared to be sacrificial, much like those of Jean le Bon, or even like the burghers of Calais. To focus on the Battle of Agincourt is to forget that Henry V and his men resemble not the allies, but the German aggressors. However, Olivier was able to turn an arrogant assumption about ownership—Henry's tenacious hold on a fragile dynastic claim of France—into a vehicle for nationalistic propaganda to serve the interests, as he himself notes, of the descendants of the original aggressors.

Olivier's film accomplished several things at once. First and most important, it portrayed the English as heroic and superior soldiers in the most adverse conditions against their traditional enemies. Long after Normandy had been lost to the French in 1450, England once again invades victoriously in this re-representation of the Hundred Years' War. Through careful staging and redirecting of Shakespeare's play, the film, like Eisenstein's *Nevskii*, does create "analogue history." Further, it serves to comment on the role of the English and French in World War II. In this film the French lack leadership; disorganized and factious, they sit playing mindless children's games; weak and effeminate, they present a surface culture with little depth, a clever indictment of the Vichy government. Second, it is designed to present the allies, led by the British in their version of nationalism, as victorious over the fascist Germans. Working through the Russian nationalism against the Germans in *Alexandr Nevskii*, Olivier's *Henry V* also strikes at the Germans' position in Normandy and their reliance on advanced weaponry and steel-reinforced concrete garrisons. The film suggests that an English invasion will be successful, despite the seemingly superior defenses of the Germans. Olivier's *Henry V* may be seen as attacking at once both the French and the Germans: the weakness of the French in succumbing to the occupying army, and the weakness of the occupying army despite its much vaunted military superiority. Olivier's film captures nationalistic feeling by staging a counter-invasion, not against the Germans, but against the French as they have been Germanized, or as they have been reduced by the Germans, or perhaps merely allowed themselves to be reduced, as "we" always suspected they might.

Raymond Durgnat accepts the film's "rousing jingoism" but finds the topical references confusing. He remarks that in the wooing scene, "whether France here = France our ally, to whom Churchill had in 1940 impulsively proposed 'marriage,' or Germany our enemy whom we mustn't hate forever, is quite ambiguous."[42] The references are layered rather than ambiguous. The French are the French of the playworld, England's traditional enemy and Other. The French are further, via the representation of their effeminacy, also traditional, the French in submission to the Germans, that is, the Vichy government. The French are also the Germans outright, via the stated intentions of the filmmakers and backers, and implicitly, via unmistakable allusions to *Alexandr Nevskii*. The set speeches, "Once more unto the breach" and "We happy few," are those both of an invader and a defender. Harfleur is successfully besieged while Henry's position at Agincourt is defensive, yet both are played to comment on the war with Germany.

Following the lead of Olivier's filming of *Henry V*, critical assertions about Shakespeare's history plays have been consciously and unconsciously shaped to a large degree by the events of World War II and the reactions and attitudes of scholars who lived through or fought in that war. It would seem that as the West has grown aware of the origins and dangers of nationalism through that war itself, the analogical reconstructions in those plays would become transparent. The pull of the "national hero," however, is still quite strong, as the confused agenda of Branagh's *Henry V* reveals.[43]

Like their earlier counterparts, many contemporary critics read *Henry V* through their own experience of war; for a younger generation of American critics in the late twentieth century, this is the Vietnam war, which, beyond addressing the question of war itself also interrogated the authority of political and military leaders, the value of nationalism, and the necessity of playing world police. Despite this new antiwar interpretation, many English and American representations of the Hundred Years' War, especially those deriving from Shakespeare's English histories, are nonetheless still markedly influenced by historical narratives of England's heroism, deriving at least from the nineteenth-century response to the Napoleonic wars and further hardened by attitudes toward the French and Germans in World War II. Reading Shakespeare against the grain of uncritical nationalism thus continues to be controversial. Since the recent fiftieth anniversary of the allied invasion of Normandy, that reading is very delicate and to some even blasphemous to maintain.

HENRY VI, PART 2 AND THE CRITIQUE OF THE WAR

Historians who in some way treat the Hundred Years' War do not look with the same intensity at all of its long series of events. If Henry's invasion of Normandy and his claiming of it for his son are difficult to discuss outside nationalistic attitudes, it is far more difficult to address the end of the Hundred Years' War without becoming immured in chauvinistic rhetoric. What French historians call the "recovery of Normandy" is to the English the "loss of France," a phrase which appears to capture genuine contemporary responses to the events, but which may also treat them with all the feeling of a much later era of nationalism built against the French. Of the full-scale English histories or more detailed articles on various segments of the Hundred Years' War, I have read few which do not to some degree regret, for complex reasons, that the English "lost" Normandy. The Hundred Years' War does seem to be on the consciences of some historians, such as Griffiths and Postan. But others, particularly McFarlane and his followers, assert that the war was morally justifiable and on the whole beneficial to the populace of England.[44] Most English historians, whatever they may think of the series of events during the English occupation, are of one mind about the end of the war: it was a mistake that could have been prevented.

By contrast, earlier and modern French historians, as do French writers and artists of various types and from various periods, as I have suggested above, inscribe the war in narratives differing greatly from those produced by the English. French historians emphasize the social and economic effects of invasion and of warfare. For the most part they consider the English attempt to bastardize the dauphin and the reversion of the French succession to Henry V as humiliations, viewing the latter's exploits in terms of the damage they inflicted on soldiers and civilians, and stressing his cruelty and ruthlessness. In historical surveys, the Hundred Years' War does not always claim the large place it does in English histories. Agincourt often receives only a brief account, and sometimes French histories do not separate the events from 1415 to 1453, seeing the first date as the beginning of the end of the Hundred Years' War.[45] One history which treats the entire period at length considers it "une occupation."[46] The experience of World War II exerts great pressure on these historians as well, as they readily admit.

Competing narratives of the war and its effects were also accessible *within* late Elizabethan England; they, too, are narratives of resistance. The events portrayed in Shakespeare's *Henry V* can be played in opposing ways; the drama has the potential for military heroics and chauvinistic razzing of a traditional enemy, as well as for a dark and skeptical, even cynical reading of those very attitudes. It includes the visions of people from various orders of society. And it ends with a stark reminder that although this play is about the exploits of the warrior king everyone loves to admire, the playwright knows quite well what followed those military conquests: lingering foreign war and military defeat leading to internal strife and civil war. In a backward glance to the beginnings of his own career in the theater, Shakespeare ends *Henry V* with this sonnet epilogue:

> Thus far, with rough and all-unable pen
> Our bending author hath pursu'd the story,
> In little room confining mighty men,
> Mangling by starts the full course of their glory.
> Small time, but in that small, most greatly lived

> This star of England. Fortune made his sword
> By which the world's best garden he achieved,
> And of it left his son imperial lord.
> Henry the Sixth, in infant bands crowned king
> Of France and England, did this king succeed,
> Whose state so many had the managing
> *That they lost France and made his England bleed,*
> *Which oft our stage hath shown*—and for their sake,
> In your fair minds let this acceptance take
> (V.iii.1–14; emphasis added).

If this end of the war were so shameful as historians suggest, one wonders why Shakespeare began his career with a trio of plays about the king who "lost" the Hundred Years' War, and this closely following 1588, when the English more or less "defeated" the Armada.

At a moment when feeling over home territory and anxiety over the threat of invasion were running high and before he chose to represent Henry V or the landing at Harfleur, Shakespeare staged the death of heroism, the reputedly ignominious loss of Normandy, the popular rebellion of Jack Cade, and the Yorkist uprising known as the War of the Roses. Few critics have managed, to any remarkable degree, to establish why.[47] The answer may lie in part in the convergence of the influence of the chronicle sources with the necessity for England's state of wartime readiness in the late 1580s and early 1590s. Elizabeth and her subjects seemed propelled into war, after years of "relative" peace, by the Queen of Scots, by Philip II, by *Liguers*, by the Low Countries, and by her militant Protestants. Although critics often cite the aging queen's succession crisis as giving rise to domestic anxieties at the same moment as the war, the gravest succession question between 1589 and 1593 was not who would succeed the Virgin Queen or even who would sit in the Privy Council, but who would sit on the throne of France. The consequences of that decision were fearfully projected to the English. I posit here that the "matter of France," the uncertainty of the French succession, and the complex of attitudes it fostered about war with England's traditional enemy, are the salient influences on Shakespeare's early plays.

In Act IV of *Henry VI, Part 2*, the rebel captain, Jack Cade, accuses the Lord Treasurer of a number of crimes and pronounces decisive judgment upon him: "[he] can speak French; and therefore he is a traitor" (IV.ii.155–60). This line, spoken by a character from the lower orders of society, is usually read as comic, if not ludicrous, and to some, as a measure of Shakespeare's antipopulism. Cade's anti-French attitude, in a playworld rent by factious leaders and terrorized by his popular uprising, might be read not so much as Shakespeare's demonizing of the lower classes as a negotiated representation of *la guerre de Cent ans* on the English home front. In some current historical reconstructions of the war's end, English military aggression in France is thought to have been internalized; I would add that then as later, France-bashing or the desire to conquer France and anxieties about losing it helped disguise domestic economic depression and anxieties about the succession questions both at home and in France. Through the chronicle sources of Hall, Holinshed, Stow, Grafton, and others, dramatists of the 1590s could read of an earlier period of external military failure and internal domestic distress punctuated by anti-Gallic sentiment. It played well. It was not, however, a matter of simple xenophobia or deflection to a scapegoat of frustrations about losing foreign wars.

In recent years, Leah Marcus, Phyllis Rackin, and Richard Helgerson have attempted to describe the complicity of Elizabethan drama in the development of English nationalism. To extend that effort, I should like to offer two premises, concluded in part from Charles Tilly's theoretical explanation of the role of war in the making of the state:[48] (1) Foreign war promotes nationalism in the form of chauvinism and of state centralization. (2) Internal responses to the economic pressures of war affect the ways in which nationalism proceeds; if the wars are lingering or unsuccessful, the pressures become acute and violence can turn inward. Those internal responses and effects are dispersed throughout the populace to surface in its writings, including the chronicle plays of the 1590s. In *Henry VI, Part 2*, which recounts the English response to the French recovery of Normandy, the venom, hurled not so much against France as on the Francophile activities of those who lost it, draws on accounts of the earlier period of popular anti-Gallic sentiment, the middle of the 1400s, to mediate a crisis in late Elizabethan England; the tension between national and dynastic identity filtered through continued warfare, particularly with *Liguers*-controlled France.

Even as Elizabeth's courtiers pursued a militant protestancy abroad, their wars in France, the costs of which cut deeply across the populace, were largely unfocused and unsuccessful.[49] The attitude toward France represented in *Henry VI, Part 2*, especially through the popular uprising led by Jack Cade, is as much a complex register of popular feeling about that war as it is of early modern nationalism: waging war and creating the state are inseparable, both historically and on the stage. Further, the complication of

Elizabeth's tentative backing of Henri de Navarre invites us to explore the contradiction between traditional France-bashing and the undeniable admiration the English felt for Navarre as he battled his way to his throne. As Dickens and Bell have demonstrated, from 1589 the number of newsletters pouring into England on the wars of Henri de Navarre kept the reading public aware of his progress as he struggled to gain Paris. Those published only in France are copious, but many were translated and the number of those extant indicates the extent of their popularity.[50] English hostility toward *Liguers* and their activities from 1588 to 1594 is complicated by English admiration for Henri IV, who appeared as a heroic Protestant prince who might or might not succeed in gaining the throne he claimed by Salic law, as opposed to the candidate "Charles X," or those put forward by Philip II, including the Infanta. This complexity informs Shakespeare's presentation of the French. The chronicle accounts of losing France in the 1440s and 1450s may have read to Shakespeare and other Elizabethans as a curiously familiar tale of the high price an ambivalent public pays for nationalistic or political war efforts sponsored by dynastic claimants. In the earlier period, while the public expressed a desire to retain the "French patrimony," they balked at its cost in lives and other resources. In the latter period, while the public responded positively to the idea of supporting Henri IV and of defining itself against Catholic *Liguers*, it reacted negatively to the internal pressures created by the tremendous if inadequate costs of that war, which first legitimated taxation, and, although it was lingering and indeterminate, continued to demand taxation. These costs are both named and disguised by anti-Gallic sentiment and anger over the "loss of France."

Leah Marcus has examined *Henry VI, Part 1* and its collapsing of Joan la Pucelle, the French woman warrior who consorts with demons, into Elizabeth and her lack of decisiveness in Protestant efforts abroad. "Want of men and money" led to frustration with the war effort: "When English audiences watched *1 Henry VI*, what they saw was a bustling, bloody palimpsest of past and present militarism."[51] While Marcus focuses on the relationship between war and its effects at home as it is manifested in *Part 1*'s implied criticism of Elizabeth for disgracing England by withholding funds adequate to win the war, I would like to emphasize that *Part 2* considers the effects of that even inadequate resource extraction from those who cannot bear the costs and the resulting internal violence—hardships that are difficult to analyze because of the concurrence of dynastic and incipient nationalistic agendas. According to Charles Tilly, who describes state making as "organized crime," the criticism often acts as a screen; it is in the interests of the crown and its agents to be able to "protect" their subject populations, and lingering or unsuccessful wars allude to the possibility that they cannot uphold their obligations of protection, and cannot therefore justify resource extraction.[52] Moreover, it is difficult to compute the costs to those people in various lower orders of society, although their contributions to the war efforts in both periods are substantial.[53] Complaints about the various hardships caused by the war are imbedded in many forms of chauvinism, both historically and in these plays.

In the *Henry VI* trilogy, things fall apart: the loss of France is followed by rebellion and confusion, the loss of a strong moral center, and finally, civil war, all woven into the long and tortured reign of Henry VI. That reign spanned nearly forty years, carving, from Henry's majority, the middle out of the fifteenth century. Between 1445 and 1455 occurred several of the more important events of that reign: Henry's marriage to Margaret of Anjou; the development of Henry's court faction and within it, the rise to power and the murder of the Duke of Suffolk; the contraction from Normandy; the Cade rebellion; the contraction from Gascony and the end of the Hundred Years' War; the Yorkist rebellion and the first battle of Saint Albans between the Yorkists and Lancastrians. The liminal site between those two traumatic events—the Hundred Years' War and the War of the Roses—is characterized by instability, and the transition between them is effected by widespread rebellion, particularly Cade's rebellion of 1450. Two developments have an impact on the events of 1450: Henry's personal rule and the military contraction from France, both of them underscored by economic deterioration. The rise of Henry's faction after his majority resulted in a household affinity extending from court to county, which alienated the traditional aristocracy and the smallholders of the southern and eastern counties through the perversion of justice and corruption of offices.

In the popular and chroniclers' imaginations, however, "the loss of Normandy" began in 1445, with the marriage of Henry VI to Margaret of Anjou (great granddaughter of that Louis I who commissioned the tapestries at Angers), and popular anti-Gallic sentiment is reflected in chronicle statements about her:

> THIS mariage semed to many, bothe infortunate, and vnprofitable to the realme of England, and that for many causes. First the kyng with her had not one peny, and for the fetchyng of her, the Marques of Suffolke, demaunded a whole fiftene, in open parliament: also for her mariage, the Duchie of Aniow, the citee of Mauns, and the whole

> cou[n]tie of Mayne, were deliuered and released to Kyng Reyner her father, whiche countreis were the very stayes, and backestandes to the Duchy of Normandy. Furthermore for this mariage, the Erle of Arminacke, toke suche great displeasure, that he became vtter enemy to the realme of Englande and was the chief cause, that the Englishmen, wer expulsed out of the whole duchie of Aquitayne, and lost bothe the countreis of Gascoyn and Gyen. But moste of all it should seme, that God with this matrimony was not content. For after this spousage the kynges frendes fell from hym, bothe in Englande and in Fraunce, the Lordes of his realme, fell in diuision emongest themselfes, the commons rebelled against their souereigne Lorde, and naturall Prince, feldes wer foughten, many thousandes slain, and finally, the kyng deposed, and his sonne slain, and this Quene sent home again, with as-muche misery and sorowe, as she was receiued with pompe and triumphe, such is worldly vnstablenes, and so wauerying is false flattering fortune.[54]

Not only is Margaret of Anjou blamed for the loss of Normandy, she also lost Aquitaine and, with this explusion of the English from France, she is responsible for the War of the Roses. The *French* queen caused these wars.

Drawing from several such chronicle sources, *Henry VI, Part 2* dramatizes the third phase of Lancastrian France, 1444–1453. It opens with the arrival in England of the French princess and the cession of Maine and Anjou to her father. The war party, headed by Gloucester, registers shock at the yielding of "the keys of Normandy" (I.i.113), and blames Suffolk, leading the peace party, for that loss.[55]

> What! did my brother Henry spend his youth,
> His valour, coin, and people, in the wars?
> Did he so often lodge in open field,
> In winter's cold, and summer's parching heat,
> To conquer France, his true inheritance? (1.i.77–81)

Invoking the name of the conqueror is of no avail; Henry VI does not resemble his warrior father, and the incredible costs—the expense of aristocratic blood, subject blood, and physical resources—will have been for naught. Yet the words could apply to an Henri IV still in the process of gaining his throne, which may account for the Cardinal's curious response: "For France, 'tis ours; and we will keep it still" (I.i.105).

Although each character speaks of it in terms of his own physical expenditure in getting and keeping France, York explores the value of France as equivalent to one's landed title. His first reactions parallel Gloucester's, but then become far more personal and physically acute:

> Methinks the realms of England, France, and Ireland
> Bear that proportion to my flesh and blood
> As did the fatal brand Althaea burnt
> Unto the prince's heart of Calydon.
> Anjou and Maine both given unto the French!
> Cold news for me, for I had hope of France,
> Even as I have of fertile England's soil (I.i.233–39).

Again, these lines suggests the human costs of such a patrimony. By I.iii, the court, to remove Gloucester from power, will accuse him of various crimes, including gouging the public and losing French territory. In Act III, news will arrive that all France is lost, as York, though in conspiracy, formally charges that Gloucester "took bribes of France" and "stay'd the soldiers' pay" (III.i.104–5). Two-hundred lines later in the scene, York accuses Somerset, who returns the volley, of losing France. And as soon as it *is* lost, Gloucester is removed as well, followed soon by the Cardinal. Thus all factions tying the court to Henry V and his conquest are removed and the forces of internal chaos are unleashed.

After Gloucester's death, however, the Duke of Suffolk and Margaret, as in many contemporary Yorkist-biased chronicles and witnesses, bear most of the responsibility for the loss of Normandy. Early in Act IV, a pirate tribunal charges that Suffolk "sold" Anjou and Maine to France (IV.i.85); that is, he has, like Elizabeth, alienated crown lands and brought home disabled soldiers. The accusation is telling:

> By devilish policy art thou grown great,
> And, like ambitious Sylla, overgorg'd
> With gobbets of thy mother's bleeding heart.
> By thee Anjou and Maine were sold to France,
> The false revolting Normans thorough thee
> Disdain to call us lord, and Picardy
> Hath slain their governors, surpris'd our forts,
> And sent the ragged soldiers wounded home (IV.i.86–89).

Suffolk is demonized for his cannabalizing pro-French activities, as crucial a part of the literary representation of *la guerre de Cent ans* as external demonizing is of the construction of English nationalism. His activities abroad reveal that the state can no longer justify its extraction of resources for the "ragged soldiers," who have been sent home unattended and unprepared, historically, for what little awaited them when they arrived. The analogue of Normandy 1450 /1590 must have seemed almost as strong as that of Normandy in 1415 /1944.

Aside from the costs of the unsuccessful wars inflicted and endured by the aristocracy, those costs suffered by the underclasses are far more acute. After Suffolk's execution in scene IV.i, the remainder of the act is devoted to Cade's rebellion, which further develops the complicity of state-making and war through anger over the loss of France; the transition from foreign war to civil war is effected by that uprising. Significantly, Cade's concerns are with both arenas. Against Lord Say (whose head the butcher will have for "selling the dukedom of Maine" [IV.ii.153–54]), Cade alleges the castration of the body politic; that loss is clearly France, paid for physically by the populace. Later, during the mock tribunal, Cade charges that Lord Say is he "which sold the towns in France" (IV.vii.18); the formal accusation uses Francophobic language: "What canst thou answer to my Majesty for giving up of Normandy unto Mounsieur Basimecu, the Dauphin of France?" (IV.vii.25). Cade also orders the execution of (Sheriff) William Crowmer (Say's son-in-law), and then has their two heads paraded on poles, to kiss at every corner and then to part "lest they consult about the giving up of some more towns in France" (IV.vii.126–27). These actions, almost straight from the chronicle sources, visually reinforce Cade's complaint of the loss of France and the human costs of these unsuccessful foreign wars.

Those responsible for the aftermath of the war, socially mobile members of the king's faction, are conveniently executed outside the king's tribunal. Yet, the concessions to the subject population do not end here; in the ensuing years the king's concessions will include, eventually, his own title. The struggle among various sectors of the population will also continue; Cade's rebels must be accused of using illegitimate forms of violence and must, in turn, be executed by the king's faction, that the select portion of the subject population may be protected from them. Apart from anger over the loss of France, Shakespeare's Cade's most insistent grievance is economic hardship, and his "program" includes radical reforms for access to property and power, the lowering of prices, with something like a subsistence economy assured for all. Thus between the two complaints, Cade glances at the economic effects of protracted and unsuccessful war; Shakespeare writes his own analogue history, applying the internal effects of the end of the French war to the effects of war in France in the early 1590s.[56]

In its representation of Cade's rebellion, the play manages to expose those who bore responsibility for the extraordinary costs of waging a losing war on the territory of an historical rival: the agents of the state. In representing the end of the Hundred Years' War as turning in on England, the play allows Cade, an artisan suborned by the Duke of York, brutally to punish those whose most notorious crime is having "lost France" and extorted funds from the populace to exacerbate economic conditions. After the nobler characters accuse each other, Cade steps in to accuse his superiors as a class, using their own rhetoric. The common soldier has not lost the war. Cade's intended social reform glances at the institutions and agents of the "state," and in his judgment on the war having ended with the "loss of France," Cade reveals the economic costs of Elizabethan "war making and state making."[57] He also embodies the costs in human life by initiating the first battles on the stage. In this excessively violent play, strewn with bodies and heads, the only battles occur at home, with Cade's uprising followed by York's. At the end of the play, Old Clifford dies fighting for Henry not against the French, but against York. Clifford's last words comment about the honor that is to be assessed through one's final actions, but the sentiment extends to the end of the French war and their lingering effects; he dies speaking axiomatic French: "la fin couronne les oeuvres."

French and English narratives of the events of the Hundred Years' War, as the *Apocalypse* tapestries suggest, have always been in conflict. Further, the narratives produced on either side of the Channel have had conflicting claims within their own cultures. Examining these representations of the Hundred Years' War may lead us to a greater understanding of the varied constructions of nationalism: they justify the sacrifice of subjects, resources, and victims through selective memories and rhetoric. Now, perhaps, it is easier than during World War II, when dangers were severe and during which the rhetoric of "allied" nationalism seemed a mere statement of truth, to see the nature of these constructions as they have been made the vehicles for upholding the sanctity of the nation and those who proclaim themselves its authorities.[58] By contrast, earlier narratives, particularly Shakespeare's history plays, with their concerns about the increasingly negative effects of war on the invaders' home front made manifest through anti-Gallic sentiment, reveal his criticism of the role of continual warfare in the making of what was increasingly called the "state."[59] In twentieth-century assessments and revisions of those plays, the focus has been on *Henry V* and its potential as the very stay and prop of nationalism, or its continued use by the British government to justify sacrifices and resources from the public.[60] It is thus perhaps in some measure corrective to remember that Shakespeare's first vision of the Hundred Years' War is far more cynical. *Henry VI, Part 2* questions the practice of using foreign war to promote the interests of the state: the war's end exposed its costs and its futility.

NOTES

1. The tapestries are divided into six sections (each more than 23 meters by 5 meters) of fourteen panels each. Details about the tapestries may be found in several sources; see *La tenture de l'Apocalypse d'Angers* (Nantes: l'Inventaire Général des Monuments et des Richesses Artistiques en Région des Pays de la Loire, 1993), especially 11–13, 35, 43, 84.

2. This frequently cited statement appears, for example, in Fabienne Joubert, "L'Apocalypse d'Angers et les débuts de la tapisserie historiée," *Bulletin Monumental* 139 (1981): 125. This Apocalypse manuscript is MS. Fr. 403 in the Bibliothèque nationale. A comparison of the tapestry with various manuscripts reveals the extent of this iconographical tradition. See René Planchenault, *L'Apocalypse d'Angers* (Paris: Caisse Nationale des Monuments Historiques et des Sites, 1966), 26–27. A striking comparison may be made with the photographs of leaves from the Burckhardt-Wildt album (York, c. 1270–1280), in *Catalogue of Single Leaves and Miniatures from Western Illuminated Manuscripts* (London: Sotheby's, 1983), 34–121.

3. Francis Muel, "Notices," in *La tenture*, 116, 149.

4. There is always the possibility that such interpretations are offered solely for the benefit of English tourists, just as those of Jeanne d'Arc are tendered at various monuments in Rouen.

5. Francis Salet, "Prologue," in *La tenture*, 11.

6. For these and other details of Louis's captivity, see Edouard Perroy, *La Guerre de Cent ans* (Paris: Gallimard, 1943), 117; and Jean Favier, *La Guerre de Cent ans* (Paris: Fayard, 1980), 285.

7. In fact, the history of the tapestries and of the payment of ransom is interwoven; in 1363, taxes were owed on certain tapestries that Louis d'Anjou had bought, taxes destined for the payment of the ransom; see Joubert, "L'Apocalypse d'Angers," 138, n. 6.

8. Perroy, *La Guerre de Cent ans*, 160.

9. Françoise Autrand, "La déconfiture. La Bataille de Poitiers (1356) à travers quelques textes français des XIVe et XVe siècles," in *Guerre et société en France, en Angleterre et en Bourgogne XIVe–XVe siècles*, ed. Philippe Contamine, Charles Giry-Deloison, and Maurice Keen (Lille: Université de Charles de Gaulle, 1991), 93–121.

10. See Frank Anderson Trapp, *The Attainment of Delacroix* (Baltimore: Johns Hopkins, 1971), 179; and René Huyghe, *Delacroix* (New York: Harry N. Abrams, 1963), 191.

11. Although it is unclear exactly who erected the monument or authored the *panneaux* at the site of the battle, that account may to some degree be considered France's official though abridged version of what transpired.

12. Michel Mollat du Jourdin, *La guerre de Cent ans vue par ceux qui l'ont vécue* (1975; reprint. Paris: Éditions du Seuil, 1992), 35, citing MatteoVillani, *Istorie Fiorentine* (republished Florence, 1823), chapter 18.

13. Thomas D. Hardy, *Syllabus (in English) of the Documents . . . in the Collection Known as 'Rymer's Foedera'* (London: Longmans, Green & Co., 1869–1885), 1:357: "12 Aug. 1347. Proclamation to be made throughout England that houses will be assigned to English persons willing to reside at Calais. Reading. R. iii. p.i.130. O.v.575. H.iii.p.i.16."

14. Jean le Bel, *Chronique*, ed. Jules Viard and Eugène Déprez (Paris: Librairie Renouard, 1904–1905), 1:162–63.

15. Ruth Butler, *Rodin: The Shape of Genius* (New Haven: Yale University Press, 1993), 204.

16. Butler, *Rodin*, 211.

17. Jean le Bel, *Chronique*, 1:166–67. Although Froissart's elaboration on the burghers and their fate has become famous, he in fact took it from this passage in Jean le Bel. This scene also appears in Shakespeare's *Edward III*, only recently included in the canon primarily because of Eric Sams's argument in *Shakespeare's Edward III: An Early Play Restored to the Canon* (New Haven: Yale University Press, 1996). In the play there is no indication that Edward intends to depopulate the city after he releases the burghers.

18. Butler, *Rodin*, 496.

19. Representations of Jeanne d'Arc are also, of course, in this vein.

20. The famous genealogical tree is in BM Royal 15, E. vi, fol. 3; the Jesse tree is in BM Add. MS 42, 131, fol. 73; and the depiction of St. Louis and Henry VI is in BM MS Cotton Dom. A. xii, fol. 50. For discussions, see J. W. McKenna, "Henry VI of England and the Dual Monarchy: Aspects of Royal Political Propaganda, 1422–1432," *Journal of the Warburg and Courtauld Institutes* 23 (1965): 145–62; P. S. Lewis, "War Propaganda and Historiography in Fifteenth-Century France and England," *Transactions of the Royal Historical Society*, 5th series, 15 (1965): 1–21; J. H. Rowe, "King Henry VI's Claim to France in Picture and Poem," *The Library*, 4th series, 13 (June 1932): 77–88.

21. Shakespeare's hand in *Edward III* has long been suspected, but since the play has only recently been added to the canon, I defer discussion of it to another time.

22. Between 1898 and 1970, at least nineteen films were produced on the heroine. Directors include Pathé, Cecil B. De Mille, Roberto Rossellini, Otto Preminger, Victor Fleming; actresses include Ingrid Bergman, Jean Seberg, and Sandrine Bonnaire (Musée Jeanne d'Arc, Rouen). In 1999 two films on Joan of Arc premiered: one was produced for CBS and aired in the United States in May 1999; the second, "The Messenger," was directed by Luc Besson.

23. For this debate, which still rages, see the chapter entitled "De la modernité de la guerre de Cent ans: conflit féodal, dynastique ou national?" in Philippe Contamine, *De Jeanne d'Arc aux guerres d'Italie: Figures, images et problèmes du XVe siècle* (Orléans: Paradigme, 1994), 13–37.

24. There is simply no room to discuss here representations of Jeanne d'Arc. It must be acknowledged, however, that since the nineteenth century she has become *the* figure of French nationalism. To what presumably national crisis this version of her life responds is the subject of another inquiry.

25. Desmond Seward, *The Hundred Years War: The English in France, 1337–1453* (New York: Athenaeum, 1978), 17.

26. Andrew Gurr, ed., *King Henry V*, by William Shakespeare (Cambridge: Cambridge University Press, 1992), 43–52.

27. Jonathan Dollimore and Alan Sinfield, "History and Ideology: The Instance of *Henry V*," in *Alternative Shakespeares*, ed. John Drakakis (London and New York: Methuen, 1985), 206–27; here, 226.

28. Chris Fitter, "A Tale of Two Branaghs: *Henry V*, Ideology, and the Mekong Agincourt," in *Shakespeare Left and Right*, ed. Ivo Kamps (New York and London: Routledge, 1991), 259–75; here, 274.

29. Gurr, *King Henry V*, 52. For the date, see DeWitt Bodeen, "*Henry V*," in *The International Directory of Films and Filmmakers*, ed. Christopher Lyon (New York: Putnam, 1985), 195.

30. Harry M. Geduld, *Filmguide to Henry V* (Bloomington: Indiana University Press, 1973), 13–17. Supporters included Dallas Bower, "a sound engineer turned filmmaker," who conceived the idea of the film, had earlier written a script for *Henry V*, and worked with Olivier at the BBC during the war; and Del Giudice, who helped back the film financially.

31. Bodeen, "*Henry V*," 196, remarks that "Olivier, preparing his own screenplay from the Shakespearean text, cut the play nearly a quarter so that he could give ample time to the staging of the Battle of Agincourt."

32. Geduld, *Filmguide*, 52.

33. Graham Holderness, *Shakespeare Recycled: The Making of Historical Drama* (New York: Harvester Wheatsheaf, 1992), 178–227, esp. 190.

34. Geduld, *Filmguide*, 19.

35. Laurence Olivier, *Confessions of an Actor* (London: Weidenfeld and Nicolson, 1982), 162. He recalls that while working on *Richard III* in 1954, he was unhappy with the battle scene: "Somehow, after Henry V, I couldn't find another battle in me and even that one, which did seem to come off, was littered with petty larcenies from our Master of All, Eisenstein."

36. Geoff Andrew, *The Film Handbook* (Essex: Longman Group, 1989), 95, calls the film "[a]n historical epic serving as an allegory of Nazi aggression and Soviet heroism."

37. Sergei Eisenstein, "My Subject is Patriotism," *International Literature* 2 (1939): 91–94, especially 92.

38. Arthur Knight, *The Liveliest Art* (New York: MacMillan, 1957), 218.

39. Sergei Eisenstein, "The Structure of Film" [1939], in *Film Form: Essays in Film Theory*, ed. and trans. Jay Leyda (1949; reprint. New York: Harcourt Brace Jovanovich, 1977), 152–53.

40. He cites Griffith's failure to perceive social injustice and castigates him as "an open apologist for racism, erecting a celluloid monument to the Ku Klux Klan, and joining their attack on Negroes in *The Birth of a Nation*," in "Dickens, Griffith, and the Film Today," *Film Form*, 234.

41. Gurr, *King Henry V*, 52: "The central section of the film, the realistically portrayed battle, almost completely abandons speech (the whole script at 1,500 lines is not much above half the full text) for visual effects. Since there is no battle scene in the play itself apart from Pistol and Le Fer, that was an inevitable adjustment. It is all Hollywood, with a great charge of French horsemen taken from Griffiths [sic], an Eisenstein-like flight of arrows through the sky, and English soldiers dropping from branches to pull the French knights from their horses as in Errol Flynn's Robin Hood films." All other critics, including Olivier himself, cite Eisenstein directly as the source for the horsemen, which seems very likely, given the nature of film distribution.

42. Raymond Durgnat, *A Mirror for England*, 109, cited in Geduld, *Filmguide*, 68–69.

43. Holderness, *Shakespeare Recycled*, is the best discussion on the film, but see also Kenneth Branagh himself, *Beginning* (New York and London: W. W. Norton, 1989).

44. Ralph Griffiths, *The Reign of King Henry VI: The Exercise of Royal Authority, 1422–1461* (Berkeley: University of California Press, 1981); C. T. Allmand, "The War and the Non-combatant," in *The Hundred Years War*, ed. Kenneth Fowler (London: Macmillan, 1971), 163–83; M. M. Postan, "Some Social Consequences of the Hundred Years' War," *Economic History Review* 12 (1942): 1–12. Opposed to these is the majority view of K. B. McFarlane, "War, the Economy and Social Change: England and the Hundred Years War," *Past and Present* 22 (1962): 3–15.

45. See, for instance, Guy Bois, *The Crisis of Feudalism: Economy and Society in Eastern Normandy c. 1300–1550* (Cambridge: Cambridge University Press, 1984); Alain Demurger, *Temps de crises, temps d'espoirs: XIVe–XVe siècle* (Paris: Éditions du Seuil, 1990); Michel Mollat du Jourdin, *La guerre de Cent ans*; Philippe Contamine, *La Guerre de Cent ans*, 6e ed (Paris: Presses universitaires de France, 1992).

46. Emmanuel Bourassin, *La France anglais 1415–1453: Chronique d'une occupation* (Paris: Librarie Jules Tallandier, 1981).

47. For example, here is the analysis of Peter Womack in "Imagining Communities: Theatres and the English Nation in the Sixteenth Century," in *Culture and*

History 1350–1600: Essays on English Communities, Identities and Writing, ed. David Aers (New York: Harvester Wheatsheaf, 1992), 126: "The answer is that so long as the dynastic legitimation of the monarch and the nobility is more or less working, the stage does not afford any space for anyone else. The community of the nation is not needed, so to speak, and so there is no call to imagine it. It is only when that hierarchical order fails that the undifferentiated totality of the realm appears, as *that which is harmed by its failure*. The theatre's obsession with the contentions of noble houses is not a reflection of contemporary political reality: Elizabeth by the 1590s seems not to have been particularly threatened either by lawless magnates or by rival claimants to her throne. Rather, the *enactment* of such conflicts operates like a ritual, in which the degradation of the institutional forms of the realm generates a manifestation of the *comitatus*, the prior, underlying body to which all—characters and spectators—can feel they belong" (emphasis in original).

48. Charles Tilly, "Western State-Making and Theories of Political Transformation," in *The Formation of National States in Western Europe*, ed. Charles Tilly (Princeton: Princeton University Press, 1975), 630.

49. Perry Anderson, *Lineages of the Absolutist State* (London: New Left Books, 1974), 130, claims that "The lack of any positive continental strategy inevitably resulted in the wasteful and pointless diversions of the last decade of the century."

50. See A. G. Dickens, "The Elizabethans and St. Bartholomew," in *The Massacre of St. Bartholomew: Reappraisals and Documents*, ed. Alfred Soman (The Hague: Martinus Nijhoff, 1974), 52–70; and David Bell, "Unmasking a King: The Political Uses of Popular Literature Under the French Catholic League, 1588–89," *Sixteenth Century Journal* 20 (1989): 371–86.

51. Leah Marcus, *Puzzling Shakespeare: Local Reading and Its Discontents* (Berkeley: University of California Press, 1988), 52, 70, 76–80.

52. Charles Tilly, "War Making and State Making as Organized Crime," in *Bringing the State Back In*, ed. Peter B. Evans, Dietrich Rueschmeyer, and Theda Skocpol (Cambridge: Cambridge University Press, 1985), 169–91.

53. Several historians have computed the cost in large terms: John Guy, *Tudor England* (Oxford: Oxford University Press, 1988), 343–47, 384–90; R. B. Wernham, *After the Armada: Elizabethan England and the Struggle for Western Europe, 1588–1595* (Oxford: Oxford University Press, 1984), 564–67; Wallace T. MacCaffrey, *Elizabeth I: War and Politics 1588–1603* (Princeton: Princeton University Press, 1992), 45–69.

54. Edward Hall, " The troubleous season of Kyng Henry the Sixt," in *The Vnion of the Two Noble and Illustre Famelies of Lancastre and Yorke*, ([London: Richard Grafton,] 1548), chapter 46. Most of the material is from Robert Fabyan, *The New Chronicles of England and France* [1516], ed. Henry Ellis (London: C. and J. Rivington et al., 1811).

55. Fabyan, *New Chronicles*, 617–18, who first mentions that Anjou and Maine "are called the keyes of Normandy."

56. For a discussion of the debates on the economic conditions, see Ellen C. Caldwell, "Jack Cade and Shakespeare's *Henry VI, Part 2*," *Studies in Philology* 92 (1995): 18–79.

57. This paper thus both appeals to and questions the theory of hegemonic containment as it has been applied to Cade. See Stephen Greenblatt's reading in "Murdering Peasants: Status, Genre, and the Representation of Rebellion," *Representations* 1 (1983): 1–29; Phyllis Rackin's refinement of this reading in *Stages of History: Shakespeare's English Chronicles* (Ithaca, N.Y.: Cornell University Press, 1990), 207–22; Richard Wilson, "'A mingled yarn': Shakespeare and the Cloth Workers," *Literature and History* 12 (1986): 164–80; Brents Stirling, "Shakespeare's Mob Scenes: A Reinterpretation," *Huntington Library Quarterly* 3 (1945): 213–40. Against these readings see Annabel Patterson, *Shakespeare and the Popular Voice* (Oxford: Basil Blackwell, 1989), passim; Alexander Leggatt, *Shakespeare's Political Drama: The History Plays and the Roman Plays* (London and New York: Routledge, 1988), 17, 18, 20; and Michael Hattaway, "Rebellion, Class Consciousness, and Shakespeare's 2 Henry VI," *Cahiers élisabéthains* 33 (1988): 15.

58. See the discussion on such demands for sacrifice in Benedict Anderson, *Imagined Communities: Reflections on the Origin and Spread of Nationalism* (London: Verso, 1991), 187–206.

59. MacCaffrey, *Elizabeth I*, 23.

60. Holderness, *Shakespeare Recycled*, 191–210.

CONTRIBUTORS

DENISE N. BAKER is a professor and head of the English Department at the University of North Carolina at Greensboro. In addition to essays on Gower, Langland, Chaucer, and the Middle English mystics, she has published *Julian of Norwich's Showings: From Vision to Book*.

JOHN M. BOWERS has published more than twenty articles on writers from St. Augustine to Shakespeare. He is the author of three books on major medieval works: *The Crisis of Will in "Piers Plowman," "The Canterbury Tales": Fifteenth-Century Continuations and Additions*, and *The Politics of "Pearl": Court Poetry in the Age of Richard II*. He currently chairs the English Department at the University of Nevada, Las Vegas.

ELLEN C. CALDWELL is an associate professor of Humanities at Clarkson University. She has published essays on Shakespeare's *Henry VI* plays, Marlowe's *Edward II*, and the poetry of Sir Thomas Wyatt. Her current project is a book on Shakespeare's history plays.

SUSAN CRANE is a professor of English at Rutgers University. She has published on English, French, and Anglo-Norman literature and culture. Her essay on Joan of Arc comes from a book in progress concerning the place of clothing in late medieval self-presentation.

PATRICIA DEMARCO, an assistant professor at West Virginia University, is currently working on a book on chivalric culture, violence, and masculinity in late medieval romance. She has a Ph.D. from Duke University.

JUDITH FERSTER, who received her Ph.D. from Brown University in 1974, is the author of *Chaucer on Interpretation* and *Fictions of Advice: The Literature and Politics of Counsel in Late Medieval England*. She is a professor of English at North Carolina State University.

NORRIS J. LACY is the Edwin Erle Sparks Professor of French at Pennsylvania State University. He holds his doctorate from Indiana University and has previously taught at Indiana, the University of Kansas, and Washington University in St. Louis. He is the past international President (and now Honorary President) of the International Arthurian Society; he has been decorated by the French government as a Knight in the Order of Academic Palms. His publications deal primarily with Arthurian studies, medieval romance, and fabliaux.

ANNE D. LUTKUS is Language Coordinator in the Department of Modern Languages and Cultures at the University of Rochester, with graduate degrees in French from Indiana University. Her research interests include Renaissance portraiture and language methodology. She participated in NEH seminars in 1980 and 1983 and in the Southeastern Medieval and Renaissance Institute at Duke University in 1976.

EARL JEFFREY RICHARDS, a professor of Romance Languages and Literature at the University of Wuppertal in Germany, has published numerous essays and books, including a translation of Christine de Pizan's *Book of the City of Ladies* and a collection of essays entitled *Reinterpreting Christine de Pizan*. He is currently working on editions of Christine's *Epistre Othea* and the collected works of Charity Cannon Willard, a study of German Romanists and German identity, and a monograph on the literary origins of nationalism.

MICHELLE SZKILNIK was appointed Maître de Conférences in the Department of Lettres Modernes of the Universitè of Nantes, after teaching at Smith College and the University of Wisconsin. In 1999 she defended her Habilitation à Diriger des Recherches at the University of Paris III-Sorbonne Nouvelle. She has edited several French romances and published extensively on medieval French literature.

JULIA M. WALKER is an associate professor of English and coordinator of Women's Studies at the State University of New York at Geneseo. She is the editor of *Dissing Elizabeth: Narrative Representations of Gloriana* and author of *Medusa's Mirrors: Spenser, Shakespeare, Milton and the Metamorphosis of the Female Self*. She received the James Holly Hanford Award for the most distinguished Milton essay of 1997 from the Milton Society of America.

R. F. YEAGER is a professor of Literature and Languages at the University of North Carolina at Asheville. He has written and edited books and articles on Old and Middle English subjects as well as Dante, Spanish and Portuguese manuscripts, and Umberto Eco.

Index

Abberbury, Richard, 141
Aers, David, 72n. 52, 84
Albertano of Brescia, 10, 74
Allmand, Christopher, 6, 8, 60–61, 67
Anderson, Benedict, 106
Angle, Guichard d', 141
anglicus caudatus ("Englishmen with tails"), 96, 169–70
Anne of Bohemia (Queen of Richard II), 109–10
Anonimalle Chronicle, 56, 57, 65
Anson, John, 204
Apocalypse tapestries, 13, 238–39; 240–41, 244
Appellants, 74, 80–81, 103, 107, 108
 and Chaucer, 81–82
 Tale of Melibee, 6, 10, 82–84, 85–86
 and Richard II, 75, 134, 145–46
L'Arbre des Batailles (Bonet), 34–35, 38–39, 47, 62
Artois, Robert d', 18
 as character in *Voeux du heron*, 4, 17, 18, 19, 20, 22, 23 24, 29, 36–37, 38, 39, 40–41, 42, 47
Arundel, Thomas, 150, 151
Augustine of Canterbury, 169
Augustine of Hippo, 33–34, 49–50n. 25, 162–63
Austin, J. L., 33
Autrand, Françoise, 240

Auvergne, Pierre d', 169
Avesbury's chronicle, 61
Ayton, Andrew, 62

Balades (see Deschamps)
Balades de moralitez (see Deschamps)
Baldwin, Anna, 68n. 2
Barnie, John, 14, 57, 60
Bataille de Poitiers (Delacroix), 5, 13, 241–42, 243, 244
Beaune, Colette, 16n. 22, 172
Bell, David, 254
Bennett, J.A.W., 68n. 2
Black Prince, 5, 6, 56
 and *Apocalypse* tapestries, 239
 in Chandos Herald's *Life of the Black Prince*, 30–32, 35, 61, 94
 and profits of war, 60, 61, 62
Bohun, Humphrey de, 57
Bonet, Honoré (*L'Arbre des Batailles*), 34–35, 38–39, 62
Book of the Duchess, 97, 100, 101–102, 104
Bordo, Susan, 46
Bowers, John, 144
Boucicault, Jean (*Livre de cent ballades*), 92
Bourgeois de Calais (Rodin), 5, 12, 242–44
Bradwardine, Thomas, 92
Brimeu, David de, 181
Bruges, Hennequin de, 238
Brut, 48n. 14, 65, 141

Buigne, Gace de la (*Roman des Deduits*), 92
Bullough, Vern, 207
Burley, Simon, 141, 145
Butler, Judith, 33, 196
Bynum, Caroline Walker, 207

Cagny, Percival de, 200
Calin, William, 137
Canterbury Tales, 98, 101, 104, 110, 112, 111, 137
    Tale of Melibee, 6, 10, 73–87, 95
Chalon, Renier H. G., 44
Chançons royaulx (*see* Deschamps)
Chandos Herald (*Life of the Black Prince*), 61, 94
    and chivalric violence, 30–32, 35
Chanson de Roland, 172
Charlemagne, 165
Charles V (King of France), 6, 56, 92, 137, 240
Charles VI (King of France), 6–7, 107, 108, 151, 165
Charles VII (King of France), 7, 12,
    and Christine de Pizan, 183
    and Joan of Arc, 177–78, 180, 183, 198
Chaucer, Geoffrey, 5, 6, 10–11, 14, 73–86, 91, 93–113, 144
    capture in France, 5, 91, 94–96
    as translator, 99–100
    Book of the Duchess, 97, 100, 101–102, 104
    Canterbury Tales, 98, 101, 104, 110, 112, 111, 137
        Tale of Melibee, 6, 10, 73–86, 95
    House of Fame, 101, 103–105
    Legend of Good Women, 98, 99, 100, 109–12
    Parliament of Fowls, 105–106
    Troilus and Criseyde, 95, 104, 106–107
Chaucer, Thomas, 112

chivalry, 55, 59–63, 66–67
    and violence, 29–33
    in *Cleriadus et Meliadice*, 226–28
    according to just war theory, 34–35, 39
    against Saracens, 168, 226–27
    in *Voeux du heron*, 27–29, 32, 36–69, 43–45, 47
Chrétien de Troyes, 41, 161
Christian universalism, 162–63
Christine de Pizan, 7, 12, 177–91
    and Charles VII, 183
    and Henry IV, 150
    Ditié de Jehanne d'Arc, 7, 12, 168, 177–91, 211–12
    dating of, 177–80, 182, 183, 190–91
    as prophetic history, 180, 183, 186–91
Chronique de la Pucelle, 200
Chronique du cordeliers, 206
Chroniques (Froissart), 4, 13, 31–32, 65–66, 93, 241, 242, 244
Cicero, 101
Cinkante Balades (Gower), 129, 130, 131, 132, 133, 148, 150
civilians, suffering of, 28, 30–32, 33–35, 38–39, 44–47
Cleriadus et Meliadice, 8, 13, 14, 221–33
    and contemporary events, 221–22
    date of, 223
    and Froissart, 223–26, 227, 232–33
Clifford, Sir Lewis, 111
Clin, Marie-Véronique, 181
Clovis, 165, 172
Collette, Carolyn, 79
Confessio Amantis (Gower), 130, 131, 132, 133, 137, 142, 144–46, 147–48, 149–50, 151
Coucy, Enguerrand de, 92, 93
Courcelles, Thomas de, 210
Crawford, Donna, 48n. 10

Creton, Jean, 108
Cronica Tripertita (Gower), 130, 133, 148, 150
Curtius, Ernst Robert, 161

Deguileville, Guillaume (*Pelerinage de la vie humaine*), 99
Delacroix, Eugène (*Bataille de Poitiers*), 5, 13, 241–42, 243, 244
Delcourt, Marie, 209
Delecourt, Charles J. B., 44
De quadam puella, 206, 211
De Regimine Principum (Egidio Colonna), 141
Deschamps, Eustache, 6–7, 11–12, 159–72
   and Chaucer, 99, 100, 110, 171
   and French national identity, 6–7, 11–12, 159–61, 165–67, 171, 172
   representation of English in, 95–96, 169–70
   Balades
      no. 812, 175n. 24
      no. 868, 169
      no. 883, 168
      no. 893, 169
      no. 980, 165
      no. 1124, 166
      no. 1142, 171
      no. 1148, 166
      no. 1154, 170–71
      no. 1171, 168
      no. 1181, 168
      no. 1200, 170
      no. 1317, 171
      no. 1331, 171
      no. 1472, 160
   Balades de moralitez
      no. 16, 175n. 24
      no. 17, 175n. 24
      no. 23, 164
      no. 26, 174n. 19
      no. 48, 167
      no. 53, 164
      no. 67, 174n. 19
      no. 81, 174n. 19
      no. 94, 175n. 24
      no. 140, 165
      no. 141, 165
      no. 159, 174n. 15
      no. 163, 164
      no. 180, 175n. 19
      no. 182, 175n. 19
      no. 185, 163
      no. 211, 175n. 19
      no. 229, 175n. 19
      no. 253, 167
      no. 255, 163
      no. 263, 165
      no. 284, 162
      no. 285, 171
   Chançons royaulx
      no. 324, 166–67
      no. 327, 175n. 19
      no. 337, 170
      no. 344, 170, 174n. 17, 175n. 24
      no. 359, 174n. 17
      no. 378, 164
      no. 379, 164
      no. 387, 165
      no. 394, 167–68
      no. 395, 168
   Fiction du lyon, 169, 172
   Lay VI, 163
   Rondeau
      no. 671, 169
      no. 673, 167
      no. 1113, 167
Derby, Earl of, 18
   as character in *Voeux du heron*, 19, 21, 37, 38
   daughter of, as character in *Voeux du heron*, 18, 19, 21, 22
Derrida, Jacques, 33, 112

De Vere, Robert, 75, 83, 143, 146
Dickens, A. G., 254
Ditié de Jehanne d'Arc (Christine de Pizan), 7, 12, 168, 177–91, 211–12
    dating of, 177–80, 182, 183, 190–91
    as prophetic history, 180, 183, 186–91
Dollimore, Jonathan, 246
Dulac, Liliane, 165
Durgnat, Raymond, 249

Eagleton, Terry, 98
Eckhardt, Caroline, 99
Edward III (King of England), 4–6, 17, 52n. 45, 60–63, 64, 242–43
    and *Apocalypse* tapestries, 239, 240
    as character in *Voeux du heron*, 18, 19, 20, 27, 29, 36–37, 40–41, 42–44
    French culture at court of, 92–93, 96, 97
    in Froissart's *Chroniques*, 31, 65–66
    and Gower, 133, 134
    and *Piers Plowman*, 9–10, 59–60, 63–67
    and Treaty of Brétigny, 55–56, 58–59, 64–66, 137–38, 139
Eisenstein, Sergei, 247–49
Erghome, John (*Prophecy of John of Bridlington*), 57
estatist tradition, 163–66
Estivet, Jean d', 211

Fauquemont (or Faukemont), Jean de
    as John of Valkenberg in *Voeux du heron*, 19, 22, 38–39, 41, 44, 45
Ferster, Judith, 146
Fiction du lyon (*see* Deschamps)
Fisher, John, 110, 134
Fitter, Chris, 246
Foucault, Michel, 196
Fraioli, Deborah, 184
French culture
    claims for superiority of, 161–62
    at court of Edward III, 92–93, 96
    at court of Richard II, 108–109, 110
    and English nationalism, 97–98
    and *studium*, 166–67
Froissart, Jean, 15n. 5, 21, 39, 91–92, 94, 108, 244
    and Chaucer, 97, 101, 110
    and *Cleriadus et Meliadice*, 223–26, 227, 232–33
    influence in England, 96
    Chroniques, 4, 13, 31–32, 65–66, 93, 241, 242, 244
    Meliador, 233
    Voyage en Béarn, 226
Fulcher of Chartres, 161

Gadamer, Hans-Georg, 197
Garber, Marjorie, 205–206
Gaunt, Simon, 202–203, 204
Geduld, Harry, 246
Geoffrey le Baker (*Chronicon*), 61
Godfrey of Harcourt, 31
Gower, John, 6–7, 11, 14, 127–54
    antiwar sentiments of, 14, 142
    dating of poetry, 129–33
    and Henry IV, 148–53
    and Richard II, 141–48
    Cinkante Balades, 129, 130, 131, 132, 133, 148, 150
    Confessio Amantis, 130, 131, 132, 133, 137, 142, 144–46, 147–48, 149–50, 151
    Cronica Tripertita, 130, 133, 148, 150
    Mirour de l'Omme, 129, 130, 131, 133, 134–35, 137–39, 140, 142, 145, 148, 149, 150
    Speculum Hominis or *Speculum Meditantis* (on Gower's tomb), 131, 139, 140, 148, 153
    "To King Henry IV, In Praise of Peace," 132, 133, 148, 149, 150, 151, 152–53

Traité pour essampler les amantz marietz,
  129, 130, 132, 148, 150
Vox Clamantis, 130, 131, 133, 137,
  139–40, 141, 142, 145, 146, 147, 148
Grady, Frank, 152
Grandes Chroniques de France, 161
Gransden, Antonia, 57
Granson, Oton de, 96, 102
Graus, Frantisek, 173n. 8
Gray, Sir Thomas (*Scalacronica*), 52n. 45,
  56, 58–59, 65, 94
Griffiths, Ralph, 251
Grigsby, John, 44
Guesclin, Bertand du, 6, 240
Gurr, Andrew, 245–46, 248

Hanawalt, Barbara, 46
Hastrup, Kirsten, 204
Helgerson, Richard, 253
Henry IV (King of England), 7, 51n. 34,
  151–52
  and Gower, 132, 148, 149–51, 153
  as Bolingbroke, Henry, 83, 112, 133
  as Henry of Lancaster, Earl of Derby,
    148
Henry V (King of England), 5, 7
  as Duke of Aquitaine, 152
Henry V, 13, 177, 180, 189, 241, 244–50,
  251–52
  Branagh's film of, 13, 245, 246, 250
  Olivier's film of, 13, 246–50
Henry VI (King of England), 7, 8
Henry VI, Part 1, 254
Henry VI, Part 2, 13, 237, 238, 244, 245
  and anti-French sentiments, 252–53,
    255–56
  Cade's rebellion in, 252, 253, 258–59
  as critique of war, 250–59
  economic costs of war, 258–59
  loss of France in, 256–58
Henry of Grosmont, Duke of Lancaster,
  62, 66

Hewitt, H. J., 61
Higden, Ranulf, 93
historical criticism, 1–3, 15 n.5, 197
  and Chaucer's Tale of Melibee, 73–75,
    80, 82–84, 85
Holderness, Graham, 247, 248
Holland, Sir Thomas, 31
Homer, 104, 111
House of Fame (Chaucer), 101, 103–105
Huizinga, J,, 44
Hundred Years' War, 3–8, 60–63, 64, 103
  and chronology of Chaucer's canon,
    97–98, 102–103, 106, 107–108
  and chronology of Gower's life,
    133–35
  and Elizabethan politics, 250–56
  Normandy campaign (1359–1360) of,
    52n. 45, 55–60, 63, 64–66, 94–96
  and representations of national identity, 237–50
Huppé, Bernard, 68n. 2, 71nn. 41, 45, 46

Jameson, Fredric, 99
Jean II (King of France), 5, 55, 56, 61, 63,
  136
  as prisoner of war in England, 91–92,
    239, 240
Jean, Duke du Berry, 92, 101, 102, 240
Jean le Bel (*Chronique*), 48n. 14, 242, 243
Jerome, Saint, 101
Joan of Arc, 7, 12, 177–83, 195–213
  and Charles VII, 177–78, 180, 183, 198
  crossdressing of, 12, 195–96, 100–207,
    208–10, 212–13
  and documentary record, 197
  relations with women, 208–10
  representations of, 245
  sexuality of, 210–12
  and taking of Paris, 180–83
  trials of, 197–99
  (*see also* Christine de Pizan, *Ditié de
    Jehanne d'Arc*)

John II (see Jean II)
John of Hainault, 19, 48n. 14
   as Beaumont in *Voeux du heron*, 19,
     21–22, 23, 24, 25n. 10, 38
John of Legnano, 34–35
John of Valkenberg (see Jean de
   Fauquemont)
Joinville, Jean de, 161
Jourdin, Michel Mollat du, 241
just war theory, 28, 33, 36–69, 45

Kane, George, 98
Kauper, Richard, 68, n.7
Keen, Maurice, 62
Kempton, Daniel, 75, 80
Kennedy, Angus, 178, 188, 190, 191–92n. 3
Knapp, Peggy, 84
Knight, Stephen, 84, 85

Lacy, Norris, 37, 40, 44
Langland, William, 5–6, 9–10, 14, 55–67,
   137
   Piers Plowman, 55–67
     antiwar sentiments of, 63–67
     and criticism of chivalric greed,
       63–64, 66–67
     and Treaty of Brétigny, 56–59
Lay VI (see Deschamps)
Legend of Good Women (Chaucer), 98, 99,
   100, 109–12
Leicester, H. Marshall, Jr., 75, 84
Liber consolationis et consilii (Albertano of
   Brescia), 10, 74
Life of the Black Prince (Chandos Herald),
   30–32, 35, 61, 94
Liguers, 252, 253, 254
Liocourt, Colonel de, 182
Livre de Mellibée et de Dame Prudence, 74
Lorris, Guillaume de, 101
Louis of Anjou, 92, 238–40, 255
Lowe, Ben, 14
Luxembourg, Jeanne de, 209, 210

Machaut, Guillaume de, 92, 96
   and Chaucer's poetry, 94, 97, 99, 101,
     110
Macherey, Pierre, 84
Mahdia, battle of, 227
Man, Paul de, 1–2
Marcus, Leah, 253, 254
Margaret of Anjou (Queen of Henry VI),
   255–56, 257
Matthew of Paris, 170
McFarlane, K. B., 61. 63, 251
McKisack, May, 64, 141
Mézières, Philippe de (*Epistre du Roi
   Richart*), 108
Minot, Laurence, 93
Mirour de l'Omme (Gower), 129, 130,
   131, 133, 134–35, 137–39, 140, 142,
   145, 148, 149, 150
Montacute, William of (Earl of
   Salisbury), 18, 48n. 14
   as Salebrin in *Voeux du heron*, 18, 19,
     20–21, 22, 41–42, 43, 44
Montebelluna, François de, 240
Morte Arthure, 33
Mote, Jean de le, 92
Mowbray, Thomas, 83
Müller, Franz Walther, 165, 166
Muscatine, Charles, 98

nation, meaning of, 160–61, 165–66
national identity, 13, 110–12, 160–61,
   172, 237–50
Navarre, Henri de, 254
Neillands, Robin, 97
Nicopolis, battle of, 108, 227
Nietzsche, Friedrich, 101, 197
Nogent, Guibert de, 161
Normandy campaign (1359–1360)
   and Chaucer, 94–96
   and *Piers Plowman*, 55, 57–58, 60, 63,
     64–66
   and Gray's *Scalacronica*, 52n. 45, 56,
     58–59, 65, 94

Orléans, Girard d', 92
Orwell, George, 127, 128
Otto of Saint Blaisin, 170

Parliament of Fowls (Chaucer), 105–106
Pasquerel, Jean, 209
Patterson, Lee, 2–3, 76, 82, 85, 98
Payne, Robert, 110
Pearl poet, 137, 144
Pearsall, Derek, 81
"perfidious Albion," 170
Pernoud, Régine, 180, 181
Perrers, Alice, 68n. 2, 75
Phebus, Gaston, Count of Foix, 226, 233
Philippa of Hainault (Queen of Edward III), 19
  as character in *Voeux du heron*, 19, 23–24, 27–28, 42–47
  and Froissart, 92, 93, 223, 244
  and surrender of Calais, 243
Philippe VI (King of France), 4, 17, 18, 64
  in *Voeux du heron*, 36
Philippe, Duke of Burgundy, 240, 241
Philippe, Duke of Orléans, 92
Piers Plowman (Langland), 55–67
  antiwar sentiments of, 63–67
  and criticism of chivalric greed, 63–64, 66–67
  and Treaty of Brétigny, 56–59
Pintoin, Michel, 160
Pole, Michael de la, 107, 143
Postan, M. M., 251
Prestwich, Michael, 4, 68n. 8
Prophecy of John of Bridlington (John Erghome), 56, 57
Prudentius *(Psychomachia)*, 169

Quilligan, Maureen, 184

Racklin, Phyllis, 253
Régnier, Jean, 96

Renart, Jean *(Guillaume de Dole)*, 224
Richard II (King of England), 6, 10, 41, 98, 108, 110, 141–46, 147–48
  and Apellants, 75, 134, 145–46
  and Chaucer, 75, 80–81, 82–84, 85–86, 111–12
  French culture at the court of, 108–109, 110
  and Gower, 133, 134, 139–40, 141–43, 144, 145–48
Richard of Bury, 93
Rickard, Peter, 161
Roche, Katharine de la, 209
Rodin, Auguste *(Les Bourgeois de Calais)*, 5, 12, 242–44
Rondeau (see Deschamps)

Saint-Pierre, Eustache de, 242
Salisbury, Sir John, 145–46
Saracens, 168, 227
Scalacronica (Gray), 52n. 45, 56, 58–59, 65, 94
Scaliger, Guilio Caesare *(Poetices libri septem)*, 170
Scanlon, Larry, 85
Scarry, Elaine, 28, 30, 32, 49–50n. 25
Second Charlemagne Prophecy, 179, 185, 186–88
Secretum Secretorum, 76, 79
Selzer, John, 68n. 2
Seward, Desmond, 6, 245
Shakespeare, William
  Henry V, 13, 177, 180, 189, 241, 244–50, 251–52
    Branagh's film of, 13, 245, 246, 250
    Olivier's film of, 13, 246–50
  Henry VI, Part 1, 254
  Henry VI, Part 2, 13, 237, 238, 244, 245, 250–59
    and anti-French sentiments, 252–53, 255–56

Shakespeare, William *(continued)*
    Cade's rebellion in, 252, 253, 258–59
    as critique of war, 250–59
    economic costs of war, 258–59
    loss of France in, 256–58
Sibyl, 162–63, 180, 185, 187–88
Sinfield, Alan, 246
Speculum Hominis or *Speculum Meditantis* (on Gower's effigy), 131, 139, 140, 148, 153
Spiegel, Gabrielle, 2–3, 8
Staley (Johnson), Lynn, 82
Statute of Pleading (1362), 135–37, 146
Steiner, George, 99, 101
Stow, George, 147
Strohm, Paul, 46, 81, 84, 106, 109

Thucydides, 180
Tilly, Charles, 253, 254
"To King Henry IV, In Praise of Peace" (Gower), 132, 133, 148, 149, 150, 151, 152–53
Traité pour essampler les amantz marietz (Gower), 129, 130, 132, 148, 150
Treaty of Brétigny, 5–6, 9–10, 55–56, 61, 64, 66, 91, 94, 134, 136–37, 138
    critiques of, 57–59
    and Henry IV, 152
    and *Piers Plowman*, 56–67, 59–60, 63, 64, 66–67, 68n. 2
Treaty of Troyes, 7
Troilus and Criseyde (Chaucer), 95, 104, 106–107
Truce of Tours, 8, 223
Tuck, Anthony, 80
Turville-Petre, Thorlac, 10

Uberti, Fazio degli (*Dittamondo*), 170
Ufford, Robert, Earl of Suffolk, 19, 48n. 14
    as Suffort in *Voeux du heron*, 19, 21–22, 22–23, 37, 38

Vale, Juliet, 33
Varty, Kenneth, 178, 199, 190
Venette, Jean de (*Chronicle*), 48–49n. 14, 95
Villani, Matteo, 241
violence
    chivalric, 29–33
        in *Cleriadus et Meliadice*, 226–28
        in just war theory, 34–35, 39
        against Saracens, 168, 226–27
        in *Voeux du heron*, 27–29, 32, 36–69, 43–45, 47
        internal in Elizabethan period, 254, 258
Virgil, 97, 104, 180, 185, 188
Vitry, Jacques de (*Historia occidentalis*), 169–70
Voeux du heron, 8–9, 17–24, 27–29, 32–33, 35–47
    as antiwar poem, 14, 24
    courtly love in, 40–42
    as critique of chivalric violence, 27–29, 32, 36–39, 43–45, 47
    historical counterparts of characters in, 18–19
    and inception of Hundred Years' War, 4–5, 17, 29
Vows of the heron (see *Voeux du heron*)
Vox Clamantis (Gower), 130, 131, 133, 137, 139–40, 141, 142, 145, 146, 147, 148

Wallace, David, 78, 84
Walsingham, Thomas, 41, 107
Walter of Manny (or Mauny), 18, 25n. 5, 242
    as character in *Voeux du heron*, 19, 21, 22, 37, 38, 41
Warner, Marina, 181, 212

Whiting, B. J., 18, 21, 22, 25n. 3, 47n. 2
Willard, Charity Cannon, 179
Wilton Diptych, 144
Wimsatt, James, 98

Womack, Peter, 264n. 47
Wood, Charles, 181, 183

Zink, Gaston, 22–23, 232

www.ingramcontent.com/pod-product-compliance
Lightning Source LLC
Chambersburg PA
CBHW020641230426
43665CB00008B/272